DATE DUE

Keep 2018	
Lane S.	

DEMCO, INC. 38-2931

RACING

THE

ENEMY

RACING
THE
ENEMY

STALIN, TRUMAN, AND THE
SURRENDER OF JAPAN

TSUYOSHI HASEGAWA

THE BELKNAP PRESS OF
HARVARD UNIVERSITY PRESS
Cambridge, Massachusetts · London, England

Library of Congress Cataloging-in-Publication Data

Hasegawa, Tsuyoshi, 1941–
Racing the enemy : Stalin, Truman, and the surrender
of Japan / Tsuyoshi Hasegawa.
p. cm.
Includes bibliographical references and index.
ISBN 0-674-01693-9 (alk. paper)
1. World War, 1939–1945—Armistices. 2. World War, 1939–1945—Japan.
3. World War, 1939–1945—Soviet Union. 4. World War, 1939–1945—
United States. 5. World politics—1933–1945. I. Title.

D813.J3H37 2005
940.53'2452—dc22   2004059786

In memory of
BORIS NIKOLAEVICH SLAVINSKY,
my friend and colleague,
who did not see the fruit of our collaboration

Contents

Illustrations follow pages 132 and 204

Maps

Note on Transliteration and Spelling

For Russian words, I have used the Library of Congress transliteration system except for well-known terms such as Yalta and Mikoyan when they appear in the text; in the citations, I retain Ialtinskaia konferentsiia and Mikoian. Soft signs in proper nouns are omitted in the text but retained in the notes; hence "Komsomolsk" instead of "Komsomol'sk." I employ the strict Library of Congress transliteration system for the ending "ii" rather than the more popular ending "y"; hence "Maiskii" instead of "Maisky" and "Lozovskii" instead of "Lozovsky."

For Japanese words, I use the Hepburn transliteration system with some modifications; hence "Konoe" instead of the more commonly used "Konoye." But I use "nenpyo" instead of the strict Hepburn rendering "nempyo." In addition, I use an apostrophe in some cases for ease of reading; for instance, "Shun'ichi" instead of "Shunichi," to separate "shun" and "ichi." Macrons in Japanese names and terms are omitted.

Japanese given names come before surnames in the text, but the order of surnames and given names follows the Japanese custom in the endnotes, except for Japanese authors of English- or Russian-language books and articles. For instance, Sadao Asada's Japanese article is cited as "Asada Sadao," but his English article is cited as "Sadao Asada."

For Chinese geographical names I use the Postal Atlas system. For Chinese personal names I follow contemporary style rather than the pinyin system; hence "Chiang Kai-shek" rather than "Jiang Jieshi," and "T.V. Soong" rather than "Song Ziwen."

For proper names in direct quotes from original documents I retain the usage in the original, although these renderings may not conform to the system I use in the text. Thus, the "Kurils" may appear as the "Kuriles" and "Konoe" as "Konoye" in direct quotes.

RACING
THE
ENEMY

Race to the Finish

Sixty years after the dropping of the atomic bomb and the Japanese surrender, we still lack a clear understanding of how the Pacific War ended. Historians in the United States, Japan, and the Soviet Union, the three crucial players in the drama of the war's end, have focused on a small piece of a large picture: Americans on the atomic bomb, Japanese on how Emperor Hirohito decided to end the war, and Russians on Soviet military actions in the Far East. But a complete story has not yet been told.

In the United States debate has continued as to whether the atomic bomb was directly responsible for Japan's surrender. As the 1995 controversy over the *Enola Gay* exhibit at the Smithsonian's National Air and Space Museum reveals, the atomic bombs used on Hiroshima and Nagasaki continue to strike America's raw nerves. But this debate has been strangely parochial, concerned almost entirely with the American story.

The intense drama leading to Japan's decision to surrender in the last days of the Pacific War has likewise fascinated the Japanese. Despite a continuous stream of publications on this subject, no serious scholarly work has critically analyzed Japan's decision in the broader international context. Until now, Robert Butow's study of Japan's surrender has been the most complete scholarly analysis on the topic in both Japan and the United States.[1]

The works of Soviet historians bear the marks of the ideological straitjacket the Marxist-Leninist state imposed during the postwar period.

These state-approved histories depict the end of the Pacific War as the concluding chapter of the Soviet's Great Patriotic War, in which the USSR played the heroic role of liberating the oppressed peoples of Asia from the yoke of Japanese militarism and imperialism. During perestroika, some scholars began to look at their country's history from a new perspective. Despite the significant new materials that have become available in the wake of the Soviet collapse, however, Russian historians continue to adhere to the interpretations established during the Soviet period. Boris Slavinskii remains the notable exception.[2]

Significantly, American and Japanese historians have almost completely ignored the role of the Soviet Union in ending the Pacific War. To be sure, the issue of whether the Truman administration viewed the use of the bomb as a diplomatic weapon against the Soviets has created a sharp division between revisionist and orthodox historians in the United States. Yet even here, the focus remains on Washington, and the main point of contention is over American perceptions of Soviet intentions. Standard accounts of the end of the Pacific War depict Soviet actions as a sideshow and assign to Moscow a secondary role at best.

An International History

This book closely examines the end of the Pacific War from an international perspective. It considers the complex interactions among the three major actors: the United States, the Soviet Union, and Japan. The story consists of three subplots. The first is the combination of competition and cooperation that played out between Stalin and Truman in the war against Japan. Although the United States and the Soviet Union were allies, Stalin and Truman distrusted each other; each suspected that the other would be the first to violate the Yalta Agreement governing their relationship in the Far East. The Potsdam Conference, which met from July 17 to August 2, 1945, triggered a fierce race between the two leaders. While it became imperative for Truman to drop the atomic bomb to achieve Japan's surrender before the Soviet entry into the war, it became equally essential for Stalin to invade Manchuria before Japan surrendered. This book examines how the Allies' Potsdam Proclamation issued to Japan, the atomic bombs, and the Soviet entry into the war were intertwined to compel Japan's acceptance of unconditional surrender.

The Soviet-American rivalry is carried beyond the emperor's acceptance of unconditional surrender on August 14. Far from abating, Soviet military maneuvers in the Far East accelerated after Moscow learned of

Japan's intention to surrender, a point often missed in existing accounts of the war's end. It was only after Japan's acceptance of the Potsdam surrender terms that Stalin ordered the Kuril and Hokkaido operations. While the Japanese were preparing to accept surrender, Stalin and Truman were engaged in an intense tug of war to gain an advantage in the postwar Far East.

The second subplot is the tangled relationship between Japan and the Soviet Union, characterized by Japanese courtship and Soviet betrayal. The more the military situation deteriorated, the more Japanese policymakers focused on the Soviet Union. For the army, determined to wage a last-ditch battle to defend the homeland, it became essential to keep the Soviet Union out of the war. For the peace party, the termination of the war through Moscow's mediation seemed to offer the only alternative to unconditional surrender. At the same time, Japan's overtures served Stalin's interests by providing an opportunity to prolong the war long enough for the Soviets to join it. Even after the Potsdam Proclamation was issued, the Japanese clung to the hope that Moscow mediation would bring about more favorable surrender terms. Thus Soviet entry into the war shocked the Japanese even more than the atomic bombs because it meant the end of any hope of achieving a settlement short of unconditional surrender. Eventually, the fear of Soviet political influence in Japan's occupation drove the emperor to accept unconditionally the Potsdam surrender terms.

The third subplot is the fateful competition between the war party and the peace party within the Japanese government over the terms of surrender. While Stalin and Truman were competing in a deadly race to achieve Japan's surrender, Japanese policymakers were hopelessly divided into two camps: those who wanted to terminate the war as quickly as possible in order to save the emperor and the imperial house; and those who wanted to fight the last decisive battle against the enemy in the homeland to preserve the national spirit embodied in the emperor system. In this debate, the nebulous Japanese concept *kokutai*—national polity—became the central focus of the disagreements between the peace party and the war party. Both sides sought their goals in the name of the *kokutai*.

Kokutai: Defining the Japanese Nation

Japan's Meiji Constitution of 1889 defined the emperor as "sacred and inviolable" and placed him at the pinnacle of power: all legislative, executive, and judicial power emanated from his person. The emperor was also the supreme military commander, whose authority was beyond the reach of the cabinet.

In addition, the emperor served as a symbol of the Japanese national community. As such, he embodied what it meant to be Japanese. Compulsory national education and military conscription inculcated in the Japanese a strong sense of nationalism and the importance of emperor worship. The emperor thus held absolute power in political, cultural, and religious terms. The *kokutai* was a symbolic expression of both the political and the spiritual essence of the emperor system.[3]

Despite the political and cultural centrality of the emperor, he nonetheless remained a figurehead when it came to actual policy making. This system led to what Masao Maruyama, Japan's foremost authority on political thought, called "a system of irresponsibility" whereby policymakers made decisions in the name of the emperor, who could not exercise power over policies thus adopted.[4] During the 1930s, Tatsukichi Minobe, a professor of constitutional law at Tokyo University, attempted to transform the Meiji Constitution into a modern constitutional monarchy by defining the emperor as an organ of the state whose power was limited by law. But his "Emperor as Organ Theory" provoked an ultranationalist backlash that only served to validate the mythical notion of the *kokutai* that transcended the political system. In 1937, the Ministry of Education published *The Essence of the Kokutai,* which defined the emperor as a living God, one and united with the Creator of the imperial system and the eternal essence of his subjects and the imperial land. From then on this mythical notion of the *kokutai* became the orthodoxy. Central to this new notion was the emperor's monopolistic power over the military command, which provided the major impetus for Japan's unbridled military expansion.[5] These ideas reinforced the centrality of the emperor—both politically and culturally—to Japanese national identity. Changing the role of the emperor would require redefining the terms of the national community and of Japanese identity.

Japan's decision to surrender in the Pacific War forced Japanese policymakers to reconceive this central element of nationalism. In a desperate attempt to save himself and the imperial house, the emperor, in conjunction with the peace party, redefined national mythology to fit Japan's new circumstances. Departing from the tradition that the emperor was merely a figurehead, Hirohito actively involved himself in the decision to accept Japan's unconditional surrender. In doing so he separated the idea of the national community from his own person.

The Blind Men and the Elephant

In this book I show that Stalin was an active participant, not a secondary player, as historians have hitherto depicted, in the drama of Japan's surrender. He was engaged in skillful Machiavellian diplomacy to manipulate Japanese desires for negotiated peace to his own ends. He was involved in intense negotiations with the Americans and reacted decisively to American maneuvers. He bullied the Chinese into accepting the Soviet terms, and ruthlessly pursued diplomacy and military operations to secure the territories to which he felt entitled.

This study also casts the American use of the atomic bomb in a wider setting. The bomb provided a solution to the previously unsolvable dilemma that faced Truman: to achieve Japan's unconditional surrender before Soviet entry into the war. Truman issued the Potsdam Proclamation, not as a warning to Japan, but to justify the use of the atomic bomb. I challenge the commonly held view that the atomic bomb provided the immediate and decisive knockout blow to Japan's will to fight. Indeed, the Soviet entry into the war played a greater role than the atomic bombs in inducing Japan to surrender.[6]

Moreover, the *kokutai* had a tremendous impact on the outcome of the war, as did a group of Japanese advisers who have not figured prominently in the standard account. Although historians have examined Japan's decision-making process with due attention to the highest policymakers in the cabinet, the military, the imperial court, and a few influential politicians outside the government, I reveal a more complex scenario in which a group of second-echelon advisers played a decisive role in directing the actions of the peace party.

Finally, unlike other studies on the end of the Pacific War, this book examines the crucial period after Japan's acceptance of unconditional surrender on August 15 to the final date of the Soviet operation in the Kurils on September 5, a time of frantic Soviet maneuvering. Japan's surrender triggered Stalin's order to implement military operations in the Kurils and Hokkaido. While Stalin skillfully combined diplomacy and military operations, Truman had to balance the need to bring about Japan's surrender quickly and smoothly with the need to check Soviet expansion beyond the limits defined by the Yalta Agreement. In the end Stalin gained the Kurils but had to abandon his plan to capture Hokkaido. Despite mutual distrust and tension, however, both sides in the end observed the boundaries set by the Yalta Agreement. The Cold War had not yet begun.

Like the blind men touching the elephant, historians have perceived only parts of the complex drama of the ending of the Pacific War. Sixty years after the signing of surrender terms on the decks of the USS *Missouri*, this book offers the first behind-the-scene's look at the intricate negotiations and machinations that led to Japan's decision to accept unconditional surrender.

CHAPTER 1

Triangular Relations
and the Pacific War

O N THE EVENING of April 13, 1941, Stalin hosted Japan's foreign minister, Yosuke Matsuoka, at a banquet in the Kremlin to celebrate the Neutrality Pact that had been signed that afternoon. Jubilant and quite drunk, Matsuoka pledged: "The treaty has been made. I do not lie. If I lie, my head shall be yours. If you lie, be sure I will come for your head." Stalin replied: "My head is important to my country. So is yours to your country. Let's take care to keep both our heads on our shoulders." Then Stalin told Matsuoka: "You are an Asiatic. So am I." "We're all Asiatics," Matsuoka chimed in. "Let us drink to the Asiatics!"

The two men met again the following day. Stalin made a rare appearance at Yaroslavl Station to bid farewell to Matsuoka. He embraced and kissed the Japanese foreign minister and saw to it that the scene was photographed. Stalin carefully staged his appearance to demonstrate—as much to the Japanese as to the German ambassador also present at the railway station—the importance of the Neutrality Pact.[1]

A quick glance at the tortured history of Russo-Japanese relations since the late nineteenth century is sufficient to appreciate the uniqueness of this ostentatious display of friendship. But it is also important to bear in mind that two other powers, the United States and China, were closely intertwined with Russo-Japanese affairs. Exploiting China's weakness, Russia acquired enormous territories north of the Amur and west of the Ussuri in the middle of the nineteenth century. Russia founded the port city of Vladivostok in 1860 as its gate to the Pacific Ocean. Its next ambition was to extend its influence into Manchuria and Korea. But there, Russia encountered Japan, a formidable rival who, having embarked on modernization after 1868, began its own imperialist expansion into its neighbors' territory. Japan's aggressive policy toward Korea soon enraged China, the nominal suzerain of the hermit kingdom, and the two Asian countries went to war in 1894–1895. Japan defeated China, which was obliged to cede to the victor Taiwan, the Pescadores Islands, and the Liaotung Peninsula in Manchuria, and to recognize Korea's independence. Japan had now acquired a foothold into the Asian continent. (See Map 1.)

Alarmed by Japan's intrusion into Asia, Russia persuaded Germany and France to force the Japanese to abandon the newly acquired Liaotung Peninsula. In addition, in the 1890s Russia began to build the Chinese Eastern Railway through Manchuria to Vladivostok. Japan was further humiliated when in 1898 Russia acquired the lease for the Liaotung Peninsula and the right to construct the South Manchurian Railway connecting the Eastern Chinese Railway to the warm-water port of Dairen and the naval fortress of Port Arthur. Russia and Japan were on a collision course.

When the Chinese revolted against foreign powers in the Boxer Uprising in 1900, Japan and Russia sent a large contingent of expeditionary forces. To Japan's alarm, Russia not only refused to withdraw its forces after the uprising was quelled but also began sending significant reinforcements over the Trans-Siberian Railway. In 1902, as tension between Russia and Japan intensified, Japan concluded the Anglo-Japanese Alliance, thereby securing a powerful ally. In February 1904 Japan broke off relations with Russia and launched a surprise attack on the Russian fleet in Port Arthur two days before it declared war against Russia. The Japanese laid siege to Port Arthur, which fell in January 1905. The Japanese Army crossed the Yalu into Manchuria and captured Mukden in March. Russia pinned its last hope on the Baltic fleet, which sailed all the way across the world to attack Japan. But the Japanese Navy, which waited in the Straits of Tsushima, annihilated the Russian fleet in a one-day battle. Russia lost the war. The Portsmouth Treaty, mediated by President Theodore Roosevelt in 1905, granted to Japan southern Sakhalin and the South Manchurian Railway as far north as Changchun and Liaotung Peninsula. The Japanese Empire gradually turned Manchuria into a virtual colony by sending Japanese settlers, who displaced Chinese villagers. Once this colonial outpost was created, it had to be protected from Rus-

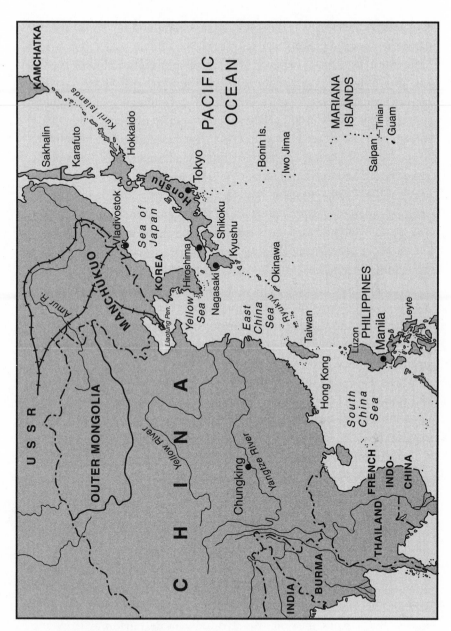

Map 1. Japan at War, 1945

sian encroachments. The Japanese troops stationed in Manchuria became the Kwantung Army in 1919. (See Map 1.)

Defeat in the Russo-Japanese war delivered a profound blow to Russia.[2] Not only did it acquire the dubious distinction of being the first European great power to suffer defeat at the hands of a non-European
power, but it also was compelled to cede to Japan southern Sakhalin, an
integral part of its territory. Moreover, Russia lost the strategically important city of Dairen and Port Arthur. This humiliation lived well beyond the Russian Revolution.

After the Russo-Japanese War, however, Russia and Japan quickly
reached rapprochement by concluding three conventions in 1907, 1911,
and 1912, which divided their respective spheres of influence. Whereas
Outer Mongolia became Russia's protectorate, Japan annexed Korea.
Manchuria was divided in half, the southern half under Japan's sphere of
influence and the northern half under Russia's. These conventions were
also designed to exclude from Manchuria other Western powers, especially the United States, which was making aggressive attempts to expand
its influence through commercial and financial deals in the name of the
open door policy.

World War I gave the Japanese an opportunity to expand their territorial ambition in China. Taking advantage of the European powers' preoccupation with the war in Europe, the Japanese sent troops to Tsingtao to
repulse the Germans and imposed the infamous Twenty-one Demands on
China. All the major powers protested against Japan's brazen opportun-
ism. Only Russia refrained from joining the chorus of protest in the hope
that its silence would earn the gratitude of Japan and prevent it from in-
fringing on Russia's territory in Manchuria. In 1916, Russia and Japan
concluded an alliance whereby they pledged to support each other if a
third party were to threaten their respective spheres of influence.

The Russian Revolution and the civil war, however, exacerbated Soviet-Japanese relations. Together with the United States, Japan sent its
expeditionary forces into the Soviet Far East to assist anti-Communist
forces. But Japan's mission was avowedly more territorial than anti-
Communist; Japan intended not only to invade northern Manchuria but
also to extend its reach far into Siberia and northern Sakhalin. Japan's
"Siberian intervention" resulted in strong feelings of hostility on the part
of the Russians toward the Japanese and validated the Soviets' suspicion
that Japan was always ready to pounce on Russia.

Just as the Versailles Treaty was the foundation on which the post–

World War I order was constructed in Europe, the Washington Treaty system that resulted from the Washington Conference in 1921–1922 was the basic framework of Asian international relations. Japan agreed to adhere, together with the United States and Britain, to naval disarmament and concluded the Nine-Power Agreement, which guaranteed China's independence and territorial integrity. The Soviet Union was excluded from both the Versailles Treaty and the Washington Treaties. Left isolated, the Soviet Union had to fend off Japan's expansion alone. In accordance with the agreement reached between the Far Eastern Republic, a buffer state created by the Soviet Union, and the Japanese government, Japan finally withdrew its troops from the Soviet Union, except for northern Sakhalin. Not feeling completely comfortable with international cooperation with Western powers, and facing mounting domestic criticism against the cost of continuing the intervention, Japan also found it convenient to reach rapprochement with the Soviet Union in order to settle the new demarcation between their respective spheres of influence in Manchuria. Both countries restored diplomatic relations in the Basic Convention of 1925. Japan finally withdrew its troops from northern Sakhalin in exchange for oil concessions.

Japan Invades Manchuria

Japan's invasion of Manchuria in 1931 marked a new era in international relations in the Far East. In 1932, Japan created the puppet state of Manchukuo. In 1933 it withdrew from the League of Nations. In 1934 it annulled the Washington Naval Disarmament Treaty. Despite Japan's brazen aggression and open challenge to the Washington system, however, the reaction of Western powers was muted. The British government was reluctant to challenge Japan, as it was not completely averse to the possibility of a Soviet-Japanese war. President Franklin Delano Roosevelt, inaugurated into office in 1933, was initially preoccupied with domestic problems and lacked a clear vision for a new international system in the Far East.[3]

Japan's invasion and annexation of Manchuria posed a serious threat to the Soviet Union. Still isolated diplomatically, the Soviet government had to devise ways to fend off the constant threat coming from Japan, which was under the increasing control of the military. Its first line of defense was appeasement. During the invasion, the Soviets kept strict neutrality. When Japan rejected the Soviets' repeated attempts to conclude a

12   RACING the ENEMY

non-aggression pact, the Soviet government negotiated with Japan for the sale of the Chinese Eastern Railway. The deal went through in 1935.

Between 1933 and 1937 international relations in the Far East were marked by uncertainty. The Japanese government under the leadership of the foreign minister and later prime minister Koki Hirota attempted to establish a new international order that recognized the gains Japan had obtained from its aggression. The Nationalist government in China was divided over peace with Japan: Chiang Kai-shek sided with the pro-peace faction against the pro-war faction headed by his brother-in-law, T. V. Soong. To complicate the matter, Nazi Germany maintained close relations with the Nationalist government in China during that period and even provided it with substantial military aid and advisers. The British government vacillated between appeasement and confrontation with Japan. The Americans, though more alarmed by Japan's expansionism than the British, remained largely passive.

Facing the danger of the Japanese military threat in the East and the rise of Nazi Germany in the West, the Kremlin adopted a new foreign policy designed to seek collective security with Western powers. The Soviet Union gained the diplomatic recognition of the United States in 1933 and joined the League of Nations in 1934. In 1935 the Comintern, the headquarters of the Moscow-led international Communist movement, adopted a new policy calling for the formation of a popular front against fascism. Nevertheless, U.S. recognition of the Soviet Union did not immediately lead to a meaningful coalition with Western powers against the Japanese threat. The continuing dispute over payment of debts that the Bolshevik government had canceled after the Russian Revolution became the insurmountable obstacle to further improvement in relations with the United States. The British government under Exchequer Neville Chamberlain and Prime Minister Stanley Baldwin preferred instead to establish "permanent friendly relations" with Japan by recognizing Manchukuo. This situation left the Soviet Union with one option to guard against possible Japanese aggression: to rely on its own military strength and demonstrate its determination in border incidents.

The Soviet military buildup in the Far East began in earnest. In 1931, the Kwantung Army outnumbered the Red Army by a large margin, but by 1939 the situation was reversed. In 1932 the Pacific Fleet was created. The double-tracking of the Trans-Siberian Railway was completed in 1937. The Soviets also began building fortifications along the Manchurian border and the Maritime Province.

While the Soviets were quickly fortifying the Manchurian border, Japanese militants were loudly advocating war against the Soviet Union. General Sadao Araki, the army minister from 1931 to 1934, repeated his conviction that war against the Soviet Union was Japan's national mission. But this policy met with the opposition of the navy, which preferred war against the United States and Britain. In August 1936, the Japanese Government and the Imperial General Headquarters adopted three basic principles for Japan's foreign policy: to maintain Japan's position in the Asian continent; to prevent Soviet expansion in the continent; and to advance to the south. The prototype of Japan's direction in the Pacific War was formulated. And yet Japan remained decidedly anti-Soviet. In 1936 it concluded the anti-Comintern Pact with Germany. Its secret protocol stipulated that if one party went to war with the Soviet Union, the other party was obligated to remain neutral. This pact, which was concluded one month after the formation of the German-Italian Axis, meant that Japan took the decisive step toward siding with the Axis powers.

The second Sino-Japanese War, in July 1937, forced the major powers to abandon their past policy of non-intervention. As Japan quickly expanded the war in China, President Roosevelt made a speech in Chicago in October stressing the need to "quarantine" those who were spreading "the epidemic of world lawlessness." This was Roosevelt's first signal that the United States would abandon isolationism. In November, Japanese troops pursued the retreating Nationalist forces to Nanking and committed the Nanking massacre. This brutal action invited international outcry and contributed further to the isolation of Japan in world public opinion. In 1938, Roosevelt initiated the U.S.–British military cooperation for joint operations against Japan, and moved the major portion of the U.S. fleet to the Pacific. He also approved a loan to China to support the Nationalist government's resistance to Japanese aggression. The United States was emerging as the major power to block Japan's military expansion. While the United States was asserting its strong stand against Japan, Hitler abandoned Germany's long-standing assistance to China and recognized Manchukuo. The clear line between the Axis powers and Western liberal allies was now clearly drawn. The question was, Which side would the Soviet Union take?

The Sino-Japanese War was a godsend for the Soviet Union. The more the Japanese became bogged down in the quagmire of the war in China, the less likely they were to invade the Soviet Union. In the initial phase of the Sino-Japanese War, the Soviets were China's most reliable ally;

they concluded a non-aggression pact with the Nationalist government and shipped weapons, planes, and tanks to China to help the Chinese resist Japan's aggression.

From 1937 on, the Soviets became more aggressive in responding to border skirmishes with the use of force. In 1938 the Soviets and the Japanese clashed in a major border battle at Lake Khasan (Changkufeng) near the Korean border. In 1939 they again clashed in a full-fledged war in Nomonhan (Khalkin Gol) along the Mongolian-Manchukuo border that resulted in a Soviet victory. The defeat had a sobering effect on the Japanese military. Japan's offensive against the Soviet Union would require careful planning and enormous military buildup along the Soviet borders.

Conclusion of the Neutrality Pact

The outbreak of World War II dictated to both countries the temporary suspension of hostilities for their respective strategic interests. The Munich Conference in 1938 had convinced Stalin that the only way to keep the impending war from being fought on Soviet soil was to conclude the Nazi-Soviet Non-Aggression Pact. Despite the pact, however, Nazi-Soviet relations quickly deteriorated by the end of 1940, raising the ominous possibility that the Nazis might invade the Soviet Union. To avoid a war on two fronts, Stalin needed Japan's neutrality.

The Japanese were shocked to learn of the Non-Aggression Pact. But they very quickly decided to exploit the changing vicissitudes in the international situation, and in 1940 they concluded the Tripartite Pact with Germany and Italy. Matsuoka declared that the pact was "a military alliance directed against the United States." Foreign Minister Matsuoka had a grandiose plan to form an anti-Western alliance consisting of Germany, Italy, Japan, and the Soviet Union. For this purpose, he made a grand tour in March and April 1941, visiting Moscow, Berlin, and Rome. While in Moscow, Matsuoka negotiated with Stalin and Viacheslav Molotov to conclude a neutrality pact. But the negotiations were anything but smooth. To conclude the pact, Stalin had to intervene personally and Matsuoka had to pledge to abandon oil concessions in northern Sakhalin.[4]

The Neutrality Pact stipulated that both countries would maintain "peaceful and friendly relations" and respect the territorial integrity of the other. Both parties were to observe neutrality "throughout the duration of the conflict" if one party were attacked by a third party. The pact was to be effective for five years from the time of ratification, and "in case neither of the contracting parties denounces the pact one year before expiration of the term, it will be considered automatically prolonged for the next five years."[5] The pact was ratified by both countries and went into effect on April 25, 1941. Thus began the "strange neutrality" between the Soviet Union and Japan.

The United States had been watching the direction of Japan's foreign policy with apprehension. Since the Munich Conference in 1938, the political forces favoring a more aggressive policy against Japan gained power within the Roosevelt administration. But Roosevelt had to balance the U.S. security interest in Europe and Asia. When the British alone were engaged in a heroic struggle against Nazi Germany in the Battle of Britain, Roosevelt made Europe his top priority. In the latter half of 1940, the United States passed a compulsory draft law and concluded a defense agreement with Britain. Responding to Japan's military action in northern Indochina, the United States imposed an embargo on scrap iron against Japan.

Congress passed the Lend-Lease Act in March 1941, allowing the president to send war materiel to Britain and other countries whose defense he deemed vital to U.S. security. Meanwhile, the United States kept a watchful eye on the Japanese. The situation in the Far East was closely connected with the war in Europe. If Germany attacked the Soviet Union, as American policymakers expected it would, the United States did not wish to see its potential ally weakened or defeated. The United States government, therefore, received the news of the Soviet-Japanese Neutrality Pact with mixed feelings. Needless to say, the pact meant that Japan's aggression would be directed southward, increasing the likelihood of Japan's ultimate confrontation with the United States. Nevertheless, the U.S. government did not betray any sense of disappointment. It was more concerned with the imminent danger of a German attack on the Soviet Union than with the Far Eastern situation.[6]

The conclusion of the Neutrality Pact coincided with the formation of the ABCD (American, British, Chinese, and Dutch) alliance against Japan, the objective of which was to stem Japanese aggression in Asia and support Chinese resistance to the Japanese. But the United States also wished to avoid war, and so continued negotiations. But the principles that Secretary of State Cordell Hull insisted on to maintain peace in Asia, such as respect for territorial integrity and peaceful change of the status quo, represented a direct challenge to the mission that the Japanese were attempting to accomplish: the creation of a Greater Asia Co-Prosperity Sphere.

On June 22, less than two months after the ratification of the Neutrality Pact, Nazi Germany invaded the Soviet Union. This meant an end to Matsuoka's grandiose plan to lure the Soviet Union into the Axis bloc against the Anglo-American bloc. Roosevelt made a crucial decision that all his political and military policies would be based on the assumption that the Soviet Union would ultimately win a victory in the war against Germany. Toward that goal, he extended Lend-Lease aid to the Soviet Union. Even before the United States entered the war, the framework for the Grand Alliance among the United States, Britain, and the Soviet Union was formed.[7]

The German invasion of the Soviet Union threw the Japanese government into turmoil. Japan was torn between two alternatives: move north and wage war against the Soviet Union in collaboration with Germany, or move south, which meant war with the United States. On June 24 the army and navy adopted a draft proposal "not to intervene in the German-Soviet war for the time being," but "to make secret military preparations for unilateral action, and furthermore, to use force for the resolution of the northern question and the establishment of security in the north if the German-Soviet war becomes extremely advantageous for the empire."[8] With the memory of defeat at Nomonhan still fresh in their minds, the Japanese military was not eager to rush into war against the Soviet Union.

Just two months after committing to the Neutrality Pact at the risk of his head, Matsuoka advocated war against the Soviet Union. He insisted at the Liaison Conference between the government and military high commands—Japan's highest decision-making body at that time—that Japan immediately invade the Soviet Union and postpone its southern advance. But those present felt the timing was not propitious. Army Chief of Staff Hajime Sugiyama advocated a wait-and-see policy until the military situation in the German-Soviet war became decisively favorable to the Germans. Japan should patiently wait for the ripe persimmon to fall to the ground.[9]

Finally, on July 2 the imperial conference decided to advance south while carefully monitoring the German-Soviet war. Japan would make preparations to attack the Soviet Union should the circumstances become favorable. Under the pretext of "special maneuvers," the Imperial Army carried out a large-scale mobilization of Kwantung Army troops in prep-aration for a possible attack on the Soviet Union along the Manchurian border. The number of Japanese troops in Manchuria almost doubled, from nearly 400,000 to 700,000.[10]

The Kremlin nervously watched Japan's reactions to the outbreak of the Nazi-Soviet war. Matsuoka told Soviet Ambassador Konstantin Smetanin that Japan's commitment to the Tripartite Pact took precedence over the Neutrality Pact with the Soviet Union. But Matsuoka's saber-rattling overstepped the decision of the Liaison Conference, and Prime Minister Fumimaro Konoe summarily dismissed Matsuoka. The new foreign minister, Toyojiro Toyoda, reversing Matsuoka's policy, assured Smetanin that Japan would continue to honor the Neutrality Pact. De-spite this assurance, however, Stalin feared that Japan might launch a surprise attack, and he ordered the Far Eastern Military District to do ab-solutely nothing to provoke Japan into conflict. Richard Sorge, an impor-tant Soviet military intelligence spy planted in the German Embassy in Tokyo, kept sending high-quality information to Moscow. Sorge warned Moscow that the Japanese might start a war without any declaration. He also reported persistent German pressure on Japan to enter the war against the Soviet Union. In view of such information, Stalin did not dare transfer troops from the Far East to the European theater in sufficient numbers lest the defense of the Far East become weakened. It was not un-til October that Sorge reported his conclusion that Japan would not at-tack the Soviet Union, at least not that year.[11]

In the end, the persimmon did not fall. The Japanese invasion of French Indochina in July led the United States to freeze Japanese assets. The War Department created a new command in the Philippines—U.S. Armed Forces Far East, and brought back former Chief of Staff Douglas MacArthur to active duty to take command. The United States further imposed an oil embargo against Japan. In August, Roosevelt and Chur-chill jointly issued the Atlantic Charter after a conference aboard the USS *Augusta* off the coast of Newfoundland, enunciating the goals of Britain and the United States in the war, including the rejection of territorial ex-pansion and the restoration of sovereign rights and self-government to those territories deprived of them. These principles overtly aimed at Eu-rope had valid application to Asia.[12]

Konoe tried desperately to avoid war against the United States. He proposed a summit meeting with Roosevelt even as the Japanese military prepared for war against the United States. In August Admiral Isoroku

Yamamoto completed a plan to launch a surprise attack on the U.S. Pacific Fleet at Pearl Harbor. On September 6, the imperial conference adopted a resolution stating that unless diplomatic negotiations settled differences with the United States, Japan should initiate war against the United States and Britain. Negotiations between the Japanese ambassador and Secretary of State Cordell Hull stalled over the question of Japanese withdrawal of troops from China. In the end, the Konoe-Roosevelt meeting did not take place.

In October the Konoe Cabinet resigned, and General Hideki Tojo took over the premiership. On November 26, Hull delivered the "Hull Note," which was tantamount to an ultimatum and put an end to any diplomatic solutions to the conflict between Japan and the United States. War against the United States became inevitable. One day after the Hull Note was handed to the Japanese, Foreign Minister Shigenori Togo instructed Ambassador Hiroshi Oshima in Berlin to tell Hitler and his foreign minister, Joachim von Ribbentrop, that Japan would not attack the Soviet Union. Thanks to this information, Stalin sent highly trained divisions from the Far East to the defense of Moscow.

Without being detected by the Americans, the Japanese attacked Pearl Harbor on the morning of December 7. Roosevelt immediately declared war against Japan. Hitler in turn declared war against the United States, whereupon the United States entered the war in Europe as well as in the Pacific. Stalin must have been pleased with this development. Japan's involvement in the war against the United States would surely make the possibility of a Japanese attack on the Soviet Union more remote.[13]

The triangular relationship among the Soviet Union, the United States, and Japan was a strange one. To carry out the war against the United States, Japan needed to maintain the Neutrality Pact with the Soviet Union. To concentrate on the war against Nazi Germany, Stalin needed Japan's neutrality in the Far East. What existed between Japan and the Soviet Union from 1941 until 1945 was indeed "strange neutrality," as George Alexander Lensen has termed it. While the Soviets were at war with Japan's ally Germany, Japan was fighting a war against the United States, a Soviet ally against Germany. The United States sent Lend-Lease war supplies to the Soviet Union across the Pacific on Soviet merchant ships. Some of these weapons found their way to China, and others were later directed against Japan. A number of American pilots escaped to the safety of Soviet territory after they completed their bombing missions against Japan. The Soviet government, in turn, accused Japan of lending military assistance to Germany and providing its enemy with important military information through diplomatic channels. The neutrality that existed between Japan and the Soviet Union was therefore a precarious peace that lasted only as long as it served the strategic interests of both sides.[14]

On December 8, one day after the Japanese attacked Pearl Harbor, Roosevelt and Hull requested of the new Soviet ambassador, Maksim Litvinov, that the Soviet Union join the war against Japan. On December 11, Molotov instructed Litvinov to reply that the Soviet Union would be unable to join the war while it was fighting with Germany, and as long as it remained committed to the Neutrality Pact with Japan. Nevertheless, it would be a mistake to conclude that Stalin had no intention at this time of waging war against Japan. Only ten days after Litvinov rejected Roosevelt's request, Stalin told British Foreign Secretary Anthony Eden that the Soviet Union would eventually join the war against Japan, that it would require only four months to move troops from the European Front to the Far East, and that the best scenario would be to induce Japan to violate the Neutrality Pact. At the end of December, Deputy Foreign Commissar Solomon Lozovskii sent a memorandum to Stalin and Molotov in which he formulated his ideas about postwar Soviet foreign policy. Two points are noteworthy in this memorandum. First, he foresaw that the primary conflict in the postwar world would be between the Soviet Union and the capitalist world. Second, the most important task for the Soviet Union would be security. He suggested that the major objective regarding Japan should be to regain Soviet access to the Pacific Ocean by freeing the Soya Strait, the Kuril Islands, and the Tsugaru Strait. It bears emphasizing that even during those dark days, when Moscow was threatened by the advancing German troops, Stalin and his foreign policy elite already harbored a plan to attack Japan.[15]

In January 1942, Japan's Liaison Conference adopted "The Fundamental Policy on the Conduct of the War." Japan was for the time being to "attempt to maintain tranquility between Japan and the Soviet Union, to prevent the strengthening of relations between the Soviet Union and its Anglo-American Allies, and to separate the two camps." It should be noted, however, that the maintenance of tranquility concealed an aggressive design to attack the Soviet Union when an opportunity arose. On July 10, 1942, Ribbentrop requested Japan's participation in the war against the Soviet Union, but the Japanese government rejected the German request. Major General Kenryo Sato, chief of the Army Ministry's Bureau of Military Affairs, stated that "the persimmon is not ripe yet."[16]

After their initial success, the fortunes of war began to turn against the

Japanese. They lost a major battle at Midway in June 1942, and then another battle in February 1943 in Guadalcanal, which coincided with the Soviet victory over the German forces in Stalingrad. The new military situation forced Japan to change its policy toward the Soviet Union.

Switching to Appeasement

In February 1943, when the German defeat in the Battle of Stalingrad became evident, Japanese Ambassador Naotake Sato urged the Japanese government to improve Soviet-Japanese relations by liquidating the North Sakhalin concessions of oil and coal, and concluding a fishing agreement.[17] In April 1943, veteran diplomat Mamoru Shigemitsu became foreign minister and accepted Sato's recommendation. Shigemitsu's appointment had great significance for the subsequent peace maneuvers. The Lord Keeper of the Privy Seal and Hirohito's most trusted confidant, Marquis Koichi Kido, was an old acquaintance of Shigemitsu's, and the two secretly began to study ways to terminate the war.[18] Nevertheless, mindful of Hirohito's still-firm confidence in Tojo and his military policy, Kido was reluctant to arrange a meeting of senior statesmen with the emperor.

On June 19, the Liaison Conference adopted a new policy toward the Soviet Union. This policy aimed to "preserve the tranquility between Japan and the Soviet Union" and "to make the Soviet Union strictly observe the Neutrality Pact." For this purpose, Japan should transfer the northern Sakhalin concessions of oil and coal to the Soviet Union, a promise that Matsuoka had made before the conclusion of the Neutrality Pact, but that had remained unfulfilled. Negotiations began in June 1943.

At a minimum, it was necessary to keep the Soviet Union out of the war, and it was even desirable, if possible, to take Soviet-Japanese relations to a higher, more cooperative level. The Soviet Union began to assume a central place in Japan's foreign and military policy. On September 10, Shigemitsu instructed Sato to sound out the possibility of dispatching a special envoy to Moscow for the purpose of conveying Japan's desire to improve Soviet-Japanese relations. But, as Sato had predicted, Molotov replied that the Soviet government was not prepared to receive such an envoy; not only was the envoy's objective unclear, but his visit would be construed as an attempt to mediate peace between the Soviet Union and Germany. On September 25, the Liaison Conference adopted "the Outline of War Guidance to Be Followed in the Future," which listed Soviet neutrality as the most important precondition for the continuation of war against the United States and Britain. The Japanese government had switched its policy to appeasement.[19] The relationship between the Soviet Union and Japan was reversed. It was now the Soviet Union that waited for the ripe persimmon to fall to the ground.

The Kremlin quickly suspended the negotiations for northern Sakhalin oil and fishing rights when the Japanese Navy seized three Soviet ships transporting American Lend-Lease goods. Although the government and the Ministry of Foreign Affairs realized that the transport of Lend-Lease goods was a trifling matter compared with the need to improve relations with the Soviet Union, they could not overcome the strenuous opposition from the Naval General Staff. Moscow exploited this incident to put its relationship with Japan on hold indefinitely. By the time the problem of the seizure of Soviet ships was resolved in November, the Soviet government had already held the Moscow Foreign Ministers' Conference and the Teheran Conference, through which it succeeded in strengthening its relations with the Allies. The negotiations on the Sakhalin concessions and the fisheries concessions resumed in November but were not completed until March 1944. Japan had wasted a precious nine months.[20]

Roosevelt Demands Unconditional Surrender

In January 1943, Roosevelt announced at a press conference at Casablanca that the Allies should impose unconditional surrender on the Axis powers.[21] The concept of unconditional surrender was born partly from the experience of World War I, in which the armistice gave rise to the "stab in the back" myth in Germany, partly from the desire to eradicate Nazism, fascism, and militarism, and partly from the desire to ensure the unity of the Allies. By unconditional surrender Roosevelt meant not only the capitulation of the armed forces, but also the elimination of the "philosophy" that made expansion and militarism possible. Moreover, the victor would impose his will on the vanquished until such time as the "peace-loving" nations could be certain that the defeated would pose no threat to peace. As Winston Churchill explained, unconditional surrender meant the victor would be given "a free hand" in dealing with the defeated. He added that it meant that the Atlantic Charter would not apply to the defeated.[22]

Roosevelt was indifferent to the question of how to translate the prin-

ciple of unconditional surrender into specific policies, leaving the formulation of the policies to the State Department's Committee on Post-War
Foreign Policy. Since 1942 three important Japan specialists, Joseph Ballantine, George Blakeslee, and Hugh Borton, had been actively involved
in the formulation of U.S. postwar policy in Japan.[23] Inspired by the ide-
alism of the Atlantic Charter, but dismayed by the unconditional surrender demand declared by Roosevelt, the Japan specialists attempted to
craft a policy whereby Japan would be able to return to the international community as a peaceful, constructive member after the war. They
shared with those who advocated "hard peace" against Japan the need
to destroy Japan's military power and rid it of the sources of militarism.
But the trio adamantly opposed the notion of hard peace advocated by
the Roosevelt administration. Proponents of hard peace argued that Japan's militarism would not be eradicated so long as the emperor system
survived. Thus, they stood for disestablishing the monarchy, punishing
Hirohito as a war criminal, and imposing a democratic, republican system on Japan.

Ballantine, Borton, and Blakeslee adamantly disagreed with the proponents of "hard peace." They insisted that a political system, even democracy, would not be easily grafted onto a country whose political, cultural,
and religious traditions were so different from those of the United States.
Their knowledge of Japanese history taught them that the emperor system had little to do with the resurgence of Japanese militarism and that
the symbiotic relationship between the emperor system and militarism as
expressed in the kokutai had only a recent pedigree. Emperor worship
had profound religious and emotional roots among the Japanese, and
only a handful of radicals, mostly Communists, would advocate the abolition of the monarchical system. Imposition of a republican form of government in Japan would mean that the American occupation would last
for a long time, and even then there would be no guarantee that the monarchy would not be restored after the Americans left.

Proponents of soft peace argued that America's interest would be best
served if Japan were turned into a peaceful, constructive power. To that
end, preservation of the monarchy was crucial. This view also gained a
spokesman in Joseph Grew, who became a lightning rod for the attack
from the New Deal liberals, who assailed him as "an appeaser" and "an
apologist of Hirohito."[24]

Although Roosevelt did not pay much attention to the details of the
Far Eastern question, he clearly favored punitive peace against Japan.

Even Hull criticized the views expressed by the Japan specialists as overly conciliatory. American public opinion was overwhelmingly against Japan and Hirohito. Amid the loud chorus against Japan, specialists within the State Department had to refashion their views to fit the virulent anti-Japanese sentiment. They paid lip service to the president's avowed goal of unconditional surrender. Nevertheless, they held their ground in insisting on the need to revise unconditional surrender to allow Japan's monarchical system to be preserved.

Stalin Promises War on Japan

October 1943 was the turning point in U.S.-Soviet cooperation in the Pacific War. W. Averell Harriman became the new ambassador to the Soviet Union, and the Joint Chiefs of Staff (JCS) appointed Major General John R. Deane as head of the United States Military Mission in Moscow. The Foreign Ministers' Conference, which opened in Moscow on October 19, 1943, primarily dealt with the question of a second front in Europe. It was at this conference, however, that the Soviet leaders first indicated their intention to join the war against Japan. Hull reported that Stalin had told him "clearly and unequivocally that, when the Allies succeeded in defeating Germany, the Soviet Union would then join in defeating Japan." One evening after dinner, the Soviets showed a movie about the Japanese invasion of Siberia. "It was distinctly anti-Japanese propaganda," Deane reported, "and we all felt it was an indirect method of telling us their attitude with regard to Japan." When Eden expressed concern that this might not be an appropriate film for a neutral country to show, Harriman insisted that it was and offered a toast to the day when the Americans and the Russians would be "fighting together against the Japs." Although Harriman told Molotov that he would understand if the Soviet commissar of foreign affairs did not join the toast, Molotov replied, "Why not? Gladly—the time will come," and downed the drink.[25]

At the Foreign Ministers' Conference in Moscow the Allies issued a declaration in which they pledged collaboration. Paragraph 5 of this declaration stipulated that the Allies would consult with one another and when necessary with other members of the United Nations "with a view to joint action on behalf of the community of nations" until a new system of general security was established.[26] In July and August 1945, this provision was to become an important issue between the United States and the Soviet Union.

Stalin's promise to join the war against Japan was closely connected with the question of opening a second front in Europe. The Soviet Union had borne the brunt of the European war, confronting 80 percent of the German forces in the previous two years. Stalin's demand for Anglo-American forces to open the second front had been repeatedly denied. His promise to join the war against Japan at the Moscow Foreign Ministers' Conference was his bargaining chip with the Allies in return for opening the second front.[27]

But his pledge to enter the war against Japan was more than a negotiation ploy; he had already begun preparations for it. The Soviet victory at Stalingrad gave Stalin a sense of confidence, prompting him to take the first concrete step toward war with Japan. In August 1943, the State Committee of Defense ordered the construction of a railway from Komsomolsk-na-Amure to Sovetskaia Gavan as the top-priority project under the jurisdiction of the People's Commissariat of Internal Affairs (NKVD), for the transport of troops to the Pacific theater.[28] Nevertheless, if Stalin intended to attack Japan, he kept his intentions close to his chest, revealing his plan to only a few key Politburo members such as Molotov and Lavrentii Beria.

The quick pace with which the Allies pledged collaboration with the Soviet Union worried Ambassador Sato. On November 10, he asked Molotov if the Moscow Conference signaled any change in Soviet policy toward Japan. Molotov assured the ambassador that it did not. When Sato inquired further about the Four Power Declaration, Molotov cut him short, and asked Sato about the meaning of the recent reaffirmation of the Tripartite Pact between Germany, Italy, and Japan on September 15. By taking an aggressive stance, Molotov managed to cover up the true meaning of the Moscow Declaration.[29]

The Moscow Conference was a prelude to the first summit conference of the Allied leaders. But Stalin vetoed the idea of inviting Chiang Kai-shek. He did not regard China as an equal with the other three powers, and he did not want Chiang Kai-shek to form a coalition with the others to pressure the Soviet Union to join the war in the Far East. Thus, on November 27, 1943, Roosevelt, Churchill, and Chiang Kai-shek met in Cairo without Stalin. There they issued the Cairo Declaration, which enunciated the principle of non-expansion of territory and declared their aim to have Japan return all the territories it had acquired from others "by force and greed"—specifically, the Pacific islands, Manchuria, Taiwan, the Pescadores Islands, and Korea.

On November 28, the Big Three (Roosevelt, Churchill, and Stalin) met at Teheran. At this conference Roosevelt and Churchill finally agreed to open the second front in Europe by May 1944. In return, Stalin pledged to enter the war against Japan after the defeat of Germany. Stalin also said that he would make known in due course his "desiderata" for Soviet entry into the Pacific War. Although no record exists, it is likely that Roosevelt and Stalin discussed the reward for Soviet entry into the war. On January 12, 1944, Roosevelt revealed at the Pacific War Council that he and Stalin had agreed to return Manchuria, Formosa, and the Pescadores to China, to place Korea under a forty-year trusteeship, to grant to the Soviet Union Dairen and the Manchurian railways on bonds, and to return southern Sakhalin and hand over the Kurils to the Soviet Union. Stalin and Roosevelt had secretly discussed the specific concessions to the Soviets at Teheran, though they would have to be formally agreed upon.[30]

Meanwhile, Stalin requested from his foreign policy experts their position papers on Soviet policy toward Japan. On January 11, 1944, Ivan Maiskii, deputy commissar of foreign affairs, sent Molotov a long memorandum expounding his notions of the Soviet global strategy to be pursued in the postwar world. The primary objective for Soviet policy, Maiskii argued, should be to create conditions conducive to long-term peace and security for the Soviet Union not merely in Europe but also in Asia. For this reason the Soviet Union should obtain borders strategically favorable to Soviet security. In the Far East, he suggested that the Soviet Union secure the return of southern Sakhalin and the transfer of the Kurils in order to secure access to the Pacific Ocean. Maiskii, however, did not consider Soviet entry into the war essential to achieving these objectives. It would be more advantageous for the Soviet Union to stay out of the war and let the Americans and British defeat Japan at an enormous cost in human lives and resources. At the subsequent peace conference, the Soviet Union would be able to obtain southern Sakhalin and the Kurils "without firing a shot in the Far East."[31]

In June 1944 Ambassador Iakov Malik was summoned back to Moscow. In July, he submitted a seventy-three-page report on Soviet-Japanese relations.[32] This document had two important sections, the first devoted to analysis of the current situation, and the second to the future perspective. In the first section, Malik documented in detail how the Japanese had become dependent on the Soviet Union. Not only did the preservation of the Neutrality Pact constitute the precondition for continuing the war against the United States, but the cultivation of good relations with the Soviet Union was also the only way for Japan to extricate itself from the war. Malik asserted that Japan believed it would be possible to exploit the conflict between the U.S.-British Allies and the Soviet Union, and as the military situation became desperate the Japanese government would make substantial concessions to the Soviet Union to play the Soviets against the Allies. Although the Kwantung Army still maintained substantial strength, there was no reason to believe that Japan would attack the Soviet Union in the near future. Malik recommended, therefore, that the Soviet government expand the current level of cooperation with the Japanese.[33]

The second part of Malik's report was devoted to his view on the future of Soviet-Japanese relations. He concluded that Japan's defeat was only a matter of time. He recommended, therefore, that the Soviet Union act before the United States and Britain dissolved the Japanese Empire. The first Soviet objective should be to secure passage to the Pacific Ocean by occupying strategic points such as Manchuria, Korea, Tsushima, and the Kurils. The second should be to prevent other countries from occupying these strategic territories. Malik further enumerated twenty-seven specific goals that the Soviet Union could reach without ever joining the war.[34]

Two common threads ran through the three recommendations presented by the foreign policy elite—Lozovskii in December 1941, Maiskii in January 1944, and Malik in June 1944—with regard to Soviet policy toward Japan. They all emphasized the importance of Soviet security requirements, especially the need to secure a free passage to the Pacific Ocean. It was for this reason that they advocated the return of southern Sakhalin and the occupation of the Kurils. It is important to note that they constructed their argument of the postwar territorial settlement not on historical legitimacy, the basis of the Atlantic Charter and the Cairo Declaration, but on security needs. More than anyone else, Malik was aware of the contradiction between these two principles, and yet he pushed for the Kurils nonetheless. These foreign policy advisers also shared the conviction that the Soviet government could best accomplish its objectives by staying out of the war, though Malik had his doubts.

Stalin shared his advisers' view that the postwar territorial settlement should be dictated by the requirements of the Soviet state, not by its historical claim. He especially valued Malik's report. In fact, there were striking similarities between Malik's list and Stalin's proposal for the

Yalta Agreement. Stalin did not, however, accept their recommendation that the Soviet state could accomplish these territorial objectives by staying out of the war.

Unbeknownst to Malik, Maiskii, and Lozovskii, Stalin and Molotov had made up their minds by this time to wage war against Japan. Sometime in the summer, Stalin recalled Marshal Aleksandr M. Vasilevskii from the Belorussian front, and indicated his intention to appoint him commander of the Far Eastern front to oversee the Soviet preparations for the war against Japan. In September, in strict secrecy, Stalin ordered the General Staff to draw up estimates for the concentration and logistical support of troops in the Far East. The General Staff completed the estimates at the beginning of October before Stalin's meeting with Churchill.[35]

While Stalin was secretly plotting to wage war against Japan, the United States began to review its strategy for the Pacific War. Despite turning the tide of the war since Midway and Guadalcanal, the United States was fighting in the Pacific without a coherent, long-term strategy. Preoccupied with the war in Europe, the Joint Chiefs of Staff gave the two commanders, Admiral Chester W. Nimitz in the central Pacific and General Douglas MacArthur in the southwest Pacific, considerable autonomy. The two-prong advance was dictated more by circumstances and short-term goals than by long-term strategic plans. But in the latter half of 1943 the Allies could confidently think about defeating Germany, and the Combined Chiefs of Staff made a decision to defeat Japan within one year after the German defeat. In the beginning of 1944, Nimitz's forces were advancing to take the Marianas, while MacArthur's forces were poised to recapture the Philippines.[36] It became necessary to craft a coherent long-term strategy to defeat Japan.

American military leaders disagreed on the best method to achieve Japan's surrender. The navy, led by Fleet Admiral Ernest King, commander in chief of the United States Fleet and chief of naval operations, and the Army Air Force, headed by its chief, General H. H. "Hap" Arnold, believed that combined naval blockades and aerial bombardments would yield Japan's surrender without ground invasion. In contrast, Army Chief of Staff General George Marshall and his planners considered it necessary to invade Japan's homeland to secure the enemy's unconditional surrender. In the spring and summer of 1944 they reached a compromise consensus: the United States would launch a ground invasion in the Japanese industrial heartland while simultaneously initiating a sea and air blockade and intensive air bombardment. In July 1944, the Joint Chiefs of Staff approved the two-stage invasion of Japan's homeland, first on Kyushu, and then a decisive invasion on the Kanto plain.[37]

Soviet entry into the war against Japan was considered an essential component of this plan. But the Americans found it exceedingly difficult to coordinate military plans with the Soviet Union against Japan. Deane's efforts to obtain detailed information on Soviet capabilities and intentions met with stonewalling. Thus, when the Combined Chiefs approved the overall strategy for the defeat of Japan at the Quebec Conference in September 1944, it had no choice but to proceed without counting on Soviet participation in the war.[38]

The Fall of Tojo

The changing tide of the war inspired Stalin to contemplate how to bargain for the best conditions from the Allies for Soviet entry into the Pacific War. Meanwhile, in Japan, the fall of Saipan in July 1944 provoked widespread criticism of Tojo's policies. Senior statesmen centered around Keisuke Okada, Reijiro Wakatsuki, and Konoe hatched a conspiracy to oust Tojo. Even Kido, who had until then supported Tojo, found it necessary to sacrifice the unpopular prime minister.[39] The next cabinet was headed by General Kuniaki Koiso.

The fall of Tojo coincided with the beginning of a secret plan to seek the termination of the war. At the end of August, Navy Minister Mitsumasa Yonai ordered Rear Admiral Sokichi Takagi released from active duty and placed on sick leave. The real purpose of this order was to have Takagi secretly study how to end the war. Takagi had a sharp, analytical mind, amazingly free of the jingoism that blinded many of his countrymen. With a wide network of connections, including Konoe and Okada as well as the scholarly community, he had access to all important documents from the cabinet and the Supreme War Leadership Council, which had replaced the Liaison Conference as the highest decision-making body in Japan. Takagi soon established an important link with Colonel Makoto Matsutani of the Army Ministry, Yasumasa Matsudaira, Kido's secretary, and Toshikazu Kase, Shigemitsu's secretary. Takagi's group concluded that the only way to end the war was for the emperor to impose his decision on the military and the government.[40]

In the meantime, the more the military situation worsened, the more important the Soviet Union became in Japan's foreign and military policy. On September 12, 1944, the Supreme War Leadership Council decided to maintain Soviet-Japanese neutrality and improve relations between the two countries, to mediate peace between the Soviet Union and Germany, and to pursue active diplomatic actions to influence the Soviet Union in Japan's favor after the defeat of Germany. The government decided to send an envoy to Moscow to achieve these goals.

The specific concessions the Japanese government was willing to make included allowing Soviet ships to pass through the Tsugaru Strait; abolishing the Soviet-Japanese Basic Agreement of 1925; abandoning fishing rights in Soviet waters; giving up the Chinese Eastern Railway; accepting peaceful Soviet activities in Manchuria, Inner Mongolia, China, and other parts of East Asia; recognizing the Soviet spheres of influence in Manchuria and Inner Mongolia; abolishing the Anti-Communist Pact and the Tripartite Pact; returning southern Sakhalin; and surrendering the Northern Kurils. Japan was prepared to make considerable concessions to keep the Soviet Union out of the war. Nonetheless, they were not enough to satisfy Stalin's appetite. The extent of Soviet spheres of influence in Manchuria was left ambiguous; the South Manchurian Railway, Dairen, and Port Arthur were not mentioned, nor were Korea and the Southern Kurils included in the concessions. The list reveals the extent to which the Japanese misjudged Stalin's intentions.[41] Whereas the Soviet foreign policy elite were demanding a territorial settlement dictated by Soviet security requirements, the Japanese government believed that minimal concessions based on historical legitimacy would be sufficient.

Under Shigemitsu's instructions, Sato approached Molotov and requested that the Soviet government receive a Japanese envoy. Molotov flatly rejected Japan's request. He pointed out that Soviet-Japanese relations were firmly based on the Neutrality Pact, and he saw no reason that any issues could not be dealt with through normal diplomatic channels. Furthermore, other countries would interpret such a move as Soviet-Japanese rapprochement against the Allies.[42] While preparing for delicate negotiations with the United States to set the price for Soviet entry into the war, Stalin did not want to give the Americans the impression that he was simultaneously bargaining with the Japanese.

In October 1944, Takagi completed the first comprehensive study on the termination of the war. He pondered the pros and cons of approaching the United States, Britain, and the Soviet Union. He listed four possible American objectives: elimination of the Japanese race; elimination of the *kokutai;* reform of the political system; and international cooperation and recognition of U.S. hegemony in East Asia. Of these Takagi dismissed the first as counterproductive to American interests, while the elimination of the *kokutai* would have advantages as well as disadvantages for the United States. He believed that the United States would likely implement the third and fourth objectives. Therefore, peace through the United States might be Japan's best chance to preserve the *kokutai*.

Approaching the Soviet Union might have some advantages: Japan and the Soviet Union shared common interests against the United States and Britain, and peace through the neutral Soviet Union would not provoke a strong negative reaction from the Japanese public. But these advantages needed to be weighed against the disadvantages of possible Communist propaganda and little hope of establishing a long-lasting friendship with this unreliable partner, whose interests in China conflicted with Japan's.

As for the specific conditions Japan should demand to terminate the war, Takagi listed preservation of the *kokutai* as the most important. Other conditions included the establishment of democracy and the elimination of military cliques; non-interference in internal affairs; the securing of economic survival for citizens; non-occupation; punishment of war criminals by the Japanese themselves; and the independence of East Asian countries. In terms of territorial possession after the defeat, Takagi considered retention of Japan's four main islands to be the absolute minimum, but he did not include the Kuril, Bonin, and Ryukyu islands in this list.[43]

Needless to say, Takagi did not represent the Japanese government. Nonetheless, his ideas cannot be dismissed as having no relation to Japan's political reality, since he represented the still small, disunited, but potentially important group favoring the termination of the war. At this point Takagi clearly preferred to deal with the United States, believing that such an approach represented the best possibility for preserving the *kokutai*. There existed a narrow strip of common ground between the Japanese peace party and Grew and the Japan specialists in the United States.

Stalin Bargains with the United States

While Japan was flirting with the Soviet Union to gain its neutrality, Stalin was engaged in hard bargaining with the United States for the price of Soviet entry into the war. When Harriman and British Ambassador Archibald Clark Kerr met Stalin on September 23, 1944, to report the results of the Quebec Conference, Stalin said twice that he was surprised the United States and Britain had not taken Soviet participation into consideration in formulating the strategy to defeat Japan. He asked the ambassadors whether the Allies wished to bring Japan to its knees without Russian assistance or whether they wanted the Russians involved, as he had suggested at Teheran. After Harriman hastened to answer that the United States of course desired Soviet participation, Stalin reaffirmed his commitment to enter the war, and solicitously asked Harriman what role the United States wished to assign to the Soviet Union. Harriman asked Stalin about the use of Soviet air bases in the Maritime Province, which Stalin had earlier approved. Brushing aside Harriman's question, Stalin replied: "That is not the most important question." The most crucial concern was moving twenty to thirty Soviet divisions to the Far East.

The United States bent over backwards to appease Stalin. Harriman recommended to Roosevelt that the United States propose the operations it wanted the Soviets to undertake rather than waiting for their proposal. Roosevelt confided to Churchill that "Stalin was . . . sensitive about any doubt as to his intention to help us in the Orient," and wrote to Harriman that he had entertained no doubts whatsoever about Stalin's Teheran pledge.[44]

In October, during Churchill's visit to Moscow, Stalin had a series of conversations with Harriman. He told Harriman that he was not yet ready to give a definite date for the Soviet attack on Japan but that "planning should begin at once." He also emphasized that "consideration would have to be given to certain political aspects," implying that he needed something in return for his commitment to enter the war. He promised to make air fields and naval bases in Kamchatka available for American use, but he demanded in turn "food, and fuel for aircraft and motor transport, sufficient to constitute a two to three months' reserve" and "rails and other transportation equipment." He also expressed his readiness to begin receiving a regular flow of four-engine aircraft for the Soviet Strategic Air Force, and agreed to begin meetings between the Soviet and American military staffs in Moscow.[45]

Harriman readily agreed to provide the supplies. Stalin did not expect the war against Japan to last very long, so two months' stockpiles should be sufficient. He added that certain political aspects would have to be considered. "The Russians would have to know what they were fighting for," Stalin said, as they had certain claims against Japan. But at that time, Stalin did not clarify what these "claims" were.[46]

While Stalin was bargaining with the United States, he was simulta-

neously preparing the country for war. In recent years the Soviet government had been careful not to make any anti-Japanese statements lest they
provoke a Japanese attack on the Soviet Union. On November 6, in his
October Revolution anniversary speech, Stalin for the first time identified
Japan as an aggressor and compared Japan's attack on Pearl Harbor with
the Nazis' attack on the Soviet Union. At the same time, Stalin loosened
controls on the Soviet press to allow the release of anti-Japanese views in
preparation for forthcoming war against Japan.[47]

If Stalin believed that he could extract concessions from the United
States by promising to enter the war against Japan, he read the U.S. motivations correctly. In November 1944, the Joint Chiefs of Staff completed
a study of Soviet participation in the war against Japan which recognized
that the self-interest of the Soviet Union, irrespective of U.S. strategic interests, would inevitably bring it into the Pacific War. "However," the
study hastened to add, "there is also general recognition of the desirabil-
ity, from our standpoint, of Russia's early entry into the war." The paper
concluded that the Joint Chiefs of Staff would "desire Russian entry at
the earliest possible date," and that the JCS would be "prepared to offer
the maximum support possible without prejudice to our main effort
against Japan." Soviet military action was necessary not only to pin
down Japanese forces in Manchuria and North China but also "to inter-
dict lines of communication between Japan and the Mainland of Asia."[48]

On December 14 Harriman met Stalin and discussed the shipping of
Lend-Lease supplies to the Soviet Far East. Harriman informed Stalin
that despite shortages in the European theater and the requirements for
operations in the Philippines, Roosevelt and the Joint Chiefs of Staff had
agreed to meet the Soviet requirements as soon as and to the fullest extent possible. Harriman asked what Stalin had had in mind in October
when he had referred to "the political questions" connected with Soviet
entry into the war against Japan. Stalin brought out a map from the next
room, and said that southern Sakhalin and the Kuril Islands should be returned to the Soviet Union. "Approaches to Vladivostok are now con-
trolled by the Japanese," he explained. "The USSR is entitled to protection for its communications to this important port. All outlets to the
Pacific Ocean are now held or blocked by the enemy." Stalin then drew a
line around the southern part of the Liaotung Peninsula including Dairen
and Port Arthur, and said that the Soviet Union wished to secure the lease
for these ports again. In addition, Stalin wished to obtain the lease for the
Chinese Eastern Railway and the Southern Manchurian Railway. He demanded recognition of the status quo in Outer Mongolia.[49]

Harriman did not seem surprised by Stalin's demands. His only objection was the lease of Dairen. Internationalizing the port would be a better approach than leasing to the Soviets, Harriman suggested. Stalin replied simply: "We will discuss this issue later."

The Dilemma of the Neutrality Pact

As Stalin prepared for war against Japan, the Soviet government had to confront the issue of the Neutrality Pact, which stipulated that unless one party notified the other of the intention not to renew the agreement one year before the term expired, the pact would automatically be renewed for another five years. There was no question that the Soviet government was going to renounce the treaty before the deadline. But clearly this action would alert the Japanese to Soviet intentions. It might even provoke preemptive military action by Japan before Soviet military preparations were completed. Stalin did not want to be bound by the Neutrality Pact. But in order to attack Japan by surprise, he would have to convince the Japanese that the pact would be in force until the term expired in April 1946.

On January 10, 1945, Lozovskii sent a memorandum to Molotov recommending that the Soviet government renounce the Neutrality Pact before the deadline passed. Lozovskii suggested that the Soviets should announce the renunciation in such a way as to give the Japanese hope that their concessions might lead to negotiations for the renewal of the pact. Lozovskii recommended that the Soviet government resume negotiations for renewing the pact sometime in October-November 1945, by which time the situation in Europe and Asia would become clear.[50] Lozovskii continued to advocate that the Soviet Union stay out of the war, and he fully expected that the Neutrality Pact would continue to be in force until it expired.

There is little doubt that this question was carefully examined at the highest level. Stalin and Molotov agreed with Lozovskii on the need to renounce the Neutrality Pact, but contrary to Lozovskii's recommendation, Stalin had already decided to enter the war against Japan, and Molotov most likely shared that secret. But in order to fool Japan, they also had to fool their foreign policy elite. Neither Lozovskii nor Malik was informed of Stalin's secret plan. But still Stalin and Molotov failed to resolve several fundamental dilemmas: how to renounce the Neutrality Pact without provoking Japan's preemptive attack; whether to continue the fiction that the pact would be in force for another year or to take the unilateral action of renouncing the pact altogether in order to gain a free hand; and, if they decided to deceive the Japanese into believing that the pact was still in force, how to launch a surprise attack without being accused of violating the pact.

The Big Three at Yalta

Roosevelt, Stalin, and Churchill met at Yalta from February 4 through February 11, 1945. The Far Eastern question was taken up on February 8, the fifth day of the conference, in an unofficial meeting between Roosevelt and Stalin. Stalin raised the specific conditions he had already outlined to Harriman in return for Soviet entry into the war against Japan, and it took Roosevelt only fifteen minutes to accept the conditions. According to Andrei Gromyko, Soviet ambassador to the United States, Roosevelt had sent a note to Stalin before the meeting, accepting Stalin's demand for southern Sakhalin and the Kurils. When Gromyko translated Roosevelt's letter, Stalin was elated; he walked back and forth in his room repeating: "Good, very good!"[51] Stalin had already obtained a copy of the Blakeslee memorandum, prepared for Roosevelt before the Yalta Conference, which recommended that Japan retain the southern Kurils, but that the northern and central Kurils be placed under the jurisdiction of an international organization administered by the Soviet Union. Stalin was overjoyed that Roosevelt did not follow Blakeslee's recommendation.[52] He succeeded in getting the United States to accept the principles of the Soviets' security requirements, not their legitimate historical claims, as the basis of the postwar settlements.

On February 10, Molotov gave Harriman the English translation of Stalin's draft proposal. Harriman made two amendments to the draft. While Stalin's draft included the lease of Dairen and Port Arthur, Harriman proposed that the two ports become international ports. Stalin also stipulated that Russian rights to the Chinese Eastern Railway and the South Manchurian Railway be restored, but Harriman suggested that the railways be operated by a Chinese-Soviet commission. Stalin told Harriman that he would agree with Dairen's free port status but insisted on the lease of Port Arthur. Roosevelt accepted Stalin's proposal. Stalin also accepted Harriman's other amendment regarding the railways, but he made it conditional on Chiang Kai-shek's concurrence to the status quo in Outer Mongolia.

Harriman's note omits one important point. Stalin slipped in one sentence with regard to the railways: "Russia's preeminent interests shall be safeguarded." Harriman disliked the term "preeminent interests" and said so to Roosevelt. But Roosevelt "was not disposed to fuss over words." Little did he know that this sentence was to play an important role in subsequent Sino-Soviet negotiations. After the draft of the Yalta Secret Agreement was decided upon, Churchill, who did not attend any meetings, decided to append his signature to the document without notifying his cabinet, presumably to protect British interests in the Far East.[53]

According to the Yalta Agreement, the Big Three had agreed that, "in two or three months" after Germany's surrender, "the Soviet Union shall enter into the war against Japan on the side of the Allies" on the following conditions:

1. The status quo in Outer Mongolia . . . shall be preserved;
2. The former rights of Russia violated by the treacherous attack of Japan in 1904 shall be restored, viz:
    (a) the southern part of Sakhalin as well as all the islands adjacent to it shall be returned to the Soviet Union;
    (b) the commercial port of Dairen shall be internationalized, the preeminent interests of the Soviet Union in this port being safeguarded and the lease of Port Arthur as a naval base of the USSR restored;
    (c) the Chinese-Eastern Railroad and the South-Manchurian Railroad which provides an outlet to Dairen shall be jointly operated by the establishment of a joint Soviet-Chinese Company[,] it being understood that the preeminent interests of the Soviet Union shall be safeguarded and that China shall retain full sovereignty in Manchuria;
3. The Kuril islands shall be handed over to the Soviet Union.

The agreement was conditional on the approval of Chiang Kai-shek, and Roosevelt was to "take measures in order to obtain this concurrence on advice of Marshal Stalin." The Soviet Union indicated its readiness to conclude with the Nationalist Government of China a pact of friendship and alliance.[54]

The wording reflects Stalin's careful maneuvering. Article 3, which dealt with the Kurils, was separated from Article 2, which stipulated the restoration of Russia's former rights "violated by the treacherous attack of Japan in 1904." The islands were to be "handed over" to the Soviet Union rather than "restored," as were the items in Article 2. By indicating that this independent article was as important as the others and by carefully using the expression "handed over" rather than "restored," Stalin precluded the possibility that the Kurils would be taken away later as a violation of the Atlantic Charter and the Cairo Declaration that proclaimed the principle of territorial integrity of all nations. Moreover, by having Roosevelt and Churchill pledge that these claims "shall be unquestionably fulfilled after Japan has been defeated," he made doubly sure that these promises would not be ignored. Harriman questioned this paragraph, but Roosevelt replied that it was "just language."[55]

Stalin also scored a major victory on the matter of rights to the Chinese railways, ports, and Outer Mongolia. These rewards were a direct infringement on China as a sovereign nation, and Roosevelt and Churchill in a cavalier fashion granted them behind the back of a major ally. In addition, Stalin slipped in the claim for Soviet "preeminent interests" in the railways and Port Dairen, while the joint partnership over the railways and the port were made contingent on Chiang Kai-shek's approval of the Soviet sphere of influence in Outer Mongolia. In order to secure Stalin's pledge to enter the war, Roosevelt did not hesitate to sacrifice China's sovereign rights. He was even less concerned that Soviet entry would violate the Neutrality Pact with Japan. Harriman showed the document to the Joint Chiefs of Staff, hoping that they might raise objections, but Marshall, King, and William Leahy, chief of staff to the commander in chief of the army and navy, approved the document without raising any questions. Leahy carried the signed document to Washington and locked it in the president's personal safe. Secretary of State Edward Stettinius and the State Department with the exception of Harriman did not know of its existence.[56]

Another incident at Yalta had important implications for subsequent events. On February 9, at the Combined Chiefs of Staff meeting, Churchill spoke about the possibility of Russia's joining Britain, China, and the United States in issuing a four-power ultimatum calling on Japan to surrender unconditionally. Japan might ask what the Allies meant by unconditional surrender. In this event, Churchill suggested, "there was no doubt that some mitigation would be worth while if it led to the saving of a year or a year and half of a war in which so much blood and treasure would be poured out." Roosevelt, however, doubted "whether the ultimatum would have much effect on the Japanese, who did not seem to realize what was going on in the world outside, and still seemed to think that they might get a satisfactory compromise." Churchill's statement was the first suggestion that Roosevelt should amend unconditional surrender. As Churchill expected, Roosevelt rejected it out of hand. It is important to note, however, that Churchill's speech was made at the Combined Chiefs of Staff meeting, where Leahy, Marshall, and King were present. Churchill planted seeds in their minds about the possibility of amending unconditional surrender.[57]

Yalta marked a turning point in Soviet military planning for the war against Japan. Although nothing concrete had been done before the Yalta Conference, afterward Vasilevskii and the General Staff began a detailed study of how best to launch an offensive.[58]

Japan's Last-Ditch Defense Plans

As U.S.-Soviet collaboration intensified, Japan's military fortunes worsened day by day. In November 1944, Japan lost the Battle of Leyte. American forces landed in Luzon in the Philippines in January 1945, while air raids on mainland Japan intensified. Hirohito's concern grew. Since the beginning of the war, the emperor and Kido had adamantly refused to seek advice from senior statesmen, but by February 1945, Hirohito was inviting them one by one to the Imperial Palace to express their views.

While the Big Three were meeting at Yalta on February 14, Konoe submitted his memorandum to Hirohito. "I regret to say that Japan's defeat is inevitable," the prince began. "Defeat will damage the *kokutai*, but public opinion in America and England has not gone far enough to destroy the *kokutai* . . . Therefore, we should not be worried about defeat itself. What we must worry about is a Communist revolution that might accompany defeat." Konoe then indicated that the Soviet Union would be interested in expanding its influence in Asia, just as it had in eastern Europe. Sooner or later the Soviets would interfere in Japan's domestic situation. Economic turmoil had caused profound discontent among the Japanese people. If the discontent of the masses were to combine with the radical young officers' movement, the result would be a dangerous threat to the *kokutai*. Therefore, Konoe recommended, the only way to save the *kokutai* would be to negotiate with the United States and Britain as soon as possible, an action that would require the direct intervention of the emperor against the military.[59]

Considering the upsurge of the Communist Party in the immediate postwar period, Konoe's fear of a Communist revolution cannot be easily dismissed. Furthermore, the possibility that popular discontent could develop into a military coup was a concern widely shared among Japan's policymakers. Members of the imperial household in particular keenly sensed this danger. In particular, Prince Takamatsu, Hirohito's younger brother, and Prince Higashikuni, uncle of the empress, shared the fear that military defeat might spell the end of the imperial house. To them, the notion of preserving the imperial house was already beginning to be divorced from the preservation of the *kokutai*.

Kido agreed with Konoe's view of the inevitability of defeat and the need to seek peace to save the imperial house. But Kido knew they must tread carefully to avoid alienating the military in their quest to end the war. The peace party was hardly united. The Koiso government had no plan to terminate the war, even as Japan's military continued to suffer defeat. As the prospect of defeat became certain, no plan for surrender was in sight.

Kido's fear was justified, since the Japanese Imperial Army was adamantly clinging to the course of war. On February 15, the Imperial General Headquarters submitted its report on the world situation to the Supreme War Leadership Council. The report anticipated that the United States would concentrate on securing the Philippines and the Marianas for use as launching pads to attack Japan's homeland. It anticipated that the United States would try to induce the Soviet Union to participate in the war against Japan. Although the Soviet Union might announce its intention to renounce the Neutrality Pact in the spring, the council expected the Soviet Union to maintain neutrality. Only when it judged that Japan's power had become extremely weakened might it take military action against Japan in order to "secure its voice to determine the future of the Far East." The most vulnerable point for the United States would be the cost of lives inflicted by Japan's "bleeding" strategy, a euphemism for kamikaze attacks. Thus, the report concluded that despite difficulties, Japan would be able to triumph as long as it continued to fight with courage and determination. In the middle of March, the Imperial General Headquarters adopted the last-ditch defense strategy called "Ketsu-go," expecting correctly that the U.S. landing would be launched on Kyushu.[60]

The Japanese government nervously watched the Big Three conference at Yalta. On February 22 Sato visited Molotov, who had just returned from the Crimea. The Japanese ambassador asked Molotov point-blank if the war in the Far East had been discussed at Yalta. "The relationship between the Soviet Union and Japan is different from the relationship between Japan and America and England," Molotov answered. "America and England are fighting with Japan, but the Soviet Union has the Neutrality Pact with Japan. We consider questions about Soviet-Japanese relations the affair of our two countries. It has been so, and it will remain so." Sato assured Molotov that the Japanese government intended to renew the Neutrality Pact for another five years, and he asked how the Soviet government felt about the issue. Molotov said that he listened to Japan's view on the Neutrality Pact with satisfaction, and promised to convey it to the Soviet government.[61] If diplomacy is an art of deception, Molotov was a consummate diplomat. Unlike Malik and Lozovskii, he knew Stalin's secret plan to attack Japan as well as the prize he had obtained at Yalta.

Japan's Foreign Ministry did not sit idly by. In February its Treaty Division wrote a report on the Allies' policies toward Japan on unconditional surrender, occupation, disarmament, elimination of militarism, democratic reforms, punishment of war criminals, and status of the emperor. The report concluded that the Allies would most likely demand unconditional surrender, but that they were divided on the issue of the emperor. Some felt that the emperor could serve as a stabilizing force after the war, whereas others saw the emperor system as the source of militarism. The report also paid special attention to Grew's statement that the question of the emperor should be left undecided until the war was over to find out whether the institution of the emperor would be an asset or a liability. The report emphatically stated that though public opinion remained divided on the status of the emperor, on the subject of the need for democratic reforms to eradicate militarism there was no dissent.

On the basis of open publications alone, the Foreign Ministry accurately gauged the Allies' public opinion. Like Takagi, the ministry knew that the only hope for terminating the war and saving the emperor, if not the *kokutai* itself, would be to rely on those policymakers and public figures who took the position close to Grew's. As a result of this diligent information gathering, the Foreign Ministry was poised to play an important role at the decisive moment in the termination of the war.

The Foreign Ministry's top officials were not the only ones waiting in the wings to act when an opportune moment arrived. On March 13, Takagi completed the second draft of his secret peace plan. He predicted that after the impending defeat of Germany, anti-Axis powers would concentrate on the postwar settlement of Europe and the war against Japan. The United States would attempt to finish the war in the Pacific by the end of the year, relying only on its superior military power. As in his previous study in October 1944, Takagi believed that the United States would not likely aim to eliminate the Japanese state and the Japanese race nor destroy the *kokutai*. Its goal would be to establish a peaceful regime that would cooperate with the United States. For this purpose, it would implement reforms to establish a liberal democratic regime by removing the military influence. It would also likely leave political reforms in the hands of the Japanese. Clearly, Takagi believed that the "soft peace" advocated by Grew and the Japan specialists would become the predominant policy of the United States, as Grew and the Japan specialists in the United States placed their trust in the power of Japan's "moderate" wing of political leaders. Japan's peace party and the American advocates for soft peace spoke a common language across the ocean that could become the basis for an earlier termination of the war. But the terms they advocated were acceptable on both sides for only a tiny minority.

As for Soviet policy in Asia, Takagi expected the Soviet Union to play power politics "with cold-blooded realism." While sending troops to the Manchurian border, it would carefully monitor the outcome of the deadly struggle between the United States and Japan. Both sides would be weakened from the fight, creating an opportunity to expand Soviet influence in Asia. The United States might have the upper hand against Japan, but this would inevitably lead the Japanese leaders to maintain close relations with the Soviet Union. The Soviets' first priority would be to increase their influence in Asia. Nonetheless, when Japan became considerably weakened, one could not exclude the possibility that the Soviets would engage in political pressure, military intervention, military occupation, seizure of military bases, and even entry into the war against Japan. Which option the Soviet Union might choose would depend on its relationship with the United States and Britain and the military situation in Asia. Here, Takagi's assessment was off the mark, but if he erred, he was not alone; the American Joint Chiefs of Staff, Ambassador Sato, and even Soviet diplomats like Malik, Lozovskii, and Maiskii had reached the same conclusion.

On the basis of this analysis, Takagi felt the time was now ripe to end the war. Japan should insist only on maintaining the "sanctity of the emperor's position" and the "preservation of the *kokutai*." As in his previous study, Takagi made a distinction between the emperor's position and the *kokutai*. Now, however, he implied that if push came to shove, he might jettison the broader definition of the *kokutai* and attempt to save only the emperor's status.[62]

The peace party had a plan; the challenge was how to implement it. As Takagi pointed out, the support of the army staff officers was essential, as was the support of the emperor. Since the Koiso cabinet was utterly incapable of implementing a peace plan, it would have to be forced to resign.

MacArthur Calls for Soviet Entry

Whereas the Japanese Army constructed its strategy on the assumption that the Soviet Union could be kept out of the war, the United States considered Soviet entry into the war a precondition for the successful invasion of Japan's homeland. MacArthur told Brigadier General George A. Lincoln, chief of the Strategy and Policy Group of the War Department's Operation Division, that the Soviets needed to enter the war against Japan before any U.S. invasion, in order to pin down Japanese forces on the Asian continent.

In a letter to George Marshall, MacArthur agreed that the only way to defeat Japan would be to invade the industrial heart of the country, but he warned of "the potency of the Japanese army" and emphatically stated: "we must not invade Japan proper unless the Russian army is previously committed to action in Manchuria." He was fully aware of the Soviet ambition to acquire all of Manchuria, Korea, and part of North China, but the Soviet seizure of these territories would be inevitable. "The United States must insist," MacArthur stated, "that Russia pay her way by invading Manchuria at the earliest possible date after the defeat of Germany."[63]

Roosevelt and MacArthur underestimated Stalin's intention. They judged that Stalin would wait for an opportune moment to minimize the Soviet sacrifices in the Far Eastern War. But they did not understand that regardless of the Yalta Agreement, Stalin had been prepared to wage war against Japan. Now that he had secured the Yalta Agreement, Stalin was ready to sacrifice thousands of Soviet lives to obtain what was promised.

Despite assurances from the Soviet General Staff that it would vigorously pursue coordination of military plans with the U.S. Mission in Moscow, the combined planning group, which held a series of meetings in Moscow from January through March, stalled without producing any results.[64] The lack of cooperation on the Soviet side stemmed partly from the excessive caution taken to keep the Soviet military plan secret in order to maximize the effect of surprise. But it also reflected Stalin's reluctance to allow U.S. forces to operate on Soviet soil. In particular, Stalin was not pleased with the extensive operations the United States planned in the Kurils. He did not want to foreclose this possibility, but he did not actively pursue it.

The Manhattan Project

The story of the development of the atomic bomb in the United States is so well known that it does not need to be told here in detail. The Manhattan Project, which developed the atomic bomb at the cost of $2 billion over three years, began its practical start in 1943 under the leadership of Brigadier General Leslie Groves with the ultimate responsibility residing with Secretary of War Henry Stimson. It suffices to note only several important ways the Manhattan Project influenced the tripartite relationship among the United States, Japan, and the Soviet Union.

At least in the beginning of 1945, the possibility of the United States possessing the atomic bomb did not seriously enter into the strategy crafted by the military planners. Knowledge of the atomic bomb was limited to those officers who worked directly with or under General Groves. The Operations Division of the War Department (OPD), officially termed "command post" of the Chief of Staff, was responsible for preparing plans and prosecuting the war, but few OPD officers had knowledge of the Manhattan Project. According to George Lincoln, who was one of only a few people who knew about the atomic bomb project, "prior to 6 August 1945 no reference to the atomic bomb appeared in OPD records." In December 1944, the president read a report prepared by Groves "outlining the expected schedule for the production of atomic bombs." One bomb would be ready by August 1, 1945, and another, more complicated one might be ready for testing in July. The bombs were still too far in the future to be integrated into military planning. Nevertheless, it was already assumed that when completed, the bombs would be used against the Japanese. In September 1944, Churchill visited Roosevelt and they reached an agreement: "When a bomb is finally available, it might perhaps . . . be used against the Japanese, who should be warned that this bombardment will be repeated until they surrender."[65]

The atomic bomb was also important in the context of U.S.-Soviet relations. Fissures and strains had already emerged over Eastern Europe, especially over Poland. At Yalta, Roosevelt and Churchill conceded to the Soviet preponderant power in Eastern Europe, although for public relations purposes they had the Soviet Union pay lip service to the Declaration of Liberated Europe, which promised "free elections." But the manner in which Stalin asserted the Soviets' preeminent position in Poland alarmed even Roosevelt. Churchill began harping on Roosevelt to make Poland a "test case between us and the Russians."[66] But Roosevelt told Churchill not to create a public showdown with Stalin. In his last letter to Churchill, on April 11, Roosevelt counseled the prime minister: "I would minimize the general Soviet problem as much as possible because these problems in one form or another, seem to arise every day and most of them straighten out . . . We must be firm, however, and our course thus far is correct." He died the next day, but as Arnold Offner concludes, "There is no reason to think . . . that he intended to challenge Stalin over Poland or to forge an anti-Soviet coalition."[67]

Harriman was alarmed. In December, he wrote in the unsent memorandum to the president that a disturbing pattern of U.S.-Soviet relations was emerging: "Russians decide what they want and announce their decisions. We are given no reasons for their decisions and no real opportunity to discuss them. The Russians appear to expect us to accept without question whatever they decide and don't seem to care what effect these arbitrary decisions have on our general attitude and on American opinion."[68]

After the Yalta Conference, Harriman became more worried about Roosevelt's appeasement policy, and his critical advice became more strident. He vented his frustrations in another undelivered memo to the president. The Soviets were violating the agreement on Poland, and when the United States stood firm, they started to retaliate, hoping to force the United States to back down. Since a magnanimous act on the part of America was interpreted as a sign of weakness, Harriman recommended that it was about time to "abandon our conciliatory policies and put our reliance on a four square basis."[69]

Harriman's recommendations might have had little impact on Roosevelt, but they influenced Stimson. The secretary of war had been thinking hard about the issue of international control of atomic energy in the postwar world. He had come to the conclusion that the secret of atomic energy could not be kept for long from the Soviet Union. But Harriman's clarion call made Stimson think twice about the implications of sharing the atomic secret with the Soviets. He decided at the end of December 1944 "not to take them into our confidence until we were sure to get a real *quid pro quo* from our frankness."[70]

The Manhattan Project also reveals the extent to which the Soviets were involved in espionage activities. In April 1943 the State Defense Committee decided to initiate the Soviet atomic bomb project, and the NKVD and the Soviet military intelligence instructed their agents, including Klaus Fuchs, David Greenglass, and Theodore Hall, to gather information about the Manhattan Project. In addition, Harry Gold and Julius Rosenberg were involved as conduits of information. Thanks to the information given by these spies, Stalin knew about the bomb. He understood that the Soviet Union had to join the war before the Americans used the atomic bomb.

In the two months since the Yalta Conference, so much had changed. The Japanese suffered defeat in the Philippines, and in March the Japanese forces in Iwo Jima were annihilated. Curtis LeMay's strategic air command began bombarding Japanese cities relentlessly. The Americans were now poised to attack Okinawa, the last step before the homeland invasion. In Europe, the Allies were moving from East and West to strangle the remnants of Nazi Germany, but as victory came near, fissures emerged among the Allies over Poland and Eastern Europe. Churchill fumed, Roosevelt's health deteriorated, and Stalin plotted his next move. March was ending, and April was bound to bring drastic changes.

CHAPTER 2

Stalin, Truman, and Hirohito Face New Challenges

C HANGE FIRST BEGAN in the Pacific. On April 1, American troops landed on Okinawa, initiating the last battle before the planned invasion of Japan's homeland. On April 3, the Joint Chiefs of Staff formally directed General MacArthur, commander in chief of U.S. Army forces in the Pacific, and Admiral Chester Nimitz, commander in chief of the Pacific Fleet and the Pacific Ocean Areas, to develop plans for the invasion of Kyushu. On April 5, in Moscow, Molotov notified Ambassador Sato that the Soviet Union did not intend to renew the Neutrality Pact. On the same day, in Tokyo, the Koiso cabinet fell, and on April 7 Baron Kantaro Suzuki formed what turned out to be Japan's last wartime cabinet. In Washington, on April 12, Franklin Delano Roosevelt died, and Harry S. Truman took his oath as the thirty-third president of the United States. The winds of change had begun to blow.

On April 1, 183,000 U.S. troops landed on Kadena Beach on Okinawa. By then it was clear that Japan was losing the war. Rather than face this obvious fact, however, Hirohito sought to wage a decisive battle on Okinawa. He hoped that by inflicting tremendous damage on the Allies, Japan could gain favorable terms to end the war. Although the Americans eventually won the battle, the Japanese inflicted tremendous casualties on the invading army and navy, killing 12,520 American troops and wounding 37,000. The ferocious battle gave the American military planners further proof that the Japanese were determined to fight to the end. This perception had a sobering effect on future U.S. military planning, as the question of whether to invade the Japanese homeland began to loom large.[1]

On April 5, Molotov summoned Sato to his office and read the statement renouncing the Neutrality Pact. Molotov explained that the pact had been concluded before the German attack on the Soviet Union and before the outbreak of war between Japan and the United States. The situation had drastically changed since then. "Germany attacked the Soviet Union, and Japan, an ally with Germany, is assisting Germany in its war against the Soviet Union," Molotov declared. "In addition, Japan is fighting with the United States and Britain, which are the allies of the Soviet Union." The Neutrality Pact had lost its meaning, and its extension became impossible. Molotov served notice that "in accordance with Article 3 of the Neutrality Pact," the Soviet government declared its intention to renounce the agreement.

The "strange neutrality" that existed between the Soviet Union and Japan was nothing new. The real question is, Why did the Soviet government decide to abrogate the Neutrality Pact at that time? Molotov's answers to Sato's questions indicate the Soviet government's ambiguous position. On the one hand, the Soviets wished to nullify the Neutrality Pact immediately, thereby freeing them to enter the war against Japan. On the other hand, Article 3 stipulated that the pact would remain in force for one year in the event that one party notified the other of its intention to renounce the agreement before the term expired. The unilateral abrogation of the pact might provoke Japan into launching a preemptive attack on Soviet forces. Thus the task for the Soviet government was to fool the Japanese into believing that the Soviets would maintain neutrality until the pact's full term, allowing Stalin to surreptitiously transport troops and equipment to the Manchurian border while the Japanese were "lulled to sleep," as Stalin later put it.

Sato wanted clarification. As far as the Japanese government was concerned, the Neutrality Pact would remain in force until the end of its full term. Molotov responded that with the renunciation of the pact, "Soviet-Japanese relations will virtually return to the situation in which they were before the conclusion of the pact."

Sato would not let the matter rest. He declared that the Japanese government still interpreted Article 3 to mean that even after Soviet renunciation, the pact would remain in force until the five-year term was completed. In the face of this unassailable argument, Molotov conceded that there had been a "misunderstanding." The Soviet statement was "in accordance with Article 3," which meant that the pact would remain in force until the completion of its term. For the moment Molotov opted for "strategic deception," which served Stalin's immediate tactical needs. But this option left unresolved the problem of how to justify the violation of the pact once the Soviets went to war against Japan. Molotov, most likely on Stalin's orders, chose the option that would allow the Soviets to continue sending massive reinforcements to the Far Eastern Front. Banking on Japan's gullibility, the commissar of foreign affairs left the tricky legal question to be decided by other means.[2]

There still remains the puzzling question of timing: Why did the Soviet Union choose to renounce the Neutrality Pact at that particular moment? In fact, if the Neutrality Pact was not set to expire until April 1946, why did the Soviets not take advantage of the cloak of the pact to make preparations for military action against Japan? By renouncing the Neutrality Pact, didn't Stalin risk a preemptive Japanese attack against Soviet forces in the Far East, which had not yet been sufficiently reinforced?

There were two possible reasons the Soviets declared their intention to abrogate the Neutrality Pact at that particular time. The first, most obvious reason was that if the Soviet government wished to renounce the pact, it was obligated to notify the Japanese government before April 25, one year before the term was up. As Lozovskii stressed, the Soviets had to make their intention known before the arrival of Chinese Foreign Minister T. V. Soong in Moscow, lest the Japanese interpret the Soviet action as a response to pressure from the Allies. If they could not get away with their "liberal" interpretation of Article 3 of the pact, as Molotov first attempted, violation of the pact would still carry less liability, if not legally, at least politically, than an attack on Japan without any notice of Soviet intentions to renounce the agreement. It is erroneous to assume that Stalin's regime was prepared to violate just any treaty when it was convenient. On the contrary, the Soviets took their treaty obligations seriously, even though they often interpreted the terms of such agreements as it best suited them. Stalin had to be especially careful lest his actions be compared to Hitler's violation of the Nazi-Soviet Non-Aggression Pact.

Second, and more important, the renunciation of the pact was a message to the United States that the Soviet Union was prepared to honor its commitment to enter the war against Japan after Germany's capitulation. After the honeymoon at Yalta, fissures of conflict had emerged over Poland and other European issues. The renunciation of the Neutrality Pact was the signal to the United States that the Soviet Union was eager to cooperate, despite minor irritations. As soon as the note of renunciation was handed to the Japanese ambassador, Molotov sent a telegram to the Soviet ambassador in Washington, Andrei Gromyko, to notify the U.S. government of the Soviets' intention to abrogate the Neutrality Pact.[3]

Was Stalin risking a possible Japanese attack? Kremlin leaders relied on Malik for information on the situation in Japan. On March 22, the Soviet ambassador had sent an important report to Moscow. He observed that as the ruling elite of Japan became convinced of defeat, they came to rely more and more on the Soviet Union as the mediator for peace. This analysis, buttressed by other intelligence sources, must have convinced Kremlin leaders that even if they announced the renunciation of the Neutrality Pact, the chances of a preemptive attack by Japan were slim.[4]

But Stalin was not one to leave important matters to chance. On March 26 he issued two orders, one to the commander of troops in the Maritime Province and another to the commander of the Far Eastern Front, to place Soviet troops on alert for possible Japanese attacks, to strengthen the protection of the railways, and to reinforce the defense of major cities including Vladivostok and Khabarovsk.[5] He covered all ground before informing the Japanese of his intention to abrogate the Neutrality Pact.

Suzuki Takes Over

By the time Sato received Molotov's note, the Koiso cabinet had already fallen. Kantaro Suzuki, a seventy-eight-year-old navy admiral with hearing problems, reluctantly accepted the premiership. In forming a cabinet, Suzuki was assisted by Hisatsune Sakomizu, who accepted the post of cabinet secretary. Sakomizu was the son-in-law of a senior statesman, Keisuku Okada, who had been engaged in behind-the-scenes maneuvers to terminate the war. But the most important post for the new cabinet was that of army minister, because the army, fearful of Suzuki's intention to terminate the war, was prepared to oppose his nomination. Suzuki decided on General Korechika Anami, a true believer in the continuation of the war. Anami, however, would accept the post only if Suzuki agreed to fight the war to the end and implement the army's plan for victory. To the surprise of the army officers, the admiral accepted these conditions without any resistance. To counterbalance the war hawk Anami, Suzuki appointed as navy minister Mitsumasa Yonai, known as an advocate for the termination of the war.[6]

Another important appointment was that of foreign minister. Although Kido preferred his personal friend Shigemitsu, Suzuki decided to appoint his own candidate, Shigenori Togo, who as ambassador to Moscow in 1938–1939 had negotiated with the Soviet government for the settlement of the Nomonhan War, and who had been foreign minister when Japan attacked Pearl Harbor in 1941. When Suzuki asked him to accept the position, Togo responded that in view of the worsening military situation it was time to think about terminating the war. Suzuki stated that he believed Japan could continue to fight for two or three more years. Finding this view unsatisfactory, Togo at first rejected the offer. Under pressure from Matsudaira and Sakomizu, however, he ultimately accepted the position of foreign minister.[7]

The powerful combination of Kido and Togo, joined by Navy Minister Yonai, formed the core of the peace party. Within this party Prime Minister Suzuki was the weakest link. In fact, it is impossible to put him in the ranks of the "peace party," at least initially. His messages on April 7 and 8 were drumbeat calls for the Japanese people to continue defending the *kokutai*. In an interview with the newspaper *Asahi*, Suzuki stated that he felt Japan would win the war. Like the emperor, he believed in waging one more decisive battle before ending the war.[8]

Truman Becomes President

Across the Pacific Ocean there was another change in government. At 5 P.M. on April 12, Vice President Truman was in Sam Rayburn's office when he received a call from the president's press secretary, asking him to come to the White House as quickly as possible. Once there, he was ushered into Mrs. Roosevelt's study on the second floor. Eleanor Roosevelt put her arm around Truman's shoulder, and said: "The president is dead." Truman asked her what he could do. Mrs. Roosevelt immediately responded: "Is there anything we can do for you? For you are the one in trouble now." At 7:08 P.M., Truman took the oath as the thirty-third president of the United States. Immediately after, he called his first cabinet meeting.[9]

Roosevelt had not prepared the vice president for the enormous task facing a wartime president. In fact, Truman had been consciously excluded from all deliberations on foreign and military policy. On the first full day of his presidency, Truman drove to the Hill for lunch and asked his former colleagues for advice. After lunch, he told the reporters waiting in the hallway: "Boys, if you ever pray, pray for me now. I don't know whether you fellows ever had a load of hay fall on you, but when they told me yesterday what had happened, I felt like the moon, the stars, and all the planets had fallen on me." "Good luck, Mr. President," a reporter responded. "I wish you didn't have to call me that," Truman replied.[10] Those were the words of a frightened man who was all too aware of his inadequacies and lack of preparedness for the enormous tasks suddenly thrust on him.

Truman attempted to compensate for his insecurity with quick decisions that gave him the appearance of being decisive. John J. McCloy, assistant secretary of war, noted in his diary: "He is a simple man, prone to make up his mind quickly and decisively, perhaps too quickly . . . He spoke at length of how he had made the decisions which he had made since he had taken office, and constantly emphasized how lucky he had been in his decisions as he realized that many of them had been made very much on the spur of the moment."[11]

Truman's first major preoccupation was to carry on Roosevelt's legacy. On April 13 he called a meeting of his predecessor's cabinet. To ensure continuity, he asked the secretaries of war and the navy and the Chiefs of Staff to stay on and serve him. Despite his age, a profound sense of duty to the country compelled Henry Stimson to stay on as secretary of war. James Forrestal also continued to serve as secretary of the navy. Admiral William Leahy offered to resign as Chief of Staff to the president, a position that Roosevelt had created, but Truman asked him to stay. After all the cabinet members had left the room, Stimson remained alone with Truman. He told him about "a new explosive of almost unbelievable destructive power." "That's all I feel free to say at the moment," the secretary of war stated, and left the room. Stimson's elliptical remark must have left Truman puzzled.

To compensate for his lack of experience in foreign policy, however, Truman wanted to bring in someone he could trust as secretary of state. On their way back from Roosevelt's funeral at Hyde Park, Truman offered the post to James Byrnes, a powerful senator from South Carolina. The two men met on April 13 and "discussed everything from Teheran to Yalta . . . and everything under the sun."[12]

On Monday afternoon, April 16, Truman appeared at the Joint Session of the Congress and made his first speech as president. He declared: "Our demand has been and it remains—unconditional surrender." Thunderous applause followed. Truman was to carry the banner of unconditional surrender, not merely because he wanted to stress the consistency of his policy with Roosevelt's, but also because he was convinced that the United States had the right to demand retribution for the infamy of Pearl Harbor.[13]

Truman was also determined to honor the Yalta Agreements. On April 17, Ambassador to China Patrick Hurley, who had been sent to Moscow by Roosevelt, sent a telegram to Truman informing the president of the meeting he had had with Stalin and Molotov. According to Hurley, Molotov told the ambassador that "the Chinese Communists are not in fact Communist at all." The Soviets were not supporting the Chinese Communist Party and had no intention of intervening in internal disputes or civil war in China. During the meeting Stalin had asked Hurley if Truman and Chiang Kai-shek had been informed about the specific provisions of the Yalta Agreement. Hurley answered that Truman had been informed, but that Chiang Kai-shek had not. Hurley advised Truman to decide when to tell the Chinese leader about the agreement. Despite the widely held view that Truman did not know about the secret Yalta Agreement until he opened Roosevelt's safe, he surely must have known of its existence by the time Hurley sent this telegram. On April 19, Truman met China's foreign minister, T. V. Soong. Without revealing the Yalta Agreement, Truman encouraged Soong to travel to Moscow to reach an accord with the Soviet Union.[14] Truman was convinced that to ensure the continuity of his policy with Roosevelt's he must strictly adhere to the agreements reached at Yalta.

Pressure to Revise Unconditional Surrender

Truman's assumption of the presidency coincided with the final decision of the American military planners to implement the Kyushu invasion, codenamed Olympic. On May 25, the JCS designated MacArthur as the primary commander of the invasion of Kyushu, and set the date of the invasion as November 1, 1945.[15]

As the military planners began preparing to invade Japan, the movement to make the terms of surrender more acceptable to the Japanese was picking up speed. Three diverse groups raised the possibility of redefining unconditional surrender. In the first group were Joseph Grew, Eugene

Dooman, and the trio of Japan specialists Ballantine, Blakeslee, and Borton. At the end of 1944 Grew became undersecretary of state. Grew's trusted aide, Eugene Dooman, was appointed chairman of the Far Eastern subcommittee of the State-War-Navy Coordinating Committee (SWNCC) and quickly recruited Borton and Blakeslee to write policy papers for the committee. Ballantine was appointed head of the Far Eastern Affairs of the State Department. Thus the soft-peace advocates positioned themselves in strategic posts and were ready to strike back.

With the help of Borton, Blakeslee, Ballantine, and Dooman, the Far Eastern Regional Committee of the State Department adopted document "CAC 93, the Emperor System," which presented three alternative ways to preserve the monarchical system in Japan. The first was "total suspension," according to which the emperor and his relatives would be placed in protective custody. The emperor would become a nominal sovereign without any political power; all power would be transferred to the Supreme Commander of Allied Powers. The second alternative was "total continuation," by which the emperor would exercise all power. The third alternative was "partial continuation," in which the emperor would carry out a limited number of government functions. The first alternative might provoke Japanese resentment, thereby making it difficult for the Supreme Commander of Allied Powers to implement occupation policies. But in view of American public opinion, the committee felt that the second alternative would be impossible to implement. The committee therefore recommended the adoption of the third alternative, and specifically mentioned that the emperor's power to veto laws and his exclusive control of the military command [tosuiken] should be abolished. The idea of preserving the emperor as the "symbol" of the nation but depriving him of real power originated from this document.[16]

Most important for the advocates of soft peace was Grew's emergence as their most powerful spokesman. Since his famous speech in Chicago in 1943, in which he passionately advocated the need to resurrect Japan as a peaceful and constructive member of the international community, Grew had been criticized as the nation's foremost "appeaser." During his confirmation hearings for the post of undersecretary of state, he had to tone down his sympathy for the Japanese emperor. As the lightning rod for vicious attacks from the Left, he found it necessary to retreat from his position and state that the question of the emperor should remain "fluid and unprejudiced." But the retreat was merely tactical. He wrote on April 14: "Surrender by Japan would be highly unlikely regardless of military defeat, in the absence of a public undertaking by the President that unconditional surrender would not mean the elimination of the present dynasty if the Japanese people desire its retention."[17] It was clear that he would strike back at the opportune moment to lobby for the revision of unconditional surrender.

The second initiative to modify unconditional surrender came from Captain Ellis Zacharias of the Office of Naval Intelligence, who was assigned to the Office of War Information in April. Since 1944, the Office of Naval Intelligence had been gathering information about Japan's domestic situation. It detected the existence of a "peace party" within Japan centering around Yonai and his adviser Takagi. Having obtained seemingly reliable information about the divisions within the Japanese government from a captured navy officer and a diplomat of a neutral Scandinavian country, most likely Widar Bagge of Sweden, Zacharias convinced Navy Secretary Forrestal to begin a psychological warfare program in Japan. The program, called OP-16-W, would involve sending a series of broadcast messages to Japan aiming to convince Japanese policymakers that unconditional surrender would not mean the destruction of the Japanese nation and state. Zacharias's view eventually contributed to Forrestal's effort to revise unconditional surrender.[18]

The Joint Chiefs of Staff was the third group interested in revising unconditional surrender. In the beginning of April, aware that Japan's defeat might come soon, the JCS ordered the Joint Intelligence Committee to study the implication of Japan's surrender. The committee submitted two reports to the Joint Chiefs of Staff in April. The first memorandum stated that "the increasing effects of air-sea blockade, the progressive and cumulative devastation wrought by strategic bombing, and the collapse of Germany" would make the Japanese realize that "absolute defeat is inevitable." It went on to state: "The entry of the U.S.S.R. into the war would, together with the foregoing factors, convince most Japanese at once of the inevitability of complete defeat." The memorandum suggested one possible way to induce Japan to early surrender: "If . . . the Japanese people, as well as their leaders, were persuaded both that absolute defeat was inevitable and that unconditional surrender did not imply national annihilation, surrender might follow fairly quickly." The JCS was picking up the theme that Churchill had planted at the Yalta Conference. The question of defining unconditional surrender was raised as an alternative not only to the homeland invasion but also to Soviet entry into the war.

The Joint Intelligence Committee's second memorandum recommended a more specific redefinition of unconditional surrender: "there is a possibility that some constitutional Japanese central government, backed by the Emperor, may seek and accept a rationalized version of unconditional surrender before the end of 1945." Prompted by these memoranda, George Lincoln decided to study the question of unconditional surrender further at the end of April. His study concluded: "Japanese will to resist might break down psychologically before its physical capacity to resist [has] been completely destroyed, and this pressure could take the form of a definition of unconditional surrender." It added: "Unless a definition of unconditional surrender can be given which is acceptable to the Japanese, there is no alternative to annihilation and no prospect that the threat of absolute defeat will bring about capitulation."[19]

These three initiatives to redefine unconditional surrender still remained unconnected, but the movement was gathering momentum from below. Sooner or later the president who had just pledged to uphold the principle of unconditional surrender would be forced to reconsider his position.

The Soviet factor was closely connected with this impetus. While the JCS was contemplating the redefinition of unconditional surrender, it also began to reexamine the wisdom of military collaboration with the Soviet Union. The combined planning group, which had held a series of meetings in Moscow from January to March, turned out to be a complete failure. Together with Harriman, Deane became a strong advocate of the "quid pro quo" policy toward the Soviet Union. He insisted that further collaboration with the Soviets "won't be worth a hoot, unless it is based on mutual respect and made to work both ways." He warned that the United States was "steering perilously close to 'suckerdom.'" Americans were put in the position "of being at the same time the givers and the supplicants," a situation that was neither dignified nor healthy for U.S. prestige.

Deane returned to Washington at the beginning of April and recommended that the Joint Chiefs of Staff abandon the idea of establishing strategic bomber forces in the Komsomolsk-Nikolaevsk area, and make no further plans with Soviet authorities regarding maintenance of a Pacific supply route. When Deane arrived in Washington, he found that the Chiefs were more disturbed by the situation than he was. The Joint Chiefs of Staff at once directed Deane to inform Soviet Chief of Staff Aleksei Antonov that the United States had decided to cancel the project to establish strategic bases. As for the Pacific supply route, on April 17, the Joint Chiefs of Staff decided to "withdraw from all projects involving military operations." Plans for the establishment of the route would "continue insofar as may be practicable without interfering with the main effort," but the JCS also stipulated that "no mention be made of the route to the Russians and no action involving Russian collaboration be taken to establish the route until the Soviets on their own initiative so request."[20]

This did not mean, however, the end of collaboration with the Soviet Union. Soviet entry into the war, if not essential to the American invasion of Japan, was still considered desirable in order to shorten the war. According to Deane, "we continued to do our utmost to build up the Russian supply reserve in Siberia because we still felt that a Russian offensive against the Japanese would shorten the war and because we had committed ourselves to the project." While Deane and Harriman insisted on retaliatory measures for the Soviet lack of cooperation, Marshall rejected such measures, fearing that they might bring about undesirable results.[21]

By April military planners were confident that as a result of strategic conventional bombing on Japanese cities, the effective naval blockade against the Japanese mainland, and control of the air and the sea to intercede the transfer of the Japanese Army from the continent to Japan, the United States would be able to carry out the invasion on its own without relying on the Soviet Union to pin down the Kwantung Army in Manchuria. On April 25, the Joint Chiefs of Staff adopted policy JCS 924/15, which strongly supported Olympic and dismissed both bombardment and blockade as insufficient. In view of the heavy casualties that were being inflicted on the American troops on Okinawa, it was only prudent for Marshall to ensure Soviet entry into the war. King reluctantly endorsed the invasion but recommended that the plan be placed before the president for final approval.

Why was the JCS rushing headlong into the invasion of Japan's homeland when the Americans had suffered such horrendous casualties in Luzson, Iwo Jima, and Okinawa? As Dale Hellegers argues, behind this judgment "lay the unspoken fear that time was on the side of Japan—that time would perfect Japanese defenses and bolster Japanese manpower, that time would dishearten the American public and encourage Japanese hopes for a brokered settlement, that time might find the Americans bogged down far from Japan and the Soviets ready and able to move into the enemy's homeland."[22] This was precisely the thinking of the Japanese military leaders, who justified their policy of "one more decisive strike before peace."

Soviets Assess the New Situation

Although Malik's analysis on March 22 had led Kremlin leaders to believe that an attack by Japan was unlikely, they nevertheless watched nervously to see how Japan would react to the Soviet renunciation of the Neutrality Pact. On April 12, when the dust had settled on the new cabinet, Malik cabled to Moscow that the Japanese were relieved by the Soviet assurance that the Neutrality Pact was still in force. He also reported that some in the Japanese Foreign Ministry believed that after the defeat of Germany, the Soviet Union would increase pressure on Japan, raise its demands, and even threaten to break diplomatic relations with Japan, but "without declaring war."[23]

Malik's meeting with Togo on April 20 confirmed the accuracy of his analysis. Togo regretted that the Soviet Union had decided not to renew the Neutrality Pact, but he was pleased to know that the pact would remain in effect until April of next year. This would give Japan enough time to improve its relations with the Soviet Union. He invited Molotov to stop over in Japan on his way to San Francisco. Malik answered that Molotov would most likely take the Atlantic route, which, the Soviet ambassador must have known, was not the case.[24]

From his meeting with Togo, Malik made some shrewd observations. The Japanese knew that it would be impossible to resolve the fundamental problems between the USSR and Japan by diplomatic means, Malik reported. But "as long as the . . . main task [for Japan] is to extricate itself from this war," the Soviet ambassador continued, "then Togo must secure the neutrality of the USSR [and] create the semblance . . . of the beginning of serious negotiations between the USSR and Japan." This would cause serious concerns for the United States and Britain, and eventually frighten them into reaching a compromise with Japan.[25]

Stalin did not rely on Malik's information alone to gauge Japan's reaction. He also had the military intelligence network, which operated separately from diplomatic channels. On April 11, the Tokyo *rezidentura*— the headquarters of intelligence—reported that "the new cabinet, in view of the extremely unfavorable military situation and constantly worsening difficulties in the country, is pursuing its objective to create conditions for extricating Japan from the war." More important, the *rezidentura* informed Moscow that the Japanese believed they could not continue the war for more than eight months, and that this period might be even shorter if the Americans intensified military actions.[26] This important piece of information must have reaffirmed Stalin's conviction that he could not afford to postpone the war against Japan until the following year, and that, given the weather conditions in the Far East, the only time to start the war against Japan would be the summer of 1945.

Meanwhile, Stalin was concerned about the change in the American administration. Roosevelt's death shocked him. When Harriman went to see Stalin in the Kremlin on the night of April 13, he held Harriman's hands and expressed his condolences. He said: "President Roosevelt has died but his cause will live on. We shall support President Truman with all our forces and with all our will." Harriman found his conversation with Stalin "most earnest and intimate." The American ambassador suggested that one way the Soviet Union could continue good relations with the Americans would be to send Molotov to the United States. Reversing his earlier decision, Stalin signaled his goodwill to Truman by agreeing to send Molotov to the San Francisco Conference devoted to the founding of the United Nations. Stalin also made an important point. He asked Harriman whether under Truman U.S. policy toward Japan might become more conciliatory. Harriman answered that there was no such possibility. He said: "Our policy regarding Japan as agreed to at the Crimea Conference remains unchanged." Stalin wanted to emphasize to the Americans that he had not changed his mind about his commitment to enter the war against Japan.[27]

Stalin and the Soviet government watched carefully to see how the new president would approach the Soviet Union. In his telegram to Molotov on April 21, Gromyko described Truman's speech on April 16 at the Joint Session of the Congress as the first sign of the new administration's continuity with Roosevelt. Gromyko felt that at least for the immediate future Truman would continue his predecessor's policy of cooperation with the Soviet Union, though in the past he had made some less-than-friendly remarks about the USSR. Gromyko concluded that Truman's forthcoming meeting with Molotov in Washington would be a good test of which direction Truman would move.[28]

Japan's Army Advocates Soviet Neutrality

While Stalin was courting the new American president, the Japanese were desperately trying to keep the Soviet Union out of the war. Japanese military intelligence accurately detected the transfer of troops from the European theater to the Far East. In April Lieutenant Colonel Isamu Asai, military attaché to the Japanese Embassy in Moscow, took a trip on the Trans-Siberian Railway. Observing that the Red Army was transporting twelve to fifteen military trains eastward, Asai cabled Deputy Chief of Staff Torashiro Kawabe on April 27, warning that it would take only two months for the Red Army to transport twenty divisions to the Far East. Asai concluded that Soviet entry into the war against Japan should now be considered "inevitable."[29]

The General Staff was not unanimous in its opinions about Soviet intentions. The Fifth Section, which specialized in intelligence regarding the Red Army, disagreed with the Twelfth Section, which was charged with planning and operations. The Fifth Section felt that sooner or later the Soviet Union would enter the war, a conclusion that the Twelfth Section, headed by Colonel Suketaka Tanemura, rejected.[30] Tanemura believed that in order to continue the war against the United States, it was essential to keep the Soviet Union out of the war.

At the General Staff high officials' meeting on April 18, Chief of Staff Yoshijiro Umezu supported the position that Japan should pursue "its active policy toward the Soviet Union." This position was too ambiguous for Tanemura; it left open the question of whether Japan should seek to maintain peace on the northern flank or to end the war through Soviet mediation.[31] Peace was an anathema to Tanemura, who felt that Japan's Soviet policy should be an instrument for continuing the war. There was also conflict between the radical staff officers who were in charge of actual planning of operations and the senior officers of the army. If the top leaders of the army were to seek peace through Moscow's mediation, they would have to operate behind the backs of their subordinates.

On April 22 Kawabe, accompanied by Second Section Chief Seizo Arisue, who was in charge of overall intelligence, visited Togo and recommended that the foreign minister take a bold approach toward the Soviet Union in order to ensure its neutrality. Kawabe promised that the army would give its full support to Togo's policy. Togo said that since the Soviet Union had already declared its intention not to renew the Neutrality Pact, Japan would have to be prepared to grant extraordinary concessions to the Soviet Union to keep it out of the war. Kawabe did not specify what those concessions might be.[32] Togo knew that the army wanted Soviet neutrality in order to continue the war. Nonetheless, he welcomed the army's intervention. He intended to turn negotiations for Soviet neutrality into negotiations to terminate the war.

On April 29 Tanemura wrote a memorandum entitled "Opinion Regarding Our Future Policy toward the Soviet Union" and distributed it to a select number of the highest army authorities.[33] Tanemura's memo began by underscoring the crucial importance of Japan's policy toward the Soviet Union, which would have "life or death importance" to the prosecution of the Pacific War. With the Soviet abrogation of the Neutrality Pact, Japan faced its greatest crisis. Tanemura likened this crisis to the point in Japanese Sumo wrestling when a wrestler is pushed to the end of the ring. The chance of the wrestler's throwing his opponent out with a desperate suicidal move backward, or the opponent's succeeding in pushing the wrestler out of the ring, is 9 to 1 in favor of the opponent. But Japan had no choice but to gamble on this desperate suicidal move in order to win.

Anticipating Togo's policy, Tanemura warned that some would attempt to seek Soviet mediation only to terminate the war, a policy that should be resisted at all costs. He warned that any attempt to negotiate with the United States would lead to the destruction of the *kokutai*, which would be tantamount to the extermination of the Japanese race. If there was any chance for success, it was to exploit the differences between the Soviet Union and the Anglo-American alliance in their policies toward Japan and China.

Japan's specific goal should be one of the following: conclusion of a Japanese-Soviet alliance, conclusion of a Japanese-Chinese-Soviet alliance, or Soviet neutrality. In order to attain one of these goals, Japan should be prepared to grant whatever concessions the Soviet Union might demand. Specifically, Japan should be prepared to give up Manchuria, the Liaotung Peninsula, southern Sakhalin, Taiwan, the Ryukyu Islands, the northern Kurils, and Korea. In addition, Japan should be prepared to concede the Chinese Eastern Railway to the Soviet Union, and to give up the Fishing Treaty. This would be equal to the conditions that had existed before the Sino-Japanese War of 1894–1895.

Tanemura's whole argument was constructed on the fundamental assumption that the war had to continue. To keep Soviet neutrality was a sine qua non for that goal. Even though the chances for success in achieving Soviet neutrality were one in ten, Japan would have no choice but to try. Tanemura refused to say what Japan should do if it failed to achieve its goal. Implied, however, was the apocalyptic vision of turning the entire population of Japan into warriors on a suicidal mission, a vision based on the conviction that the annihilation of the Japanese nation and the Japanese race was better than acceptance of surrender. Tanemura's vision had resonance with the majority of officers in the General Staff and the Army Ministry, giving some indication of how they would react to the end of the war in August.

Tanemura proposed making greater territorial concessions to the Soviets than the Japanese government had been prepared to offer in September 1944. For instance, he recommended that Japan abandon Manchuria, including the Liaotung Peninsula, Taiwan, the Ryukyu Islands, and Korea, which were not included in the previous proposal. While the Yalta Agreement stipulated that the Kurils should be handed over to the Soviet Union, Tanemura's concessions were limited to the northern Kurils. Tanemura justified these concessions on the grounds that Japan was prepared to return to the situation that existed before the Sino-Japanese War of 1894–1895. When Soviet policymakers were contemplating the postwar territorial settlements on the principle of Soviet security requirements rather than the principle of historical legitimacy, there was little room for the Soviet leaders to accept Japan's concessions.

Tanemura's memorandum also gave some indication as to how the army staff officers would have reacted to the American offer to modify the demand for unconditional surrender. The officers were convinced that the United States would attempt to destroy the *kokutai*. They firmly believed that the principle of democracy advocated by the United States was diametrically opposed to the essence of *kokutai*. Thus, it is doubtful that they would have accepted even the promise of a constitutional monarchy.

Finally, the conflict between Tanemura's view and the Fifth Section's more anti-Soviet assessment raises a question as to the importance of the Soviet Union in the military's strategic thinking. It is true that Japanese intelligence had an accurate picture of the Soviet military buildup, and that the Fifth Section had advocated the adoption of countermeasures in anticipation of an attack. Nevertheless, the Fifth Section's view was not the policy adopted by the army high command. The "brains" of the army, which consisted of the Twelfth Section and above all of the Army Ministry's Military Affairs Bureau, endorsed Tanemura's view, and it became the official policy supported by Umezu, Kawabe, and Anami. Their "Ketsu-go" strategy was built on the assumption that the Soviets would remain neutral. When the Soviets joined the war, the entire edifice on which "Ketsu-go" was built was destined to crumble.

Whereas the army sought to secure Soviet neutrality in order to continue the war, Togo intended to use Moscow's mediation to terminate the conflict. But Togo encountered unexpected opposition from the Japanese Embassy in Moscow. Ambassador Sato considered it unrealistic and unwise for Japan to rely on the Soviet Union to terminate the war. He had already sent back his trusted aide, Minister Goro Morishima, from Moscow to Tokyo to coordinate Japan's policy toward the Soviet Union. On April 27, at the dinner meeting with Togo, Morishima warned against Japan's offering any proposals beneficial to the Soviet Union under any circumstances.[34] In order to carry out his Soviet policy, Togo had to navigate the treacherous channel between the Imperial Army and the Moscow Embassy.

Truman's Tough Talk with Molotov

Truman asked himself often what Roosevelt would have done in a given situation. But what Roosevelt would have done was not the same as what Truman thought Roosevelt would have done. Although he believed he was faithfully pursuing Roosevelt's policy, it was inevitable that Truman's personality, the personal preferences of his advisers, his style of policy making, and his own ideas about Russia and Japan would eventually be reflected in the policies that he adopted and rejected. In the end, Truman's foreign policy had his distinct imprint.

Roosevelt did not have a structured mechanism for making foreign policy decisions. Different groups of actors had often presented conflicting views. As Melvyn Leffler states, "Roosevelt had been able to sit at the pinnacle of this diffuse structure to suit his administrative style." Truman found this system confusing and intolerable. Leffler describes Truman's style as born of his insecurity: "Because he was insecure and fearful of displaying his own ignorance, he hesitated to discuss his views and rarely thought through a problem aloud. Almost everyone commented on his snap judgments. He conveyed a sense of authority, but at the expense of thoughtfulness and consistent policy."[35]

Truman's policy toward the Soviet Union reflected the ambivalence of American policymakers toward the emerging colossus. Cooperation with the Soviet Union was an essential ingredient in the creation of a stable world order after the war. In addition, Soviet entry into the Pacific War was still considered desirable, if no longer essential. But Soviet actions in the newly occupied territories of Eastern Europe, especially in Poland, raised concerns about the consequences of Soviet expansion. Officials

within the Truman administration voiced different opinions about U.S–
Soviet relations, and Truman adopted the recommendation of the adviser
he happened to be around at a given moment. As a result, his Soviet policy took a zigzag course.

As soon as Truman took his oath, he was confronted with the Polish
question. Churchill was alarmed: Stalin was installing a puppet government in Poland in violation of the Yalta Agreements. On April 13, Truman replied to Churchill's letter to Roosevelt of April 11, endorsing the
prime minister's suggestion that they write a joint letter to Stalin. On
April 16, he instructed Harriman to submit the letter to the Soviet leader,
reminding him that the Soviet Union had an obligation to observe the
agreements reached at Yalta. A subtle change of attitude toward Stalin
and the Soviet Union was already taking place. Whereas Roosevelt had
cautioned Churchill "not to excoriate the Russians publicly," Truman
was eager to confront Stalin.[36]

With Truman in the White House, State Department officials who had
been largely ignored by Roosevelt began to campaign actively to gain access to the new president. Especially important was the role of Harriman,
who returned to Washington in the middle of April itching to bring his
warning about Soviet expansionism straight to the Oval Office. Harriman had been critical of Roosevelt's overly conciliatory policy toward
the Soviet Union, arguing that the United States should take a hard-nosed
quid pro quo policy. He warned that "the outward thrust of Communism
was not dead," and that "we might well have to face an ideological warfare just as rigorous and dangerous as Fascism or Nazism."[37]

Whereas Roosevelt had remained unsympathetic to Harriman's views,
Truman was eager to embrace them. At his meeting with the president
on April 20, Harriman outlined the two possible options the Soviet government could take: "the policy of cooperation with the United States
and Britain" or "the extension of Soviet control over neighboring states
through unilateral action." He made the point that U.S. generosity and a
desire to cooperate had been misinterpreted by the Soviets as signs of
weakness. He then outlined a number of specific difficulties that had developed since Yalta. Truman told Harriman that he was not afraid of the
Russians, and that he intended to be firm and fair, since, in his opinion,
"the Soviet Union needed us more than we needed them." Truman also
stated that he intended to "make no concessions from American principles or traditions for the fact of winning their favor," and declared that
"only on a give and take basis" could any relations be established. Harri-

man must have felt vindicated at last by Truman's acceptance of his quid pro quo policy.

As if to release his pent-up frustrations, Harriman made a strong pitch for the reorientation of U.S. policy toward the Soviet Union. He said that the United States was faced with a "barbarian invasion of Europe." He was not pessimistic about arriving at a workable compromise with the Soviets, but "this would require a reconsideration of our policy and the abandonment of the illusion that for the immediate future the Soviet Government was going to act in accordance with the principles which the rest of the world held to in international affairs." Truman said that though he could not expect to get 100 percent of what he wanted, "he felt that we should be able to get 85 percent."[38]

Although Truman expressed his agreement with Harriman on a number of points, he wanted to be fair, and in one instance he disagreed with the ambassador. When Harriman suggested that the United States should go ahead with the creation of an international organization even without the Soviet Union, Truman curtly contradicted him: an international organization without the Soviet Union would be meaningless. Above all, Truman was disturbed by what he viewed as a Soviet violation of the Declaration of Liberated Europe. After Byrnes briefed him about the Yalta Conference, the president must have decided that the various agreements reached at Yalta should form the foundation for cooperation among the Allies. To him, a breach of contract represented a gross affront to American principles. Whereas Roosevelt was prepared to play power politics at the expense of legal niceties, Truman had a rather rigid sense of legalism that a contract should be honored by both parties.[39] Commitment to the Yalta Agreements, even if it might be disadvantageous to U.S. interests at times, was one of the consistent threads that ran through Truman's policies at least until the end of the Pacific War.

Molotov arrived in Washington on the evening of April 22. He immediately met with Truman at Blair House. Despite his promise to be firm, Truman was cordial at his first meeting with Molotov. After expressing great admiration for Stalin and the Soviet Union, he zeroed in on the Polish question. Molotov responded by stating that this issue was important to Soviet security, but that he hoped the agreements reached at Yalta would provide the basis for mutual understanding. Molotov then raised the question of the Yalta Agreement on the Far East. He understood from Ambassador Hurley's meeting with Stalin that the president was thoroughly familiar with the agreement, and he asked if Truman accepted the provisions of the accord. Truman answered that he would wholeheart-edly support the provisions. Molotov scored a major victory by extract-ing Truman's pledge to adhere to the Yalta Agreement.[40]

On Monday, April 23, Stimson was summoned to an emergency meet-ing at the White House at two o'clock "on an undisclosed subject." When Stimson arrived, he found Stettinius, Forrestal, Marshall, King, Leahy, and a number of State Department officials already assembled in the Oval Office. With obvious annoyance, Stimson wrote: "and without warning I was plunged into one of the most difficult situations I have ever had since I have been here." The participants Stimson pointedly chose not to name in his diary included Harriman, Deane, James Dunn (assis-tant secretary of state), and Bohlen, all of them in the Harriman camp.[41]

The subject of the meeting was U.S. policy toward the Soviet Union. As Stimson suspected, the meeting was engineered by the State Department in order to convert Truman to the quid pro quo policy. Stettinius and Harriman strenuously argued that the United States should take a tough stand against the Soviet Union. Forrestal and Leahy supported this posi-tion. Harriman pointed out that the Soviets had been reneging on their promise to collaborate with the United States in the Far Eastern War, and he asked Deane to corroborate his account. Deane replied that he knew from his own experience in the Soviet Union that fear of the Russians would get the United States nowhere. Stimson cautioned against break-ing with the Soviet Union over Poland. He was sympathetic to the Sovi-ets' security concerns in Eastern Europe. When it came to military mat-ters, the Soviets had kept their word, and had even performed better than their promise. Only Marshall supported Stimson. Marshall argued that Soviet participation in the war against Japan would be useful to the United States, but he warned that the possibility of a break with Russia was "very serious."

Although it is unlikely, as has often been asserted, that Truman said at this meeting, "if the Russians do not join us [at the San Francisco confer-ence], they can go to hell," he clearly supported the majority view that the United States should take a tough stand against the Russians.[42] At the end of the meeting, the president dismissed Stimson and the rest of the military leaders, asking only the secretary of state and his advisers to re-main and work out the details of the forthcoming talk with Molotov. It is clear that at this crucial White House meeting Stimson and Marshall lost the battle. Truman was planning a showdown with Molotov.

Whereas Truman had played Mr. Hyde at his first meeting with Molotov on April 22, he was transformed into Dr. Jekyl at his second meeting, on the following night. The president told Molotov that the U.S. government was deeply disappointed that the Soviets found it impossible to fulfill the points listed in the joint letter by Churchill and Truman about the composition of the Polish government. Borrowing the same expression used by Harriman at the meeting several hours before, the president, "using plain American language," that is, "the language that cannot be at all diplomatic," said that the United States government could not be a party to a Polish government that did not represent all Polish democratic elements.[43]

Apparently taken aback by the sharpness of Truman's tone, Molotov reiterated Soviet intentions to cooperate with the United States. The basis for that collaboration had been established by the Yalta Agreements. Truman replied "with great firmness" that an agreement on Poland already existed, and that "it only remained for Marshal Stalin to carry it out." Molotov declared that the Soviets would also remain committed to the Yalta Agreements, but that the Polish question was of great interest to the Soviet government. Growing impatient, Truman repeated: the U.S. government was prepared to honor all the agreements reached at the Yalta Conference, and he only asked that the Soviet government do the same. Molotov protested: "I have never been talked to like that in my life." "Carry out your agreements," Truman shot back, "and you won't get talked to like that." He then stood up suddenly, ending the conversation, and handed Molotov a copy of the statement he was to give to the press.[44]

Molotov was known as a tough negotiator who displayed dogged persistence and bluntness. Thus, if this conversation did in fact take place, as Harriman commented, "the idea that his sensibilities were offended seemed . . . rather silly." But even Harriman was "a little taken aback" by Truman's hostility toward Molotov. "I did regret that Truman went at it so hard," Harriman commented, "because his behavior gave Molotov an excuse to tell Stalin that the Roosevelt policy was being abandoned."[45]

What mattered, of course, was not how Truman's words wounded Molotov's feelings, but how the Kremlin perceived Truman's treatment of Molotov. Gromyko, who was present during this meeting, wrote in his memoirs: "Truman acted tough. Coldness was shown in his every gesture. The new President rejected whatever was proposed to him and whatever topic the conversation touched on. It appeared at times that he did not even hear the interlocutor." According to the Soviet ambassador,

Truman, with "cock-like belligerency, contradicted almost every point raised by the Soviet side about the significance of the future world organization and about the measures designed to prevent further aggression from Germany," and "he suddenly stood up in the middle of the conversation, and gestured that the conversation was over."[46]

Stalin's reaction was immediate. On April 24 he sent a telegram to Truman responding to the Truman-Churchill joint letter. He rejected the American-British proposal as a violation of the Yalta Agreement. He said that he had not raised any objections when the Americans and the British created governments to their liking in Belgium and Greece; therefore, he demanded the same treatment for Poland, which was vital to Soviet security. Stalin's tone was almost as strident as Truman's.[47]

Determining the Targets of the Atomic Bombs

After he was dismissed from the April 23 White House meeting, Stimson met with Groves and George Harrison, special assistant to the secretary of war, to discuss Stimson's forthcoming meeting with the president on the Manhattan Project. The following day, Stimson had a short talk with Marshall. Still upset that the State Department had upstaged the War Department on a major foreign policy matter, they discussed how to restore the military's influence on international matters. Stimson then wrote a letter to the president, requesting a meeting to talk about "a highly secret matter."[48]

On April 25, Stimson and Groves presented the first full report on the Manhattan Project to the president. They first submitted a memorandum that reported: "Within four months we shall in all probability have completed the most terrible weapon ever known in human history, one bomb of which could destroy a whole city." The memo went on to say that although at present the United States had a monopoly on the weapon, this monopoly would not last long. It predicted that "the only nation which could enter into production within the next few years is Russia." It further stated: "The world in its present state of moral advancement compared with its technical development would be eventually at the mercy of such a weapon. In other words, modern civilization might be completely destroyed." Thus the problem of sharing information about this weapon would become a primary question in U.S. foreign relations.[49]

Stimson then gave the president a second memorandum, written by

Groves, that dealt with the technical aspect of the atomic bomb. The most important part of this report was the detailed schedule of the production of the bomb. It promised that the first "gun-type" bomb "should be ready about 1 August 1945." The first implosion-type bomb should be available for testing "in the early part of July."[50] Stimson was concerned with what he considered the most fundamental issue of the postwar world: international control of nuclear weapons. In Stimson's view, it was still premature to confront the Soviet Union on the question of Poland. Such time should come only when the United States had successfully completed production of the atomic bombs.

Truman's meeting with Stimson and Groves was an important turning point in the Pacific War: the president now had another card to play in the game of forcing Japan to surrender. On May 1 Truman approved Stimson's recommendation to establish the Interim Committee, a high-level advisory group that would report to the president on the atomic bomb. It is important to note, however, that without the president's knowledge, an important decision on the use of the bomb had already been made. The Target Committee set up under Groves on April 27 had selected eighteen Japanese cities as possible targets, including Hiroshima, Tokyo Bay, Yawata, and others. The governing factor in selecting the targets was to achieve the maximum impact on breaking the Japanese will to continue the war. For that reason, Groves had considered it essential to have at least two bombs: the first to show the effect of the new weapon and the second to show that the United States could produce the atomic bombs in quantity.[51]

At the May 12–13 meetings, the Target Committee chose Kyoto, Hiroshima, Yokohama, and Kokura, with Niigata as an alternative. Kyoto, the ancient capital with a population of more than one million, hitherto untouched by air raids, was at the top of the list. The May 28 meeting confirmed three targets in order of priority: Kyoto, Hiroshima, and Niigata. This list greatly troubled Stimson. He knew the cultural value of the ancient capital and worried that the destruction of the city might provoke anti-American sentiments and solidify Japan's resolve to continue the war. At the meeting on May 31, Stimson and Groves clashed on Kyoto, when Stimson demanded that Groves's favorite target be taken off the list altogether. Groves did not yield, and Arnold supported him. Unable to convince his subordinates, Stimson appealed directly to Truman, arguing that if the United States dropped the atomic bomb on

Kyoto, the entire world would equate the U.S. action with Hitler's barbarism.[52] Truman agreed with Stimson. Kyoto was removed from the list, but only temporarily.

Reaction to the German Defeat

Germany's defeat could have been a good excuse for Japan to seek peace. But Japan failed to take advantage of this opportunity. Anticipating German defeat, on April 30, the Supreme War Leadership Council had decided "to continue the war until the objective of the Greater East Asia War is achieved," and to promote a policy intended to decouple the Soviet Union from the United States and Britain. On May 3, after Hitler's suicide and the fall of Berlin, Suzuki in his radio announcement appealed to his people to continue fighting the war with the spirit of a kamikaze pilot. Even Togo joined the chorus: "German actions [will] not affect the Empire's determination to pursue the war against the United States and Britain." On May 9, one day after Germany formally surrendered, the Japanese government declared that since its objective in the war was self-preservation and self-defense, regardless of the change in the situation in Europe, Japan should strive with more determination to crush the aspirations of the United States and Britain.[53] Thus, the Japanese government brazenly broadcast to the world its intention to continue the war despite the German defeat.

But what about the emperor and his advisers? On May 5, Kido confided to Konoe that though the emperor had previously been unwilling to make any concessions on disarmament and the punishment of war criminals, now, after long discussion with Kido, he was reluctantly inclined to withdraw these conditions. Nevertheless, when on May 13 Konoe warned Hirohito about the danger of Soviet military intervention and the possibility of a Communist government in Japan, the emperor insisted that Japan still had a chance to deal a heavy blow to the Americans. He had not given up the policy of one more strike before ending the war.[54]

The defeat on Okinawa and the German surrender belatedly led Hirohito to jettison all conditions for surrender but preservation of the *kokutai,* and for this condition, he was still willing to risk one last battle. But if this was his thinking, there was no evidence to indicate that he immediately ordered his advisers to act on his wishes.

Behind the bravado of public pronouncements, the key players of the peace party were slowly reaching a consensus that Japan should seek peace, and that the only way to do so was through the emperor's active intervention. Matsutani received an intelligence report that Soviet forces along the Manchurian border had reached thirty-five divisions and two thousand tanks. The report predicted that the Soviets would send forces from Europe to the Far East in July and August. Matsutani, Takagi, Matsudaira, and Kase concluded that it was necessary to end the war as quickly as possible. Konoe and Kido agreed.[55] But this strategy would require careful orchestration. First and foremost, the expected opposition from the military would have to be neutralized; various forces favoring peace would have to be united and their actions coordinated; maneuverings for peace would have to be done carefully and in strict secrecy; and finally, Hirohito himself would have to be persuaded to take an active role in the peace process.

As the peace party in Japan gingerly began to explore the possibility of terminating the war, the pressure to redefine unconditional surrender reached the top leaders of the Truman administration. The principal advocate for modification of the term was Forrestal. At the Committee of Three meeting on May 1, Forrestal asked whether it was time to make a thorough study of U.S. political objectives in the Far East, and he raised a series of questions.[56] How far and how thoroughly should the United States beat Japan? Should the United States contemplate Japan's readmission to the society of nations after demilitarization? What should be the policy toward Soviet influence in the Far East? Should Japan be a counterweight against it? How far should the United States go toward the complete defeat of Japan—a quick, costly assault or a long, drawn-out siege? Surprisingly, Grew did not immediately pick up Forrestal's lead. He was defensive about the status of the emperor, repeating his view that the question of the emperor should remain undecided until after the American occupation. Ironically, it was Elmer Davis of the Office of War Information, an advocate of harsh peace, who picked up the questions raised by Forrestal. The following day, Davis sent a memo to the president endorsing Captain Zacharias's recommendation that unconditional surrender be redefined. Davis, however, suggested two alternative ways of making this statement public. His preferred option was to announce it in the form of a presidential declaration directly appealing to the Japanese people over the heads of the Japanese government. The second option was to publicize the statement in the form of a press release.

Grew readily endorsed the plan to publicize the redefinition of unconditional surrender. He cleverly integrated Zacharias's recommendation into the position advocated by the Japan specialists, and transformed it into the first step toward his desired goal of allowing a constitutional monarchy. Grew feared, however, that the first option, a direct appeal to the Japanese people over the heads of the Japanese government, would lead to an outright rejection. He suggested that a press release would have "some effect on the Japanese people advantageous" to the United States. Leahy accepted Grew's recommendations and on May 6 wrote a draft for the president's speech.[57]

On May 8, his sixty-first birthday, Truman received the news of the German surrender. The president summoned a press conference and read the official announcement to celebrate V-E Day. Toward the end of the speech, he turned to the war in the Pacific. He warned that Japan's further resistance would only bring utter destruction to its industrial war production, and declared: "Our blows will not cease until the Japanese military and naval forces lay down their arms in *unconditional surrender.*" Immediately after this statement, however, he asked a rhetorical question: "Just what does the unconditional surrender of the armed forces mean for the Japanese people?" qualifying the term as "unconditional surrender of the armed forces." He then defined the term as "the termination of the influence of the military leaders who brought Japan to the present brink of disaster," "provision for the return of soldiers and sailors to their families, their farms, their job," and "not prolonging the present agony and suffering of the Japanese in the vain hope of victory." He stated that it did not mean "the extermination or enslavement of the Japanese people.[58]

Modifying unconditional surrender as unconditional surrender of the armed forces and ensuring the survival of the Japanese nation were the two important goals that the Japan specialists in the State Department had persistently advocated against those who sought harsh peace. But the president's address also left the most important point ambiguous: the status of the emperor.

Curiously, the press did not seem to pick up on Truman's significant modification of unconditional surrender as unconditional surrender of the armed forces. Moreover, Truman himself did not seem to realize that his advisers had conspired to slip in this modification. But the Japanese noticed the difference. Zacharias made sure the Japanese understood by referring to Truman's address in the first of six propaganda broadcasts designed to reach Japan's peace party. Overstepping what Truman had said, Zacharias further emphasized that the president's message was compatible with the Atlantic Charter. Through Zacharias's message Togo became aware of the narrower definition of unconditional surrender.[59] Nonetheless, there was no reaction from the Japanese government to Truman's modification of this demand. The reason was that the question of the *kokutai* and the status of the emperor remained ambiguous.

Moreover, the Japanese Army had its own values that it wished to preserve. In September 1944, the army minister had produced a document that predicted the following consequences stemming from unconditional surrender: occupation of Japan by American armed forces, disarmament of the Japanese Army and Navy, abolition of the *kokutai* and establishment of a democratic form of government, and forced emigration of the Japanese male population overseas.[60] Truman's address eliminated the last possibility, but as far as the army was concerned, the three other consequences would still be imposed. To the army, therefore, unconditional surrender was anathema, even if Truman had allowed the preservation of a constitutional monarchy. Since the army enjoyed veto power in Japan's peculiar decision-making process, there was no chance that civilians in the government could explore the possibility of surrender under the conditions specified by Truman's address without serious opposition from the military. The war party was considerably stronger than the peace party at this point. Redressing this imbalance and weakening the army's position would require a shocking event much bigger than the German defeat.

Big Six Policy toward the Soviet Union

Ambassador Malik's sensitive antennae clearly picked up the growing peace sentiments among the ruling elite in Japan. On May 4, Malik observed that high officials in the government and other public figures now found it necessary to explore the possibility of extricating Japan from the war. But they feared that if they were to begin peace negotiations, the Americans would demand unconditional surrender. High officials revealed that they were now prepared to abandon Manchuria, Korea, and Formosa. The only conditions Japan would insist on would be the territorial integrity of Japan proper and the maintenance of the emperor system. Malik observed: "Japan would never accept unconditional surrender." It was valuable information for Stalin. If he wished to prolong the war, he had only to insist on unconditional surrender.

Influential officials within the Japanese government believed that the

Soviet Union would employ diplomatic pressure on Japan rather than wage war, waiting for the most opportune moment to achieve its objectives. Japanese leaders rested their hopes on using the conflict between the United States/Britain and the Soviet Union on Eastern Europe and the settlement over Germany to their advantage in seeking peace.[61]

As Malik accurately observed, the Japanese policymakers, while barking loudly to fight on, were secretly making preparations to end the war. The first step was to create a mechanism through which the secret plan could be plotted without interference from outside. The highest decision-making body up to this point was the Supreme War Leadership Council, but this body was attended by deputy ministers and had become a rubber stamp organization that adopted the position papers prepared by staff members, the most powerful of which were the Army General Staff officers. On May 5, Togo, following Takagi's and Kase's advice, suggested that this body be reorganized into the Supreme War Leadership Composing Members Council (hereafter Supreme War Council) to include only the Big Six, consisting of the prime minister, foreign minister, army and navy ministers, and army and navy chiefs of staff, with no staff members allowed. All the meetings would be kept secret even from respective staff members, thereby ensuring the free exchange of opinions without pressure from below. Togo's proposal was supported by Admiral Koshiro Oikawa, the naval chief, but also surprisingly by Umezu and Anami. It appears that even the top army leaders desired a forum in which they could express their views freely without worrying about reactions from their subordinates. As such, this new organization was an important step toward the termination of the war.[62]

The first Big Six meetings were held on May 11, 12, and 14. The topic of discussion was policy toward the Soviet Union. The army's objective was to secure Soviet neutrality, while the navy wished, unrealistically, to negotiate with the Soviet Union to trade Soviet oil and airplanes for Japanese cruisers. It is not clear why Yonai insisted on such an unrealistic position at the meeting. But this was the first and last time that Yonai and Togo violently disagreed. Togo dismissed both views as unrealistic, but seized on the military's willingness to negotiate with the Soviet Union with the intention of turning the negotiations toward the termination of the war.[63]

In the end, the Big Six adopted a document that defined Japan's policy toward the Soviet Union. "At the present moment, when Japan is waging a life-or-death struggle against the United States and Britain," the document began, "Soviet entry into the war will deal a death blow to the Empire. Therefore, whatever development the war against the United States and Britain might take, it is necessary for the Empire to try its best to prevent Soviet entry into the war." It then advised immediate negotiations with the Soviet Union to implement the following three objectives: (1) to prevent its entry into the war; (2) to attain its "favorable neutrality"; and (3) to request its mediation to terminate the war in terms favorable to Japan. In these negotiations, Japan should persuade the Soviet Union of the advantage of maintaining neutrality by stressing the importance of Japan's international influence when it came time for the Soviet Union to deal with the United States. In view of increased Soviet confidence after the German defeat, Japan would most likely pay a high price to gain Soviet neutrality. Specifically, Japan should be prepared to abrogate the Portsmouth Treaty as well as the Soviet-Japanese Basic Convention of 1925, and to give up southern Sakhalin, annul the Fishing Agreement, open the Tsugaru Strait, grant the railways in northern Manchuria, recognize Outer Mongolia as a Soviet sphere of influence, grant a lease for Port Arthur and Dairen, and, if necessary, surrender the northern half of the Kurils. Nevertheless, Japan should insist on the retention of Korea and the maintenance of Manchukuo as an independent state.

The document, prepared by the Army General Staff, followed the basic idea presented by Tanemura in April, but by clinging to Korea and Manchuria, it fell far short of Tanemura's proposal for territorial concessions. But even these concessions met with Anami's opposition. He insisted: "Japan is not losing the war, since we have not lost any homeland territory. I object to conducting negotiations on the assumption that we are defeated." Yonai intervened, and proposed that the government should carry out negotiations to achieve only the first and the second options, but postpone for the time being negotiations for the termination of the war.[64]

The Big Six meetings revealed the fundamental divisions within the Japanese government. The Moscow route was chosen as the lowest common denominator that combined Togo's desire to attain peace and the army's desire to continue the war. As Leon Sigal states: "The critical issues—Japan's capacity to continue the war and the concessions required for peace—were sidestepped because they threatened to disrupt any attempt at reaching consensus." One important consequence of this decision was that the Japanese government, at Togo's initiative, decided to put all its eggs in one basket and pursue negotiations with the Soviets while precluding all other possibilities. Togo, Yonai, and Umezu ordered all the private contacts that had been gingerly explored through the Vatican, Swedish diplomats, and Allen Dulles in Berne to be terminated. Thus the narrow thread that barely connected the United States and Japan was cut off.[65]

In the meantime, Matsutani had a secret meeting with Anami to discuss the possibility of seeking an end to the war through Moscow's mediation. Matsutani told Anami that the only condition Japan should attach to surrender should be the preservation of the *kokutai*. In his view, Moscow's mediation would have a better chance to achieve this goal than direct negotiations with the United States. Matsutani thought that Anami agreed with his view.[66] If Anami's position was softening, however, he was certainly not abandoning other conditions that the army considered essential.

Lend-Lease Fiasco

On May 12, the subcommittee for shipping of the Lend-Lease Protocol Committee met in Washington to implement a presidential directive signed two days before. On the basis of this directive, the subcommittee issued orders to cut off shipments to the Soviet Union. American officials in Atlantic and Gulf ports were to cease loading supplies bound for the Soviet Union and call back ships already at sea.[67]

Two factors converged into this decision. As George Herring points out, Truman would have to reduce substantially shipments to the Soviet Union after V-E day owing to strong domestic pressure. But this policy also reflected Truman's decision to take a tough stand against the Soviets. Foreign Economic Administrator (FEA) Leo Crowley wanted to stop the earlier liberal policy of economic aid to the Soviet Union and stick with the legal limits as specified by the Lend-Lease Act. Grew welcomed this chance to steer the policy in a direction less accommodating to the Soviet Union. Stetinnius and Harriman wished to use Lend-Lease as an instrument to extract Soviet concessions on the Polish question. But Harriman did not want the change in American Lend-Lease policy to be so abrupt as to be perceived by the Soviets as a hostile action against their country.[68]

The abrupt stoppage of Lend-Lease shipments without any prior consultation immediately provoked strong protest from Soviet officials. I. A. Eremin, head of the Soviet Purchasing Commission, immediately contacted General John York, acting chairman of the Protocol Committee. York explained to Eremin that the decision had been made by the president, and that this decision was directly connected with the Polish question. Nikolai Novikov, Soviet chargé d'affaires, concluded that Truman's Lend-Lease decision was not an accidental mistake but a deliberate and hostile policy toward the Soviet Union.[69]

Harriman was horrified. Like Truman's April 23 meeting with Molotov, the May 12 Lend-Lease decision radically exceeded the dosage of toughness that he had prescribed to the new president. After all, unlike Grew, Harriman did not want a deterioration of U.S.-Soviet relations; he wanted continued cooperation, but on a quid pro quo basis. Using Lend-Lease aid as bait, he was planning to have a heart-to-heart talk with Stalin to extract concessions on the Polish issue. He now feared that the May 12 decision might push the Soviet government to conclude that Truman was prepared to have a complete break with the Soviet Union.[70]

Truman, too, was taken by surprise at how quickly his actions had worsened U.S.-Soviet relations. His confidence in Grew was shaken by this incident, and he never again trusted the acting secretary of state. His confidence in Harriman was also diminished. He now turned for advice to Joseph Davies and Harry Hopkins, two pro-Soviet advisers to Roosevelt. He expressed his concern that the previous course had gone too far. After the meeting with Molotov the president asked Davies, as if a student asking his tutor after an examination: "Did I do right?" Unlike Harriman, Davies pointed out the danger of breaking with the Soviet Union. While earlier Truman had paid scant attention to Stimson's view, he now listened to Davies's advice that "he give the Russians the benefit of the doubt, treat them with tolerance, and try to understand their point of view."[71]

Renegotiating the Yalta Agreement

While the Japanese government was defining its policy toward the Soviet Union, top American policymakers were also moving to define U.S. policy toward the Soviet Union and Japan. Whereas Forrestal had brought the question of revising unconditional surrender to the top level, it was Grew who took the lead in connecting the question of modifying unconditional surrender with American policy toward the Soviet Union. Forrestal and Grew were engaged in a two-pronged attack aimed at recruiting Stimson to their camp. On May 11, Forrestal had a meeting with

Harriman, Vice-Admiral Charles Cooke (chief of staff to the commander in chief, U.S. Fleet), and Vice Admiral Edwards (deputy commander in chief, U.S. Fleet). Harriman warned about Soviet expansion in China after the USSR entered the war against Japan. Cooke said that recent events considerably lessened the need for the Soviets to join the war. Edwards remarked: "The best thing for us would be if the Japanese could agree to a basis of unconditional surrender which will still leave them in their own minds some face and honor." On May 12, Grew held a meeting with Harriman, McCloy, Bohlen, and Forrestal in which he raised the possibility of Soviet entry into the war. If that happened, he said, the Soviets would most certainly demand participation in the occupation of Japan. Presumably, Harriman told Grew about the Yalta Agreement at this meeting. The acting secretary of state was horrified. He immediately raised the possibility of renegotiating the Yalta Agreement. To that end, he wrote a letter of inquiry to the War and Navy Departments.[72]

Grew asked the secretaries of war and the navy three questions. Would Soviet entry into the war against Japan be of vital interest to the United States? Should the Yalta provisions be reconsidered? Should the Soviet Union participate in the occupation of Japan? The State Department was of the opinion, Grew continued, that the following demands should be made of the Soviet government before its entry into the war: a pledge to use its influence with the Chinese Communists to persuade them to support the unification of China under the Nationalist Government headed by Chiang Kai-shek; unequivocal adherence to the Cairo Declaration regarding the return of Manchuria to Chinese sovereignty and the future status of Korea; a pledge to support the trusteeship of Korea under the United States, Britain, China, and the Soviet Union. In addition, before giving final approval to the Soviet Union's annexation of the Kurils, it might be desirable to receive from the Soviet government emergency landing rights for commercial planes on certain of these islands.[73]

Stimson was annoyed by Grew's inquiry. He expressed his irritation in his diary: "The questions cut very deep and in my opinion are powerfully connected with our success with S-1 [The Manhattan Project]." As far as Stimson was concerned, the answer to Grew's questions depended on whether the United States succeeded in developing the atomic bomb, and it was not the opportune time to answer them. On May 14, Stimson consulted Marshall and McCloy. His diary entry for that day reveals his thinking about the usefulness of the atomic bomb:

I told him [McCloy] that my own opinion was that the time now and the method now to deal with Russia was to keep our mouths shut and let our actions speak for words. The Russians will understand them better than anything else. It is a case where we have got to regain the lead and perhaps do it in a pretty rough and realistic way. They have rather taken it away from us because we have talked too much and have been too lavish with our beneficences to them. I told him this was a place where we really held all the cards. I called it a royal straight flush and we mustn't be a fool about the way we play it. They can't get along without our help and industries and we have coming into action a weapon which will be unique. Now the thing is not to get into unnecessary quarrels by talking too much and not to indicate any weakness by talking too much; let our actions speak for themselves.

In Stimson's mind the entire Soviet issue, and especially the issue of Soviet entry into the war, was integrally connected with the atomic bomb. As a consummate poker player and politician who had come from Pandergast's machine politics, Truman could identify with Stimson's "royal straight flush" analogy. Truman fully embraced Stimson's idea about the political utility of the atomic bomb in dealing with the Soviets. But there was a difference in their thinking: whereas Stimson was concerned about Soviet cooperation on international control of the atomic bomb, Truman was mainly interested in forestalling Soviet expansion in the Far East. A race had begun between the atomic bomb and Soviet entry into the war against Japan.[74]

The following day, May 15, the Committee of Three met with each secretary accompanied by his deputy, McCloy, Harriman, and Major Mathias Correa (special assistant to Forrestal). As Stimson described it, it was a "pretty red hot session." Grew and Harriman must have pressed hard for reopening the Yalta Agreement. The Battle of Okinawa was not over yet, and the redefining of unconditional surrender might be interpreted by the Japanese as a weakening of American will. Stimson argued that it was still premature to renegotiate the agreement. In view of the forthcoming Big Three meeting, it would be best to postpone these issues. In Stimson's mind, Truman's handling of the issues at the conference would also depend on the outcome of the S-1 project. "It seems a terrible thing," Stimson wrote in his diary, "to gamble with such big stakes in diplomacy without having your master card in your hand." After the Committee of Three meeting, he discussed the Far Eastern campaign with Marshall and McCloy. Stimson wrote: "The Japanese campaign involved therefore two great uncertainties; first, whether Russia will come in though we think that will be all right; and second, when and how S-1 will resolve itself."[75]

On May 15 Grew, accompanied by Harriman, had a meeting with the president. Grew and Harriman impatiently urged Truman to meet with Stalin as soon as possible. Among other items, they urged the president to reopen the Yalta provisions, especially on China and Korea. Truman no longer had confidence in Grew and Harriman, but he politely listened to their entreaties. After they finished, he told them that because of domestic concerns, especially the need to prepare a budget message, he would not be able to go to the Big Three meeting until July.[76] Truman's priorities must have shocked Grew and Harriman, but what they did not know was that Truman wanted to possess the atomic bomb before the Big Three meeting.

Pressure to change Stimson's thinking came from two unexpected quarters. Grew had obtained a powerful ally in former President Herbert Hoover, whom Truman invited back to policy circles as an elder statesman. Like Harriman and Grew, Hoover was alarmed by the possibility that U.S. insistence on unconditional surrender of Japan would inevitably invite Soviet expansion in Asia. On May 15, Hoover wrote a letter to Stimson suggesting that "the United States, Britain, and China waste no time in offering the Japanese peace upon specified terms" before the Soviets captured Manchuria, North China, and Korea.[77]

Pressure also came from Major General Clayton Bissell of G-2, the intelligence section of the Army General Staff, who recommended to Stimson on May 15 that a revised demand for unconditional surrender be issued to Japan as soon as possible, as defeat on Okinawa was near at hand. Bissell suggested that if Japanese leaders were convinced that the Soviets would enter the war, now was the time to secure their capitulation, when Japan could be assured that surrender would be made to the Anglo-Americans only.[78]

The OPD disagreed with Hoover and Bissell on the Soviets' role. In its view, the United States should not breach its commitment to the Yalta Agreement. The OPD also disagreed with Hoover's assessment that a quick negotiated peace with Japan would prevent Soviet expansion. The OPD was in favor of formulating "specific terms" for Japan's surrender, as Hoover suggested, but felt that a joint declaration by the United

States, Britain, and China, excluding the Soviet Union, "might jeopardize her desired military participation in the war."[79] On May 20 McCloy rejected G-2's recommendation, explaining that it would be unwise to issue a modified demand until after the Okinawa campaign was completed. Any signs of softening the position might lead the Japanese to believe that the Americans were backing down because of Japan's heroic defense of Okinawa. But Stimson and McCloy also considered the issuance of such a statement premature before the completion of the atomic bomb.[80]

On May 21, Stimson sent Grew the War Department's reply to Grew's initial inquiry on the Yalta Agreement. First, it stated that the War Department believed that the Soviets would decide whether to enter the war against Japan "on their own military and political basis with little regard to any political actions taken by the United States." The Soviets would exploit any political inducements proffered by the United States, but such inducements would not affect when the Soviets would enter the war. The letter stated: "Russian entry will have a profound military effect in that almost certainly it will materially shorten the war and thus save American lives." The War Department expressed fundamental disagreement with Grew's assumption that Soviet entry into the war would have a negative impact on U.S. interests. It also disagreed with the navy's view that the United States no longer needed Soviet help to force Japan to surrender.

As for the Yalta provisions, Stimson's answer went on to state:

> The concessions to Russia on Far Eastern matters which were made at Yalta are generally matters which are within the military power of Russia to obtain regardless of U.S. military action short of war. The War Department believes that Russia is militarily capable of defeating the Japanese and occupying Karafuto [southern Sakhalin], Manchuria, Korea and Northern China before it would be possible for the U.S. military forces to occupy these areas. Only in the Kuriles is the United States in a position to circumvent Russian initiative. If the United States were to occupy these islands to forestall Russian designs, it would be at the direct expense of the campaign to defeat Japan and would involve an unacceptable cost in American lives.

The War Department's position was clear: the United States might as well forget about what Roosevelt had promised to give Stalin at Yalta. The territories were already gone, unless the United States was prepared to take military action to regain them. As for the occupation of Japan, the War Department made a statement that must have shocked Grew: "From one military standpoint, this participation appears desirable, since it would reduce the military requirements of the U.S. for occupation purposes." The War Department was entertaining the possibility of sharing the occupation duties in Japan with the Allies, including the Soviet Union. Stimson then concluded: "we can bring little, if any, military leverage to bear on the Russians . . . unless we choose to use force." Although it would be desirable to have a complete understanding and agreement with the Soviets concerning the Far East, the War Department did not believe that much good would come from reopening the Yalta Agreement.[81] Nonetheless, Stimson's recommendation should not be read as a complete abandonment of the territories promised to Stalin at Yalta. Rather, Stimson's emphasis was on the last sentence: now was not the most opportune time to reopen this question, because S-1 would have the ultimate impact on the fate of these territories.

Grew Attempts to Modify Unconditional Surrender

Grew might not have succeeded in modifying the Yalta Agreement, but he still worked relentlessly on the other front: modifying the terms of unconditional surrender. On the night of May 25–26, massive incendiary bombings on Tokyo wiped out the western and northeastern parts of the city, burning down the government offices, including the Foreign Ministry building and the palaces of Princes Mikasa and Chichibu. The emperor's residence at the Imperial Palace was also burned.[82]

On Saturday, May 26, Grew summoned Dooman to his office just before Dooman was about to leave for the weekend. Grew told him to prepare a draft of the president's statement to be issued to the Japanese government at the conclusion of the Battle of Okinawa so that the United States could induce the Japanese to accept a modified form of unconditional surrender.[83] He wanted to clarify what had remained ambiguous in Truman's V-E Day statement, namely, the status and institution of the emperor.

Dooman relied on the original SWNCC document 150, "Initial U.S. Post Surrender Politics," and worked all weekend to produce the statement. Dooman had to compromise on unconditional surrender. He did not like the term, but he felt that he had to adhere to it, since it had been "enthusiastically espoused by President Truman as well as his predecessor." But he knew that the "phrase was more of a shibboleth—a bugle call as it were." While paying lip service to unconditional surrender, however, Dooman slipped in a phrase that allowed the possibility of preserving the monarchy. The key part of this document included the following passage:

> The occupying forces of the Allies shall be withdrawn from Japan as soon as these objectives have been accomplished and there has been established beyond doubt a peacefully inclined, responsible government of a character representative of the Japanese people. *This may include a constitutional monarchy under the present dynasty* if the peace-loving nations can be convinced of the genuine determination of [the] seed of a government to follow politics of peace which will render impossible the future development of aggressive militarism in Japan.[84]

Thus the laborious work that Ballantine, Borton, Blakeslee, and Dooman had managed to synthesize into SWNCC 150 leapt onto the draft of what would serve as the prototype of the Potsdam Proclamation.

When Grew received Dooman's draft and presented it at the State Department's senior staff meeting, however, it was savagely attacked by Dean Acheson and Archibald McLeish, who stood for punitive peace by abolishing the emperor system altogether as the very source of Japan's militarism. Countering that "the institution of the throne could well be the cornerstone of a peaceful regime for the future," Grew angrily told them that he would exercise the prerogatives of the acting secretary of state and submit Dooman's draft to the president regardless of their opposition.[85]

Grew submitted Dooman's draft to the president. He explained that in waging the war against Japan, "nothing must be sacrificed." This meant that the United States should never compromise the American objectives of "the destruction of Japan's tools for war and of the capacity of the Japanese again to make those tools." Nevertheless, the Japanese were fanatic people, "capable of fighting . . . to the last man." Thus it was time, Grew insisted, that the United States consider steps "which, without sacrificing in any degree our principles or objectives, might render it easier for the Japanese to surrender unconditionally now." Grew then came to his major objective: "The greatest obstacle to unconditional surrender by the

Japanese is their belief that this would entail the destruction or permanent removal of the emperor and the institution of the Throne. If some indication can now be given the Japanese that they themselves . . . will be permitted to determine their own future political structure, they will be afforded a method of saving face without which surrender will be highly unlikely."

Grew then explained that the Japanese emperors, including Hirohito, had not exercised actual power in eight hundred years. He admitted that Hirohito could not escape responsibility for signing the declaration of war against the United States. Nevertheless, once the military clique was removed, the institution of the emperor could become a cornerstone for building a peaceful Japan. After listening to Grew's presentation, Truman said that he was interested in what the acting secretary of state said "because his own thoughts had been following the same line." But he asked Grew to arrange a meeting to discuss this matter with Stimson, Forrestal, Marshall, and King.[86]

On May 29 Grew, accompanied by Dooman, had a meeting with Stimson, Forrestal, Elmer Davis, and Marshall in Stimson's office. Stimson was annoyed at Grew for calling the meeting, since "there were people . . . in the presence of whom I could not discuss the real feature which would govern the whole situation, namely S-1." Grew read Dooman's draft. Stimson praised the document, saying that his only criticism was that it did not go far enough in promising the retention of the monarchical system. Forrestal asked if it would not suffice to say that unconditional surrender did not mean the destruction of Japan as a nation. Dooman answered that this would not be sufficient, since "he believed that if the Japanese became imbued with the idea that the United States was set on the destruction of their philosophy of government and of their religion, we would be faced with a truly national suicidal defense." Stimson, Forrestal, and Marshall agreed with the principle, but "for certain military reasons, not divulged, it was considered inadvisable for the President to make such a statement now." Grew's proposal was shelved for the time being, for reasons he was not supposed to disclose. They had to wait for the outcome of the Manhattan Project.[87]

Hopkins Goes to Moscow

After the Lend-Lease fiasco, Truman asked Harry Hopkins to go to Moscow and meet Stalin in order to get the damaged U.S.-Soviet relations back on track. Although gravely ill, Hopkins agreed. He stayed in Moscow from May 26 until June 6, and had a series of meetings with Stalin.[88] He was successful in patching things up; he helped to ease the tension created by the Lend-Lease fiasco, assuring Stalin that the crisis stemmed from a "misunderstanding" and that the shipments needed for the Soviet Far Eastern campaign would continue. They agreed to begin the Big Three meeting on July 15. Even on the vexing Polish question, Hopkins managed to have Stalin agree to invite some members from the London Poles into the government.

The Far Eastern question was covered at the third meeting, on May 28. To Hopkins's question of when the Soviet Union would enter the war, Stalin replied that the Soviet Army would be "in sufficient preparedness" by August 8. Contrary to the claim that has often been made by historians, Stalin promised not that the Soviets would enter the war precisely on August 8, but that preparations would be complete by that date. Later in the conversation, Stalin remarked that the opening of operations would depend on the weather, since the autumn fogs would make the campaign difficult. Moreover, Stalin connected the actual date of operations with the acceptance of the Yalta Agreement by the Chinese. Stalin explained that he would need to justify entry into the war to the Soviet people.

Hopkins inquired how Stalin felt about demanding unconditional surrender from Japan. Stalin replied that he had heard the rumors of talks between the British and the Japanese regarding conditional surrender. Japan might be ready to surrender, Stalin said, but only conditionally. In that case, the Allies should occupy Japan but treat the country more softly than Germany. The other alternative would be unconditional surrender, which would give the Allies an opportunity to destroy Japan completely. Stalin personally preferred unconditional surrender, since it would mean the complete military destruction of Japan. Hopkins inquired whether Stalin thought the Japanese would surrender unconditionally before they were utterly destroyed. Stalin answered that Japan would not surrender unconditionally.[89]

When Hopkins asked Stalin about the position of the emperor, Stalin said that Hirohito himself was merely a figurehead, but "it would be better to do away with the institution of the emperor," since "an energetic and vigorous figure" might replace Hirohito in the future and cause trouble. Stalin's position on unconditional surrender left such a strong impression on Hopkins that he reported to Truman: "Stalin made it quite clear that the Soviet Union wants to go through with unconditional surrender and all that is implied in it. However, he feels that if we stick to unconditional surrender the Japs will not give up and we will have to destroy them as we did Germany."

Stalin was interested in completely destroying Japan's military potential. But the demand for unconditional surrender was also a convenient way to prolong the war. In addition, Stalin raised the possibility of discussing "the zone of operations for the armies and zones of occupation in Japan." Hopkins then cabled to Truman: "The Marshal expects that Russia will share in the actual occupation of Japan and wants an agreement with the British and us as to occupation zones."[90] Hopkins suggested to the Soviet leader that at the forthcoming Big Three meeting Stalin and Truman would discuss concrete proposals for Japan's surrender as well as plans for the occupation. This important point has thus far been ignored by historians. It was Hopkins who suggested the idea of a joint U.S.-Soviet ultimatum to Japan. Stalin expected this issue to be placed on the agenda of the forthcoming Potsdam Conference. It was on the basis of this understanding that Stalin most likely instructed his foreign policy advisers to draw up a draft for the ultimatum.[91]

The meeting also touched on other issues in the Far Eastern War. As for China, Stalin stated that the Soviet Union did not intend to infringe on Chinese sovereignty over Manchuria or any other parts of China. Hopkins reported that Stalin "did not believe that the Chinese communist leaders were as good or would be able to bring about the unification of China." As for Korea, Stalin readily agreed with the four-power trusteeship.[92]

As far as the Pacific War was concerned, Hopkins's talk with Stalin was a huge success. After Hopkins left for London, Harriman cabled to Truman: "I feel that Harry's visit has been more successful than I had hoped. Although there are and will continue to be many unresolved problems with the Soviet Government, I believe that his visit has produced a much better atmosphere for your meeting with Stalin."[93]

Stalin Prepares for War against Japan

Soviet planning for the war against Japan was carried out in three stages. First, the General Staff made an operational plan, which involved complicated calculations of necessary forces and equipment and selection of suitable commanders and units. To coordinate military operations on three fronts in a vast area that covered 1.5 million square kilometers, three times as large as France, and integrate the army, the Pacific Fleet, and the air force, the General Staff decided to create a Main Command of Soviet Forces of the Far East, headed by Marshal Vasilevskii and assisted by Chief of Staff General S. P. Ivanov. The second stage was to transport these units to the Far East. The final stage was to implement the operation according to the plan.[94]

By March 1945, the General Staff had completed the first stage of planning. Some shipments of war equipment had begun in April, but the transfer of troops began in earnest only in May, after the German defeat. The Soviet High Command, known as Stavka, chose to send experienced headquarter staff and combat units from the European theater to the Far East and carefully selected the units whose experience would suit the peculiarities of the Far Eastern operations. For instance, the 39th Army and the 5th Army, which had fought in the heavily fortified area of Königsberg, were reassigned to a fortified region in eastern Manchuria, while the 6th Guards Tank Army and 53rd Army, which had fought through the Carpathian Mountains, were assigned to attack the Grand Khingan Mountains of western Manchuria.[95]

Transporting more than one million men, combat units, engineer units, major headquarters, tanks, artillery, and other weapons for the distance of 9,000 to 12,000 kilometers eastward within less than four months was an extraordinary achievement. Moreover, it was accomplished relying on only a single railway line, and mostly on night movements to deceive the Japanese. The Soviets used 136,000 rail cars, and in the peak period of June and July, 20 to 30 trains each day on the Trans-Siberian Railroad, far exceeding what the Japanese intelligence estimated. In the end, the High Command had doubled the strength of Soviet forces in the Far East from 40 to more than 80 divisions. In the meantime, Japan's Kwantung Army had been considerably weakened. By April, 16 divisions had been transferred from Manchuria to the homeland defense. The United States had accurate information about Japanese troop movements through Ultra intercepts, and transmitted this information to the Soviets.[96]

Everything appeared to be going smoothly for Stalin. While he was making preparations with breakneck speed for the war against Japan, he succeeded in reaffirming the U.S. pledge to honor the Yalta Agreement. He managed to confirm a mutual commitment to the unconditional surrender demand to Japan, and even to extract a promise from the United States that the two countries would consult each other to issue a joint ultimatum to Japan at the forthcoming Big Three conference. So far so good, but one fundamental question greatly concerned Stalin: How long was the war going to last? To his mind the war would have to last long enough for the Soviet Union to join it. In this respect, he had two fears. First, in view of Truman's tough stand against the Soviet Union, he was not sure how long the United States would maintain friendly relations with the USSR. He knew that the United States would support Soviet entry into the war as long as it would help the Americans achieve Japan's surrender. But he feared that as soon as the Americans became convinced that they could achieve their goal without Soviet help, they might decide against Soviet participation in the war. Should this happen, the United States would likely renege on its commitment to the Yalta Agreement. One uncertain factor remained the development of the atomic bomb. Stalin was thus closely following the intelligence reports provided by NKVD chief Lavrentii Beria.

Stalin also feared the early termination of the war as a result of Japan's premature acceptance of surrender. In order to prolong the war long enough for the Soviets to complete their preparations to attack Japan, he urged the United States to adhere to the unconditional surrender demand. Simultaneously, he attempted to deceive Japan into believing that the Soviet Union could be kept out of the war. He confided to Hopkins that after the first part of July it would be "impossible to conceal from the Japanese very much longer the movement of Soviet troops."[97] The Japanese were willing to cooperate, making his task easier. Nevertheless, Stalin had to monitor Japan's moves closely.

Malik was busy in the second half of May gathering information from various contacts he had established among Japanese high officials. On May 20, he wrote about a conversation he had with a "leading naval officer." According to his informant, Japan would not win the war, but it would not be crushed like Germany, since Japan was in a position to exploit the fundamental conflict between the United States and the Soviet Union. "The Soviet Union fears the increasing influence of the United States and Britain in the Far East after the war as a result of their cooperation with Chiang Kai-shek," the naval officer stated. "The United States and Britain also fear that the complete destruction of Japan will make Eastern Asia and China 'red.' They are learning a painful lesson in Eastern Europe." Malik observed that Japan's major objective was to intensify efforts to maintain Soviet neutrality, while taking maximum advantage of conflict between the Soviet Union and the United States by attempting to frighten the latter with the notion of a "red scare" in the

Far East in the event of Japan's complete destruction. Malik warned that the most important question for the Soviet Union was whether the United States would soften the demand of unconditional surrender to induce Japan to agree to early capitulation.[98]

On May 25 Malik noted that the Foreign Ministry was attempting to seek Moscow's mediation between Japan and the United States. For this purpose, Japan was prepared to give up fishing rights in the Soviet waters and abandon southern Sakhalin and the Kurils to the Soviet Union. Giving up the Kurils to the Soviet Union would, in Japan's calculations, provoke conflict between the Soviet Union and the United States. In addition, Japan would withdraw Japanese troops from China and grant independence to Manchuria and Korea. As long as Manchukuo became independent, the issue of who controls the Chinese Eastern Railway would cease to be Japan's problem.[99]

On May 30, Danish Minister Lars Tillitze came to see Malik to obtain a Soviet visa to return home after Japan had broken off diplomatic relations with Denmark. Tillitze was a shrewd political observer with a wide network of contacts in influential circles. During his visit, he had very interesting and important information to offer Malik, who duly reported the conversation to Moscow. Tillitze remarked that the military situation was becoming hopeless for Japan, as Japan's defeat in the Battle of Okinawa was just a matter of time. Therefore, Japan was seriously looking for ways to get out of the war. In Tillitze's view, Japan would give up everything that it had acquired since 1905, including Manchuria and Korea. The only conditions it would insist upon would be avoidance of unconditional surrender and preservation of the territorial integrity of Japan proper. As for U.S. intentions, Tillitze expressed his firm conviction that the Americans were committed to pursuing a hard line against the Japanese in order to destroy Japan under the slogan "Remember Pearl Harbor." The Danish diplomat remarked, however, that as long as the Americans considered the roots of militarism destroyed and the revenge of Pearl Harbor fulfilled, they would consider softer conditions for Japan's surrender.

Tillitze also mentioned that the emperor was now in favor of terminating the war and had broken with Japan's High Command, which was still determined to continue the fight. The most difficult opposition to the termination of war would come, in his view, not from the highest leadership of the army but from mid-level army officers. The navy high officials had already reached the conclusion that they would have to find ways to get out of the war. It would be difficult for Japan to come up with concrete peace proposals since no one thus far had emerged to take charge of negotiations with the United States and Britain. A peace party, however, was emerging in Japan, which was centered around the Imperial Court and led by Marquis Kido.[100]

Malik's analysis at the end of May provided Stalin with valuable insight. Japan was seriously attempting to find ways to terminate the war. One possibility was the Moscow route, which would serve Stalin's purpose of prolonging the war. But Stalin had to watch for other possibilities, such as Japan's attempts to send peace feelers through Sweden and Switzerland. In the meantime, Malik was doing his best to convince the Japanese that the Neutrality Pact was still in force, though Stalin intended to violate it when the right moment came.

April and May were times of change. For Japan, the Battle of Okinawa was going badly. The Japanese could no longer count on Soviet neutrality, and the newly formed Suzuki government was divided on whether peace should be sought before the decisive battle. After being unexpectedly thrust into the presidency, Truman immediately faced the challenge of how to deal with the Soviet Union. His inconsistent policy of first toughness and then leniency revealed his uncertainties about the role of the Soviet Union not merely in the postwar world after the German defeat but also in the Pacific War. He was simultaneously faced with the dilemma of whether to modify the demand for unconditional surrender from the Japanese and whether to welcome Soviet entry into the war against Japan. Stalin, for his part, adjusted his policy to the rapidly changing circumstances. The Soviet government renounced the Neutrality Pact, partly to signal to the United States its commitment to the Yalta Agreement, and partly to free itself from the shackles of legal commitment while it prepared a surprise attack on Japan. Although things seemed to be going his way, Stalin had two major concerns: that the war might be terminated before the Soviets were ready to join it, and that the new American president, whom he did not completely trust, would renege on the Yalta Agreement. In the coming months, the three leaders would each be forced to make a momentous decision.

CHAPTER 3

Decisions for War and Peace

THE MONTH AND A HALF from June to mid-July was a time of decision. In Tokyo, after Japan was defeated in the Battle of Okinawa, the peace party finally took a decisive step toward ending the war by approaching the Soviet Union. In Moscow, the State Defense Committee and the Politburo formally adopted a plan to wage war against Japan. In Washington, the United States moved in several directions to hasten the termination of the Pacific War: the Interim Committee made the decision to drop the atomic bomb on Japan; the president approved a plan to invade Japan; and, finally, influential policymakers adopted a draft ultimatum to Japan that included a provision ensuring the maintenance of a constitutional monarchy under the current dynasty. While Japan began its desperate effort to extricate itself from the war, the race between the Soviet Union and the United States to achieve Japan's surrender had begun.

The Interim Committee made two important decisions at a meeting on May 31. The major item on the agenda was international control of the atomic bomb. Stimson opened the meeting by stressing "a revolutionary change in the relations of man to the universe" that would result from the new weapon. Robert Oppenheimer, director of the atomic program, recommended that the United States share information on the atomic bomb with the Soviets, and Marshall suggested that the United States invite Soviet scientists to the testing of the bomb, codenamed "Trinity." Byrnes put an end to such illusions. To him the new weapon's implications for civilization were irrelevant. All he could think about was the threat the Russians would pose if they succeeded in possessing the bomb. "If information were given to the Russians, even in general terms," Byrnes warned, "Stalin would ask to be brought into the partnership." The United States should push forward in production and research without informing the Soviets. Byrnes browbeat the skeptics into acquiescence.[1]

The Interim Committee also discussed the question of whether the atomic bomb should be used against Japan and, if so, in what manner. This question was not placed on the formal agenda but was discussed casually at the lunch table during recess. Byrnes argued against giving warning or a demonstration. The bomb might not work; the Japanese might intercept the bombers; or the Japanese might bring American prisoners to the target site. No one challenged Byrnes's argument. The following day, June 1, the Interim Committee made a decision: "*Mr. Byrnes recommended,* and the Committee *agreed,* that the Secretary of War should be advised that, while recognizing that the final selection of the target was essentially a military decision, the present view of the Committee was that the bomb should be used against Japan as soon as possible; that it be used on a war plant surrounded by workers' homes, and that it be used without prior warning."[2]

This was a momentous decision. Since the Target Committee had already approved the use of two bombs, as historian Martin Sherwin wrote, this decision "not only confirmed the assumption that the new weapon was to be used, but that the *two* bombs that would be available early in August should be used. The destruction of both Hiroshima and Nagasaki was the result of a *single* decision." Stimson informed the president of this decision on June 6. The secretary of war also advised Truman that the Russians should be told nothing until the first bomb had successfully been dropped on Japan. After that, information would be given on a quid pro quo basis. The president admitted to thinking the same thing, especially with regard to the "settlement of the Polish, Rumanian, Yugoslavian, and Manchurian problems." Stimson reported that he had a hard time trying to hold the air force down to precision bombing rather than area bombing. He was concerned about this feature of the war for two reasons. First, he did not want the United States to receive the reputation of outdoing Hitler's atrocities, and second, he feared that "the Air Force might have Japan so thoroughly bombed out that the new weapon would not have a fair background to show its strength." Truman laughed and said he understood. Neither Stimson nor Truman seemed to be concerned about the inherent contradiction between Stimson's two fears.[3]

At this moment, the clock began ticking on the dropping of the atomic bomb. In order to stop the clock, the president would have to undo his decision, but to do so would require an overwhelming justification and incredible courage. Meanwhile, the discussion of the atomic bomb took so much time that Stimson never got around to raising other important issues, in particular, "the possible abandonment of the unconditional surrender doctrine and the achievement of our strategic objectives without this formula."[4]

Hirota Meets Malik

By the end of May it became clear to the Japanese policymakers that the fall of Okinawa was inevitable. Once the island fell, the United States would acquire a powerful foothold into the Japanese homeland. In the meantime, American air raids continued to rain incendiary bombs on Japanese cities. Japan's ruling elite became frightened at the prospect of continuing the war. Would the Japanese people withstand the pressure or turn against the government and the emperor?

This fear drove the hitherto timid peace party to seek termination of the war as quickly as possible. But the major obstacle continued to be the Japanese Imperial Army, which was determined to wage a final battle to defend the homeland. But how to attach the bell to the beast? The problem was compounded by the indecision of Prime Minister Suzuki. Private conversations in which Suzuki confided his desire to terminate the war were often contradicted by public speeches in which he exhorted his countrymen to fight the war to the bitter end and die for the country like kamikaze suicide pilots.

Togo initiated an active policy of seeking Soviet neutrality. On May 21, he had instructed Sato to meet Molotov and find out if there was any change in the Soviets' attitude toward Japan after the San Francisco conference. Sato met Molotov on May 29 and found the foreign commissar "extremely friendly." Molotov stated that the Soviet abrogation of the Neutrality Pact had brought about no change in the existing situation. The Soviet Union "has her fill of war in Europe," Molotov explained, and must give her "immediate and deep attention" to the "domestic problem." Molotov in turn asked Sato how long Japan thought the

Pacific War would last. "As a result of America's attitude," Sato replied, "we have no choice but to continue the fight." Even Sato, usually a savvy observer, concluded incorrectly that Molotov's friendly attitude stemmed from a Soviet policy focused on domestic problems without much attention to Far Eastern questions.[5]

On June 1, Togo instructed Sato to "miss no opportunity to talk to the Soviet leaders." Togo told him that he had delegated former Prime Minister Hirota to talk to Malik, knowing full well that Sato opposed this policy.[6] Togo felt he was doing his best to end the war within the domestic constraints, and he was irritated by critical comments expressed by Sato, who was far removed from the domestic scene. Togo thus decided to pursue secret negotiations without informing Sato of the details of the talks, apparently afraid that his actions might invite the ambassador's scathing criticism. Moreover, instead of directly conducting negotiations with the Soviet ambassador, he chose to use a private channel to approach Malik.

Togo chose Koki Hirota as his unofficial envoy. Hirota, a professional diplomat, had served as ambassador to the Soviet Union from 1930 to 1932, as foreign minister from 1933 to 1935 and 1937 to 1938, and as prime minister from 1936 to 1937. Togo emphasized to Hirota that it was necessary not only to keep the Soviet Union out of the war but also to develop friendly relations with the Soviets. He should avoid requesting Moscow's mediation to terminate the war, but if the Soviet side were to make such an offer, Hirota was to let the Japanese government know immediately. If necessary, Hirota could say that his talks were initiated by the government. While pointing out that Japan's neutrality had contributed to the Soviet victory over Germany, Hirota should stress that maintaining Japan's international position would be beneficial to the Soviet Union in its conflict with the United States. Hirota could say that Japan was prepared to grant the Soviet Union substantial compensation for its neutrality, but he should avoid discussing specific concessions.[7]

On June 3, a Foreign Ministry councilor visited Malik's temporary residence at Hotel Gora in Hakone, where the Soviet ambassador had sought temporary shelter from American air raids on Tokyo. He told Malik that Hirota had been evacuated to Hakone after his house had been burned. Given that he was now Malik's neighbor, Hirota wanted to pay a visit to the ambassador. Malik told him that he would be happy to have Hirota for a visit the following week. Twenty minutes later, Hirota showed up without warning at Malik's doorstep. After a shower of sycophantic admiration for the Soviet victory over Germany and effusive praise of Malik as a young but extraordinary diplomat, Hirota told the ambassador that he wanted to discuss how to improve Japan's relations with the Soviet Union. He then asked Malik to invite him again the following day to discuss specific problems concerning Soviet-Japanese relations.[8]

The following day Hirota again invited himself to Malik's quarters at the hotel. "The Soviet Union will be preoccupied with domestic reconstruction," Hirota started, "but it must also be concerned about guaranteeing peace in the future." Hirota observed that the Soviet Union had taken back land that had belonged to it in the west and carried out "a policy of friendship and peace" with its neighbors. "I think," Hirota stated, without noticing the irony that was to haunt Japan later, "the Soviet government will approach the East in the same way." Hirota then moved on to talk about the Neutrality Pact. As long as the Neutrality Pact was in force, Japan would not worry, but it would have to start thinking about what would happen when the pact expired. If there were any difficulties, he wanted to know about them in advance. Thus began a general pattern in the Hirota-Malik talks, by which the two kept asking each other what specific proposals the other had in mind without revealing their own intentions.

Malik responded to Hirota's effusive praise of the Soviet Union by reminding him that the past behaviors of the Japanese government were not exactly conducive to establishing confidence in Japan's intentions; in fact, they had led to a feeling of suspicion and mistrust among the Soviets. Malik wanted to know what specific measures Hirota proposed to improve relations with the Soviet Union. Hirota, however, could not give his host any specific proposals, since he had none. He dwelt only on generalities. He wanted to know what form the Soviet government thought improved relations should take. Malik asked if Hirota's views were merely his own or those of specific political circles in Japan. Hirota replied: "I want you to understand that this is the view of the Japanese government as well as the view of the Japanese people as a whole."[9]

Malik correctly concluded from Hirota's sudden visits that Japan was desperately trying to find ways to terminate the war, and that Hirota was sent to sound out the possibility of a long-term agreement between the Soviet Union and Japan. During these conversations Hirota had made no sharp attacks on the United States or Britain, leading Malik to think that strengthening relations with the Soviet Union was a prelude to peace negotiations with the Allies.[10]

After reporting to Molotov about his June 3–4 meetings with Hirota, Malik recommended that it might serve Soviet interests to take advantage of Japan's difficult situation and extract the maximum concessions as outlined in his summer 1944 memorandum. Specifically, he suggested that the Japanese would now be willing to return southern Sakhalin to the Soviet Union, abandon fishing rights in Soviet waters, and even return part of the Kuril islands. But he predicted that obtaining Japan's concessions on Manchuria, Korea, and the Liaotung Peninsula would be difficult. "Such concessions would be possible," Malik stated, "only as a result of a complete military defeat and unconditional surrender of Japan. Without them, any negotiations with Japan will not provide a fundamental resolution of problems for long-lasting peace and security in the Far East." Malik suggested that if Hirota still persisted in holding urgent meetings with him, he would remind him that he was not in a position to make any statement until he received specific proposals. Malik requested further instructions from Molotov.[11]

Malik most likely did not know that Stalin had already made up his mind to wage war against Japan and that diplomacy was used only to mask his secret design. An astute, well-informed diplomat like Malik must have known that Soviet troops were being transported to the Far East, and he must have guessed the general line that Stalin was pursuing. It was therefore prudent for him to make a recommendation in tune with what he considered to be Stalin's intention. In his opinion the ultimate objective of the Soviet Union would not be obtainable without war, and yet he left open the possibility of negotiations. Stalin and Molotov preferred to keep Malik ignorant of their war plans. As far as they were concerned, matters of war did not concern a diplomat.

Japan Seeks Moscow's Mediation

Malik was not the only diplomat who was kept in the dark. Sato had no knowledge of the Hirota-Malik negotiations. Togo's June 1 telegram instructing Sato to approach Molotov in order to seek better relations with the Soviet Union had greatly disturbed the ambassador. In his reply to Togo on June 8, Sato expressed his candid view that there was "absolutely no hope" that Russia might take a "favorable attitude" toward Japan. If the Soviets had not shown any interest in improving relations with Japan while they were engaged in their life-or-death struggle with Germany, he asked, why would they be more interested in improving relations with Japan after the German defeat? Their abrogation of the Neutrality Pact should be taken as a clear sign of their intentions. Sato did not mince words: he was flabbergasted by the naiveté of a diplomacy that continued to cling to this pipe dream. Having received this stinging indictment of his policy, Togo was determined to keep Sato out of the loop on the Hirota-Malik negotiations.

Sato further touched on a delicate but fundamental issue: appraisal of the military situation. He ventured to state that "under conditions of modern warfare it would be unthinkable to continue hostilities once our means of resistance has been crushed." These comments must have especially irritated Togo, precisely because he shared the same view. But Togo also knew how delicate the domestic situation was. One false step and the cabinet might implode, or political figures who worked for peace might be assassinated. Any design to end the war would have to be approved by the army.

At the end of his telegram, Sato raised another important point: Japan would be able to do nothing if the Soviet Union decided to take advantage of its weaknesses and join the war. The superiority of the Red Army was beyond doubt even in the eyes of a civilian observer. Before that happened, Sato urged, Japan should do everything to terminate the war with the single aim of preserving the *kokutai*.[12] Togo considered Sato arrogant, pig-headed, and totally ignorant of Japan's domestic constraints. But since he could not replace him, he decided to conduct diplomacy behind the back of his own ambassador.

Two days after Hirota finished his still inconclusive second talk with Malik, the Supreme War Council adopted three mutually contradictory documents to guide Japan's policy in the war: "The Basic Outline to Be Followed in the Future for Guiding the War" and two supporting documents, "The Current Condition of National Strength" and "The World Situation." The main document stressed that although the United States would strengthen its effort to win the war in the Pacific after the victory over Germany, Japan would be able to inflict tremendous damage on the enemy, whose will to continue the war would be shaken by the end of the year. But this document was contradicted by the first supporting document, which drew a pessimistic picture of Japan's economic conditions, food supplies, transport, and general morale.[13]

As for Soviet intentions, the second document explained that the Russians planned to expand their influence in the Far East by striking at the most opportune moment. To that end, the Soviet Union was engaged in a massive buildup of forces on the Manchurian border to prepare for war against Japan. However, it judged that the Soviets would not likely resort to military action soon. The most dangerous moment for a potential attack would come in the summer and fall of 1945.[14] Again, this document was a curious combination of analysis and wishful thinking. If it was true that the Soviets were amassing enormous forces in the Far East, that the Soviets were looking for the most opportune moment to strike against Japan, and that the summer and fall would be the most dangerous time for Soviet military action against Japan, then logically it should follow that Japan would prepare for such an eventuality. Instead, the document deduced from this information that Japan should try its utmost to keep the Soviet Union out of the war.

The last-ditch defense that the army officers envisaged was based on a fanatical suicidal mission to show the superiority of the Japanese fighting spirit. For this mission, the army was prepared to mobilize the entire Japanese population in a *levée en masse*. In April, the army issued the Field Manual for the Decisive Battle in the Homeland. This manual ordered soldiers to abandon the wounded, not to retreat, to be prepared to fight even with their bare hands, and not to hesitate to kill Japanese residents, women, elderly, and children, who might be used as a shield for the approaching enemy.[15] The expected Kyushu battle was to be a suicidal fight on a larger scale than Iwo Jima, Guadalcanal, and Okinawa.

In the end the Big Six accepted all three documents, the most important of which was the document stating that Japan would continue the war to preserve the *kokutai* and to defend the homeland. For this purpose, the government would engage in active diplomacy toward the Soviet Union, and implement a domestic system to mobilize the entire population and all resources for the pursuit of war. On June 8, the imperial conference approved these documents. The army railroaded the entire process, and no protest was raised. Suzuki thought the documents were appropriate. Togo, who was excluded from the process of adopting these important documents, bitterly complained about Suzuki's lack of leadership. But Yonai thought the Japanese leadership should be united in its objective at that point, perhaps already contemplating betraying the army at the crucial moment. He kept silent during the meetings.[16] Kido decided to let the process run its course, thinking that it might be better to let the army have its say at this point. The emperor did not say a word during the conference. Although in the end everyone agreed, this decision prompted the peace party to act more decisively for peace.

After the Japanese government adopted the policy to continue the war, the Suzuki cabinet opened the Emergency Diet Session from June 9 to 13. The diet passed an emergency military mobilization bill, and under pressure from the right-wing Diet members, Suzuki was forced to make a series of brave declarations that showed Japan's determination to fight the war to the bitter end. Japan's precipitous descent into national suicide convinced Togo and Yonai to do something to arrest this momentum. On June 13, they agreed to implement Option Three of the May 14 Supreme War Council decision: to seek Moscow's mediation to terminate the war. Kido's approval of this plan helped Togo and Yonai to persuade Suzuki to accept their decision. Japan's attempt to end the war with Moscow's help was beginning to gain momentum.[17]

Stimson, Grew, and Forrestal Redefine Unconditional Surrender

While Japan's Big Six secretly decided to seek Moscow's mediation, Truman met with China's foreign minister, T. V. Soong, on June 9, and officially informed him of the contents of the Yalta Agreement. He made it clear that he was committed to observing the agreement. Soong expressed his profound misgivings about specific provisions that violated Chinese sovereignty. Citing Stalin's assurance to Hopkins that he would support Nationalist China, Truman encouraged Soong to reach an agreement with Stalin. Soong then inquired whether the president contemplated issuing an Allied joint agreement regarding surrender terms for Japan. Truman answered that such a general statement was desirable, but should wait until the Soviets entered the war. He added that he hoped that time would come early enough to shorten the war and save American and Chinese lives.[18]

But influential policymakers in the United States began to discuss how to revise the American demand for unconditional surrender so that more moderate leaders in Japan would be induced to accept an early end to the war. Even after his unsuccessful attempt to persuade Stimson, Forrestal, and Marshall on May 29, Grew was relentlessly campaigning for the modification of unconditional surrender. At the beginning of June, McCloy had "extensive" talks with Grew, who argued that "we would have nothing to lose by warning the Japanese of the cataclysmic consequences of the weapon we possessed and indicating that we would be prepared to allow Japan to continue as a constitutional monarchy."[19] It is reasonable to assume that McCloy and Stimson discussed this issue, and concluded that they should support Grew's campaign.

Previously, Stimson had opposed the idea of a presidential statement modifying the unconditional surrender term. But sometime in the beginning of June he changed his mind. The impending victory in the Battle of Okinawa allayed Stimson's fear that the Japanese might see any revision of unconditional surrender as a sign of weakness. Hoover's opinion must also have influenced Stimson's thinking. In the beginning of June, Hoover wrote a letter to Truman, a copy of which the president sent to Stimson for comment. The Japanese moderate element "desirous of preserving both nation and the emperor," Hoover wrote, would find it easier to accept the terms, "if Britain and American could persuade the Japanese they had no intention of eradicating them, eliminating their system of government, or interfering with their way of life." On June 12 Stimson, Grew, McCloy, and Forrestal revisited the question of unconditional surrender. At this meeting, Stimson raised the points mentioned in Hoover's letter. According to Forrestal, "this was one of the most serious questions," and Stimson concurred. Stimson now took a firm stand that he had "no hesitation in abandoning" the unconditional surrender formula so long as the United States could "accomplish all of our strategic objectives without the use of this phrase."[20] The Committee of Three (Stimson, Grew, and Forrestal) agreed to coordinate their activities. Forrestal then brought this matter to the president the following day. Truman said that before his departure for the Potsdam Conference, he wanted to have a meeting of the State, War, and Navy departments, plus the Joint Chiefs of Staff, to obtain a clear outline of national objectives in Asia.[21] This became Truman's favorite method of dealing with unpleasant advice: whenever he received suggestions to modify unconditional surrender, he evaded the question by referring it to a joint conference.

The pressure to redefine unconditional surrender mounted in crescendo. On June 16, Grew sent a memo to the president about Hoover's letter. In this memorandum the acting secretary of state pleaded that the president issue a statement at the conclusion of the Battle of Okinawa, clarifying that the Japanese would be "permitted to determine for themselves the nature of their future political structure." Grew observed that "the preservation of the Throne and 'non-molestation' of Hirohito were likely to be the 'irreducible Japanese terms.'" Without clarifying unconditional surrender, which would ensure these terms, there would be no way the Japanese would terminate the war.[22]

On the morning of June 18, before the president convened a meeting with military leaders to discuss the invasion plan, Grew met the president for a second time to petition for the modification of unconditional surrender. Disappointingly, however, Truman told Grew that he decided to postpone the decision until it could be discussed at the Big Three meeting.[23] The president promised to have the subject entered on the agenda of the Potsdam Conference. Again he evaded the issue. His consistent avoidance of the problem points to the inevitable conclusion that Truman did not want to modify the unconditional surrender demand. He was bent on avenging the humiliation of Pearl Harbor by imposing on the enemy unconditional surrender. But he would still have to find ways to minimize the cost of American lives while satisfying his thirst for revenge. He was not yet holding all the cards.

While the Americans were exploring ways to end the war by amending the terms of surrender, Kremlin leaders were busy trying to keep the war going. On June 15, Molotov sent instructions to Malik on how to handle his talks with Hirota. Malik was not to initiate any meetings. "If he again requests a meeting," Molotov instructed, "then you may receive him and listen to him. If he again talks about general matters, you must limit yourself to stating that you will inform Moscow of the talks at the first possibility (but through diplomatic courier). You should not go beyond that."[24]

Molotov's telegram reveals several important points. Although the foreign commissar ordered Malik not to take the initiative in seeking out Hirota, he did not tell him to reject his request. Molotov also suggested that Malik send Japan's proposal via diplomatic courier, the slowest method of communication, rather than coded telegram. Molotov's intention was unmistakable: he wanted to use the Hirota-Malik talks as a tool to prolong the war. A photocopy of Molotov's message includes his handwritten remarks: "To Stalin, Request approval, V. Molotov, 13/VI," and Stalin's signature indicating his approval. There is no question that Stalin and Molotov carefully monitored the Hirota-Malik talks. Togo's clumsy ploy to send Hirota to Malik to "sound out" Moscow's intention unwittingly played right into the Soviets' hand.

Kido's Plan to Terminate the War

As Malik correctly detected, the Japanese political elite were beginning to coalesce secretly to seek the termination of the war. Professor Shigeru

Nambara and five professors at the University of Tokyo had studied the possibility of ending the war by negotiating directly with the United States. They proposed that the Japanese government accept "unconditional surrender" with the only condition being preservation of the imperial house. They would count on the navy to prevail on the army and impose the end of the war by the emperor's decision. After the war, the emperor should abdicate. The six professors also secretly consulted Konoe, Togo, and Sokichi Takagi, and a few other important peace advocates. Nambara and Yasaka Takagi, Japan's foremost authority on America, visited Kido twice (May 7 and June 1) to discuss their ideas. On June 8, Nambara visited Sokichi Takagi and asked him to adopt the policy of ending the war through direct negotiations with the United States. Nambara explained that American public opinion was divided into those who advocated soft peace and those who insisted on hard peace. The policy to continue the war to the bitter end would alienate the soft-peace advocates in the United States, inevitably endangering the imperial house. Domestically, this policy would feed the people's discontent, which would be directed against the emperor. This was exactly what the Soviet Union wanted to achieve.

A week later, Nambara again visited Sokichi Takagi, this time accompanied by Professor Yasaka Takagi. The two professors called Takagi's attention to the views expressed by Grew and Edwin Reischauer, who stressed the need to preserve the institution of the emperor. Japan should achieve a negotiated peace through direct negotiations with the United States instead of relying on the mediation of the Soviet Union. Hirohito was familiar with the views expressed by the Tokyo University professors. It is not known, however, how he reacted to their recommendations.[25]

The adoption of the Basic Outline for Conduct of the War greatly disturbed Kido. What troubled him most was the possibility for popular discontent, which might be directed against the emperor. If Japan missed the chance to terminate the war, it would follow the same fate as Germany, and the preservation of the *kokutai* could not be guaranteed. He reached almost the same conclusions as the six University of Tokyo professors with two important exceptions. Kido saw no prospect of the army's accepting peace. Thus he, too, concluded that the only way to terminate the war would be to rely on the emperor's authority to silence the army's opposition. But unlike the professors, who advocated direct negotiations with the United States and Britain, Kido believed that Japan might be able to secure better terms by seeking Moscow's mediation. The emperor's personal letter to Moscow leaders would seek "peace with honor," abandonment of Japanese occupied territories, withdrawal of Japanese troops from overseas, and the partial disarmament of armed forces. On June 8 he wrote Kido's Tentative Plan for the Termination of the War, expressing these ideas. The marquis showed his plan to the emperor the same day. Hirohito told Kido to implement the plan immediately.[26]

It is important to note that Kido had consulted Matsudaira, Kase, Matsutani, and Takagi on his plan. The *modus operandii* of the peace party was gradually being established. The four men constituted a clandestine link among more powerful actors such as Kido, Shigemitsu, Togo, Yonai, and Konoe, who could not openly meet and plot for peace.

The discrepancies between rapidly deteriorating domestic conditions and the decision to continue the war at the Imperial Conference on June 8 did not escape Hirohito's attention, though he said nothing during the conference. On the morning of June 9, before he was shown Kido's plan, the emperor received Chief of Staff Umezu, who had just returned from an inspection tour in Manchuria. Umezu's report was shocking, revealing that the Kwantung Army had shrunk to a mere skeleton, and that the ammunition reserve would be exhausted after the first major encounter. Hirohito commented that since military units in the homeland were equipped with inferior weapons, the homeland defense would be questionable. Takagi suspected that by making this gloomy report, Umezu was signaling to the emperor that he had to intervene to terminate the war.[27] Nevertheless, the army's strategy was to reinforce the Kyushu defense at the expense of other areas, following the policy of "one decisive strike before peace." Reducing the Kwantung Army to a skeleton made sense from the army's point of view, since it expected that Japan could keep the Soviet Union out of the war.

On June 12, the emperor received another depressing report from retired Admiral Kiyoshi Hasegawa, who, as the emperor's special inspector, had investigated the conditions of various military districts and weapons depots throughout Japan. Hirohito, who had trusted the efficacy of the military until the fall of Okinawa, had finally come to question the validity of the army's plan for homeland defense. This was the first sign that Hirohito was abandoning the policy of one decisive strike before peace.[28]

From June 9 to 14, Kido was busily engaged in *nemawashi*, informal negotiations behind the scenes, with key policymakers. On June 13 he showed his plan to Yonai and received his approval. But Kido had to use the emperor's sanction of the plan to keep Suzuki from wandering into the war camp. On June 15, Kido met Togo. The foreign minister supported the plan, but he was shocked to learn that Suzuki had not apprised Kido and the emperor of the ongoing talks between Hirota and Malik. Kido obtained the approval of three of the Big Six, but in order to implement his plan he had to gain one more vote from the war party. Since he ruled out Umezu and Toyoda as hopeless, the marquis decided to approach Anami. The Lord Keeper met the army minister on June 18. Kido explained that it was essential to seek the termination of the war before an invasion of the homeland. Anami disagreed, since he firmly believed that the best guarantee to preserve the *kokutai* would be to wage the last defense against the Americans in the homeland. To counter Anami's argument, Kido asked what would happen if the Americans succeeded in invading Japan and capturing Three Divine Objects, symbols of Japan's imperial house. To convince the fanatic believer in the emperor system, Kido cunningly used this mythic symbol, which was sufficient to soften Anami's objection. Although Kido did not obtain Anami's full approval, at least he secured a promise that he would not oppose the emperor's letter seeking Moscow's mediation for the termination of the war.[29]

On the same day, the Big Six approved the plan to ask for Moscow's mediation by the end of July so that the war could be terminated by September. In this way, the Big Six went behind the backs of military planners who were still determined to continue the war. Hirohito urged Togo to implement the plan to end the war as expeditiously as possible in view of the insufficient preparations for operations in the homeland.[30] While the army planners were preparing for the last-ditch defense of the homeland without knowing their highest superiors had given a nod to the peace overtures through Moscow, the peace party began secret maneuvers to outwit the army.

Truman Approves Operation Olympic

Truman remained undecided about modifying unconditional surrender. In order to solve this question, he had to find out what would happen if he stuck to this demand. On June 14, Admiral Leahy informed the Joint Chiefs of Staff that the president wanted to discuss the military plans for the invasion of Japan at the White House on June 18. Specifically, the president wanted to know the number of men and ships necessary to defeat Japan, the estimated time required to invade Japan proper and how many casualties could be expected, the estimated time and losses of alternative plans for blockade and bombardment, and the advisability of Soviet entry into the war. The president's top priority, Leahy's memo made clear, was to minimize the loss of American lives.[31]

On June 15, the Joint War Plans Committee submitted a briefing paper to the Joint Chiefs of Staff, reaffirming the decision that had already been made on the invasion of Kyushu as the only strategy to force Japan's surrender. The committee predicted that there would be 193,500 casualties in the Kyushu and the Kanto Plain operations combined, of which 40,000 would be combat deaths. It considered Soviet entry into the war against Japan no longer essential, though the Red Army could contribute to pinning down the Japanese troops in Manchuria and North China.[32]

Having received the president's summons to this important conference, Stimson engaged in a small conspiracy. The night before he called McCloy and told him that since he was not feeling well, McCloy should attend the meeting in his place. Stimson and McCloy then discussed what line of argument McCloy should take at the meeting. With the overwhelming preponderance of power that the United States would bring to bear on Japan, McCloy recalled telling Stimson that "we should have our heads examined if we did not consider the possibility of bringing the war to a conclusion without further loss of life. I felt we could readily agree to let the Japanese retain the emperor as a constitutional monarch." They talked about "the possibility of a message to the Japanese government, what form it might take, and whether or not we should mention the possession of the bomb."[33]

On the afternoon of June 18, the Chiefs of Staff (Marshall, King, and Lieutenant General Ira Eaker, deputy commander of the army air forces, in place of Arnold), Forrestal, and McCloy gathered at the White House. To McCloy's surprise and pleasure, Stimson also attended. Marshall began by reading the Joint War Plans Committee's report defending the strategy of invading Kyushu on November 1 (Operation Olympic), but he omitted any reference to the casualties. The invasion of Kyushu was essential to tighten the stranglehold of blockade and bombardment on Japan as well as to force capitulation before the United States launched its invasion of the Kanto Plain (Operation Coronet), planned for March 1. Marshall asserted that for the Japanese to capitulate short of complete military defeat, they would have to be faced with utter hopelessness occasioned by "(1) destruction already wrought by air bombardment and sea blockade, coupled with (2) a landing on Japan indicating the firmness of our resolution, and (3) the entry or threat of entry of Russia into the war."

It is important to note that Marshall considered *both* an American landing *and* the Soviet entry into the war essential for Japan's surrender. He thought the role of the Soviet Union should be "to deal with the Japanese in Manchuria (and Korea if necessary)." He stated that Russian entry into the war might well be "the decisive action levering them [the Japanese] into capitulation" after the Americans landed in Japan. King and Eaker concurred that Operation Olympic was necessary. King, however, disagreed with Marshall on the Soviet role. He argued that they were not indispensable. He did not think the United States should "go so far as to beg them to come in," since there was no question in his mind that the United States could handle it alone. "One of [the] objectives in connection with the coming conference [at Potsdam]," the president said, "would be to get from Russia all the assistance in the war that was possible." To this end he wanted to know "all the decisions that he would have to make in advance in order to occupy the strongest possible position in the discussion." The entry of the Soviet Union thus still remained a card in Truman's hand, but how he would play that card depended on other factors.[34]

The chiefs then moved on to discuss the estimated casualties. Citing the casualty rate in Leyte, Luzon, Iwo Jima, and Okinawa, Marshall estimated that the Kyushu operation would not exceed the ratio of Luzon (one U.S. casualty to five Japanese). Leahy said that the Okinawa Battle had a 35 percent casualty rate, but King thought the rate would be much lower in the Kyushu operation. Marshall gave the estimated casualty figure as 63,000 of 190,000 troops. Although these numbers were far lower than the numbers that Truman and Stimson later claimed in their postwar memoirs to justify the dropping of the atomic bombs, they were still huge numbers that must have weighed heavily on the president's mind. McCloy felt that a full discussion of all alternatives was inhibited because the attendees who knew about the atomic bomb avoided bringing it in front of others who knew nothing about it.[35]

After ascertaining that the chiefs were unanimous in recommending Operation Olympic, the president asked for Stimson's view. The secretary of War endorsed the chiefs' recommendation, but he then turned to the "political" side of considerations. "There is a large submerged class in

Japan who do not favor the present war," he observed. "This submerged class would fight and fight tenaciously if attacked on their own ground." He suggested, therefore, that something should be done to "arouse them and to develop any possible influence they might have before it became necessary to come to grips with them." Leahy recommended that the demand for unconditional surrender be amended to avoid Japan's desperate resistance and an increase in the casualty lists.[36] At the end of the meeting the president polled all present about whether the United States should go ahead with the invasion plan. No one suggested any alternative, and Truman gave his approval to preparations for Operation Olympic. He remained undecided about Coronet.

As the participants were packing up to leave, Truman noticed McCloy and said, "McCloy, you didn't express yourself, and nobody gets out of this room without standing up and being counted. Do you think I have any reasonable alternative to the decision that has just been taken?" Stimson nodded and told McCloy to feel entirely free to express his view. "I think you have an alternative that ought to be fully explored," McCloy began, "and that, really, we ought to have our heads examined if we do not seek some other method by which we can terminate this war successfully other than by another conventional attack and landing." McCloy then suggested that the United States send "a strong communication to the emperor" that it would demand a full surrender but that it would recognize Japan's right to continue to exist as a nation, including the preservation of the emperor under a constitutional monarchy. If such an offer were rejected, he suggested, the United States would reveal that it possessed the atomic bomb. As soon as McCloy spoke of an atomic bomb, there was a gasp in the room.[37]

Truman said that he was thinking along the same lines, but he asked McCloy to elaborate on his suggestion and take the matter up with Byrnes. As Truman must have expected, Byrnes killed McCloy's idea. "He would have to oppose my proposal," McCloy recalled, "because it appeared to him that it might be considered a weakness on our part. Mr. Byrnes inferred he might not insist on treating the emperor as a war criminal, but he would oppose any 'deal' as a concomitant of a demand for surrender." McCloy argued for amending the unconditional surrender demand to avoid the use of the atomic bomb, but Byrnes was beginning to think that the atomic bomb would be the means by which to secure unconditional surrender. McCloy later expressed his regret that the United States "had not at least tried at this attempt."[38]

Hirohito Seeks Moscow's Mediation

While Truman held a crucial White House meeting with military leaders, Hirohito also had an unprecedented imperial conference. Frustrated by Suzuki's inaction, Yonai and Kido, with Matsudaira serving as a conduit, conspired to arrange a conference. On June 22, the Big Six were summoned to the Imperial Palace for an audience with the emperor, though in a break with tradition they were not given an agenda. In the beginning the emperor asked their views about the possibility of terminating the war. Although Hirohito's opinion was masked in the form of a question, such direct intervention from the emperor was unprecedented. Suzuki answered: "Needless to say, the war must be continued at all cost, but I deem it necessary to try diplomacy as well." Not satisfied with this equivocating statement, Hirohito impatiently turned to Yonai, presumably according to a scenario arranged by Yonai and Kido. Upstaging Togo, Yonai explained that the Supreme War Council on June 18 had concluded that Option Three, that is, to ask Moscow's mediation to terminate the war, should be implemented. Umezu cautioned that any proposal for peace had to be handled carefully. The emperor asked Umezu if acting too carefully might end up costing them the opportunity. Umezu was forced to concede that he would support the idea of approaching Moscow before the last battle to defend the homeland. Anami also approved the idea. Toyoda Soemu, a new naval chief who replaced Oikawa, was silent, perhaps not knowing how to behave at his first imperial conference. Having received the approval of the Big Six, Hirohito concluded the meeting by urging them to proceed with negotiations with the Soviet Union.

This was the crucial moment when Hirohito became actively involved in the effort to terminate the war. Two weeks after the imperial conference had decided to continue the war, the Big Six decided to seek peace with Moscow's help. These two decisions were not necessarily contradictory: the Japanese could try for peace over the summer and still wage the last battle in the fall. This decision was kept strictly confidential, especially from the staff officers in the Army Ministry and the Army General Staff. After the imperial conference, Yonai told Takagi that the die was cast. From then on specific contents of the conditions would be debated. He stated that an army uprising similar to the February 26th Incident could not be ruled out.[39]

Despite the strict code of silence, staff officers suspected that an important decision to terminate the war had been made. Since the decision Konoe had been visited by three staff officers of the Army Ministry. One of them was Tanemura, who explained to Konoe that half a million troops—a sufficient number, according to him—would be deployed for the expected invasion of a million American soldiers. Konoe wondered if Anami could control these radical officers. The prince also observed that there were two interpretations of the *kokutai*. The first interpretation was to obey the emperor's will unconditionally, and the second was to act against the imperial order if it was considered contrary to the interests of the state. Konoe believed that the army staff officers subscribed to the latter.[40]

The Foreign Ministry's secret approach to Malik through Hirota proceeded in tandem with Kido's maneuvering against the army. From June 17 Foreign Ministry officials made daily calls to the Soviet interpreter N. Adrykhaev, trying to arrange a meeting between Hirota and Malik, but each call was answered evasively. Malik was too busy, and besides, he had not received any instructions from Moscow after sending the report on his previous talks with Hirota. The Foreign Ministry was shocked to learn that this report had been sent to Moscow via courier. Malik was faithfully following Molotov's instructions. Togo visited Hirota on June 23 and urged him to meet Malik again. Hirota was skeptical about looking too eager to seek Moscow's mediation, but Togo prodded the reluctant Hirota into seeing Malik as soon as possible. If the Soviet Union was not interested, Togo argued, Japan would have to turn elsewhere.[41]

Thus far, Togo had concealed the Hirota-Malik talks from the Japanese Embassy in Moscow. But on June 22 he told Morishima for the first time about these secret negotiations. Sato's envoy was stunned to learn that Togo had been conducting a policy that he and Sato had consistently opposed. "If Togo and Hirota can come up with a brilliant idea to attract the Soviet Union," Morishima said, "Mr. Sato will, of course, work very hard. But if there is such a brilliant idea, what is it?" Togo had no answer. Morishima was further dumbfounded to learn that the foreign minister had kept information of the Malik-Hirota talks from Sato. He protested that unless the embassy was informed, such negotiations would have no chance of bringing favorable results. Togo promised that he would tell Sato about the negotiations in due course.[42]

Malik reluctantly agreed to meet with Hirota on June 24 in Hakone. Malik immediately informed his guest that he had heard on Radio Moscow that the Supreme Soviet had adopted a law to demobilize older soldiers from the acting army, and that the country was now making a peacetime transition to reconstruction of the economy. When the conversation turned to substantive issues, however, the two men talked past each other. Whereas Hirota kept asking Malik about specific obstacles to improving Soviet-Japanese relations, Malik repeatedly asked Hirota to give him specific proposals that he could transmit to Moscow. After Malik asked Hirota a fourth time to be more specific, Hirota vaguely implied that Japan was ready to make a deal with the Soviet Union on Manchuria, China, and Southeast Asia, but he insisted that he could not negotiate until he knew what the Soviets wanted. Despite the decision made at the Supreme War Council, Hirota did not request Moscow's help to end the war. In fact, he basically repeated what he had said in his two previous meetings without mentioning any new proposals.

Hirota did, however, secure an important commitment from Malik. The Soviet ambassador stated that the relationship between the two countries was based on the Neutrality Pact, and that the pact would play a positive role until it expired. "I am inclined to think," Malik declared, "that the relationship between our countries is developing normally on the basis of this pact. The Soviet government renounced the pact, but it did not break it." Hirota still continued to dwell on generalities, asking Malik if the Soviet side would prefer to renegotiate a neutrality pact or conclude a non-aggression pact or entente.[43]

With the Potsdam Conference just one month away, the Japanese government was wasting precious time by conducting inept diplomacy. Malik must have been irritated by Hirota's long-winded tirade about the need to improve relations absent any concrete proposals. He must also have been shocked by Hirota's preposterous suggestion that the Soviet army and the Japanese navy be combined to create an invincible force in the world, especially when this fantasy was followed by Hirota's outlandish request that the Soviet Union provide Japan with oil in exchange for rubber, tin, lead, and tungsten.

Hirota brought back to Togo little information from Malik. Togo finally concluded that generalities would no longer suffice, and so he decided to present Moscow with Japan's specific concessions. He also decided to inform Sato of the Hirota-Malik negotiations. On June 28 he sent a telegram to the ambassador instructing him to "obtain some sort of commitment [from Molotov] as to the continuation of Russia's neutrality." Overruling Sato's objections to approaching Moscow, Togo insisted: "In view of the urgency of our situation . . . it is our pressing duty to make a desperate effort at this time to obtain more favorable relations than mere neutrality." Togo promised that Japan was prepared to "make considerable sacrifices in this connection," but he did not specifically tell the ambassador what these "sacrifices" might be.[44]

On June 29 Hirota had his third visit with Malik, this time at the Soviet Embassy. Hirota submitted Japan's proposal for the conclusion of a non-aggression treaty, for which Japan was prepared to make the following concessions: (1) the independence of Manchukuo, the withdrawal of all Japanese forces from Manchuria, and a Soviet-Japanese guarantee of the territorial integrity and non-interference in internal matters of Manchukuo; (2) abandonment of Japanese fishing rights in exchange for oil from the Soviet Union; (3) a willingness to settle all the problems the Soviet Union was interested in settling.

These "specific concessions" reveal the fantasy world in which the Japanese government was living. To Malik, Hirota's concessions were still generalities and did not touch on the question of the railways in Manchuria, Dairen and Port Arthur, north China, Korea, and even southern Sakhalin and the Kurils. What Hirota proposed was far less than the Americans had promised in the Yalta Agreement. Even worse, in this desperate situation the Japanese still sought to exchange fishing rights for oil. In fact, Malik must have considered this patently silly proposal insulting. The Soviet ambassador received Hirota's proposal "calmly and coldly," assuring him that it would receive serious attention from higher authorities. In his report to Moscow, Malik predicted that Hirota would undoubtedly demand an urgent meeting soon, but with obvious relish, he wrote that he would inform Hirota that he had sent the information of their conversation via courier.[45]

Having received Malik's report, Molotov observed that the more the military situation worsened, the more desperately the Japanese sought Soviet neutrality. He told Malik that he was acting correctly in his talks with Hirota, but he instructed the Soviet ambassador to be careful not to appear to enter into negotiations.[46] As we will see, Kremlin leaders had already made the final decision to wage war against Japan. Molotov's and, more important, Stalin's thinking had already shifted from the prolongation of negotiations to initiation of war.

Hirota did not give up easily. He kept calling the Soviet Embassy, but Malik refused to see him. The last time Hirota called Malik for an appointment was July 14, only three days before the Potsdam Conference. Once again Malik refused to see him. Since the formal decision to go to war had been made, it was no longer necessary to prolong the talks. The Soviet Embassy informed the Foreign Ministry that Hirota's proposal was sent to Moscow via courier, news that drove the final nail into the coffin of the Hirota-Malik talks.[47]

The Hirota-Malik talks represent a dismal failure of Japanese diplomacy. When time was precious, Togo's method of dispatching a private envoy to Malik was a colossal mistake. Neither was Hirota an ideal person to negotiate with Malik. He never departed from generalities, and he did everything to conceal the fact that Japan was seeking Moscow's mediation to terminate the war. An entire month had been wasted, and the Soviet government used this precious period to make preparations for war. Sato and Morishima, who opposed Togo's approach, were intentionally left out of the negotiations. Had Togo himself directly approached Malik and presented specific proposals to the Soviets with a definite deadline to receive their reply, the Japanese might have realized sooner that the termination of the war through Moscow's mediation was a pipedream.

What did the Japanese leaders expect from Moscow's mediation? According to Toshikazu Kase, Japan's approach to Moscow was a necessary step toward ultimate negotiations with the Allies. Because of the army's strong opposition to peace, this roundabout process was necessary. Furthermore, Kase argues in his postwar memoirs that since he believed Japan would be forced to accept nothing short of unconditional surrender or the terms close to it, Kido's "peace with honor" was wishful thinking. Sato agreed with this view, but unlike Kase, he did not believe anything positive would come from approaching Moscow.[48]

These two diplomats were exceptions. Togo, Kido, and Hirohito harbored the illusion that Japan might be able to obtain better peace terms through Moscow's mediation, most crucially the preservation of the emperor system in some form. "Had we not approached the Soviet Union," Togo stated, "we would clearly have had to accept the terms of unconditional surrender. Only through Soviet mediation could we expect to turn unconditional surrender into conditional surrender."[49] This was precisely the major point of Kido's Tentative Plan. Thus the illusion of Moscow's mediation provided an opiate for most Japanese policymakers.

Stimson's Draft Ultimatum to Japan

The day after the decisive June 18 White House meeting, the Committee of Three met. Although Forrestal was absent, Grew and Stimson reaffirmed the need to issue a warning to Japan before the homeland invasion specifying that the terms of surrender would allow the Japanese to "retain their own form of government and religious institutions," a euphemism for the retention of the monarchical system. Grew read his recent memo to the president strongly advocating a warning as soon as Okinawa had fallen, but this memo had not met Truman's approval. Stimson believed that Truman's reticence stemmed from his desire not to abate military preparations for the attack. According to Stimson, "it became very evident today in the discussion that we all feel that some way should be found of inducing Japan to yield without a fight to the finish." Stimson and Grew also concurred that their view had the support of Leahy, King, and Nimitz. Stimson noted in his diary: "My only fixed date is the last chance warning which must be given before an actual landing of the ground forces on Japan, and fortunately the plans provide for enough time to bring in the sanctions to our warning in the shape of heavy ordinary bombing attack and an attack of S-1."[50] Stimson then took the lead role in preparing a draft proclamation to Japan, gradually easing Grew out.

On June 26, the Committee of Three (Stimson, Grew, and Forrestal, with McCloy and Major Correa also present) met again. Stimson presented a draft proposal of the ultimatum to Japan. The first draft had been written by McCloy, but it did not contain the guarantee of the monarchy. In its margin Stimson penciled in: "I personally think that if in saying this we should add that we do not exclude a constitutional monarchy under her present Dynasty, it would substantially add to the chances of acceptance." This expression came directly from the memorandum that Grew had prepared for the president in May. The participants agreed that this warning should be issued before the invasion of the Japanese homeland, and that the forthcoming Potsdam Conference might be an appropriate forum for reaching agreement on the final form of the ultimatum issued by "the chief representatives of the United States, Great Britain, and, if then a belligerent, Russia." The committee accepted the conceptual framework of Stimson's draft but decided to have the subcommittee work on it further.[51]

It is interesting to note that as soon as the lead role in drafting a warning shifted to Stimson, the Soviet factor began to assume a different importance. As noted, one of the motivations influencing Grew's urgency was the desire to exclude the Soviet Union from the process of Japan's capitulation. Now that the center of gravity had shifted to the War Department, the Soviets were included as a party to such a warning.

The following day, June 27, the subcommittee, consisting of the representatives of the State Department (Ballantine), the Operation Division
(Colonel Charles Bonesteel), G-2 (John Weckerling), and the War Department Civil Affairs Division, assembled in John McCloy's office.
There Stimson's draft memo to the president and the draft "Proclamation
to the Japanese Government and People," prepared by Ballantine, were
presented and discussed.[52]

The problem of reaching agreement on the final form stemmed from
the multiple objectives the proclamation was to serve. The principal idea
behind issuing such a proclamation to Japan was to clarify the terms of
surrender so that Japan would accept them. But such terms should not
contradict the stated war aims of the United State. The policymakers
were cognizant of the impact of such a statement on American public
opinion. The central issue was the relationship between unconditional
surrender and the status of the emperor. But there were other issues involved the timing, modality, and signatories to the proclamation—when
the proclamation should be issued, by what means (through diplomatic
channels or through propaganda channels?), and by which countries
(should China and the Soviet Union be invited to sign the proclamation?).

Ballantine's draft met with opposition. Conceding to the State Department's harsh-peace advocates, it called for unconditional surrender and
total defeat, after which the Allies would establish a military government
to exercise supreme authority. As for the form of government, the draft
echoed Chiang Kai-shek's sentiment: "all the Japanese political systems
must be purged of every vestige of aggressive elements. As to what form
of government Japan should adopt, that question can better be left to the
awakened and repentant Japanese people to decide for themselves." The
subcommittee immediately rejected Ballantine's draft, since it was unlikely the Japanese would accept it. The subcommittee instead accepted
Stimson's draft, but added comments to it. These comments were handed
to McCloy on June 28. As for when the proposal would be issued, three
options were considered: as soon as possible; at a time to coincide with
Soviet entry into the war; or at a time related to impending operations
against Japan proper. On the punishment of war criminals, the subcommittee commented that the United States should handle this matter in
such a way as to prevent "any resulting bitterness" that would cause
the Japanese to be more "easily turned against the U.S. than, for instance,
against Russia." The subcommittee members were aware that Soviet

intrusion into the war would inevitably pit the United States against the USSR in the competition for the hearts and minds of the Japanese people.[53]

The second subcommittee meeting was held in McCloy's office on the morning of June 28. At that time opposition to Stimson's draft came from an unexpected quarter. Dooman from the State Department argued against including retention of the emperor system on the grounds that it would not be supported by American public opinion. It is not clear why Dooman opposed the inclusion of the promise; it may well be that he and Grew, faced with passionate opposition in public opinion surveys and within the State Department, decided to tone down their argument and suggest that the decision on the monarchy be postponed until a later date. This was not the position that Stimson preferred. According to George Lincoln, "Mr. Stimson is searching for terms which might be *acceptable* to Japan and still *satisfactory* to us, whereas Mr. Dooman apparently has so little hope of Japanese acceptance that he is trying really only to insure that the terms will *cause no criticism* in the US."[54] The positions of Stimson and Grew had reversed, and with this reversal, Stimson assumed leadership of the movement to modify unconditional surrender.

The Operation Division concluded, after considering several options, that the best time to issue the ultimatum would be immediately after the Soviets entered the war. It suggested: "If this date could be about 15 August to 1 September and if surrender were accepted, the Allies would be in the best military position to exploit the situation." The Operation Division foresaw Truman coming to an agreement with Stalin about the date of Soviet entry into the war, and then setting the date of issuance of the proclamation "sometime late in August or early September."[55] Interestingly, this timing coincided perfectly with Stalin's plan.

On June 29, McCloy sent Stimson a short form of the proposed proclamation by the heads of state, presumably worked out by the Operation Division, ignoring the State Department draft. McCloy also sent a paper dealing with the timing, which included the following important remarks: "You will appreciate that this has no relation to S-1 but as it discusses other factors which relate to the timing, I think that the S-1 element can be readily introduced in it."[56] To McCloy and Stimson, the atomic bomb was not a weapon to prevent Soviet entry into the war but a means to, in conjunction with the Soviet entry into the war, ensure Japan's surrender.

McCloy's letter to Stimson also referred to the method by which the proclamation should be delivered. McCloy stated that "both the State Department and ourselves" were unanimous in recommending that "it should not be done through diplomatic channels but should come by way of a declaration with all the usual propaganda following it up." As for the question of whether the proclamation should be issued unilaterally or in conjunction with other countries, McCloy recommended that the United States, Britain, and China should join the declaration, but if Russia was "then or about to become a belligerent," it should also join. As for the maintenance of the emperor, McCloy wrote: "This point seems to be the most controversial one and one on which there is a split in opinion in the State Department. The draft suggests the language we have used in the memorandum to the President. This may cause repercussions at home but without it those who seem to know most about Japan feel there would be very little likelihood of acceptance."[57]

The Operation Division's Colonel Charles Bonesteel wrote a draft proposal of the proclamation which he brought to McCloy on the morning of June 29. McCloy then convened the third subcommittee meeting, where Bonesteel's draft obtained substantial agreement from the Navy and the State Departments. He then hand-delivered the draft to Stimson's house in Long Island on July 1. Stimson was generally satisfied with this draft, but he made his own corrections. Bonesteel later explained the motivation behind the draft he had penned: "About a million American GIs out there didn't give a damn whether the emperor stayed if they didn't have to go in and invade the home islands, because the Japs were pretty rough to dig out of caves." These views would "go back to their wives and gal friends and mothers and fathers." According to Bonesteel, the State Department's view that public opinion would not tolerate any departure from unconditional surrender was "an exaggerated and incorrect evaluation of what the American public view would be."[58]

The subcommittee's discussions from June 27 through June 29 reveal some interesting facts. First, the divisions among American policymakers were more complex and subtle than hitherto argued.[59] Dooman, Grew's most trusted spokesman, did not argue for retention of the monarchy. In fact, he was more concerned about how the American public would react to a revision of the unconditional surrender demand. The War Department insisted on retaining the term "unconditional surrender" but advocated defining it in such a way as to include "conditions" more acceptable to the Japanese. Policymakers also differed on how to interpret public opinion. While Dooman and Grew were concerned about the virulent anti-emperor sentiments of the American public at the moment, military planners were more worried about the war-weariness of Americans, who would sooner or later demand to bring the boys home as quickly as possible. They knew the fickleness of public opinion, which might swing quickly when the first American soldiers were killed on the beachheads of homeland Japan, when the possibility of terminating the war had existed.

It bears emphasizing that when the draft proclamation was prepared, the major goal was, above all, to induce Japan to surrender. The Soviet factor posed a major dilemma to American policymakers. They struggled to balance the expected negative consequences of Soviet entry into the war with the positive payoff the United States would expect to obtain in speeding up Japan's capitulation. The military planners took it for granted at that time that Soviet entry into the war was a necessary and important ingredient to secure Japanese surrender. The optimal timing for issuing the proclamation would thus be upon Soviet entry into the war, which the OPD anticipated sometime in the middle of August. It was for this reason that the original proclamation was to be issued by the United States, Britain, China, and the Soviet Union.

The Politburo Decides to Go to War

The end of June was also a decisive time for Stalin. On June 26 and 27 he held a combined meeting of the Politburo (the highest decision-making body of the Communist Party), the government, and the military. This meeting decided to launch an all-out offensive against Japanese forces in Manchuria in August. The General Staff's recommendation that three fronts simultaneously move toward the center of Manchuria met with final approval.[60] War against Japan was no longer a secret confined to Stalin and a small circle of his advisers: it became the official policy of the Soviet government.

At this conference the geographical parameters of the military operation were discussed. The major objective of the Soviet military operation was to secure all the territories promised by the Yalta Agreement, including Manchuria, southern Sakhalin, and the Kuril Islands. The occupation of northern Korea was considered essential to cut off the escape route of the Japanese forces. Opinions were divided about Hokkaido. Without the occupation of Hokkaido, the Soviets could not secure control of the

Soya Strait and the Kurils. Marshal K. A. Meretskov thus proposed that they occupy the island. This measure was supported by Nikita Khrushchev, but Nikolai Voznesenskii, Molotov, and Marshal Georgii Zhukov opposed the operation as too risky and likely to provoke counteraction from American forces. Molotov pointed out that the seizure of Hokkaido would provide the Allies with justifiable grounds to accuse the Soviets of a serious violation of the Yalta Agreement. Stalin asked Zhukov how many additional divisions would be needed to carry out this operation. Zhukov answered at least four. Stalin said nothing. The question of Hokkaido remained undecided.[61]

On June 28 Stalin issued three directives, the first to the commander in chief of the Far Eastern Front to complete all the preparations for the attack by August 1; the second to the commander of the troops of the Maritime groups to complete the preparations for attack by July 25; and the third to the commander of the Transbaikal Front to complete preparations by July 25.[62] These directives did not set the precise date of attack, which would most likely be decided later in consultation with Vasilevskii. According to Shtemenko, however, the offensive was set to begin sometime between August 20 and August 25. Meretskov, who was to become the commander of the First Far Eastern Front, was sent to the Far East under the pseudonym Colonel General Maksimov. Marshal Rodion Malinovskii, who was to assume the post of commander of the Transbaikal Front, arrived in Chita as Colonel General Morozov on July 4. Finally, Marshal Vasilevskii, the commander of the entire Far Eastern operation, arrived in Chita on July 5 as Deputy People's Commissar for Defense Colonel General Vasiliev.[63] The die was cast. The gigantic war machine in the Far East was set in motion.

Stimson Submits a Memorandum to Truman

On July 2, five days before Truman's departure for Potsdam, Stimson submitted to the president a memorandum with a draft ultimatum to Japan. The secretary of war warned that "the operation for the occupation of Japan following the landing may be a very long, costly and arduous struggle," an even more difficult fight than the United States had experienced in Germany. He suggested that an alternative to such a costly fight would be to convince the moderate elements in Japan that the United States was not interested in exterminating Japan as a nation. For this purpose Stimson proposed that "a carefully timed warning be given to Japan by the chief representatives of the United States, Great Britain, China and, if then a belligerent, Russia, calling upon Japan to surrender and permit the occupation of her country in order to insure its complete demilitarization for the sake of the future peace."[64]

The Soviet factor assumed great importance in Stimson's recommendation. He reasoned: "If Russia is a part of the threat, the Russian attack, if actual, must not have progressed too far. Our own bombing should be confined to military objectives as far as possible." Whereas the Operation Division took for granted that Soviet entry would be needed to secure Japan's surrender, Stimson was more focused on what would happen after its defeat, when the United States and the Soviet Union would compete for Japan's support. Stimson went on to list the "elements" to be included in this proclamation. He then came to the heart of his recommendation: "if . . . we should add that we do not exclude a constitutional monarchy under her present dynasty, it would substantially add to the chances of acceptance."[65]

Attached to this memorandum was the draft proposal Stimson had approved the previous day. The first important feature of this draft was that it anticipated that the Soviet Union would be a signatory to the document. In the title and the text, Stimson's draft placed in brackets all the parts that dealt with the Soviet Union, noting that these sections would be deleted if the Soviet Union was not at war.[66] This indicates both that Stimson and U.S. planners anticipated Stalin's signature on the proclamation, and that they expected the ultimatum to be issued at the time of or just after the Soviet Union entered the war. These assumptions coincided with Stalin's expectations.

The second important feature of Stimson's draft was that it defined the terms of surrender in detail, spelling out the U.S. determination to punish "those who embarked upon the policy of conquest," adhere to the Cairo Declaration and limit Japan's territory to four main islands and "such adjacent minor islands as we determine," and disarm the military. At the same time, the draft made clear that the United States did not intend to destroy Japan as a nation nor enslave the Japanese as a race. The most important paragraphs of Stimson's draft are paragraphs 12 and 13:

(12) The occupying forces of the Allies shall be withdrawn from Japan as soon as our objectives are accomplished and there has been established beyond doubt a peacefully inclined, responsible government of a character representative of the Japanese people. This may

include a constitutional monarchy under the present dynasty if it be
shown to the complete satisfaction of the world that such a government will never again aspire to aggression.

(13) We call upon those in authority in Japan to proclaim now the
unconditional surrender of all the Japanese armed forces under the
authority of the Japanese Government and High Command, and to
provide proper and adequate assurances of their good faith in such
action.[67]

By modifying "unconditional surrender" to "unconditional surrender of
all the Japanese armed forces," and by implying that "a constitutional
monarchy under the present dynasty" was possible, Stimson's draft intended to make the terms easier for Japan to accept, although it formally
clung to the term "unconditional surrender."

Stimson's draft was sent to the State Department on July 2. Grew,
Dooman, and Ballantine then modified the proclamation to preclude
any possibility that militarists might exploit loopholes for future resurgence. Moreover, their revised draft was directed not to the Japanese government but directly to the Japanese people. Although they endorsed
Stimson's provision to allow "a constitutional monarchy under the present dynasty," they added the following condition: "if the peace-loving
nations can be convinced of the genuine determination of such a government to follow policies of peace which will render impossible the future
development of aggressive militarism in Japan." Finally, they changed
paragraph 13 of Stimson's draft to read as follows:

We call upon the Japanese people and those in authority in Japan
to proclaim now the unconditional surrender of all the Japanese
armed forces and to provide proper and adequate assurances of
their good faith in such action. The alternative for Japan is prompt
and utter destruction.[68]

As experts on Japan, Grew, Dooman, and Ballantine knew the danger
of allowing the emperor system to continue unchecked. Stimson fully
shared this objective, but he was not an expert on Japan, and his language lacked necessary precision. The difference between Grew and
Stimson was destined to play a major part in the last stage of the drama
ending the war.

Grew most likely inserted the last phrase, "prompt and utter destruction," with the atomic bomb in mind. Dooman and Ballantine had no knowledge of the atomic bomb project at that time, but Grew had been informed of the Manhattan Project. The bombing of Tokyo on May 26 greatly saddened him. Now, given his knowledge of the bomb, Grew must have been tormented by the apocalyptic vision of the atomic devastation of Japan. He wished to give the Japanese a warning without revealing the secret of the bomb.

On July 3, one day after Stimson submitted the draft proclamation to the president, James F. Byrnes was sworn in as secretary of state. Seeing in Byrnes a spokesman for their view, the hard liners in the State Department struck back with a vengeance. On July 4, Dean Acheson called a staff committee meeting at which he strongly registered his opposition to the draft proclamation prepared by Stimson and approved by Grew. The hard liners were enraged by Stimson and Grew's attempt to retain the monarchical system. On July 6 Assistant Secretary of State Archibald MacLeish sent a memo to the new secretary of state strongly denouncing the Stimson-Grew draft as a major departure from the declared war aims, given that "nonmolestation of the person of the present emperor and the preservation of the institution of the throne *comprise irreducible Japanese terms*" tantamount to abandoning unconditional surrender.[69]

Anticipating strenuous opposition from hard liners, Grew gave his amended proposal to Byrnes before his departure for Potsdam. On July 6, Grew talked to Forrestal before the navy secretary departed for Europe, and expressed his fear that the draft "would be ditched on the way over [to the Potsdam Conference] by people who accompany the President." Forrestal named Bohlen as the person most likely to sabotage Grew's draft, but Grew must have had Byrnes in mind.[70]

On July 7, the day Byrnes left Washington for Potsdam with the president, the State Department had a stormy staff meeting, with Grew presiding, and Acheson, MacLeish, and others attending. As soon as the meeting began, MacLeish opened the attack. A heated argument ensued about the advisability of retaining the monarchical system. While Grew argued that it would be impossible to abolish the institution, MacLeish and Acheson argued that the emperor system constituted part and parcel of Japan's militarism. Acheson demanded that the staff committee's opposition to the proposed statement be put on record. Grew said that despite the opposition he would exercise his prerogatives as undersecretary of state to present his draft.[71]

Byrnes noted in his memoirs: "Immediately upon becoming Secretary of State, I learned about the differences of opinion in the State Department as to whether, at the time of surrender, we should insist on the removal of the Emperor. Before I left for Potsdam, I was presented with memoranda setting forth the varying views. These went into a brief case bulging with the problems of war and peace in the Pacific." He was inclined to side with the hard liners if only to assert his power over Grew and Stimson. One day before his departure, he had a twenty-minute conversation with Cordell Hull, who expressed fear that paragraph 12 of the draft proclamation would be "too much like appeasement of Japan." Hull recommended delaying issuance of the proclamation in order to "await the climax of allied bombing and Russia's entry into the war."[72]

The draft proclamation was written and safely kept in Byrnes's briefcase. But the problems of how to issue this proclamation, when to issue it, and who should sign it remained undecided.

Hirohito Appoints Konoe Special Envoy to Moscow

The impending Potsdam Conference was a grave concern of the Japanese government. On July 5, after learning about T. V. Soong's visit to Moscow, Togo was seized by the fear that Sino-Soviet negotiations might result in the signing of a treaty, and that "the Soviet Union will soon enter into the war against Japan." Togo instructed Sato to meet Molotov before his departure for Potsdam to sound out the Soviet reaction to the policy outlined in his June 30 dispatch: lasting friendship, neutralization of Manchuria, and renunciation of fishing rights in exchange for Soviet oil.[73]

Sato was not in a hurry, however, and it was not until July 11 that the ambassador managed to meet Molotov for twenty minutes. As Sato predicted, Molotov engaged in his typical evasion, merely stating: "We shall study Japan's proposal very carefully and make up our minds," without saying anything about the Potsdam Conference. The following day, Sato sent a long dispatch to Tokyo, launching a scathing attack on Togo's approach: "Your proposal that Japan and the Soviet Union cooperate to maintain peace in East Asia, as well as the whole question of the neutralization of Manchukuo, are both based on the assumption that Japan and Manchukuo will continue to exist." Sato went on to remind Togo: "as the very existence of Japan has become problematical [sic], we can easily see that the whole foundation on which our efforts are based is shattered." He warned that "such an idea as that of winning Russia over to our side, even to the point of making her desert her own Allies, is nothing but pinning our hopes on the utterly impossible."[74]

While Sato was meeting Molotov, however, there was a major shift in Japan's policy. The Japanese government decided to send Prince Konoe to Moscow as the emperor's special envoy before the Potsdam Conference. The idea for this special mission came directly from Hirohito himself.[75] On July 7, on the advice of Kido, the emperor summoned Suzuki to the palace and inquired about the progress of negotiations with the Soviet Union. Hirohito bluntly suggested: "since it is not a good idea to miss our chance, why not frankly ask for their mediation? What if we arrange to send an envoy with a special letter from me?" On July 10, the Big Six approved the decision without specifying the envoy's name. Finally, on July 12, the emperor received Prince Konoe at the palace and appointed him as his special envoy to Moscow.[76]

At this point Hirohito excluded the possibility of direct negotiations with the United States and Britain, who, he knew, insisted on unconditional surrender. Uppermost in his mind was the preservation of the *kokutai,* and he was even prepared to use the failure of Moscow's mediation to justify the continuation of war. It is doubtful that at this stage the emperor made a distinction between the emperor system embodied in the concept of *kokutai* and the preservation of the imperial house.[77]

Togo had a different agenda. He had to tread a treacherous path between his conviction that the war had to be terminated as soon as possible and the strenuous opposition of the war party. He was not completely opposed to direct negotiations with the United States and Britain, but he knew that he would have no chance of ending the war without the support of the war party.[78] He was convinced that before he could directly negotiate with the United States, he would have to try the Moscow route. When the Supreme War Council met, Togo and Suzuki never named Konoe as the emperor's special envoy lest the three war hawks veto Konoe. Only through such delicate maneuvers did Togo narrowly manage to obtain the Big Six's approval for probing Moscow's willingness to mediate.

When the Supreme War Council met on July 14, Anami insisted that despite the setbacks in Iwo Jima and Okinawa, Japan had not suffered a defeat. He therefore adamantly opposed any negotiations for peace that admitted Japan's defeat. Yonai dissuaded Togo from pursuing specific conditions any further, lest the cabinet implode over this issue. Incredible as it might seem, the Japanese government decided to send Konoe to negotiate the termination of the war without specific conditions. This suited Konoe, however, since it gave him carte blanche to determine on the spot the conditions acceptable to Moscow.[79]

Nevertheless, Konoe's private circles had been secretly working on the conditions for peace. They prepared two drafts of position papers for Konoe. The first draft was written by Toshikazu Kase on July 3 on Togo's instructions. It was then discussed by Matsudaira, Matsutani, and Takagi. It endorsed the Atlantic Charter and called for an immediate cease-fire and Japan's voluntary withdrawal of troops from all occupied territories. The terms of peace consisted of two categories: the first included the preservation of the imperial house and the maintenance of the *kokutai*, non-interference in domestic politics, a guarantee of the nation's economic survival, no occupation, voluntary prosecution of war criminals, and independence of East Asian nations. The second category contained cessions of territories, reparations, and voluntary control of armament. Matsutani objected that these conditions were too detailed, and he insisted that the special envoy demand only the maintenance of the *kokutai*. Takagi disagreed. Negotiations with Moscow would not be the same as negotiations with the United States; it would be better to talk about all possible conditions at the outset. Clearly, Takagi believed that the Moscow negotiations represented only a prelude to ultimate negotiations with the United States. He did, however, suggest that the maintenance of the *kokutai* be revised to the maintenance of the right of the emperor to rule.[80]

This draft is important for two reasons. First, it separated the preservation of the imperial house from the *kokutai*. Takagi defined the *kokutai* as the emperor's right to rule, thus placing this concept within the political system and removing all other mythical and spiritual trappings from it. Second, this draft contained three conditions—non-occupation, self-disarmament, and self-prosecution of war criminals—that became the central focus of top policymakers during the crucial days of August.

Kase's draft was not submitted to Konoe, however. Instead, a second proposal was drafted by Konoe's close adviser, Army Major General Koji Sakai, on the night of July 12. Singling out the maintenance of the *kokutai* as the sole condition that should not be compromised under any circumstances, it recommended territorial concessions except for the homeland, acceptance of a democratic form of government headed by the emperor, acceptance of the occupation government and occupation force for a limited period, acceptance of punishment of war criminals by the occupation powers, and complete disarmament for a definite period. The draft further stipulated that in case Soviet mediation should fail, Japan should immediately begin direct negotiations with the United States and Britain. Distrustful of the Soviet Union, Konoe and Sakai did not harbor much hope for the success of Soviet mediation, and thus they prepared themselves for direct negotiations with the United States. In this draft, maintenance of the *kokutai* meant securing imperial rule and the imperial political system, though Sakai conceded that in the worst case scenario they should consider the abdication of the emperor. As for territorial concessions, Sakai took the view that Japan should accept the loss of Okinawa, the Bonin Islands, and southern Sakhalin, and should be satisfied with the maintenance of the southern half of the Kurils.[81] His draft indicated that Konoe was prepared to accept Japan's surrender, provided that the continuity of the imperial house was assured. There was a remarkable similarity between Stimson's draft ultimatum and Sakai's conditions.

On July 11, after the Supreme War Council adopted the resolution to send the special mission to Moscow, Togo sent an "Extremely Urgent" and "Strictly Secret" telegram to Sato in Moscow, informing him for the first time of Japan's intention to seek an end to the war. Sato was instructed to "sound out to what extent it is possible to make use of Russia in ending the war" at his meeting with Molotov. Somewhat incongruously, however, Togo added: "While there is no question of your adroitness, in this conference with the Russians, please be careful not to give the impression that our plan is to make use of the Russians in ending the war." In a supplementary dispatch the same day, Togo said: "We consider maintenance of peace in East Asia to be one aspect of the maintenance of world peace. Japan in preparation for the ending of the war has absolutely no ideas of annexing or holding the territories occupied as a result of the war, out of concern for the establishment and maintenance of lasting peace."[82]

Togo's last dispatch exasperated Sato, who replied that the foreign minister's instructions were "nothing more than academic fine phrases." Now that Japan had already lost Burma, the Philippines, and even Okinawa, he asked point-blank, "how much of an effect do you expect our statements regarding the non-annexation and non-possession of territories [to have] on the Soviet authorities?" The Soviets are very realistic, Sato warned, and therefore "it is extremely difficult to persuade them with abstract arguments. We certainly will not convince them with pretty little phrases devoid of all connection with reality." He continued his stinging condemnation: "If the Japanese Empire is really faced with the necessity of terminating the war, we must first of all make up our own minds to terminate the war. Unless we make up our own minds, there is absolutely no point in sounding out the views of the Soviet Government." He then broke the taboo: "there can be no doubt that the result which faces us is . . . virtually equivalent to unconditional surrender."[83]

Before Togo received the ambassador's scathing rebuke, he had dispatched another extremely urgent telegram on July 12, instructing Sato to request Molotov's audience immediately: "We think it would be appropriate to go a step further on this occasion and, before the opening of the Three Power Conference, inform the Russians of the imperial will concerning the ending of the war." Togo then told Sato to present the following message to Molotov:

> His Majesty the Emperor, mindful of the fact that the present war daily brings greater evil and sacrifice upon the peoples of all the belligerent powers, desires from his heart that it may be quickly terminated. But so long as England and the United States insist upon unconditional surrender the Japanese Empire has no alternative but to fight on with all its strength for the honor and existence of the Motherland. His Majesty is deeply reluctant to have any further blood lost among the people on both sides, and it is his desire, for the welfare of humanity, to restore peace with all possible speed. . . .
>
> It is the Emperor's private intention to send Prince Konoe to Moscow as a Special Envoy with a letter from him containing the statements given above. Please inform Molotov of this and get the Russians' consent to having the party enter the country.[84]

This was the most important message to date from the Japanese government. Not only did it clearly express the Japanese government's desire to end the war, but it also stressed that this desire came from none other than the emperor himself. It also indicated that the major obstacle for ending the war was the Allies' demand for unconditional surrender. Although it was sent to the Soviet government, Togo most likely hoped that this message would be transmitted to the United States and Britain.[85]

Sato received Togo's urgent dispatch at 1 A.M. on July 13, and attempted all day to catch Molotov, just one day before the Soviet foreign commissar was to leave for Berlin. Lozovskii informed Sato that Molotov "simply could not manage" to find time for an interview with him. The ambassador then met Lozovskii at 5 P.M. Sato stressed that this special envoy would be totally different from the ones he had mentioned to Molotov in the past, because the envoy would be sent on the initiative of the emperor.

Sato emphasized the need for a speedy response from the Soviet government, "even if simply an agreement in principle," before Molotov's departure so that the special envoy could meet Soviet authorities as soon as they returned from Berlin. Lozovskii, continuing the familiar delaying tactics, asked Sato to whom this imperial message was addressed. Taken back by this hairsplitting question, Sato replied that this message was addressed to the Soviet government, and therefore, either to Kalinin, head of the Soviet Union, or to Stalin, as chairman of the Council of Ministers. Lozovskii claimed that "since some members are supposed to be leaving this very night," it would be impossible to make any reply before Molotov's departure. Lozovskii promised to contact Berlin and then get back to Sato.[86]

Sato sent another telegram, this time to Togo, in which he candidly stated his view on the Konoe mission. He pointed out that the plan lacked any specific proposals. He expressed the fear that the Russians would ask for further information "on the grounds that the function of the envoy himself is not clear." He requested specific information about conditions that the Japanese government wished to present for the termination of the war.[87] Sato put his finger right on the problem. But from Togo's standpoint, what Sato requested was an impossible task. He could not give any concrete proposals, since there were none. Such proposals would surely split the cabinet, wrecking any chance for peace.

Despite Sato's call for haste, late at night on July 13, Lozovskii notified the Japanese ambassador that since Stalin and Molotov had already departed for Berlin, their reply would be delayed.[88] Sato discovered, however, that they did not leave Moscow until the evening of July 14, and so he realized that the delay was intentional. He surmised various reasons for the Soviets' hesitation in replying to Japan's request, but even this shrewd ambassador never entertained the possibility that the Soviet Union had decided to enter the war. But he again insisted to Togo that Japan had "no choice but to accept unconditional surrender or terms closely approximating thereto."[89]

Togo was annoyed by Sato's unsolicited opinion on Soviet mediation. On July 17, the foreign minister cabled to the ambassador, explaining that he was well aware of the difficulty of using Russia in bringing about the termination of war. "But the situation is such that we have no recourse but to try to do so." Negotiations with the Soviet Union were necessary not only to "solicit Russia's good offices in bringing the war to an end," but also to strengthen the ground for negotiations with Britain and the United States. To counter Sato's insistence on the need to accept unconditional surrender, Togo declared: "If today America and England were to recognize Japan's honor and existence, they would put an end to the war and save humanity from participation in the war, but if they insist unrelentingly upon unconditional surrender, Japan is unanimous in its resolve to wage a thoroughgoing war. The Emperor himself has deigned to express his determination."[90]

Sato was not satisfied with Togo's approach to Moscow, but Togo was looking at the big picture. To him, the passage to Moscow was a necessary road to reach Washington. By the time this telegram reached Moscow, the Potsdam Conference was already one day old.

American Intelligence and the Magic Intercepts

American intelligence intercepted the exchange of telegrams between Togo and Sato, known as the "Magic intercepts." Naval intelligence, which was responsible for the Magic intercepts, took the position that although it was not known whether the military also participated in the decision to terminate the war, "the fact that the move is stated to be an expression of the 'Emperor's will,' would appear to be of deep significance."[91] John Weckerling, deputy assistant chief of G-2, however, speculated in a memo on the reason behind Japan's change of policy. The possibilities were: (1) the emperor personally intervened for peace against military opposition; (2) the conservative groups close to the emperor triumphed over militaristic elements who favored the continuation of the war; and (3) the Japanese government was making a well-coordinated effort to stave off defeat, believing that Soviet mediation could be bought for the right price, and that an attractive peace offer from Japan would cause war weariness in the United States. Weckerling dismissed the first possibility as remote, considered the second hypothesis a possibility, but believed the most likely motivation was the third scenario. He added that Grew agreed with his assessment.[92]

It was indeed important, as Naval intelligence suggested, that the Japanese government indicated its willingness to terminate the war, and that this initiative came from the emperor himself. But this does not immediately lead to the conclusion that the Japanese government was prepared to surrender. The Japanese would have to travel a long road from willingness to terminate the war to actual acceptance of surrender. The crucial question is, On what terms was Japan prepared to surrender? On this question the government was hardly united; in fact, it could not come up with specific conditions. Even though Anami, Umezu, and Toyoda went along with the emperor's wish to seek Moscow's mediation, there was little chance that they would have accepted conditions that contained disarmament, Allied occupation, and war crimes trials. Although Hirohito took the initiative, he himself admitted that the failure of Moscow mediation would serve as a good excuse to rally the nation behind a last-ditch defense.

As for Weckerling's memorandum, each item contained an element of truth, but none was entirely correct, either. The first two assumptions, which Weckerling dismissed as unlikely, were partially true. The emperor was personally involved in the movement for peace, and the peace party close to Hirohito did succeed in imposing on reluctant military leaders the emperor's decision to send a special envoy. Weckerling's third assumption, which he considered the most likely, is not completely accurate. The peace party was convinced that Japan had to end the war by accepting defeat. Far from "staving off defeat," the peace party took a decisive gamble by seeking Moscow's mediation. Moreover, Weckerling's characterization of the Japanese political landscape as divided sharply between the military and a "conservative group close to the emperor" did not completely correspond to reality, either. The military Big Three (not the entire Japanese government) acquiesced in the Moscow peace mediation to "stave off defeat" and to cause "war-weariness in the United States," but Konoe, Kido, and Togo certainly did not share this motivation.

The naval intelligence analysts and Weckerling reached a completely different conclusion. Whereas the former implied that the Japanese peace overtures represented a serious departure from the past that the United States should explore further, Weckerling recommended that they were not worth serious consideration. Actually, common ground existed between Japan's peace party and influential policymakers in the United States. In fact, Stimson's July 2 draft for the joint ultimatum included the provision allowing Japan to retain a constitutional monarchy, while "unconditional surrender" was modified into "unconditional surrender of armed forces." In other words, Togo's dispatch left some wiggle room that the United States could have explored.

Another curious fact of Weckerling's memo is the G-2 official's claim that Grew supported his position. There is no record other than Weckerling's account indicating that Grew endorsed this analysis. In view of the dogged persistence with which he had campaigned for the retention of a constitutional monarchy, it is puzzling why Grew did not welcome Togo's July 12 dispatch as evidence to buttress his view. It may well be that, pilloried by his critics as an apologist for the emperor, he could not openly endorse Hirohito's message suggesting the revision of unconditional surrender. Or perhaps, being a confirmed anti-Soviet diplomat, Grew had no reason to support Tokyo's peace overtures to Moscow.

Stalin Negotiates with T. V. Soong

Things were moving quickly for Stalin. He had the Politburo and the State Defense Committee formally adopt the decision to attack Japan. The Japanese, however, were still requesting Moscow's help in ending the war. Stalin exploited this request to prolong the war, but he was keenly aware that Japan's surrender was imminent. He was also keeping abreast of intelligence reports from Beria concerning the progress of the American atomic bomb project. The Americans were close to possessing a nuclear weapon, and they now knew that the only obstacle to Japan's capitulation was the Allied demand for unconditional surrender. Stalin knew all of this, and he must have been consumed by the fear that the war might end before the Soviet Union could join the fray. Moreover, the two obstacles to a Soviet attack on Japan remained: Soviet commitment to the Neutrality Pact and the need to reach an agreement with China before entering the war.

Chinese Foreign Minister T. V. Soong arrived in Moscow on June 30, and the Stalin-Soong negotiations began two days later. Until then, Truman had followed a policy of upholding the Yalta Agreement, thus supporting the conclusion of a Sino-Soviet treaty. Chiang Kai-shek had once explored the possibility of gaining American support to revise the Yalta provisions, but Truman had refused. Chiang thus became convinced that China must conclude a treaty with the Soviet Union. His first priority was to gain Soviet support for the unification of China under the Nationalists as the sole legitimate government, as long as he could preserve China's sovereign rights. Stalin was prepared to accept Nationalist unification of China, as long as he could obtain a guarantee of the vital interests promised at Yalta. Thus the interests of Truman, Stalin, and Chiang Kai-shek all converged: the successful conclusion of a Sino-Soviet treaty would make everyone happy.

The negotiations screeched to a halt, however, almost as soon as they began on July 2. Stalin and Soong first clashed over Outer Mongolia. Stalin stressed the importance of Outer Mongolia for Soviet security. In fifteen or twenty years, he said, Japan would rise again as a potential threat to the Soviet Union, and therefore, the USSR should be in a position to control Outer Mongolia within its sphere of influence. Stalin then added: "If we attack Japan, what will the people say? We finished four years of war and you start a new war. Japan does not touch you and you attack Japan. How shall I be able to justify an attack only by saying that we are strengthening ourselves?" Soong, however, did not yield an inch on Outer Mongolia. Recognizing the independence of Outer Mongolia, which was an integral part of China, would greatly erode the authority of the Nationalist government.[93]

Encouraged by Stalin's commitment to support the Nationalist government, Chiang Kai-shek decided that he could give up Outer Mongolia, as long as Soong could obtain a favorable settlement regarding Manchuria, and if Stalin gave up his support of the Chinese Communists.[94] On July 9, Soong presented his new proposals to Stalin. In return for China's acceptance of the independence of Outer Mongolia and Stalin's promise not to support the Chinese Communists, Soong proposed the joint use of Port Arthur and the free port status of Dairen, both of which would be administered by the Chinese. As for the railways, Soong proposed that they be operated jointly, but that the rights belong to China. Stalin readily disavowed any intention to support the Chinese Communists, but as far as rights in Manchuria were concerned, he insisted on Soviet administration in Port Arthur, as well as Soviet possession of the railways, since the "Russians built them."[95]

Stalin was eager to conclude a treaty, but not at the expense of Soviet control over the ports and the railways. At the July 11 session Stalin urged, "We must settle before we leave for Berlin," but the differences did not diminish. At the last session on July 12, the stalemate continued, and Stalin finally gave up. The negotiations were suspended, and the two leaders decided to resume after Stalin returned from Potsdam.[96] This was merely the first of several setbacks Stalin was to experience in the coming weeks.

CHAPTER 4

Potsdam: The Turning Point

THE POTSDAM CONFERENCE, held from July 17 to August 2, 1945, was a turning point in the Pacific War. Until this conference, developments in Washington, Tokyo, and Moscow had flowed separately through different channels like small tributaries. At Potsdam all these tributaries converged into one big river as Truman, Churchill, and Stalin raced to end the Pacific War on their own terms.

But the Potsdam Conference was not only about the war in the Pacific.[1] In fact, it dealt with a variety of topics including Eastern Europe, especially Poland, and the German question. The Pacific War was also an urgent concern, however, and it was precisely on this issue that Stalin and Truman engaged in the most delicate, and in many ways duplicitous, maneuvers.

In the train going from Washington to Newport News, Virginia, on July 6, Truman wrote a letter to his wife, Bess: "I am blue as indigo about going." This was his first trip abroad as president, and what awaited him was a major encounter with Stalin and Churchill. He confessed his insecurity and inadequacy: "I'm very much afraid I've failed miserably. But there is not much I can do now to remedy the situation . . . Now I'm on the way to the high executioner. Maybe I'll save my head." Before six o'clock in the morning on July 7 the president stepped aboard the cruiser *Augusta* at Newport News. During the eight-day voyage across the Atlantic, the English Channel, and the North Sea, he studied the papers for the conference and held daily meetings in the map room with Byrnes and

Leahy. Conspicuously absent were Stimson, Harriman, and Grew. During these crucial eight days the president was deprived of specialists on both Japan and the Soviet Union. James Byrnes, who had just been sworn in on July 3 as the new secretary of state, exerted greater influence on Truman than any other member of his administration as he prepared for the conference. Overconfident but little experienced in foreign affairs, Byrnes was a skillful political manipulator, successfully keeping his chief rival Stimson off the *Augusta*. Refusing to be outmaneuvered by Byrnes, however, Stimson invited himself to Potsdam and arrived in Berlin a few hours before the president, though he was kept out of the conference.[2]

Whereas Truman was extremely nervous about the forthcoming summit, Stalin was confident but apprehensive. The Potsdam Conference was meant to be a crowning moment for the Soviet ruler. As leader of the nation that had taken the brunt of the war against Germany, Stalin was eager to validate his rightful gains in Europe. In order to underscore his "moral superiority" to Churchill and Truman, Stalin had to host the first Big Three meeting after the defeat of Germany in a territory occupied by the Red Army.

Holding a conference in the capital of defeated Germany was a splendid idea to demonstrate the power of the victorious Soviet Union, but it presented major practical problems. Berlin was so completely devastated that no buildings suitable to an international conference remained standing. The railway lines in war-ravaged Germany and Poland were completely destroyed. Undeterred by these difficulties, Stalin at the end of May ordered NKVD Chief Lavrentii Beria to make the necessary preparations for the conference.

Beria launched "Operation Palm" for this purpose. Mobilizing tens of thousands of NKVD workers and the local population, he had bridges and the railway tracks restored by June. A suitable venue for the conference was found in the Cecilienhof Palace in Potsdam, which had been used as a military hospital during the war. More than 2,000 NKVD officers and soldiers guarded the area around the Cecilienhof Palace. Foreign dignitaries were housed three miles from Potsdam in Babelsberg, a resort town that had attracted many German filmmakers before the war. By June 15, NKVD operatives had commandeered large houses for official use during the conference and had cleared the local population from the vicinity.[3]

Truman and his closest aides occupied a three-story yellow stucco house at No. 2 Kaiserstrasse, formerly owned by a filmmaker named

Gustav Müler-Grote. This yellow "Little White House" was the site of a tragedy. Just two months before Truman's arrival, Soviet soldiers had raided the house, raped Müler-Grote's daughters, destroyed furniture, paintings, and rare books, and evicted the family with one hour's notice. The other members of the U.S. delegation were housed nearby, as was Churchill. Stalin chose a villa in Babelsberg about half a mile from the Little White House.[4] We do not know what happened to the owners of these houses, but it is not hard to imagine that tragedies similar to Müler-Grote's were repeated in those locations.

The houses where the American and the British delegations stayed were remodeled before their arrival. Old furniture was thrown out, and new furniture, often totally incongruous in size, color, and taste, was brought in. In this process hidden microphones were secretly installed. Lest a single word escape without being reported to the Soviet intelligent service, all the service people—waiters, waitresses, porters, and maids—were sent from the NKVD to serve as Stalin's eyes and ears.[5] By July 2 everything was ready: two airfields and the railway stations in Potsdam and Babelsberg were rebuilt, roads between Babelsberg and Potsdam were repaired, the areas around the two towns were cleared of Germans and heavily guarded by NKVD soldiers, and all the eavesdropping devices were securely in place. Stalin was now ready to receive Truman and Churchill.

For Stalin the main objective of the Potsdam Conference was to secure recognition of the wartime gains he had so laboriously worked to attain, while obtaining an arrangement for postwar German occupation most advantageous to Soviet interests. The situation in Asia was also a high priority. Stalin was as determined to seize the trophies promised at Yalta as he was to protect his gains in Poland and Germany. But there were a few obstacles to the Soviet war plan. The first was the Soviet Union's commitment to the Neutrality Pact. To declare war against Japan the USSR would have to justify the violation of the Neutrality Pact, especially in order to avoid a comparison to the Nazis' attack on the Soviet Union in violation of the Nazi-Soviet Non-Aggression Pact. Thus Stalin was counting on Truman and Churchill to extend an invitation to enter the war against Japan.

The second obstacle was timing, which Stalin considered the nub of the matter. In order to gain the fruits promised at Yalta, the Soviet Union would have to fight the war, even if just for one day. But the Red Army would also have to score a crushing victory; thus premature attack had to

Yalta Conference, February 1945. From the left are Churchill, Roosevelt, and Stalin; Chief of Staff William Leahy stands behind Roosevelt. Stalin pledged to enter the war against Japan three months after the German surrender, and in return, Roosevelt promised to grant the Soviet Union rights and privileges in Manchuria, southern Sakhalin, and the Kurils. *(Rossiiskii gosudarstvennyi arkhiv kinofotodokumentov, Krasnogorsk)*

Truman taking the oath of office at the White House after the death of Roosevelt, April 12, 1945. In the front row are Secretary of War Henry Stimson (second from left), Secretary of Commerce Henry Wallace (third from left), and Secretary of the Navy James Forrestal (fourth from left). Between Truman and Chief Justice Harlan Stone is Truman's wife, Bess, and between the president and Bess is Secretary of State Edward Stettinius. *(Harry S Truman Library)*

Harry Hopkins returned from Moscow on June 12 after successfully mending fences with Stalin. He brought back his notes to Truman (seated) in the White House on June 13. Standing, from left to right, are Joseph Davies, William Leahy, and Harry Hopkins. *(Harry S Truman Library)*

Joseph Grew, undersecretary of state. Grew advocated the modification of the unconditional surrender demand by allowing the Japanese to retain a monarchical system. *(National Archives)*

Henry Stimson, secretary of war. He supervised the Manhattan Project. Stimson also pushed for retention of a constitutional monarchy under the current dynasty in Japan, and submitted a draft of the Potsdam Proclamation to Truman. *(National Archives)*

T. V. Soong, foreign minister of the Nationalist Government in China.
Soong negotiated with Stalin to conclude a treaty of friendship and
alliance. The Yalta Agreement stipulated that the conclusion of this
treaty be the precondition for Soviet entry into the war against Japan.
(National Archives)

Truman with James Byrnes, secretary of state (left), and William Leahy (right), studying the Potsdam papers on the U.S.S. *Augusta* on the way to the Potsdam Conference. *(Harry S Truman Library)*

Truman and Byrnes on the *Augusta* on the way to the Potsdam Conference. *(Harry S Truman Library)*

The Big Three at the Potsdam Conference: Churchill (left), Truman (center), and Stalin (right). Stalin must have felt his distance from Truman and Churchill. *(Rossiiskii gosudarstvennyi arkhiv kinofotodokumentov, Krasnogorsk)*

The Potsdam Conference in session. Stalin is in the white uniform in the middle, surrounded by Viacheslav Molotov (left) and General Aleksei Antonov (right). Next to Antonov sits Ambassador Andrei Gromyko, then Leahy, Byrnes, and Truman. Fourth and fifth from Truman's left are Ernest Bevin and Clement Attlee, respectively. Attlee and Bevin had replaced Churchill and Eden as the British delegates after their election victory in the middle of the Potsdam Conference. *(Rossiiskii gosudarstvennyi arkhiv kinofotodokumentov, Krasnogorsk)*

Truman and Stalin at the Potsdam Conference. Each leader was suspicious of the other.
(Harry S Truman Library)

A recess at the Potsdam Conference. It was during one of these occasions that
Truman nonchalantly revealed to Stalin that the United States had acquired "a weapon
of unusual destructive force." This picture was taken a few days after that revelation.
(Rossiiskii gosudarstvennyi arkhiv kinofotodokumentov, Krasnogorsk)

Emperor Hirohito inspects his troops. *(National Archives)*

The Suzuki Kantaro cabinet, formed on April 7, 1945. Front row, center, is Prime Minister Kantaro Suzuki, with Navy Minister Mitsumasa Yonai to his left. In the second row, between Suzuki and Yonai, is Director of Information Hiroshi Shimomura. In the third row, second from left, is Foreign Minister Shigenori Togo. In the last row, center, is Cabinet Secretary Hisatsune Sakomizu, with Army Minister General Korechika Anami to his left. *(Suzuki Kantaro Memorial Museum)*

Kantaro Suzuki, Japan's last prime minister during the war. He wavered between peace and war but played a decisive role in arranging the imperial conferences in August. *(Gaimusho Gaikoshiryokan)*

Japan's foreign minister Shigenori Togo. He played a leading role in the peace party in the Suzuki cabinet. *(Gaimusho Gaikoshiryokan)*

Admiral Mitsumasa Yonai, navy minister and important member of the peace
party. *(National Archives)*

Koichi Kido, Lord Keeper of the Privy
Seal, Emperor Hirohito's most trusted
adviser. He played a crucial role in
arranging the emperor's "sacred
decisions" at the imperial conferences.
(Kyodo tsushinsha)

Naotake Sato, Japanese ambassador to the Soviet Union in Moscow.
He made a scathing attack on his government's policy of seeking termina-
tion of the war through Moscow's mediation. His effort to ascertain
Moscow's response to Japan's request for mediation was rewarded by the
Soviet declaration of war. *(Gaimusho Gaikoshiryokan)*

Koki Hirota, former prime minister and foreign minister of Japan. In a nonofficial capacity, he negotiated with Ambassador Malik of the Soviet Union to keep the USSR out of the war in June 1945. *(Gaimusho Gaikoshiryokan)*

be avoided at all costs, and the timing of attack had to be carefully chosen to ensure a decisive victory. Stalin was well aware that the Americans were near completion of the atomic bomb. He also knew from the Japanese peace overtures to Moscow that Japan's capitulation was just a matter of time. He surmised that the Japanese were following with apprehension the furious pace with which the Soviets were moving troops to the Manchurian border, and he knew that he could not count on Japan's gullibility for too long. The Generalissimo was tormented by the possibility that the war might be over before the Soviet troops crossed the Manchurian border. Thus on July 16, as soon as he arrived at Potsdam, Stalin telephoned Marshal Vasilevskii, commander of the Far Eastern Front in Chita, and inquired if it would be possible to advance the attack ten days from the previously agreed date, sometime between August 20 and 25. Vasilevskii answered that "the concentration of the troops and the transportation of essential war supplies would not allow" for a change in the date of attack. Stalin for the time being accepted Vasilevskii's cautious judgment.[6]

Then there was the problem of China: the Yalta Agreement was made contingent upon China's approval. Stalin wanted badly to come to Potsdam with a treaty signed by China in his pocket, and he worked hard until the last minute to achieve this goal. But to his great disappointment, negotiations with China were broken off before an agreement could be reached. Stalin intended to obtain Truman's help to put pressure on the recalcitrant Chinese to accept the Soviet demands by using his pledge to enter the war as bait.

Americans Receive the Magic Decrypts

The Magic intercepts were sent to Leahy on the *Augusta* while the president was sailing across the ocean, and then in Babelsberg after his arrival in Germany. Leahy received a copy from Colonel Frank McCarthy, Marshall's personal aide, and informed the president of its contents, though we do not know for sure which Magic reports, if any, Truman actually read. Since a copy of some dispatches was found in the Byrnes Papers, we can assume that Byrnes had read them. In fact, Byrnes's memoirs state that "the President had learned of the Japanese 'peace feelers' a day or two before our conference with Stalin, for we had broken the Japanese code early in the war."[7] Truman and Byrnes must have known, therefore, that the emperor's involvement in the peace process marked a new departure in Japan's policy and, further, that the major stumbling block in persuading Japan to capitulate would be the demand for unconditional surrender.

Upon arriving in Babelsberg and receiving the Magic reports, Stimson noted in his diary for July 16: "I also received important paper [regarding] Japanese maneuverings for peace." McCloy's reaction was more exuberant: "News came in of the Japanese efforts to get the Russians to get them out of the war. Hirohito himself was called upon to send a message to Kalinin and Stalin. Things are moving—what a long way we have come since that Sunday morning we heard the news of Pearl Harbor!" McCloy was quick to connect this situation with the question of issuing an ultimatum: "The delivery of a warning now would hit them at the moment. It would probably bring what we are after—the successful termination of the war and at least put them in a great dither before it was turned down." Forrestal also wrote in the July 13 entry of his diary: "The first real evidence of a Japanese desire to get out of the war came today through intercepted messages from Togo to Sato." He also noted: "Togo said further that the unconditional surrender term of the Allies was about the only thing in the way of termination of the war and he said that if this were insisted upon, of course the Japanese would have to continue to fight."[8] Despite Weckerling's assessment that the Japanese were trying to stave off defeat, Stimson, Forrestal, and McCloy drew a different conclusion from Togo's telegram.

On July 16 Stimson wrote a memo to the president in which he noted that a warning to Japan, coupled with the possibility of Soviet entry into the war, would cause the Japanese to ponder "the great marshalling of the American forces." It is important to note that Stimson considered the possibility of Soviet entry into the war a positive development. "Whether the Russians are to be notified of our intentions in advance in this regard," he argued, "would depend upon whether an agreement satisfactory to us had been reached with the Russians on the terms of their entry into the Japanese war." By "the terms of their entry into the Japanese war" Stimson was most likely referring to the Soviet pledge to support the Nationalists in China. Stimson also wrote a letter to Byrnes on July 16 in which he included a draft ultimatum to Japan. He requested an urgent meeting to discuss the contents of the ultimatum, which, he emphasized, was "the supreme importance at the moment."[9]

Byrnes, however, opposed a prompt warning to the Japanese. Stimson noted in his diary: "He [Byrnes] outlined a timetable on the subject [of a] warning which apparently had been agreed to by the President, so I pressed it no further."[10] This "timetable," which was to serve as a linchpin in the subsequent Potsdam story, was most likely connected with two anticipated, and in their minds mutually related, issues: the outcome of the atomic bomb test and Soviet entry into the war.

In his memoirs Byrnes also referred to the Sato-Togo exchange on July 11–12, explaining that he ignored this information because "[Togo's] advisers . . . apparently believed they could avoid the emperor's removal and also save some of their conquered territory." Although the first conclusion could be drawn from Togo's refusal to accept unconditional surrender, Byrnes misrepresented the second point, for Togo's dispatch suggested giving up all conquered territory. Whereas Stimson, McCloy, and Forrestal interpreted the Magic intercepts as an indication of Japan's willingness to capitulate if the unconditional surrender demand were removed, Byrnes took the exchange as proof of Japan's intransigence. To his mind unconditional surrender should be fixed and unchangeable.

Given that Byrnes was not as ideologically committed to the elimination of the emperor as were the State Department hard liners, why was he so intransigent in retaining the demand for unconditional surrender? The clue to this puzzle is the connection he made between unconditional surrender and the atomic bomb. In his memoirs he noted that "had the Japanese government surrendered unconditionally, it would not have been necessary to drop the atomic bomb." But perhaps this statement can best be read in reverse: "if we insisted on unconditional surrender, we could justify the dropping of the atomic bomb."

Byrnes also makes an important point about Japan's approach to Moscow: "The Japanese Government communicated with the Soviets instead of Sweden or Switzerland in order to advise the Russians that they were prepared to meet fully their demands in the Far East. They hoped, by granting Soviet demands, to secure Soviet aid in negotiations."[11] Byrnes was alarmed by Japan's peace overtures to Moscow. He was concerned that the Soviets might gain territorial and other concessions from Japan to the detriment of U.S interests.

Given this possibility, did the U.S. policymakers really want the Soviet government to honor the Yalta commitment and enter the war in the Pacific? There was little question, as Truman indicates in his memoirs, that American military planners thought Soviet entry into the war would hasten Japan's surrender. But U.S. policymakers also pondered the political consequences of Soviet participation in the war. Thus they sought to bring about Japan's surrender, if possible, before the Soviets could join the fight. This was one factor in determining the "timetable" for the ultimatum to Japan. The unconditional surrender demand, the Soviet entry into the war, and the atomic bomb all fit together in the "timetable" of the ultimatum to Japan.

Truman's First Meeting with Stalin

The *Augusta* moored at Antwerp on the morning of July 15. From there Truman and his party traveled to the Little White House in Babelsberg. The Potsdam Conference was originally scheduled to start on July 16, but since Stalin did not arrive until the afternoon of July 16, the opening of the conference was delayed a day.

Taking advantage of the free day, Truman met with Churchill and then took a tour around Berlin in the afternoon. Two hours before he returned to the Little White House, the first atomic bomb exploded in Alamogordo. At 7:30 P.M. (1:30 P.M. Washington time, one and half hours after the explosion in New Mexico) Stimson received a top-secret telegram from George L. Harrison, his special assistant, about "Fat Man": "Operated on this morning. Diagnosis not yet completed but results seem satisfactory and already exceed expectations." Stimson walked to the Little White House to give this news to Truman and Byrnes, "who of course were greatly interested, although the information was still in very general terms." The usually careful secretary of war rather indiscreetly wrote to his wife: "I have rece'ved good news from my baby at home which has thrilled everyone."[12]

Stalin arrived in Berlin on July 16. He immediately asked Joseph Davies to arrange a meeting with Truman at 9 P.M. that evening. To Davies's horror, Truman refused this request and postponed the meeting to the following morning. Truman was "too tired, worried and irritated over something." Swallowing Truman's first snub magnanimously, Stalin came to the Little White House at noon on July 17, accompanied by Molotov and his interpreter, Vladimir Pavlov. Truman was surprised at how unimposing the Soviet dictator was, standing a mere five foot five. Dressed in a khaki uniform with a red epaulet, holding a cigarette between the yellowed fingers of his crippled left hand, Stalin was escorted to Truman's study, where the president and Byrnes waited for their guests. Stalin was in good humor and extremely polite. Truman was especially impressed by "his eyes, his face, and his expression."[13]

Stalin apologized for the delay in arriving: he was held up by negotiations with the Chinese, and his doctors had forbidden him to fly. Truman wrote in his diary: "After the usual polite remarks we got down to business. I told Stalin that I am no diplomat but usually said yes & no to questions after hearing all the argument. It pleased him." The conversation quickly turned to the question of the war against Japan. According to Bohlen's notes, Stalin talked about the British attitude toward the Pacific War, but reverted to the Yalta Agreement concerning Soviet entry into the war. He "told the President that the Soviets would be ready for such entry by the middle of August, but said that prior to acting they would need to complete their negotiations and reach agreement with the Chinese."

The Soviet version of the Stalin-Truman conversation tells a different story. After Stalin's remarks that the British seemed to think the war was now over, the account continues: "The British think that the U.S.A. and the Soviet Union will fulfill their obligation to the war against Japan. Truman said [that] . . . the United States expects assistance from the Soviet Union. Stalin answered that the Soviet Union is prepared to enter into action by the middle of August and that it will keep its word. Truman expressed his satisfaction on this matter and asked Stalin to tell him about his negotiations with Soong."[14]

The discrepancies between the Bohlen notes and the Soviet version reveal the different expectations held by both sides. Stalin was eager to obtain Truman's invitation to join the war against Japan. Truman, meanwhile, was not about to give Stalin this satisfaction. When things did not go as Stalin had hoped, the Soviets falsified the minutes of the meeting to give the impression that it was Truman who requested Soviet entry into the war and that Stalin complied with this request. Contrary to the Soviet version, the Bohlen notes indicate that Stalin, suddenly and on his own, began talking about his commitment to the Yalta Agreement.

Furthermore, in the Soviet version, it was Truman who asked about Stalin's negotiations with the Chinese, as if to encourage Stalin to come to an agreement in order to speed up Soviet entry into the war. The Bohlen notes give a completely different picture. After Stalin announced that the Soviet Union would attack Japan in the middle of August, he talked about the state of negotiations with the Chinese, as if to ask Truman to help put pressure on the Chinese to come to an agreement with the Soviet Union. While the Soviet version did not go into the differences between Stalin and Soong, the Bohlen notes described the details of the negotiations.

According to Bohlen, Stalin explained that after long negotiations, the question of Outer Mongolia had been settled, but that they had not reached an agreement on the question of railroads in Manchuria and the status of Dairen and Port Arthur. Soong had left for Chungking for consultation, but before he left, he had asked the Soviet government for a statement that ensured "that Manchuria was a part of China and subject to its sovereignty," and that the Soviet government would support only the authority of the central government, not the Communist Party, in Manchuria. Stalin reaffirmed to Truman "that the Soviet Union would give Soong full assurances on all these points." The president said that he was happy to hear that the matters between the Soviet Union and China were near settlement. Stalin repeated his assurances that "there would be one government and one army," and that the Soviets would pledge "noninterference in Chinese internal affairs." All these details were omitted from the Soviet version.

If Stalin had expected American help to pressure the Chinese, he must have been disappointed. Truman's remarks were limited to mere platitudes. Byrnes, by contrast, asked a probing question: What differences still remained? Stalin explained that the Soviets claimed preeminent interests in the Manchurian railroads, Dairen, and Port Arthur, which the Chinese did not accept. After explaining what he meant by preeminent interests, Stalin suddenly reverted to the question of Soviet entry into the war against Japan, repeating "that the Soviets would be ready in mid-August, as was agreed at Yalta, and [that] they would keep their word." This part does not appear in the Soviet version, but clearly Stalin was trying to purchase American pressure on the Chinese with a pledge to enter the war against Japan. Byrnes, for his part, would not let the matter of Sino-Soviet negotiations rest. He noted that "if the arrangements were in strict accordance with the Yalta agreement, this would be all right, but that if at any point they were in excess of that agreement, this would create difficulties."

Truman noted in his diary: "I asked [Stalin] if he had the agenda for the meeting. He said he had and that he had some more questions to present. I told him to fire away. He did and it is dynamite—but I have some dynamite too which I'm not exploding now . . . He'll be in the Jap War on August 15th. Fini Japs when that comes about." Truman also wrote in his memoirs: "There were many reasons for my going to Potsdam, but the most urgent, to my mind, was to get from Stalin a personal reaffirmation of Russia's entry into the war against Japan, a matter which our military chiefs were most anxious to clinch. This I was able to get from Stalin in the very first days of the conference." After the first day of the meeting he wrote to Bess: "I was scared I didn't know whether things were going according to Hoyle or not. Anyway a start has been made and I've gotten what I came for—Stalin goes to war August 15 with no strings on it. I'll say that we'll end the war a year sooner now, and think of the kids who won't be killed. That is the important thing."[15]

These passages are taken by some historians as convincing evidence that Truman had no intention to use the atomic bomb as a bargaining tool with the Soviet Union, since the president's main goal at Potsdam was to obtain Stalin's assurance that he would enter the war against Japan. But the record of the Stalin-Truman meeting on July 17 does not bear out this assertion. There were already subtle hints of contention between Stalin and Truman/Byrnes at their first meeting. Byrnes's probing questions about Soviet intentions in China indicated potential sources of tension arising from China's agreement with the Soviet Union. Byrnes was already suspicious of Stalin.[16]

Furthermore, if Truman had come to Potsdam primarily to obtain Stalin's commitment to entering the war against Japan, it is strange that he did not actively seek that commitment. The best we can say about Truman's attitude toward this issue is that he was ambivalent. The president wrote in his memoirs: "By the time [the Potsdam Proclamation was issued], also, we might know more about two matters of significance for our future effort: the participation of the Soviet Union and the atomic bomb. We knew that the bomb would receive its first test in mid-July. If the test of the bomb was successful, I wanted to afford Japan a clear chance to end the fighting before we made use of this newly gained power. *If the test should fail, then it would be even more important to us to bring about a surrender before we had to make a physical conquest of Japan.*"[17] At best, Soviet participation was an insurance policy, and the atomic bomb remained Truman's top option. Moreover, Truman took Stalin's announcement as "dynamite." It is clear that he saw Stalin not as an ally committed to the common cause of defeating Japan, but as a competitor in the race to see who could force Japan to surrender.

Nonetheless, there is no reason to doubt that Truman initially welcomed the news that the Soviet Union intended to attack Japan in the middle of August. Stalin's assurance precluded the possibility of any deals between Tokyo and Moscow, thus removing one potential source of worry from Truman's mind. The Soviets would not take advantage of Japan's peace overtures to gain concessions at the expense of the United

States and China, and they would not negotiate for Japan's surrender. By precluding diplomacy, the matter was simplified: the only way to force Japan to surrender would be by military means. The date Stalin gave for the Soviet attack on Japan—August 15—gave American policymakers a definite deadline to work for; if they were to force Japan to surrender without Soviet help, they would have to do so before that date. The only remaining factor was the atomic bomb. Contrary to historians' claim that Truman had no intention to use the atomic bomb as a diplomatic weapon against the Soviet Union, it is hard to ignore the fact that the Soviets figured into Truman's calculations. The date for the Soviet attack made it all the more imperative for the United States to drop the bomb in the beginning of August, before the Soviets entered the war. The race between Soviet entry into the war and the atomic bomb now reached its climax.

Why did Stalin reveal his intention to attack Japan at his very first meeting with Truman? His eagerness to show Soviet cooperation in the Far East contrasted with the obstinacy with which he insisted on his prerogatives in Europe. The most likely answer is that he was in a hurry. He had to obtain an invitation from the United States and Britain to join the war. He also hoped that the United States would exert pressure on China to reach an agreement with the Soviet Union. He was still operating on the assumption that Truman desired Soviet entry into the war, as Roosevelt had at Yalta, not knowing that the Americans were no longer eager to see the Soviets enter the war.

The Potsdam Conference Begins

The official "Terminal" conference began at five o'clock on July 17 at the Cecilienhof Palace, with a visibly nervous Truman presiding over the discussion. In less than two hours the first meeting adjourned, and the participants repaired to a banquet of "goose liver, caviar, all sorts of meats, cheeses, chicken, turkey, duck, wines and spirits." As the participants were about to leave the palace, Stimson received another cable from Harrison: "Doctor has just returned most enthusiastic and confident that the little boy is as husky as his big brother. The light in his eyes discernible from here to Highhold and I could have heard his screams from here to my farm." The decoding officer marveled at the virility of a seventy-seven-year-old Stimson producing a healthy baby. But "Doctor" was actually Groves, and "big brother" was "Fat Man," which was detonated in Alamogordo. Highhold was Stimson's residence on Long Island, and Harrison's farm in Virginia was fifty miles from the Pentagon. Stimson went off to the president's for dinner. With many guests present, Stimson could not find a satisfactory opportunity to talk with the president, and Truman was in no mood to talk business. To McCloy this missed opportunity was unfortunate, since "the Japanese matter is *so* pressing."[18]

The next morning, July 18, Stimson walked to the Little White House to deliver Harrison's second report to Truman. The president was "evidently very greatly reinforced over the message from Harrison" and said that he was glad that Stimson had come to the meeting, his first acknowledgment of Stimson's presence at Potsdam. Truman promptly told Churchill, who was delighted to hear the "earth-shaking news." They discussed what to tell Stalin. The danger was that if they told Stalin about the bomb, it might trigger immediate Soviet entry into the war. To Churchill the atomic bomb solved two nagging problems. The Allies would no longer need a costly homeland invasion against Japan. Instead of the man-by-man and yard-by-yard combat in which thousands of American and British soldiers would be killed, he now had "the vision—fair and bright indeed it seemed—of the end of the whole war in one or two violent shocks." More important, the Allies no longer needed the Soviets. He wrote to Eden: "It is quite clear that the United States does not at the present time desire Russian participation in the war against Japan." Truman decided to convey news of the bomb to Stalin as late as possible, and to tell him "that we have an entirely novel form of bomb," without specifically saying that it was the atomic bomb. Churchill agreed with Truman's plan.[19]

Churchill, for his part, had something to share with Truman. The night before, Stalin had revealed to Churchill information about Japanese peace overtures to Moscow. Churchill asked Stalin why he had not brought this news directly to Truman, to which Stalin replied that he "did not wish the President to think that the Soviet Government wanted to act as an intermediary." Stalin hastened to add that he did not mind if Churchill shared this information with Truman. Churchill then raised the issue of unconditional surrender. Sir Alan Brooke, the British Chief of Staff, had already argued that the American demand of unconditional surrender be modified. Admiral Leafy, knowing Truman's firm commitment to this demand, had suggested that Brooke bring the matter to Churchill so that the prime minister could personally persuade Truman to change his mind. Following Brooke's advice, Churchill proposed to

Truman that he amend the demand for unconditional surrender in such a way that "we got all the essentials for future peace and security, and yet left the Japanese some show of saving their military honour and some assurance of their national existence." Truman countered by saying that the Japanese had little military honor left after Pearl Harbor.[20] Truman again revealed his deep commitment to unconditional surrender. The news about the atomic bomb reinforced his conviction. In his mind the atomic bomb and unconditional surrender were now linked.

At three o'clock it was Truman's turn to pay a return visit to Stalin. At this meeting, Stalin revealed that he had received the Japanese request for mediation to terminate the war, and he showed the president a copy of Sato's note requesting the mediation in the emperor's name. Stalin explained that he had three alternatives: "ask the Japanese for more details, leading them to believe their plan had a chance; ignore the overture; or send back a definite refusal. Stalin pointed out that the Soviet Union was not at war with Japan, and that it might be desirable to "lull the Japanese to sleep." For that purpose, the first option would be the best. Truman agreed.

This was a cat and mouse game. Truman knew from the Magic intercepts about Japan's request for Moscow's mediation. Whether or not Stalin knew that the Americans had intercepted Japanese diplomatic dispatches, he was providing the most confidential information to the Americans in an attempt to impress upon Truman his good will. Truman pretended that he was hearing the news for the first time. Stalin's tactics seemed to work well. Truman felt that the Soviet leader was "honest— but smart as hell."[21]

Both Truman and Stalin preferred the first option—leading the Japanese to believe their proposal had a chance—for different reasons. For Stalin, it was advantageous to lead Japan into believing it could end the war with Moscow's help; Stalin could then prepare for war against an unguarded enemy. For Truman, the ruse of continued negotiations might allow America to drop the atomic bomb on Japan before the Soviets had a chance to enter the war. Both wanted to surprise Japan: Stalin by crossing the Manchurian border, and Truman by dropping the atomic bomb.

Walter Brown's diary suggests that Byrnes also agreed with Truman, or perhaps Truman was acting on Byrnes's advice. The entry for July 18 reads: "JFB had hoped Russian declaration of war against Japan would come out [of] this conference. No[w] he think[s] United States and United Kingdom will have to issue joint statement giving Japs two weeks to surrender or fac[e] destruction. (Secret weapon will be ready by [t]hat time)."[22] This passage provides a clue as to what Truman and Byrnes had in mind when devising the timetable for the ultimatum to Japan. First, it had to be issued before the Soviet entry into the war, and the Soviet Union would be excluded from the joint ultimatum. Second, the atomic bomb would have to be used to bring Japan to its knees before the Soviets joined the fight.

It is interesting to note that twice that day Truman referred to Japan's attack on Pearl Harbor, first at his meeting with Churchill, and then at his meeting with Stalin. He justified deceiving the Japanese because they had no sense of honor. His visceral sense of revenge, widely shared by the American public, also colored his decision to stick to unconditional surrender and drop the bomb.

Magic Continues to Intercept Japanese Cables

On the evening of July 18, Ambassador Sato received a letter from Lozovskii, who wrote: "the instructions expressed in the Japanese emperor's message are general in form and contain no specific proposals. The mission of Prince Konoe is not clear to the Soviet Government. It is, therefore, impossible for the Soviet Government to give a definite reply." That was exactly what Stalin and Truman had agreed to say to the Japanese. Two hours after replying to Lozovskii, Sato sent another telegram virtually telling Togo "I told you so." He drew the conclusion from Lozovskii's answer that Japan could not expect to win over the Russians. On July 20, Sato sent a long, desperate telegram to Tokyo with an impassioned plea to surrender to the Allies with the sole reservation that the *kokutai* be preserved. The enemy would destroy all industrial and agricultural interests in Japan before it launched the homeland invasion. If such an invasion were to take place, Sato admitted, the Japanese would fight and perish to the last man: "Nevertheless, all our officers and soldiers as well as the people, who have already lost their fighting strength due to the absolutely superior incendiary bombing of the enemy, will not save the imperial house by dying a glorious death on the field of battle. Should we be solely concerned with the safety of the emperor while his 70 million subjects are sacrificed?"[23] Sato separated the *kokutai* from the nation and narrowly defined the *kokutai* as the preservation of the emperor and the imperial house. Sato's plea was rejected by Togo, but his narrow definition of the *kokutai* began to influence high officials in the Foreign Ministry.

Sato's desperate plea must have further angered Togo, who sent two telegrams to Sato on July 21. In the first dispatch he reminded the ambassador that "Special Envoy Konoe's mission will be in obedience to the Imperial Will." But in his next dispatch, Togo made a startling revelation. He stressed that Japan would not consent to unconditional surrender. "Even if the war drags on," he warned, "and it becomes clear that it will take much more than bloodshed, the whole country as one man will pit itself against the enemy in accordance with the Imperial Will so long as the enemy demands unconditional surrender." The whole point of seeking Moscow's mediation, Togo explained, was to seek peace short of unconditional surrender. It would be "both disadvantageous and impossible, from the standpoint of foreign and domestic considerations," he continued, "to make an immediate declaration of specific terms." Togo revealed his strategy: "Consequently, we hope to deal with the British and Americans after, first: (a) having Prince Konoe transmit to the Russians our concrete intentions as expressed by the Imperial Will, and (b) holding conversations with the Russians in light of their demands with regard to East Asia." This telegram ended with a stern admonition to the ambassador to fulfill the cabinet's decision to seek Moscow's mediation.[24]

Dutifully, Sato obtained another audience with Lozovskii on July 25. In response to Lozovskii's July 18 letter asking for clarifications on the Konoe mission, Sato made an emphatic statement removing the ambiguities that might have remained in his July 12 request. The purpose of the Konoe mission was, he explained, specifically and officially to request the mediation of the Soviet government to terminate the war. Prince Konoe was personally chosen by the emperor to serve as his special envoy. He would bring to the Soviet government specific terms for ending the war, as well as concrete proposals for improving Soviet-Japanese relations during and after the war.

Despite Sato's clarifications, however, Lozovskii asked the Japanese ambassador to put his statement in writing. He further asked if the intention of the Japanese government was to terminate the war with the United States and Britain, and what concrete proposals Prince Konoe would bring to improve future Soviet-Japanese relations. Lozovskii was clearly interested in stalling the negotiations with the Japanese to earn more time to prepare the Soviet attack.[25]

On July 25, Togo advised Sato to obtain an interview with Molotov and explain to him the intentions of the Japanese government. He instructed Sato to (1) stress to Molotov "that Japan has gone first to the Russians with its request for mediation"; (2) make clear "that the dispatch of the special envoy would permit Stalin to acquire a reputation as an advocate of world peace"; (3) tell him that "we are prepared to meet fully the Russian demands in the Far East"; and (4) inform the Russians that "in the event the Soviet Government remains indifferent to our request, we will have no choice but to consider another course of action."[26]

Togo was following a two-track policy. First, he was pursuing an agreement with the Soviet Union. By offering the Soviets concessions in Manchuria, southern Sakhalin, Korea, and the northern Kurils, he thought he might be able to lure Stalin into serving as a mediator between Japan and the Allies. Given the increasing friction between the Soviet Union and its Allies over Poland and Eastern Europe, this policy cannot be dismissed as totally unrealistic.

Second, Togo was working toward direct negotiations with the United States and Britain. His dispatches to Sato can be interpreted as a warning to the United States and Britain that the major stumbling block to peace was their demand for unconditional surrender. Togo must have entertained the possibility that Japan's peace overtures to Moscow would be a topic of discussion at the Potsdam Conference. In fact, Sato surmised that since Lozovskii's reply came on July 18, one day after the opening of the conference, the Allies must have discussed the Japanese proposal.[27] In addition, the Japanese government knew from Zacharias's propaganda messages that the United States might be prepared to mitigate the demand for unconditional surrender and explore a peace based on the Atlantic Charter. Thus as far as Togo was concerned, the only unresolved issue was the status of the emperor. But the thorny question persisted: how to convince the army to accept surrender on these terms.

The JCS Modifies Stimson's Draft

While Truman and Stalin were engaged in the opening gambit of the meeting, there were important developments on the military side of the conference. On July 16 the U.S. and British chiefs held a Combined Chiefs of Staff meeting. British Chief of Staff Field Marshall Sir Alan Brooke commented on the last paragraph of the draft ultimatum, which mentioned the survival of the institution of the emperor. To the British, whose soldiers were fighting in the outlying areas, the emperor's authority to order a cease-fire was of vital importance. Brooke suggested, therefore, that the Allies make it clear to the Japanese that the emperor might be preserved "shortly after a Russian entry into the war."

The United States Chiefs of Staff explained that this problem had been discussed at a political level. Leahy suggested that "it would be useful if the Prime Minister put forward to the President his views and suggestions as to how the term 'unconditional surrender' might be explained to the Japanese."[28] Leahy secretly supported Brooke's proposal and hoped that Churchill would exert influence on Truman to amend the unconditional surrender demand. This explains Churchill's suggestion to Truman at the meeting on July 18.

On July 17, the JCS discussed Stimson's draft proclamation. At the beginning of the month the ultimatum had been sent to the Joint Strategic Survey Committee, a blue-ribbon review board of senior officers, "at times equal in influence to the joint chiefs themselves."[29] The committee commented that it considered Stimson's draft "generally satisfactory," but suggested a revision of the section dealing with the possibility of allowing Japan to maintain a constitutional monarchy. This provision, the Joint Strategic Survey Committee commented, "may be misconstrued as a commitment by the United Nations to depose or execute the present Emperor and install some other member of the Imperial family." It further commented: "To the radical elements in Japan, this phrase may be construed as a commitment to continue the institution of the Emperor and Emperor worship." Although the radicals were a small group at present, "with the disillusion of total defeat facing them, this group may assume major importance at a later stage." On these grounds, the Joint Strategic Survey Committee recommended amending Stimson's draft as follows:

> The occupying forces of the Allies shall be withdrawn from Japan as soon as our objectives are accomplished and there has been established beyond doubt a peacefully inclined, responsible government of a character representative of the Japanese people. ~~This may include a constitutional monarchy under the present dynasty if it be shown to the complete satisfaction of the world that such a government will never again aspire to aggression.~~ Subject to suitable guarantee against further acts of aggression, the Japanese people will be free to choose their own form of government.[30]

The committee's attempt to strike out this provision was a slap in the face to Stimson and those who sought to maintain a monarchical system. Furthermore, the committee's reasons for changing the draft made little sense. A promise to keep a constitutional monarchy could hardly be interpreted as a measure to "depose or execute the present Emperor." On the contrary, a constitutional monarchy "under the present dynasty" was more likely to be perceived as a modification of unconditional surrender on one crucial point: whether or not Japan would be able to maintain the monarchy. Moreover, there were hardly any "radical elements in Japan" (except for a handful of Communists in jail) violently opposed to the preservation of the institution of the emperor. It is difficult to fathom where the Joint Strategic Survey Committee obtained information that a group opposing the emperor system was growing in strength. The source of this initiative to undermine Stimson's draft remains a mystery. The committee's intervention angered the War Department's Operation Division, which had served as the principal architect of Stimson's draft. As far as the OPD was concerned, the whole point of the provision on a constitutional monarchy was to entice Japan to surrender before total defeat.

On July 13, the OPD submitted its further recommendation to General Handy, deputy Chief of Staff, countering the Joint Strategic Survey Committee's memo. The OPD found that the first point made by the committee could be resolved by further clarifying the term "constitutional monarchy." As for the second point, since "the radical element" was so small and unlikely to have any power to influence the present government in its decision to accept surrender, this argument was totally irrelevant. The OPD further stated: "The primary intention in issuing the proclamation is to induce Japan's surrender and thus avoid the heavy casualties implied in a fight to the finish. It is almost universally accepted that the basic point on which acceptance of surrender terms will hinge lies in the question of the disposition of the Emperor and his dynasty. Therefore, from the military point of view it seems necessary to state unequivocally what we intend to do with regard to the Emperor." On these grounds, the OPD further amended the Joint Strategic Survey Committee's amendment:

> ~~Subject to suitable guarantees against further acts of aggression,~~ The Japanese people will be free to choose ~~their own form of government~~ *whether they shall retain their Emperor as a constitutional monarchy.*[31]

The OPD stressed that its amendment was totally in line with the thinking of Stimson and McCloy. Handy sent this memorandum to Marshall in Babelsberg.

Thus, when the JCS discussed this matter on July 17, it had two contradictory proposals in its possession. Leahy reported the Joint Strategic Survey Committee's amendment to Stimson's draft. Leahy explained that "this matter had been considered on a political level and consideration had been given to the removal of the sentence in question." His statement strongly suggests that Truman and Byrnes had discussed this issue, and that they had already decided to remove the promise of a constitutional monarchy from the ultimatum. Marshall proposed acceptance of the committee's amendment. The next day, following Arnold's proposal, the Joint Chiefs of Staff adopted the Joint Strategic Survey Committee's amendment. The JCS then sent a memorandum to the president explaining, in the exact words of the Joint Strategic Survey Committee, the reason for the amendment. The memo said nothing about the OPD's counterarguments.[32]

In the judgment of the JCS, this statement was advantageous because it contained no commitment by the United States to support any particular form of government, while preserving the right of the United States to prevent any unsuitable government from being installed. Leahy and Marshall had been strong supporters of Stimson, Grew, and Forrestal's efforts to amend unconditional surrender. By striking out the passage promising a constitutional monarchy, over the strenuous opposition of the Operational Division, the Joint Chiefs of Staff promoted a draft that was harsher on the Japanese.

A number of unsolved mysteries surround the JCS's amendment. Who in the Joint Strategic Survey Committee proposed the amendment and why? Why did Marshall and the JCS accept the committee's revision over the objections of the OPD? Why did Stimson and McCloy accept defeat without any protest? Why did they keep silent on this crucial matter in their diaries? Stimson's meetings with Truman on July 16 and with Byrnes on July 17, and Leahy's statement on July 16, offer a clue. At that time Stimson was told that the president and Byrnes had worked out a "timetable" for the end of the Pacific War. His attempt to persuade the president to double his efforts to modify unconditional surrender in view of Japan's overtures to Moscow was rebuffed. Stimson must have felt how strongly Truman and Byrnes were committed to unconditional surrender. Likewise, informed by Leahy that Truman and Byrnes had already made up their minds to remove the promise to retain a constitutional monarchy, the JCS had to accept that decision.

Stimson Receives Groves's Report

Stimson received news of the successful detonation of the Trinity bomb on July 16 and 17, but initial reports were so sketchy that it was not until Groves's full report arrived on July 21 that the atomic bomb began to influence American decisions. Once American policymakers digested the implications of the new weapon, the atomic bomb drastically transformed the decision-making process.

In his report Groves was unable to conceal his excitement: "For the first time in history there was a nuclear explosion. And what an explosion! . . . The test was successful beyond the most optimistic expectations of anyone." He explained that the energy released by the explosion exceeded 15 to 20 kilotons of TNT, enough to evaporate the 100-foot steel tower on which the explosion had taken place. Groves added in the report: "We are all fully conscious that our real goal is still before us. The battle test is what counts in the war with Japan."[33] The clock had begun ticking faster for the first deployment of the atomic bomb.

Stimson was impressed by Groves's report, which he read aloud to Truman and Byrnes at the Little White House. After hearing the report the president looked "immensely pepped up." Truman thanked Stimson for the news, which gave him "an entirely new confidence," and again told the secretary of war that he was glad Stimson had come to Potsdam. Churchill noticed that at the meeting the next day Truman was "much fortified by something that had happened and that he stood up to the Russians in a most emphatic and decisive manner." McCloy similarly noted in his diary: "The Big Bomb stiffened Truman and Churchill after getting Groves' report. They went to the next meeting like little boys with a big red apple secreted on their persons." Many eyewitnesses have commented on Truman's reaction to news of Trinity's success, but neither eyewitnesses nor historians have ever questioned how Stalin and the Soviet side interpreted the Allies' behavior.[34]

For the next two days, Stimson was preoccupied with a battle with his subordinates back home. When he returned to his temporary residence in Babelsberg, a top secret telegram from Harrison awaited him: "All your local military advisers engaged in preparation definitely favor your pet city and would like to feel free to use it as first choice if those on the ride select it out of four possible spots in the light of local conditions at the time." Stimson thought he had succeeded in removing Kyoto from the list of target cities for atomic bombing. Groves had revived Stimson's "pet city" as the military's top priority target. Groves had wished all along to drop the first bomb on Kyoto in order to demonstrate its impact on the self-contained ancient capital surrounded by mountains. The Japanese would be shocked into submission when the ancient temples and gardens turned to dust. Infuriated by Groves's insubordination, Stimson immediately fired off a telegram without waiting for the president's agreement: "Aware of no factors to change my decision. On the contrary new factors here tend to confirm it."[35] These "new factors" were most likely the impending Soviet entry into the war.

Meanwhile, another telegram from Harrison arrived: "Patient progressing rapidly and will be ready for final operations first good break in August. Complicated preparations for use are proceeding so fast we should know not later than July 25 of any change in plans." The following day, Stimson showed Truman Harrison's two telegrams. Truman "was intensely pleased by the accelerated timetable." He was delighted to know that the atomic bomb would be available for use before the Soviets joined the war. As for the target, he approved Stimson's decision to remove Kyoto from the list. Stimson also met with Arnold and obtained his approval to exclude Kyoto as a target.[36]

At ten o'clock on the morning of July 23, Byrnes called Stimson and asked him about the timing of the S-1 program. Byrnes was most concerned about the timetable. On Byrnes's request, Stimson sent another telegram to Harrison: "We assume operation may be any time after the first of August. Whenever it is possible to give us a more definite date please immediately advise us here where information is greatly needed." He also told Harrison that Kyoto should be excluded from the list, and informed him that his decision had been confirmed "by highest authority." Shortly after he sent his telegram, Stimson received two telegrams from Harrison. The first listed the targets: Hiroshima, Kokura, and Niigata.[37] Kyoto was spared, but Hiroshima's fate was sealed.

Stimson's unflagging attempt to exclude Kyoto saved this ancient city from atomic devastation. Nevertheless, preserving Japan's national treasure was not the only motivation that spurred Stimson to save Kyoto. His action was also politically motivated. On July 24, Stimson and Truman talked about the atomic bomb. According to Stimson's diary, "he [Truman] was particularly emphatic in agreeing with my suggestion that if elimination [of Kyoto] was not done, the bitterness which would be caused by such a wanton act might make it impossible during the long post-war period to reconcile the Japanese to us in that area rather than to the Russians." By eliminating Kyoto, Stimson pointed out, the United States would be able to ensure "a sympathetic Japan to the United States in case there should be any aggression by Russia in Manchuria." Not only the target but also the timing of the atomic bomb was closely connected with Soviet entry into the war. Harrison's telegram states: "Operations may be possible any time from August 1 depending on state of preparation of patient and condition of atmosphere. From point of view of patient only, some chance August 1 to 3, good chance August 4 and 5, and barring unexpected relapse almost certain before August 10."[38]

On the morning of July 23 Harriman came to see Stimson and reported on the "expanding demands being made by the Russians." Not only were they making such demands in Europe; but they might propose solitary control of the trusteeship in Korea. When he went to the Little White House, Stimson told the president about Harriman's visit, and noted that he had asked Harrison exactly when the atomic bomb would be ready to be dropped. Stimson wrote in his diary: "He [Truman] told me that he had the warning message which we prepared on his desk, and had accepted our most recent change in it, and that he proposed to shoot it out as soon as he heard the definite day of the operation. We had a brief discussion about Stalin's recent expansions and he confirmed what I have heard. But he told me that the United States was standing firm and he was apparently relying greatly upon the information as to S-1."[39] The timing of the ultimatum, Soviet entry into the war, and the dropping of the atomic bomb became closely connected in Truman's mind.

According to Harrison, preparations for an atomic attack should be completed by July 25. The bomb would be ready to be dropped against Japan the first week of August. Given that the Soviets had pledged to enter the war in the middle of August, Truman was assured that the atomic bomb would be ready for use before the Soviets had a chance to attack. But Truman would have to issue an ultimatum to Japan before using the bomb. Thus he had a narrow window between July 25 and August 1. No wonder the president was "intensely pleased by the accelerated timetable." Everything was falling into place according to the plan that Truman had worked out with Byrnes.

The preparations for using the atomic bomb on Japan proceeded at breakneck speed, but so far no formal order to drop the bomb had been given. On July 23 General Carl Spaatz, commander of the Army Strategic Air Forces, who had left Europe and stopped by Washington on his way to the new command post at Guam, asked General Handy for a written order. The next day Groves drafted the directive for use of the bomb. It went to Harrison, who transmitted it by radio to Marshall in Potsdam "in order that your approval and the Secretary of War's approval might be obtained as soon as possible." Marshall and Stimson approved the directive. According to Richard Rhodes, they "presumably showed it to

Truman, though it does not record his formal authorization." General Handy's order was given to Spaatz on the morning of July 25: "The 509 Composite Group, 20th Air Force will deliver its first special bomb as soon as weather will permit visual bombing after about 3 August 1945, on one of the targets: Hiroshima, Kokura, Niigata and Nagasaki." It further ordered: "Additional bombs will be delivered on the above targets as soon as made ready by the project staff."[40]

Referring to this directive, Truman later noted in his memoirs: "With this order the wheels were set in motion for the first use of an atomic weapon against a military target. I had made the decision. I also instructed Stimson that the order would stand unless I notified him that the Japanese reply to our ultimatum was acceptable."[41] This three-sentence paragraph is filled with untruths and half-truths. The atomic bomb was not targeted specifically "against a military target." The order was to prepare not only a single "atomic weapon" but also "additional bombs." But the most important point is that Truman did not issue any order to drop the bomb. In fact, he was not involved in this decision but merely let the military proceed without his interference. Furthermore, it is doubtful that he gave Stimson specific instructions to let the order stand until he received a satisfactory response from Japan. No such instructions have been discovered in the archives.

It is important to note that Handy's order to Spaatz, the only existing direct order to deploy atomic bombs against Japan, was given on July 25, one day before the Potsdam Proclamation was issued. The popular myth, artificially concocted by Truman and Stimson themselves and widely believed in the United States, that Japan's rejection of the Potsdam Proclamation led to the U.S. decision to drop the bomb, cannot be supported by the facts. Truman wrote that he issued the order to drop the bomb *after* Japan rejected the Potsdam Proclamation. The truth is quite the opposite, however: the rejection of the Potsdam Proclamation was required to justify the dropping of the bomb.

Truman mulled over the implications of the atomic bomb. He had come to Potsdam to obtain a pledge from the Soviet Union to enter the war against Japan. But with the news of the atomic bomb, he began to reconsider the role of the Soviet Union. On the morning of July 23, the president met with Stimson and instructed him to find out "whether Marshall felt that we [needed] the Russians in the war or whether we could get along without them." When Stimson put the question to Marshall, he did not answer directly. American military planners' original intention in desiring Soviet participation in the war, Marshall stated, was to pin down Japanese troops in Manchuria. This objective had already been accomplished, as Soviet troops were amassed along the Manchurian border. He further remarked: "even if we went ahead in the war without the Russians, and compelled the Japanese to surrender to our terms, that would not prevent the Russians from marching into Manchuria anyhow and striking, thus permitting them to get virtually what they wanted in the surrender terms." Stimson noted in his diary: "Marshall felt as I felt sure he would, that now with new weapon we would not need the assistance of the Russians to conquer Japan."[42]

But Marshall never stated at this meeting that Soviet assistance would not be needed because of the atomic bomb. Stimson merely inferred it. In fact, Marshall appears to have believed that even with the use of the atomic bomb the war would last long enough for the Soviets to join the fight, that Soviet entry into the war would be more or less inevitable, and therefore, that the United States would be better off establishing conditions for Soviet participation in the war. Marshall also told Stimson that weather conditions might militate against the use of the atomic bomb.[43] Clearly, Marshall did not believe that the atomic bomb alone would force Japan to surrender. What Stimson's diary reveals is that Marshall and Stimson did not completely agree on the utility of the atomic bomb and Soviet entry into the war.

On the morning of July 24, Stimson told Truman about his conference with Marshall. Stimson told the president that he could infer from Marshall's words that the Russians were not needed. That Stimson misrepresented Marshall's view is clear. This misrepresentation had far-reaching implications, for it must have convinced Truman that his military leaders believed that with possession of the bomb, the United States would be able to force Japan's surrender unilaterally, without Soviet assistance.

Stimson's diary entry for July 24 contains a passage that historians have to this point curiously ignored. He wrote: "I then showed him the telegram which had come last evening from Harrison giving the dates of the operations. He [Truman] said that was just what he wanted, that he was highly delighted and that it gave him his cue for his warning." The president revealed that he had sent the draft warning to Chiang Kai-shek, and "as soon as that was cleared by Chiang Kai-shek, he, Truman, would release the warning and that would fit right in time with the program we had received from Harrison."[44] The timing of the Potsdam Proclamation was integrally connected with the schedule for deployment of the atomic bombs. The question of timing was indeed the nub of the matter.

Truman Tells Stalin about the "Weapon"

At 7:30 P.M. on July 24, the eighth plenary session of the Big Three meeting took a recess. As the participants were walking around, Truman approached Stalin without his interpreter and casually confided: "We have a new weapon of unusual destructive force." Stalin showed no interest; at least so it seemed to the president. Truman remembered: "All he said was that he was glad to hear it and hoped we would make 'good use' of it against the Japanese." Stalin's nonchalant reply fooled everyone who witnessed the exchange, including Truman. Everyone thought Stalin did not understand the significance of the information.[45]

But Stalin was not fooled. On June 2 Harry Gold, a Soviet spy, had invited Klaus Fuchs, a physicist involved in the Manhattan Project and a Soviet spy as well, for a short ride. Fuchs told Gold of the approaching bomb test.[46] In the middle of June Soviet NKVD agent Leonid Kvasikov had sent information to Moscow that the American atomic bomb test would take place on July 10. (Actually, it was scheduled on July 4 and then postponed until July 16 owing to bad weather.) This information was immediately sent to Stalin. Thus when Truman mentioned "a new weapon of unusual destructive force," the Soviet leader immediately understood what the president was talking about.

After the session, Stalin telephoned Beria and asked if he knew anything about the test. Beria answered: "Yes, Comrade Stalin. As we reported to you, they were supposed to have this test two weeks ago, but since then we have not received any information about powerful explosions." Stalin accused Beria of ignorance and proceeded to give him a tongue-lashing. He told Beria that the explosion had taken place one week earlier and that Beria was "misled by disinformation." He blamed the NKVD chief for creating a situation in which Truman could conduct negotiations from a position of strength, bossing the Soviet delegation around. According to Gromyko, when Stalin returned to his villa, he commented that with atomic monopoly the United States would force the Soviet Union to accept its plans regarding Europe. "Well, that's not going to happen," he stated, and cursed "in ripe language." Stalin then vowed to speed up Soviet production of the bomb.[47]

To Stalin, the most important revelation was that Truman was with-holding information about the atomic bomb. Stalin must have deduced from this fact that the United States, with the new weapon in hand, was about to force Japan's surrender without the Soviet Union. It was then that Stalin began to worry that the United States might outmaneuver the Soviet Union.

Several hours before Truman revealed the news of the "weapon of un-usual destructive force" to Stalin, the U.S.-British combined chiefs met with their Soviet counterparts for the first time. Leahy asked Antonov to provide an outline of the Soviet plan of action against Japan. Antonov answered that the Soviets "would be ready to commence operations in the last half of August." The actual date would depend on the outcome of negotiations with the Chinese. Antonov was clearly operating under the assumption that the Allies needed Soviet assistance in the war, and for that reason, he expressed the wish that the Allies would exert pressure on the Chinese to come to an agreement with the Soviet Union.[48]

But something must have happened to the Soviets' thinking after Tru-man's less-than-truthful revelation about the atomic bomb. After receiv-ing Sato's clarifications about the Konoe mission on July 25, Lozovskii sent his recommendations as to how to respond to Japan's latest peace overtures. He suggested that the Soviet government continue to use stall-ing tactics by requesting the specific proposals that Konoe would bring to Moscow. Molotov flatly rejected this recommendation, writing in the margin of Lozovskii's dispatch "Not necessary." The time to fool Japan was over. All efforts now had to be concentrated on waging a war against Japan.[49]

Truman Issues the Potsdam Proclamation

Stalin expected to be asked to sign the Potsdam Proclamation.[50] Such a document, signed by the United States, Britain, the Soviet Union, and China, would justify the Soviet war against Japan as a joint action of the United Nations, though it would violate the existing Neutrality Pact with Japan. A proclamation signed by the Soviet Union would therefore serve as a declaration of war against Japan. Given that Japan was pinning its last hopes on Moscow's mediation, the Soviets' joining the ultimatum would shock Japan into surrender.

The atomic bomb, however, changed the whole dynamics of the joint ultimatum. For American policymakers, the ultimatum was originally meant to secure Japan's surrender before the Allies' homeland invasion. Now with the news that the two atomic bombs would be ready for use at the beginning of August, the proclamation acquired a new urgency: it would have to be issued before the atomic bomb was dropped. The bomb had also changed the purpose of the ultimatum; rather than securing Japan's surrender before the Allies' homeland attack, the proclamation would now serve as a final warning about "prompt and utter destruction." Japan's rejection of the terms specified in the proclamation would serve as justification for dropping the bomb. Moreover, the bomb solved the dilemma of Soviet entry into the war. The United States no longer needed Soviet assistance to force Japan to surrender; in fact, it became imperative for the United States to use the bomb to hasten Japan's surrender before the Soviet Union could enter the war.

By July 24 Truman and Byrnes approved the final text of the Potsdam Proclamation. According to Byrnes, Stimson's draft "was turned over to me." Then when they learned of the atomic bomb test, Byrnes finished drafting the ultimatum: "The copy in my files indicates that several suggestions made by Churchill were incorporated, and the President inserted one or two with his pen." It is not clear which parts of the amendments were made by Byrnes and which parts by Truman, or when. But what is certain is that either Byrnes or Truman removed the part added by the Joint Chiefs of Staff in Article 12: "Subject to suitable guarantee against further acts of aggression, the Japanese people will be free to choose their own form of government." The omission made this provision more stringent and less clear about the status of the emperor. In order to obtain British approval, however, they had to accept British amendments to issue the proclamation to the Japanese government rather than directly to the Japanese people and to change the form of Allied occupation from direct occupation to indirect occupation.[51] The British government did not, however, insist on the preservation of the monarchical system. In view of strong opposition from Truman and Byrnes, Churchill and Eden decided to drop the demand that unconditional surrender be modified.

Stimson also made a gallant last attempt to revise the substance of the Potsdam Proclamation. Framing his request around the U.S. interest in forestalling Soviet expansion in Asia, he made an eleventh-hour effort to include the promise of preservation of the monarchical system in the proclamation. Stimson met with Truman on July 24 and attempted to revive the clause that had been stricken out by the Joint Chiefs of Staff.

Stimson wrote in his diary: "I then spoke of the importance which I attributed to the reassurance of the Japanese on the continuance of their dynasty, and I had felt that the insertion of that in the formal warning was important and might be just the thing that would make or mar their acceptance." Truman told him that since he had sent the draft to Chiang Kai-shek, it was impossible to change it. Stimson asked Truman to "watch carefully so that the Japanese might be reassured verbally through diplomatic channels if it was found that they were hanging fire on that one point." Truman said that this was exactly what he had in mind, and that he would take care of it.[52] Despite Stimson's intervention, Truman had already made up his mind. Byrnes had decided to maintain the term "unconditional surrender" without promising anything about the emperor, and Truman had agreed. Truman's assurance that he would keep Stimson's advice in mind was an empty promise that the president had no intention of fulfilling.

Why did Byrnes and Truman reject Stimson's recommendation to restore the provision allowing Japan to retain a constitutional monarchy? The July 24 entry of Walter Brown's diary gives the following account: "JFB told more about Jap peace bid to Russia. Japanese Ambassador to Russia warned his government that same thing which happened to Germany would happen to Japan if she stayed in the war. Emperor had said they would fight to the last man unless there was some modification of unconditional surrender."[53] We can assume that Togo's second dispatch on July 21, intercepted by Magic, played a decisive role in Byrnes and Truman's decision.

Byrnes's biographer, David Robertson, stresses that Byrnes understood the July 21 dispatch as an indication of "Japan's intention to fight on rather than accept an unconditional surrender." After the war, Byrnes wrote: "This cable . . . depressed me terribly. It meant using the atomic bomb; it probably meant Russia's entry into the war. There is no question in my mind that only the havoc wrought by our new weapon, which was used only twice, caused the warlords of Japan to surrender when they did."

Stimson and Forrestal read the same telegram but came to a totally different conclusion. Forrestal wrote: "[the Japanese leaders] final judgment and decision was that the war must be fought with all the vigor and bitterness of which the nation was capable *so long as the only alternative was the unconditional surrender.*"[54] Forrestal and Stimson concluded that

Japan might be close to surrender if the United States revised the unconditional surrender demand to include the retention of a constitutional monarchy with the current dynasty.

But Byrnes treated this demand as if it were etched in stone. Robertson explains this intransigence by citing Byrnes's concern with domestic pressure. But it is possible that another consideration also played an important role in his decision. Walter Brown wrote in his diary on July 24: "JFB still hoping for time, believing after atomic bomb Japan will surrender and Russia will not get in so much on the kill, thereby being in a position to press for claims against China." Forrestal wrote: "Byrnes said he was most anxious to get the Japanese affair over with before the Russians got in with particular reference to Dairen and Port Arthur." When Forrestal told Byrnes that Truman had said "his principal objective at Potsdam would be to get Russia in the war," Byrnes responded that "it was most probable that the President's views had changed; certainly that was not now my view."[55]

But the question remains: If Byrnes's overriding concern was Soviet expansion in China, why did he not accept Stimson's recommendation to forestall Soviet entry into the war? From the Magic intercepts, he was well aware that dropping the demand for unconditional surrender and ensuring the continuation of a constitutional monarchy under the current dynasty might quicken Japanese surrender. More important, he also knew any ultimatum that insisted upon unconditional surrender would be rejected by Japan.

The key phrase here is "believing *after atomic bomb* Japan will surrender." A different interpretation, perhaps more diabolical, is possible. In Byrnes's mind the atomic bomb, as the ace in the U.S. hand, assumed primacy. The atomic bomb would force Japan to surrender and forestall Soviet entry into the war. Thus the atomic bomb had to be used. In order to drop the bomb, the United States had to issue the ultimatum to Japan, warning that the rejection of the terms specified in the proclamation would result in "prompt and utter destruction." And this proclamation had to be rejected by the Japanese in order to justify the use of the atomic bomb. The best way to accomplish all this was to insist upon unconditional surrender. Walter Brown's diary in the Potsdam file contains the following passage for July 26: "Joint message to Japan released. This was prelude to atomic bomb."[56] Byrnes knew even before the Japanese responded to the Potsdam Proclamation that the document was the prelude to the bomb.

What about Truman? It is inconceivable that he was unaware of the implications of the timing, signatories, and substance of the Potsdam Proclamation. He knew that Handy had given Spaatz an order to prepare for the deployment of the atomic bomb. He must have known of the Magic intercepts, and through those documents he must have known that the Japanese were trying to amend the unconditional surrender demand to terminate the war. Hence, he must have known that any proclamation that contained the unconditional surrender demand would be rejected by the Japanese. The important thing for Truman was to make no decision and let the process run its course. George Elsey, a naval intelligence officer assigned to the map room, recalled: "Truman made no decision because there was no decision to be made . . . He could no more have stopped it than a train moving down a track."[57] To Truman, it was important not to impede deployment of the atomic bomb.

In the July 25 entry for his Potsdam diary, Truman marveled at the destructive power of the atomic bomb, which "caused the complete disintegration of a steel tower 60 feet high," and "knocked over a steel tower $\frac{1}{2}$ mile away." Did he translate this destructiveness into unprecedented killing and suffering of the civilian population? His diary further stated: "This weapon is to be used against Japan between now and August 10th. I have told the Sec. of War, Mr. Stimson, to use it so that military objectives and soldiers and sailors are the target and not women and children. Even if the Japs are savages, ruthless and fanatic, we as the leader of the world for the common welfare cannot drop this terrible bomb on the old capital or the new." He then repeated, as if to convince himself: "He and I are in accord. The target will be a purely military one." Thus even before the atomic bomb was deployed, the president was deceiving himself into believing that a bomb with the ability to cause "the complete disintegration of a steel tower 60 feet high" could be used solely against military targets without killing women and children. When Arnold talked with Stimson about the atomic bomb on July 23, he recalled: "We talked about the killing of women and children; the destruction of surrounding communities, the effect on other nations, and the psychological reaction of the Japanese themselves." There is no reason to believe that the commander in chief did not know what Arnold and Stimson knew.

Truman's diary then states: "we will issue a warning statement asking the Japs to surrender and save lives. I'm sure they will not do that, but we will have given them the chance."[58] In Truman's mind, the purpose of the Potsdam Proclamation was to issue a warning before dropping the atomic bomb. He was completely confident that Japan would reject the offer. He did not say that he hoped Japan would accept it so that he would not have to use the bomb. Rather, his diary implies that he would issue the ultimatum only as an excuse to justify the dropping of the bomb.

On July 24, immediately after Truman approved the final draft of the Potsdam Proclamation, he sent a telegram to Ambassador Hurley instructing him to obtain Chiang Kai-shek's approval as quickly as possible. Before his departure for London on July 25, Churchill gave his approval of the proclamation. By the evening of July 26, Truman had received Chiang Kai-shek's approval as well. At seven in the evening copies of the Potsdam Proclamation, which demanded "unconditional surrender of all the Japanese armed forces," with no reference to the fate of the emperor, were given to the press to be released at 9:20 P.M.[59] The Little White House also sent a copy to the Office of War Information in Washington so that it might disseminate the proclamation widely to Japan. As agreed upon by the State and War Departments, the proclamation was considered an instrument of propaganda rather than a diplomatic document. At 4 P.M. Washington time (5 A.M. July 27, Tokyo time) American West-Coast shortwave radio stations began transmitting the text.[60]

Stalin Reacts to the Potsdam Proclamation

The U.S. delegation came to Potsdam with a draft of the Potsdam Proclamation that included the Soviet Union as a possible signatory nation. But neither Stalin nor Molotov had been consulted on this matter even once. In fact, after the Alamogordo explosion, the major objective of Truman and Byrnes was to exclude the Soviet Union from the proclamation. This secret operation was successful, for it appears that until the proclamation was announced in the press, the Soviets were left completely in the dark. After the press release on July 26, Byrnes sent a copy of the ultimatum to Molotov as a diplomatic courtesy. Caught by surprise, Molotov immediately asked Byrnes to postpone the announcement for two or three days, but Byrnes told Molotov that it was too late, since the proclamation had already been handed to the press.[61]

Stalin must have expected that the joint ultimatum would be discussed at some point during the conference. The Russian scholar Viacheslav

Safronov recently uncovered a document that the Soviet delegation had brought to Potsdam in anticipation of joining the Allied ultimatum. The Soviet draft of the Potsdam Proclamation began: "The time has come when the Governments of the Allied democratic countries—the United States, China, Great Britain, and the Soviet Union—have recognized that it is essential to make a joint declaration about our relations with Japan." It then listed Japan's transgressions, from its attack on China to its "treacherous" attack on Pearl Harbor, "the same perfidious surprise attack by which it had attacked Russia forty years ago." The aggressive plans by the Japanese militarists, however, had been thwarted only by the "unyielding resistance of the Chinese people and the courageous struggle of the American and British armed forces." The draft then stated: "People all over the world have a burning desire to terminate the continuing war. The United States, China, Great Britain, and the Soviet Union consider it their duty to take joint, decisive measures immediately to bring the war to an end." Finally, the document called on Japan to "lay down arms and surrender without any conditions."[62]

The document reveals the Soviet approach to the Potsdam Proclamation. What is striking about this document is its conciliatory, even obsequious tone, indicating how desperately Stalin wished to issue a joint declaration against Japan together with the United States and Britain. But was Stalin not concerned that the issuance of such a joint declaration might immediately lead to Japan's surrender, thereby circumventing his ultimate objective of actually waging war against Japan to earn the trophies promised at Yalta? Stalin and Molotov must have hoped that the issuance of the ultimatum might be postponed to coincide with the Soviet attack. This expectation was by no means far-fetched, given that the U.S. War Department had originally envisaged the optimal timing of the ultimatum as the moment of Soviet entry into the war. Moreover, the last part of the draft that called for Japan's unconditional surrender would surely deter Japan from immediately accepting the joint ultimatum.

But once Byrnes told Molotov that the text of the ultimatum had already been released to the press, the game was over. The Soviet Union had been hoodwinked by the United States. Molotov did not even submit the Soviet draft, which was quietly sent to the archives.

At 6 P.M. the following day, July 27, Byrnes and Molotov had a meeting. The secretary said that Molotov's request for a two- or three-day postponement in the issuance of the Potsdam Proclamation had not reached him until morning, and that by then it was too late. This was clearly a lie. In fact, releasing the document before Soviet intervention was one of the most important objectives for Byrnes and Truman. Molotov reminded Byrnes that the request had been made the previous night, as soon as he had received a copy of the proclamation.

Byrnes explained why Truman had considered it important to issue the proclamation without consulting the Soviet Union. First, the Allies had to issue the proclamation before Churchill relinquished premiership after his loss in the British general election. Second, the United States did not consult the Soviet Union since the Soviet Union "was not at war with Japan" and it "did not wish to embarrass them." Molotov simply said that he was not authorized to discuss the matter further, and that Stalin would return to it at some point.[63]

The omission of Stalin's signature from the Potsdam Proclamation had a profound effect on Japanese policy. The Japanese immediately noticed that Stalin did not sign the proclamation. This prompted them to continue their efforts to terminate the war through Soviet mediation rather than immediately accepting the conditions stipulated by the Potsdam Proclamation. Thus Stalin's failure to affix his signature inadvertently benefited the Soviets by convincing the Japanese that the Moscow route for mediated peace still remained open. This was a purely serendipitous outcome.

On July 28 the new British delegation headed by Prime Minister Clement Attlee and Foreign Secretary Ernest Bevin joined the Potsdam Conference. Before the official plenary session began, Stalin said he wished to make an announcement and share important information he had received from Moscow. Then the Russian interpreter read Sato's statement made on July 25 to Lozovskii, and the emperor's personal request officially asking for Moscow's mediation to terminate the war. Stalin remarked that although the Soviet delegation had not been consulted by the Allies about the issuance of the Potsdam Proclamation, he nevertheless wished to keep the Allies informed of Japan's further overtures. After the interpreter read the telegram from Moscow, Stalin declared that there was nothing new in it "except that it was more definite than the previous approach," and that he would give the Japanese a more definite negative answer.[64] Truman thanked Stalin for the information.

This was the same cat and mouse game. Truman had already known the contents of the telegram through Magic. Stalin's purpose in introducing this information was presumably to impress upon the Americans how cooperative he was despite the humiliation he had suffered at not being consulted on the proclamation. He desperately needed a concession from the United States on one important matter.

Exclusion from the Potsdam Proclamation created a huge problem for Stalin. It deprived him of a justification to declare war against Japan in violation of the Neutrality Pact. On July 29, Stalin allegedly caught a cold and did not come to the plenary meeting. Molotov sat in his place. At the end of the session, Molotov raised the question of the Soviet role in the Pacific War. He explained that Stalin had instructed him to tell Truman that "the best method would be for the United States, England and the other allies in the Far Eastern war to address a formal request to the Soviet Government for its entry into the war." This request could be made on the basis of Japan's rejection of the Potsdam Proclamation, and for the purpose of "shortening the war and saving lives."

The Soviet request placed Truman and Byrnes in an awkward position. Under no circumstances could they comply. Byrnes wrote: "We had, of course, begun to hope that a Japanese surrender might be imminent and we did not want to urge the Russians to enter the war." But they could not ignore the Soviets' request, either, given that U.S. policy since Yalta had been to seek Soviet participation in the war, and Truman himself had declared publicly and privately that the main purpose of his coming to Potsdam was to secure Soviet entry. In order to get out of this dilemma, Byrnes mobilized Benjamin Cohen, his trusted State Department legal hand. Cohen came up with an ingenious legal contortion. The Soviet Union could justify entering the war against Japan even though it would violate the Neutrality Pact, on the basis of the Moscow Declaration of October 30, 1943, signed by the Soviet Union, the United States, Britain, and China, as well as the United Nations Charter Articles 103 and 106. Paragraph 5 of the Moscow Declaration and Article 106 of the United Nations Charter stipulated that the four Allied nations would consult one another and take "joint action" on behalf of the community of nations. Article 103 stated that if there was a conflict between the obligations of the members of the United Nations and their obligations under any international agreement, their obligations to the United Nations Charter should take precedence."[65] This was a flimsy legal basis at best. The Moscow Declaration was merely a declaration of four powers, and whether its legal basis could extend to other nations, and whether it overrode the existing treaty obligation, were open to question. The United Nations Charters still remained unratified.

In his memoirs, Truman states: "I did not like this [Stalin's] proposal for one important reason. I saw in it a cynical diplomatic move to make Russia's entry at this time appear to be the decisive factor to bring about victory." The Soviet Union had pledged to enter the war at Yalta, and it reaffirmed its commitment at Potsdam. Thus, as far as Truman was concerned, Soviet entry into the war was a treaty obligation, and "none obliging the United States and the Allies to provide Russia with a reason for breaking with Japan." Truman explained his reluctance to have Russia enter the war: "I was not willing to let Russia reap the fruits of a long and bitter and gallant effort in which she had had no part." Byrnes, for his part, wrote that he did not believe that "the United States should be placed in the position of asking another government to violate its agreement without good and sufficient reason," forgetting that this did not bother Roosevelt when he solicited Stalin's pledge to enter the war. "Good and sufficient reason" to violate the Neutrality Pact was what Stalin sought desperately and what Truman and Byrnes adamantly refused to give him.

Byrnes was more direct in his memoirs: "I must frankly admit that in view of what we knew of Soviet actions in eastern Germany and the violations of the Yalta agreements in Poland, Rumania and Bulgaria, I would have been satisfied had the Russians determined not to enter the war. Notwithstanding Japan's persistent refusal to surrender unconditionally, I believed the atomic bomb would be successful and would force the Japanese to accept surrender on our terms." In this sentence, the timetable that Byrnes and Truman had worked out is succinctly explained: issuance of the Potsdam Proclamation with the unconditional surrender demand—Japan's rejection—use of the atomic bomb—Japan's surrender before Soviet entry into the war.

Neither Truman nor Byrnes was willing to give the Soviets the satisfaction of receiving a U.S invitation to join the war. But neither could they ignore Molotov's request or flatly refuse it. Thus, Truman wrote a personal letter to Stalin on July 31, suggesting that Stalin justify the Soviet declaration of war against Japan on the basis of the Moscow Declaration of October 30, 1943, and Articles 103 and 106 of the United Nations Charter. According to Byrnes, Truman told Byrnes that Stalin had "expressed great appreciation" for Truman's letter. If he did, this was one of Stalin's fine performances, since the letter was tantamount to a slap in the face. In the end, Stalin did not use the legal reasons given by the United States to justify the Soviet declaration of war.[66]

As far as Stalin was concerned, the issuance of the Potsdam Proclamation was a prime example of American duplicity. The way the Americans treated the Soviets in this matter bothered him more than Truman's half-truth about the atomic bomb. His game plan was completely spoiled. Moreover, Stalin must have felt profound humiliation to see Truman and Churchill issuing, behind his back, a proclamation in the name of the very site where he had hosted them. Most important, Stalin realized that this act on the part of Truman was conclusive proof that the United States intended to obtain Japan's surrender without Soviet help. He decided to enter the war as quickly as possible before the atomic bomb would force Japan to end the war. Now the race was on in earnest.

Suzuki's "Mokusatsu" Statement

On July 26, Colonel Suenari Shiraki of the General Staff's Intelligence Division brought alarming news to the General Staff. The Soviets had already transported up to 1.5 million troops, 5,400 airplanes, and 3,400 tanks to the Far East. Soviet tanks and reconnaissance forces were spotted moving along the Manchurian border. The Soviet forces did not appear to be prepared for the winter. On the basis of this information, Shiraki predicted that the Soviets would launch an attack in August.[67] Few people paid much attention to this report.

The Japanese began receiving shortwave radio announcements of the Potsdam Proclamation from San Francisco beginning at 6 A.M. on July 27. Takagi immediately noticed the absence of Stalin's signature. As for the Potsdam terms, Takagi thought they made surrender "conditional," thus making it easier for Japan to capitulate. He believed that the government should under no circumstances make any comment on the proclamation until it decided whether to approach Moscow or to negotiate directly with the United States and Britain. The Foreign Ministry, too, discussed how to respond to the ultimatum. Deputy Foreign Minister Shun'ichi Matsumoto argued that since this proclamation defined the conditions of unconditional surrender, Japan would have no choice but to accept it. As for the emperor system, Shin'ich Shibusawa (treaty division chief) noticed that though the proclamation said nothing, neither did it say anything about abolishing or limiting the system. Yoshiro Ando (political affairs division chief) also called attention to the part of the pronouncement that left the political system to the will of the people, and argued that the Japanese people would never think of abolishing the emperor system.[68] Matsumoto, for his part, stated that the government should not attempt to hide the ultimatum from the people, arguing that under no circumstances should the government take any actions that might imply the rejection of the proclamation. Matsumoto considered it best to publish the text in toto without any comments from the government. He further suggested that this proclamation should serve as the basis for Konoe's negotiations with the Soviet Union. He even wrote a draft telegram instructing Sato to approach the Soviet government.

Togo, however, rejected Matsumoto's advice, insisting that he should wait for Molotov's answer. As far as Togo was concerned, there was ambiguity between this proclamation, on the one hand, and the Atlantic Charter and the Cairo Declaration, on the other. For instance, the Cairo Declaration called for Japan's unconditional surrender, while the Potsdam Proclamation demanded "unconditional surrender of armed forces." Whether the Soviet government would join the joint ultimatum was not clear. These ambiguities would have to be clarified before Japan accepted the Potsdam terms. Nevertheless, he felt that the Japanese government should not reject the Potsdam Proclamation under any circumstances. Togo thought it might be possible to clarify these points with Moscow's help. [69]

At 11 A.M. Togo reported to the emperor on the proclamation. He expressed his view that "since the Potsdam Proclamation is a broad, general statement, and it leaves room for further study of the concrete terms, we plan to find out what these concrete terms are through the Soviet Union." The emperor accepted this position. Hirohito had already obtained a copy of the joint proclamation and had studied it closely. When Kido came to see him that afternoon, he pointed out to the emperor that the joint proclamation contained many ambiguities, especially with regard to the absence of Stalin's signature and the position of the emperor. It was an unusually long audience. It is not difficult to imagine that Kido and Hirohito discussed the fate of the emperor and the imperial house. Both men must have agreed with Togo that they should await the outcome of negotiations with Moscow before making a decision on the Potsdam Proclamation.[70]

After his report to the emperor, Togo hurried back to attend the Big Six meeting in the morning. He insisted to those gathered that the proclamation was an offer for conditional peace. Since its immediate rejection would invite dire consequences, he argued, Japan should not express any view on the proclamation and pursue the course of negotiations with the

Soviet Union. Anami, Umezu, and Toyoda strenuously opposed this view. Toyoda advocated the issuance of a special imperial order rejecting the Potsdam Proclamation. In the end, however, Prime Minister Suzuki and Togo persuaded the military to take no action for the time being.[71]

The Potsdam Proclamation was the major topic of discussion during the regular cabinet meeting in the afternoon. There Togo expressed the view that the major objective of the United States government was to terminate the war in order to avoid further bloodshed. In his opinion, the United States had brought the proclamation to the Potsdam Conference and sought Soviet participation. Despite this request, the Soviet Union chose not to sign the document, and so there still remained room for negotiations with the Soviet Union.[72] For tactical reasons, Togo felt that the cabinet should make no decision on the Potsdam Proclamation, since to do so would reveal the hopeless division of the government. Thus the discussion of the cabinet centered around the issue of how to release the contents of the Potsdam Proclamation, not whether the government should accept it. Since American radio broadcasting had already widely disseminated news of the ultimatum, the cabinet decided to have the press treat it as small news, summarizing the contents of the proclamation without any official comments so as not to lower the morale of the people. On July 28, newspapers reported on the Potsdam Proclamation. *Yomiuri Hochi* editorialized with the heading, "Laughable Surrender Conditions to Japan," but *Asahi Shinbun* had a more mild headline, "The Government Intends to *Mokusatsu* [Ignore It]." Both articles limited themselves to the conditions specified by the proclamation rather faithfully, but omitted the reference that Japanese soldiers would be allowed to go home to resume a peaceful life.[73]

On the morning of July 28, the Imperial General Headquarters and the government held an information-exchange meeting. Since this was a routine meeting, Togo did not attend. At this gathering, however, Anami, Umezu, and Toyoda insisted that the government should denounce the Potsdam Proclamation. Yonai objected, but he was overruled. In the end, Yonai suggested that Suzuki make an announcement that the government would ignore the Allied proclamation. Under the pressure of the military's strong view, Suzuki agreed to make a short statement at a press conference scheduled for that day. According to *Yomiuri Hochi,* Suzuki announced at the press conference: "I think that the joint statement is a rehash of the Cairo Declaration. The government does not think that it has serious value. We can only ignore [*mokusatsu*] it. We will do our utmost to complete the war to the bitter end." The same statement is recorded in various sources.[74]

Suzuki's statement at the news conference is widely known as the "mokusatsu" statement. "Mokusatsu" literally means "silently kill" and can be translated as "ignore." But there is a question as to whether Suzuki made the mokusatsu statement at the news conference. The government's intention to ignore [*mokusatsu*] the ultimatum had already been bandied around in newspapers on July 28, before Suzuki's news conference. Saiji Hasegawa of Domei, who attended the news conference, distinctly remembered that, asked whether the government would accept the Potsdam Proclamation, Suzuki said: "No comment."[75] It is plausible that newspaper reporters put the term "mokusatsu" into Suzuki's mouth, and that Suzuki himself never used the word.

Japan's first reaction to the Potsdam Proclamation came from the Domei News Agency, a semi-official news organization. It first reported on the ultimatum on the afternoon of July 27, that is, one day before Suzuki's press conference. This dispatch stated that according to authoritative sources, the government would ignore the joint proclamation, and "Japan will prosecute the war of Greater East Asia to the bitter end." The Associated Press in San Francisco caught the broadcast and reported on July 27: "The semi-official Japanese Domei news agency stated today that Allied ultimatum to surrender or meet destruction would be ignored, but official response was awaited as Japan's ruling warlords debated the demand." But in the second paragraph, the AP also reported that the Japanese government rejected the joint statement. Although Akira Naka believes that the AP's leap from "ignore" to "reject" is quite natural, there is a substantial difference between the two words in English. Japan's decision to "ignore" the proclamation was not the same as to "reject" it.

Nevertheless, whether or not Suzuki himself used the word, "mokusatsu" became known as Japan's official position on the Potsdam Proclamation. The peace party leaders were aware of the U.S. press's coverage of Japan's reaction to the joint proclamation, but none, not even Togo, strongly protested Suzuki's statement. If the emperor was dissatisfied with this statement, he could have summoned Suzuki to question and reprimand him. He did not. Togo said in his memoirs that he was upset with Suzuki's statement. He lodged a strong protest, but when he was told that there was no way to correct the statement, he took no further action.[76]

The major reason for Japan's lukewarm reaction to the proclamation can be found in the ultimatum's ambiguity over the question of the emperor. But what if the Potsdam Proclamation had contained the promise of a constitutional monarchy? In all likelihood, this would not have changed Japan's course of action drastically. Togo, Kido, and Hirohito would still have preferred to wait for Moscow's answer to Japan's request for mediation. Nonetheless, there is little question that the promise of a constitutional monarchy would have made the peace party more favorably disposed to the Potsdam ultimatum, while it would have weakened the war hawks' argument against it. Thus, it would have subtly changed the relative strength of the peace party and the war party. One can also argue that had the Potsdam Proclamation contained a promise for a constitutional monarchy, Suzuki's alleged "mokusatsu statement" may not have occurred, since the peace party, and above all Hirohito, would have been more careful not to give the Allies the impression that Japan would reject it.

The question is how Suzuki's vague statement became a justification to drop the atomic bomb. In his memoirs Truman three times mentioned Japan's reaction to the Potsdam Proclamation. The first reference came after he described Stalin's revelation of the Japanese peace overtures on July 28. Truman wrote: "Our ultimatum to the Japanese people of July 26 was broadcast continuously and also had been sent through the customary neutral diplomatic channels; that is, through the intermediaries of Switzerland and Sweden." The president made a fundamental error here, for the United States government had made a conscious decision to issue the Potsdam Proclamation not as a diplomatic document but as propaganda. There was no attempt to use the intermediaries of Switzerland and Sweden. Truman then stated: "No formal reply had come from the Japanese. But on this day, July 28 . . . our radio monitors reported that Radio Tokyo had reaffirmed the Japanese government's determination to fight. Our proclamation had been referred to as 'unworthy of consideration,' 'absurd,' and 'presumptuous.'"[77] Since the Potsdam Proclamation was issued as propaganda through the Office of War Information, it is not surprising that "no formal reply had come from the Japanese." Newspaper editorials that Truman cited were not the same as the government's official policy. Most important, Truman did not think that the Japanese had made a formal reply to the Potsdam Proclamation.

Truman's second reference came when he mentioned his decision to drop the atomic bomb. He wrote: "On July 28 Radio Tokyo announced that the Japanese government would continue to fight. There was no formal reply to the joint ultimatum of the United States, the United Kingdom, and China. There was no alternative now. The bomb was scheduled to be dropped after August 3 unless Japan surrendered before that day." No formal reply; that is, the ultimatum was "ignored," not "rejected." It was therefore Japan's silence and inaction that led to the dropping of the atomic bomb.[78]

Truman's story suddenly changed, however, when he described the dropping of the atomic bomb on Hiroshima. He wrote: "It was to spare the Japanese people from utter destruction that the ultimatum of July 26 was issued at Potsdam. Their leaders promptly rejected that ultimatum." Only after the dropping of the atomic bomb on Hiroshima was this decision associated with Japan's "prompt rejection" of the Potsdam Proclamation. But this is a fiction that Truman later created, and its veracity is disproven by Truman's own words. Contrary to what millions of Americans believe, the Japanese government never rejected the proclamation. Truman succeeded in perpetuating a myth. Dooman, a conservative diplomat, wrote: "There seemed to be an eagerness for grasping at any excuse for dropping the bomb." He noted that there was no official, formal reply from the Japanese government, and that Suzuki's remarks were an off-hand comment. "This casual remark by the Prime Minister," Dooman commented, "was seized upon and the order [to drop the bomb] was issued."[79]

Magic Intercepts after the Potsdam Ultimatum

On July 27, immediately after the Potsdam Proclamation was issued, Ambassador Sato fired off a telegram to Togo. The joint ultimatum, in Sato's view, was "intended as a threatening blast against us and as a prelude to a Three Power offensive." Since it was presumed that Moscow was fully consulted on this matter, "any aid from the Soviet Union has now become extremely doubtful and there can be little doubt that this ultimatum was meant to serve as a counterblast to our peace feelers." Sato also called the foreign minister's attention to the July 26 BBC coverage of the conference, which noted that Stalin had participated in the discussions regarding the war in the Far East.

Togo's attention was focused on the Soviet position on the Potsdam Proclamation. He was "deeply concerned as to whether this was related to Japan's proposal, i.e., whether the Russian Government communicated the latter to the English and Americans, and as to what attitude the Russians will take toward Japan in the future." The telegram thus instructed Sato to meet with Molotov as quickly as possible to find out Soviet intentions.[80] Togo's dispatch makes it clear that the Japanese government suspended judgment on the Potsdam ultimatum.

In his dispatch to Togo on July 28, Sato continued to assail the foreign minister's continuing reliance on negotiations through Moscow. Calling attention to the Potsdam Proclamation, which in his view provided more lenient peace terms than those given to Germany, Sato questioned the wisdom of attempting to use Moscow's mediation to terminate the war. As for the interview with Molotov, Sato warned: "I would particularly like to be informed whether our Imperial Government has a concrete and definite plan for terminating the war; otherwise I will make no immediate request for an interview."[81]

On July 30, Sato responded to Togo's telegram of July 28. In response to Togo's question about the extent of Stalin's involvement in the Potsdam Proclamation, Sato reported that the ultimatum was most likely communicated to Stalin before being released. He further asserted that the Konoe Mission must have been communicated to the United States and Britain, and that "the Joint Proclamation was issued in order to make clear the attitude of America, England, and China in response to our proposal." Sato noted that the Allies had demanded "Japan's immediate unconditional surrender" and had stated clearly that they had no intention of softening the terms. "If it is to be understood that Stalin was completely unable to influence the intentions of America and England," Sato deduced, "it follows that he will be unable to accept our proposal to send a Special Envoy." He then concluded: "There is no alternative but immediate unconditional surrender if we are to try to make America and England moderate and to prevent [Russia's] participation in the war."[82]

Sato was not necessarily a lone wolf in the wilderness crying for acceptance of unconditional surrender. On July 30, Shun'ichi Kase, Japanese minister to Switzerland, also dispatched a telegram from Bern urging Togo to accept the terms of the Potsdam Proclamation. Director of Information Shimomura had a meeting with Japan's leading industrialists on August 3. The consensus of the industrialists was that the government should accept the Potsdam terms. On the following day, Shimomura met with Togo and urged the foreign minister to make informal contact with the United States, Britain, and China, but Togo rejected this proposal.[83]

Despite his opposition to negotiations with Moscow, Sato dutifully paid a visit to Lozovskii on July 30, demanding a reply from the Soviet government with regard to the Konoe Mission. Lozovskii repeated that no reply was given owing to the absence of Stalin and Molotov. With respect to the Potsdam Proclamation, Sato reiterated that Japan was "completely unable to surrender unconditionally," but he stressed that the Japanese government was "taking a very broad and conciliatory attitude so long as its own honor and existence are guaranteed." All Lozovskii promised was to convey Sato's opinions to Molotov.[84]

On August 2, Togo replied to Sato's telegram of July 30. He began by saying that he understood Sato's views as the ambassador on the spot, but that he should know that "it is difficult to decide on concrete peace conditions here at home all in one stroke." Clearly, Togo was referring to domestic political pressure, especially the stiff opposition that he would have to overcome to attain a consensus for surrender. Then he added an important passage: "Under the circumstances there is a disposition to make the Potsdam 3-Power Declaration the basis of our study concerning terms." He further stated that the emperor was concerned with the development of the Moscow negotiations, and that "the Premier and the leaders of the Army are now concentrating all their attention on this one point."

The Naval intelligence analysts who examined these Magic intercepts noted: "The most prominent feature of the developments reflected in this Summary is the magnetic effect of the 3-Power Joint Ultimatum, which has polarized the views of 'all quarters' in Japan." It further added: "Although not yet agreed on the method" (except that there is "unanimous determination to ask the good offices of the Russians"), "there is a disposition (or determination) of finding in its terms a sufficiently effective emollient for the tortured pride which still rebels at the words 'unconditional surrender.'"[85]

The Magic intercepts revealed that at least some of Japan's leading diplomats recognized that unconditional surrender in the proclamation was limited to unconditional surrender of armed forces, and that without mentioning a word about the emperor and the emperor system, the proclamation left open the question of the fate of the emperor. They also indicated that Japan's foreign minister was contemplating the Potsdam terms as the basis of surrender terms. It is reasonable to assume that Truman, Byrnes, and Stimson were paying close attention to the Magic intercepts to see Japan's reaction to the Potsdam Proclamation.[86] They must have known, therefore, that the reaction of the Japanese government was entirely different from what Radio Tokyo had reported. If they wanted Japan's surrender at a minimal cost in American lives, if they wished to prevent Soviet entry into the war, and if they wanted to avoid the use of the atomic bomb, as they claimed in their postwar memoirs, why did they ignore the information obtained by the Magic intercepts?

It is true that there was no realistic possibility that the Japanese government would have accepted the Potsdam terms, as they were presented, at the end of July. Had Togo proposed acceptance, he would surely have encountered a powerful veto from the war party in the Big Six. Even Suzuki's and Yonai's support could not be assured. Moreover, Hirohito and Kido might not have consented to acceptance. The Japanese political elite, including the key figures in the peace party, were not yet ready to accept the Potsdam terms without assurance of the preservation of the *kokutai*, although they had not thought seriously about the precise meaning of the term. That was the reason Togo opted for Moscow's mediation. Nevertheless, the inclusion of a promise to allow the Japanese to retain a constitutional monarchy might have tipped the delicate balance between the peace party and the war party in favor of the former.

It is unlikely that Truman and Byrnes knew about the intricate dynamics of Japanese politics, but if they read the Magic intercepts, they must have known that the Japanese foreign minister was willing to make the Potsdam terms the basis for terminating the war. Why did they not wait for the outcome of Japan's proposal to Moscow, which they knew would fail? Perhaps these "murmurs" in the Magic intercepts were too weak a signal to overturn the wheels of atomic deployment already in motion. After all, Sato's and Kase's views advocating the acceptance of the Potsdam terms were not the views the Japanese government followed. Truman and Byrnes knew that against Sato's and Kase's advice, the Japanese government was still looking for Moscow's help, and they also knew that Moscow would betray this hope by announcing its declaration of war against Japan.

Perhaps it is unfair to judge Truman's decision on the basis of what we now know about Japanese politics. But even in the face of what was known, and should have been known to Truman, Byrnes, and Stimson, one cannot escape the conclusion that the United States rushed to drop the bomb without any attempt to explore the readiness of some Japanese policymakers to seek peace through the ultimatum.

Chiang Kai-shek's Reaction to the Potsdam Proclamation

Chiang Kai-shek was not invited to the Potsdam Conference, but China's presence loomed large at the meeting. The Chinese leader was one of the three heads of state to sign the Potsdam Proclamation. Moreover, China represented a source of contention over which Stalin and Truman engaged in subtle maneuvers.

Revisionist historians argue that the United States exploited the stalemate in the Sino-Soviet negotiations and put pressure on the Chinese to hang tough in order to prevent the Soviets from entering the war.[87] Contemporary documents do not bear out this assertion, however. The Chinese had their own interests, which were not completely identical with those of the United States. In fact, independent of the American desire, the Chinese Nationalists were refashioning their posture toward the forthcoming negotiations with Stalin. Truman told Chiang Kai-shek through Hurley to "carry out the Yalta Agreement," though he cautioned him not to make any concessions in excess of the agreement. The president added: "If you and Generalissimo Stalin differ as to the correct interpretation of the Yalta agreement, I hope you will arrange for Soong to return to Moscow and continue your efforts to reach complete understanding." Byrnes also urged Hurley to "tell Soong to return to Moscow and continue discussing in hope of reaching agreement." These were hardly messages urging the Chinese to sabotage the negotiations. Ambassador Hurley repeatedly supported a Sino-Soviet treaty in his frequent meetings with Chiang and Soviet Ambassador Apollon Petrov.[88] At the meeting with Petrov on July 27, Hurley revealed that the Chinese had asked Truman to make a few revisions to the Yalta Agreement. "To this, Truman answered that he agrees with the Crimean [Yalta] decisions," Hurley told Petrov, "does not want to make any revisions, and suggested that the Chinese government agree with all its provisions with the Soviet government." Both Truman and Byrnes made it clear that the Chinese should not have an agreement with the Soviets that exceeded the Yalta limits, but they still remained committed to the Yalta Agreement.

On July 28, Petrov visited Chiang Kai-shek at his summer residence. The Soviet ambassador asked him how he thought Japan would react to the Potsdam Proclamation. Chiang Kai-shek remarked: "It is hard now to expect any kind of results. I think it will take three months for this measure to have any effect." Petrov also asked if this joint ultimatum to

Japan might significantly contribute to the demoralization of the Japanese spirit. Chiang answered that "the entry of the Soviet Union into the war against Japan would be a more significant, stronger, and more important measure than this communiqué."[89] Chiang Kai-shek rested more hope on Soviet entry into the war than on the Potsdam Proclamation as the best method to end the war, and this judgment, not American pressure, was the most important principle guiding China's policy toward the forthcoming negotiations with the Soviet Union.

Although Harriman was excluded from the decision-making process at Potsdam, the ambassador was preoccupied with the Stalin-Soong negotiations. On July 28 he wrote a memo to Byrnes, recommending that the president provide clarifications on the Yalta Agreement with regard to the port of Dairen and the operations of the railroads in Manchuria. What concerned Harriman more than anything else was ensuring an Open Door policy in the port of Dairen to protect American interests. Far from attempting to obstruct an accord, Harriman supported the conclusion of the Sino-Soviet agreement before Soviet entry into the war. The same memorandum to Byrnes stated: "Although it may not be desirable for us at this time to show any concern over the question of Russia's entry into the war against Japan, it would seem that there are substantial advantages in the reestablishment of friendly relations between the Soviet Union and China, particularly the agreement that the Soviet Government will support the Chinese National[ist] Government as the unifying force in China."[90] Contrary to the revisionist assertion, both Harriman and Hurley were in favor of an early Sino-Soviet agreement, and there is no evidence to indicate that either Truman or Byrnes put pressure on the Chinese to stall negotiations in order to prevent Soviet entry into the war.

On July 30 Truman received a telegram from Stimson, who had left Potsdam for Washington on July 25. In this telegram the secretary of war informed the president: "The time schedule on Groves' project is progressing so rapidly that it is now essential that [a] statement for release by you be available not later than Wednesday, 1 August." Stimson planned to send a draft statement by special courier, but in case he could not reach the president in time, he requested Truman's authorization to "have [the] White House release [a] revised statement as soon as necessary." In response to Stimson's request, Truman replied on July 31: "Suggestion approved. Release when ready but not sooner than August 2."[91] Although David McCullough identifies Truman's telegram as his "final go-ahead for the bomb," the dispatch was merely his approval to release the statement on the atomic bomb. In fact, despite his later claim that he issued the order to drop the bomb on his voyage back to the United States somewhere in the middle of the Atlantic, the president never issued such an order. The fact is that the atomic bomb was dropped without Truman's explicit order. Indeed, the deployment of the atomic bomb was proceeding like clockwork ever since Handy's order to Spaatz on July 25.[92]

The Big Three met for the last time on August 1. Truman, as chairman, announced the end of the conference. Stalin made a little speech praising Byrnes, "who had worked harder perhaps than any of us." We do not know if Stalin meant this sincerely or if his remarks concealed a sharp sarcasm. Stalin left Berlin that day, and Truman left early on the morning of August 2. It was on his way back to the United States, near Newfoundland, on Monday, August 6, that Truman received the news that the atomic bomb had been dropped on Hiroshima.

The race between the atomic bomb and Soviet entry into the war had finally reached its last, most dramatic moment.

CHAPTER 5

The Atomic Bombs and Soviet
Entry into the War

STALIN RESPONDED QUICKLY to what he perceived to be secret American maneuvers. At Potsdam he had told Truman that the Soviet Union would enter the war by the middle of August, but Antonov had told the American Chiefs of Staff that the Soviets would be ready to join the war in the last half of August. In all likelihood, the date of attack had remained some time between August 20 and 25, as set before the Potsdam Conference. With American possession of the atomic bomb and Truman's manipulation of the Potsdam ultimatum, however, Stalin changed the timetable for the Soviet attack. It appears that while still in Potsdam, he ordered Marshal Vasilevskii to move up the operation by ten to fourteen days.[1]

On July 30, one day after Truman rejected Stalin's request to append his signature to the Potsdam Proclamation, Stalin appointed Vasilevskii supreme commander of the Soviet troops in the Far East effective August 1. On August 2, Stavka ordered the formation of three fronts: the First Far Eastern Front, commanded by Marshal Kirill Meretskov, the Second Far Eastern Front, commanded by General Maksim Purkaev, and the Transbaikal Front, commanded by Marshal Rodion Malinovskii. The cloak of secrecy under which Stalin had prepared for the attack of Japan had been cast off, and the formidable Soviet war machine was about to be set in motion.[2]

On August 3, Chief of Staff Colonel General S. P. Ivanov and Colonel General Vasiliev (pseudonym of Marshal Vasilevskii) sent an important

report to Stalin and Antonov. Vasilevskii stated that by August 5 the Soviet forces at the First and Second Far Eastern Fronts would complete
their advance to the designated points of concentration about 50 to 60
kilometers from the border. In order to maximize the effect of surprise,
he emphasized that it would be important for the attack to begin "on
the same day and at the same hour" on the two fronts. Vasilevskii estimated that once they received the instruction to attack, it would take
three to five days to cross the border. Thus the optimal time of attack
would be August 9–10. He further requested that Stavka give him final
instructions for the precise time that military action should begin, as well
as instructions regarding questions of a "political and diplomatic nature."[3]

This report reveals two important facts. First, it was clearly sent in response to Stalin's earlier instructions to advance the date of attack by ten
to fourteen days from the previously agreed-upon date between August
20 and August 25. Since this report was sent on August 3, Stalin's order
must have been sent earlier than that date, most likely from Potsdam before he left for Moscow on August 2. There is little doubt that Stalin hastened the date of attack in response to what he perceived as an American
maneuver to achieve Japan's surrender before Soviet entry into the war.
Vasilevskii's reference to questions of a "political and diplomatic nature"
associated with the date of attack reinforces this point.

Second, though the date of attack was set some time on either August 9
or August 10, the precise timing was still left undecided. Sometime between August 3 and August 7, Stavka must have decided that the precise
timing of the attack was to be at midnight (Transbaikal time) on August
11 (6 P.M. Moscow time on August 10).[4]

Stalin returned to Moscow on the evening of August 5. His appointment log for August 5 shows that immediately after his arrival
at the Kremlin, he frantically resumed work. He met with senior officials, including Foreign Commissar Molotov, Deputy Foreign Commissar Vyshinskii, NKVD Commissar Beria, Navy Commissar
Kuznetsov, and Mikoyan, the head of Lend-Lease. It is almost certain that at least part of the meeting was devoted to the war in the Far
East and the possibility of the Americans' using the atomic bomb. It is
also safe to assume that Stalin was constantly in touch with General
Antonov of the General Staff, most likely through direct military telephone lines.[5]

The U.S. Drops the Atomic Bomb on Hiroshima

By July 31 Little Boy was ready, but a typhoon in Japan delayed the operation. Meanwhile, plans were being made for the bombing flights. Seven planes were to take part in the mission: three B-29s acting as weather observers were to fly to Hiroshima, Kokura, and Nagasaki; two planes would escort the bombing plane to the target, one with scientists, one with photographers; and one other plane would stand by at Iwo Jima to take over if the bomber experienced trouble. On August 4, Colonel Paul Tibbets held a briefing of the mission for his crew, revealing for the first time that they would be dropping the atomic bomb on Hiroshima, Kokura, or Nagasaki. Capt. William S. Parsons, the navy officer assigned to assemble the first atomic bomb, showed the flight crews a motion picture of the Trinity test. One of the crew members, Abe Spitzer, who secretly kept notes of the briefing, recorded his impressions: "It is like some weird dream, conceived by one with too vivid an imagination."[6]

On the following day, August 5, weather forecasters predicted improved conditions. At 2 P.M., Curtis LeMay, Chief of Staff of the 21st Bomber Command in Guam, "officially confirmed that the mission would take place on August 6." That afternoon, Little Boy was loaded into the B-29, which Tibbets named *Enola Gay* after his mother. By dinnertime, all preparations were completed.

Tibbets called the final briefing at midnight. A Protestant chaplain read the prayer hastily written on the back of an envelope, asking the Almighty Father "to be with those who brave the heights of Thy Heaven and who carry the battle to our enemies." After a preflight breakfast and a group picture in front of the hardstand, the crew boarded the plane. At 2:45 A.M. (11:45 on August 5 in Washington) the *Enola Gay* took off, followed by two B-29 observation planes at two-minute intervals. At 8:15 A.M. (Hiroshima time) Little Boy was dropped on Hiroshima. Tibbets announced in the interphone: "Fellows, you have just dropped the first atomic bomb in history."[7]

Little Boy exploded 1,900 feet above the courtyard of Shima Hospital, 550 feet off its target, Aioi Bridge over Ota River, with a yield equivalent to 12,500 tons of TNT. The temperature at ground zero reached 5,400°F, immediately creating a fireball within half a mile, roasting people "to bundles of smoking black char in a fraction of a second as their internal organs boiled away." Thousands of such charred bundles were strewn in the streets, sidewalks, and bridges. A man sitting on the steps of a bank waiting for it to open vaporized, leaving only his shadow on the granite steps.

The blast that followed the explosion destroyed thousands of houses, burning most of them. Of 76,000 buildings in Hiroshima, 70,000 were destroyed. Fire broke out all over the city, devouring everything in its path. People walked aimlessly in eerie silence, many black with burns, the skin peeling from their bodies. Others frantically ran to look for their missing loved ones. Thousands of dead bodies floated in the river. Everywhere there was "massive pain, suffering, and horror," unspeakable and unprecedented. Then the black rain fell, soaking everyone with radiation. Those who survived the initial shock began to die from radiation sickness. According to one study conducted by the cities of Hiroshima and Nagasaki, 110,000 civilians and 20,000 military personnel were killed instantly. By the end of 1945, 140,000 had perished.[8]

On August 6, four days after leaving Plymouth, Truman was having lunch with the *Augusta* crew when Captain Frank Graham of the White House Map Room handed him a report with the message "Big bomb dropped on Hiroshima August 5 at 7:15 P.M. Washington time. First reports indicate complete success which was even more conspicuous than earlier test." The president beamed. He jumped to his feet and shook hands with Graham. "Captain," he said, "this is the greatest thing in history." He told Graham to take the message to Byrnes, who was seated at another table. Byrnes read the message and exclaimed, "Fine! Fine!" A few minutes later the second message arrived, which reported "visible effects greater than in any test." Truman signaled the crew in the mess hall and announced: "We have just dropped a new bomb on Japan which more power than twenty thousand tons of TNT. It has been an overwhelming success!" Truman and Byrnes then went to the officers' wardroom to announce the news.[9]

Meanwhile, Eben Ayers in the White House released a previously approved message from the president: "A short time ago an American airplane dropped one bomb on Hiroshima and destroyed its usefulness to the enemy. That bomb has more power than 20,000 tons of T.N.T." The statement went on to say that the Japanese had begun the war by attacking Pearl Harbor, and that the bombing of Hiroshima was retribution for that act. The statement declared that "the bombs are now in production and even more powerful forms are in development." Truman's message ended with a dire warning:

> It was to spare the Japanese people from utter destruction that the ultimatum of July 26 was issued at Potsdam. Their leaders promptly rejected that ultimatum. If they do not now accept our terms they may expect a rain of ruin from the air, the like of which has never been seen on this earth. Behind this air attack will follow sea and land forces in such numbers and power as they have not yet seen and with the fighting skill of which they are already well aware.[10]

Three aspects of Truman's response are worth emphasizing. First, when Truman received the news that the atomic bomb had been dropped on Hiroshima, his immediate reaction was jubilation; there was no hint of remorse or pain, contrary to his later claim that the decision had been a painful one for him. How can we explain his excitement? To begin with, he had not yet received a detailed report of the damage the Hiroshima bomb had inflicted on civilians. Presumably, it took a little while to translate the 12.5 kiloton TNT explosion into a casualty figure of more than 100,000. Naturally, as any leader of a nation fighting a war, he was preoccupied with saving his own troops from further sacrifices. In this sense, his heart was with all those sailors and officers who surrounded him and shouted, "Does this mean we can go home now?"

Another key point in Truman's prepared message was the reference to Japan's attack on Pearl Harbor. In an interview with Eben Ayers in August 1951, Truman recalled that at Potsdam he was told by military leaders that at least a million American soldiers would be involved in the homeland invasion, and that casualties would be about 25 percent. According to Ayers, "He said he asked what the population of Hiroshima was and his recollection was that they said about 60,000. He said that it was far better to kill 60,000 Japanese than to have 250,000 Americans killed." In August 1945, the population of Hiroshima was 280,000 to 290,000 civilians and 43,000 servicemen, for a total of 323,000 to 333,000 people.[11] It is therefore a mystery where Truman found this figure. Nor is it clear if this was the number he later came to believe and clung to in order to justify his decision to himself. Regardless, the fact that he compared 250,000 Americans saved with 60,000 Japanese killed was indicative of his thought process in August 1945. Punishing the Japanese, soldiers and civilians alike, with atomic devastation represented in Truman's mind a just retribution against the "savage and cruel people" who had dared to make a sneak attack on Pearl Harbor and mistreat American POWs.

Equally important was Truman's reference to Japan's "prompt" rejection of the Potsdam ultimatum as a justification for the Hiroshima bomb. As noted, Truman in his memoirs twice wrote that Japan had not responded to the joint ultimatum. The naval intelligence analysts underlined the passage in Togo's July 30 dispatch stating that "there is a disposition to make the Potsdam 3-Power Declaration the basis of our study concerning the terms." Also, the OSS in Washington sent a memorandum to the president on August 2, informing him that the Japanese group in Bern had accepted the Potsdam Proclamation "as [an] astute document which left a possible way out." The Japanese group was especially impressed by the qualified term "unconditional surrender" of "Japanese armed forces." The Japanese group emphasized that the Allies should not take "too seriously what was said over Tokyo radio," since the radio comment was merely "propaganda to maintain morale in Japan." The group indicated to Allen Dulles that the real reply would be given through some "official channel."[12]

There is no evidence to show that Truman and Byrnes actually saw these reports. But if Truman wanted to avoid dropping the bomb on Japan, he would have made arrangements to scrutinize any signs of the Japanese government's willingness to negotiate surrender terms on the basis of the Potsdam Proclamation. There exists no documentary evidence indicating internal discussion at the highest level of the administration about Japan's reaction to the proclamation. If Truman was truly pained by the decision to drop the bomb, as he repeatedly asserted in his postwar statements, why did he not exploit the flicker of hope glimmering through these messages?

One possible answer is that Truman expected a ferocious last-ditch defense from the Japanese. The information coming from naval intelligence and the OSS indicating the willingness of the Japanese government to accept the Potsdam terms must be weighed against the hard evidence that the president must have received from the JCS about the massive military reinforcements the Japanese goverment had implemented in the defense of Kyushu.[13] Truman was well aware that once he insisted upon unconditional surrender in the Potsdam Proclamation, Japan would fight the war to the bitter end. His objectives were twofold: to impose unconditional surrender and to save American lives. He was not interested in a negotiated peace. He feared that any negotiations with the Japanese government might be taken as a sign of weakness. Any weakening of the U.S. stand on unconditional surrender might strengthen the war party in Japan, reinforcing their will to fight on. Domestically, such weakness would diminish his credibility as president.

This argument, however, reinforces the fact that Truman was not really interested in Japan's reaction to the Potsdam ultimatum. Suzuki's statement at the news conference, reported in the press, not through official diplomatic channels, was sufficient for him to conclude that the Japanese government "promptly rejected" the ultimatum. In fact, the atomic bomb provided Truman with the answer to the dilemma of imposing unconditional surrender on Japan and saving American lives. Thus, he was eager to use the atomic bomb rather than explore other alternatives.[14]

An important issue was conspicuously absent from the president's message: the possibility of Soviet entry into the war. Obviously, Soviet participation in the war would take the form of a surprise attack, and thus the president could not say anything about it. Nonetheless, Soviet entry played an important part in the American decision to speed up the dropping of the atomic bombs. Truman was in a hurry. He was aware that the race was on between the atomic bomb and Soviet entry into the war. That was why he concocted the story of Japan's "prompt rejection" of the Potsdam Proclamation as the justification for the atomic bomb, and that was also the reason he was ecstatic to receive the news of the Hiroshima bomb. The atomic bomb represented to Truman a solution to all the dilemmas he faced: unconditional surrender, the cost of Japan's homeland invasion, and Soviet entry into the war. He was jubilant at news of the atomic bomb on Hiroshima, not because of a perverted joy in killing the Japanese, but because of the satisfaction that everything had gone as he had planned.

Japan Reacts to the Hiroshima Bomb

As the race between Stalin and Truman accelerated, another, deadly competition was intensifying inside Japan: a race between those determined to end the war and those who wanted to wage a last-ditch defense of the homeland. In the desperate struggle for national survival, both groups redefined the previously ambiguous concept of *kokutai* to fit their own objectives.

Because the atomic bomb wiped out all means of communication, news of the devastation of Hiroshima did not reach Tokyo until the evening of August 6. The first news was brought to the Imperial General Headquarters from the Kure Navy Depot, which revealed that the United States had used "a new weapon of unprecedented destructiveness." Cabinet Secretary Sakomizu received a report from the Army Ministry in the afternoon "about the complete destruction of Hiroshima and the unspeakable damage inflicted by one bomb with unusually high effectiveness," and he immediately informed Prime Minister Suzuki and the other ministers. Sakomizu also relayed the news to the imperial palace. As soon as Deputy Chief of Staff Kawabe received word of Hiroshima's complete destruction by one bomb, he immediately surmised that it was the atomic bomb.[15] Then, before dawn on August 7, American shortwave radio stations began to broadcast Truman's message announcing that an atomic bomb had been dropped on Hiroshima. Hasegawa of Domei News relayed the information to Sakomizu and Togo at 3:30 A.M. Word of the atomic bomb was sent to the emperor on the morning of August 7, as well as to the cabinet ministers.

On the afternoon of August 7, Suzuki called a cabinet meeting. Despite the claim that this meeting was a decisive turning point, prompting some members of the cabinet to advocate openly acceptance of the Potsdam terms, there is no evidence to support this assertion. Togo informed the cabinet that Truman had announced that the United States had dropped an atomic bomb on Hiroshima. Anami cast doubt on this information and reported that the army had decided to send a special investigating team to Hiroshima. He proposed that before taking any action the government should wait for the results of this investigation. The cabinet accepted this proposal, and Togo did not protest the decision. But he did propose, and the cabinet agreed, that Japan should register strong protest through the International Red Cross and the Swiss legation about the U.S. use of the atomic bomb as a serious violation of international law prohibiting poisonous gas. Anami's diary, however, betrayed his shock. In the entry of August 7, he admitted that Hiroshima had been attacked by the atomic bomb, and he consulted Japan's leading nuclear physicists about the implication of uranium bombs.[16]

One day after the atomic bomb was dropped, neither the cabinet nor any member of the peace party believed that any change of policy was needed. Most members of the cabinet knew that unless Japan surrendered, many atomic bombs might be dropped on other cities in Japan. In fact, far from entertaining the possibility of accepting the Potsdam terms, the cabinet was outright combative against the United States. The army's investigating team immediately concluded that the device was indeed the atomic bomb, but they did not return to Tokyo until August 10.[17]

On August 7, Togo dispatched an extremely urgent telegram to Ambassador Sato in Moscow. "The situation is becoming more and more pressing," the foreign minister urged the ambassador. "We must know the Soviets' attitude immediately. Therefore, do your best once more to obtain their reply immediately." Togo still clung to the hope that the war could be ended through Moscow's intervention. Sato's reply to Togo, informing the foreign minister that Molotov had agreed to meet him at five in the afternoon on August 8, reached the Foreign Ministry at noon on August 8. All policymakers in Japan were now waiting for Molotov's reply.[18]

On the following morning, August 8, Togo went to the imperial palace for an audience with the emperor. "Now that such a new weapon has appeared," the emperor told Togo, "it has become less and less possible to continue the war. We must not miss a chance to terminate the war by bargaining for more favorable conditions now. . . . So my wish is to make such arrangements as to end the war as soon as possible."[19] Hirohito urged Togo to "do [his] utmost to bring about a prompt termination of the war," and he told the foreign minister to convey his desire to Prime Minister Suzuki. Togo met with Suzuki and proposed that the Supreme War Council be convened immediately.

There was no question that the Hiroshima bomb had a great impact on the emperor, convincing him of the urgency with which Japan had to terminate the war. Nevertheless, his statement on August 8 should not be taken as a wish to end the war by accepting the Potsdam terms. The question to the Japanese ruling elite was how to terminate the war while preserving the *kokutai,* and the Potsdam Proclamation had left the future of the emperor's position ambiguous. As long as they still felt they might preserve the *kokutai* or negotiate with the Allies with Moscow's help, they would press on. The Hiroshima bomb did not change this situation, though it certainly made the need to obtain Moscow's answer to the

Konoe mission more pressing. According to Toyoda's postwar testimony, "the situation had not progressed to the point where one atomic bomb would force us to discuss the possibility of terminating the war."[20]

There is no convincing evidence to show that the Hiroshima bomb had a direct and immediate impact on Japan's decision to surrender. All that can be said is that the damage it inflicted on Hiroshima made the determination of some leaders—including the emperor, Kido, and Togo—to terminate the war as quickly as possible even greater. Nevertheless, it did not lead to their decision to accept the Potsdam terms. If anything, the atomic bomb on Hiroshima further contributed to their desperate effort to terminate the war through Moscow's mediation.

Stalin Reacts to the Hiroshima Bomb

Pravda did not report anything about the atomic bombing of Hiroshima on August 7, and only on August 8 did it report Truman's statement on the bomb at the bottom of page 4, without comments. *Pravda*'s silence on August 7 speaks volumes about the profound shock the Soviet leadership must have felt at the news. Stalin became depressed. The Soviet dictator regarded the American decision to drop the bomb as an act of hostility directed against the Soviet Union, first, to beat the USSR in the race to force Japan's surrender before the Soviet entry into the war, and second, to bully the Soviet Union from a position of strength. Now that the atomic bomb had been used against Japan, Stalin became convinced that the Americans had beaten him in the race to the finish in the Pacific War. His appointment log shows that, though he was extremely active on August 5, conducting successive meetings with major Politburo members until 11 P.M., he refused to see anyone on August 6, the day he received news of the Hiroshima bomb. This behavior was quite reminiscent of his reaction to the Nazi invasion of the Soviet Union in June 1941.[21]

The Chinese delegation headed by T. V. Soong arrived in Moscow on the afternoon of August 7. While waiting at the airport, Harriman asked Molotov what he thought about the Japanese reaction to the atomic bomb. Molotov replied: "Well, I have not heard yet," and commented, "You Americans can keep a secret when you want to."[22] When the Chinese delegation arrived, Molotov told the Chinese that Japan was on the verge of collapse. Considering Molotov's dejected mood, it is likely that the foreign commissar did not know at that time that the Kremlin had received new information about Japan's reaction to the atomic bomb.

Something important happened on the afternoon of August 7. The day before, having learned that Molotov had returned to Moscow, Ambassador Sato had contacted Lozovskii, requesting a meeting with Molotov to find out Moscow's answer to the Konoe mission. Sato received no reply. But on August 7, he again contacted Lozovskii to make an appointment with Molotov regarding the Konoe mission. Sato's request on August 7 had special meaning: it was an unmistakable sign that Tokyo had not surrendered despite the atomic bomb.

On receiving this news, Stalin leapt into action. He ordered Vasilevskii to begin the Manchurian operation at midnight on August 9, thus moving up the date of attack by forty-eight hours. Accordingly, Vasilevskii immediately issued four directives, each ordering all forces on the Transbaikal Front, the First and the Second Far Eastern Fronts, and the Pacific Fleet to begin operations at 12:00 midnight Transbaikal time.[23]

In late afternoon on August 7, Ambassador Sato finally received the news that he had been waiting for: Molotov would see the ambassador in his office at 6 P.M. on the evening of August 8. But the appointment time was soon changed to 5 P.M. At 7:50 P.M. on August 7, Sato dispatched a telegram to Togo, informing the foreign minister that Molotov was to meet with him at 5 P.M. the following day.[24] Stalin also decided to have a meeting with the Chinese delegation at 10 P.M. at the Kremlin, giving the Chinese only a few hours to rest after their arrival that afternoon.[25]

Stalin's appointment log for the evening of August 7 shows that he suddenly resumed intensive activity. He first met with Molotov at 9:30 P.M. From 10:10 to 11:40 P.M. he met with T. V. Soong and the Chinese delegation, and after that meeting, he conferred with Voroshilov until 1:10 A.M. on August 8.[26] Stalin most likely discussed with Molotov and Voroshilov diplomatic and military preparations for the war against Japan.

Stalin Resumes Negotiations with Soong

Harriman returned to his post in Moscow on August 6. The ambassador had been preoccupied with the question of China while in Potsdam. Byrnes did not reply to Harriman's recommendation to intervene more actively in Sino-Soviet negotiations. Disturbed by Byrnes's silence, before he left Potsdam Harriman "wrote out the instructions he wanted from the State Department in order to counter Stalin's stepped-up demands on China." In this memorandum, he asked for Byrnes's permission to tell Stalin that the United States would not support Soviet insistence on a lease for Dairen, which should be an open port administered by an international commission. Byrnes's instructions, which repeated almost word-for-word Harriman's memorandum, reached Moscow on August 5.[27]

After T. V. Soong arrived in Moscow, Harriman met with him briefly. Immediately after this meeting, Harriman sent a memo to the president and Byrnes, informing them of Chiang Kai-shek's intention to comply with Stalin's demand to include the larger area surrounding Port Arthur in the Soviet military zone. Harriman stated that he and Deane had no objections to this concession as long as "the free port area of Dairen and the connecting railway are not included in the Soviet military zone and the port is under Chinese administration."[28]

Stalin's request to meet with the Chinese delegation that very night surprised Soong, but Stalin was in a hurry: he had less than twenty-four hours to conclude a treaty with the Chinese before the Soviet attack on Manchuria. Before the meeting Soong managed to slip a handwritten note to Harriman, suggesting that the ambassador also request to meet Stalin that evening.[29] A delicate maneuvering between Soong and Harriman had begun. Soong, surrounded by pro-Soviet members of the delegation and under instruction from Chiang Kai-shek to come up with an agreement, wished to resist Stalin's expected demands for concessions on the port and the railways, while Harriman attempted to use Soong to protect American interests in the open port of Dairen. Revisionist historians are wrong, however, in asserting that Harriman's actions were meant to pressure Soong to resist Stalin's demand in order to prevent Soviet entry into the war against Japan.

As soon as Soong entered the room in the Kremlin, he was greeted by Stalin's impatient question: "What news have you brought?" Soong mentioned only Chiang Kai-shek's meeting with Ambassador Petrov on July 16, which must have disappointed Stalin, who expected a breakthrough in the negotiations. Both sides once again clashed over Dairen. Soong proposed that Dairen be a free port administered by the Chinese, as Harriman had demanded, while Stalin insisted on the Soviets' preeminent position over the control of Dairen. Soong emphasized that Chinese sovereignty in Manchuria was at stake in this issue. China had already made a number of concessions on Outer Mongolia, Port Arthur, and the railways; thus it was time for the Soviet side to make a small concession. Stalin responded that the Soviet side demanded these concessions in order to prepare for the future Japanese threat. Japan would surrender only to revive in thirty years. The Soviet ports in the Far East were not connected with railways. That was the reason the Soviets insisted on Port Arthur and Dairen.[30] Differences over Dairen did not narrow, and the negotiations on August 7 failed to produce an agreement.

The Stalin-Soong talk on August 7 tells us something important about Stalin's approach to Japan. Fueling Stalin's demand for Chinese concessions on Outer Mongolia, Port Arthur, and Dairen was his fear of Japan's potential revival. His approach was governed by geostrategic concerns, not ideology. To Stalin, the most important objective for entering the war against Japan was to obtain what he thought he had been promised at Yalta. He was not prepared to sacrifice his entitlements for the sake of reaching an agreement with the Chinese, even if he was obligated to "express his readiness" to conclude an agreement. He correctly judged that once Soviet tanks penetrated into Manchuria, the Americans and the Chinese would not condemn the Soviet action against Japan as a violation of the Yalta Agreement for fear that Stalin might change his mind about supporting the Nationalist Government as the sole legitimate government in China.

Moscow Declares War against Japan

In Tokyo, at around two o'clock in the morning on August 9, Cabinet Secretary Sakomizu completed all the arrangements for the forthcoming Supreme War Council and finally went to bed, thinking about Sato's meeting with Molotov that should have been taking place in Moscow at that time, and wondering what answer Molotov would give Sato about the Konoe mission.[31] That same day in Washington, the president resumed work after returning from Potsdam. When Sakomizu went to bed in Tokyo, it was lunchtime in Washington.

Ambassador Sato, accompanied by Embassy Secretary Shigeto Yuhashi, arrived at Molotov's office at the People's Commissariat of Foreign Affairs.[32] Sato had no illusions about Molotov's reply to the Konoe Mission. Nevertheless, what happened at this fateful moment was far beyond his imagination. Ushered into Molotov's office, the ambassador began his usual greetings. Molotov interrupted him, signaled him to stop, and asked him to sit down, since he had an important declaration to read in the name of the Soviet government. Molotov then began to read the Soviet declaration of war against Japan.

The declaration asserted that since Japan had refused the Potsdam Proclamation, "the proposal of the Japanese Government to the Soviet

Union concerning mediation in the war in the Far East thereby loses all basis." It further explained: "the Allies approached the Soviet Government with a proposal to join in the war against Japanese aggression and thereby shorten the length of the war, reduce the number of victims, and assist in the prompt reestablishment of general peace." Faithful to its obligations to its Allies, the Soviet government accepted this proposal and adhered to the Potsdam Proclamation. The Soviet government considered this action to be "the only means of hastening the coming peace" and "[saving] the Japanese people from the same destruction as Germany had suffered." It concluded: "the Soviet Government declares that as of tomorrow, that is, as of August 9, the Soviet Union will consider itself in a state of war with Japan."[33]

Having read the text of the declaration aloud, Molotov handed a copy to the ambassador. Sato took the copy and asked Molotov in a low voice to read it again. Molotov told Sato that simultaneously Ambassador Malik in Tokyo was making the same declaration to the Japanese government. Sato replied that he did not quite understand the Soviet decision to enter the war in order to save the Japanese people from further destruction; he had thought that Soviet non-participation in the war in the Far East would reduce the sacrifices of the Japanese people, especially at a time when the Japanese government was asking the Soviet Union for help in ending the war.[34]

The ambassador then asked if he could send a coded telegram before "midnight tonight" to the home government about the declaration of war as well as the contents of his conversation with Molotov. Molotov raised no objection. Sato, however, did not catch the important ambiguity that was intentionally left in the text of the Soviet declaration of war. It merely announced that the state of war would begin "as of tomorrow, that is, as of August 9," without specifying which time zone the Soviet Union would use to enter the war. Sato must have taken it for granted that they were using Moscow time without realizing that Transbaikal time was six hours and Khabarovsk time seven hours ahead of Moscow time. Sato's telegram, however, never reached Tokyo; most likely it never even left Moscow. Presumably, the Soviet government halted all telegraph service to Japan to ensure that the Soviet attack was a complete surprise.

With sarcasm shrouded in old-fashioned diplomatic formality, Sato expressed his profound appreciation to Molotov for working with him to keep both countries neutral during three difficult years, insinuating that in reality Molotov had been deceiving the ambassador and the Japanese government for four months after the Soviet abrogation of the Neutrality Pact. Molotov embraced Sato, and the two bid farewell.[35]

The Soviet claim that the Allies had asked Moscow to join the Potsdam Proclamation was a brazen lie. The war was going to start within an hour, and Stalin had to find a justification for violating the Neutrality Pact. He had no choice but to fabricate a motive, hoping the Allies would swallow it. The declaration avoided any reference to the Neutrality Pact, but with this alleged invitation and the commitment to the Allies, it implied that the Soviet government could be absolved of the violation of the Neutrality Pact. In 1941, Matsuoka had told Soviet Ambassador Smetanin that Japan's commitment to the Tripartite Pact took precedence over its commitment to the Neutrality Pact. In 1945, what the Soviet government declared to the Japanese was that its commitment to the Potsdam Proclamation took precedence over its commitment to the Neutrality Pact. The only difference was that the Soviet government had neither signed the Potsdam Proclamation nor been invited to sign it.

On the way back to the embassy, Sato glumly told Yuhashi in the car: "The inevitable has now arrived."[36]

Harriman Meets Stalin

After Ambassador Sato left the room, Molotov asked British Ambassador Archibald Clerk Kerr and American Ambassador Harriman to come to his office at seven o'clock. He told both men that he had presented the Japanese ambassador with a declaration of war two hours before. He emphasized that the Soviet government had now strictly lived up to its promise to enter the war three months after the defeat of Germany. Molotov further stated that the announcement of the Soviet entry into the war would be given to press and radio correspondents at 8:30 Moscow time that evening (2:30 A.M. Tokyo time and 1:30 P.M. Washington time).[37] This information, accompanied by the text of the Soviet declaration of war against Japan, was immediately dispatched to Washington.

Harriman then met with Stalin and expressed his gratitude at the Soviet entry into the war. He told him how happy he felt that the United States and the Soviet Union were allies again. Stalin reported the situation in the Far East in surprising detail. He explained how far the Soviet troops had advanced on each front in Manchuria, and announced that an attack on southern Sakhalin would commence soon. Stalin was in a jovial mood. He was obviously delighted that he had succeeded in joining the war before Japan's surrender. He was prepared to share the details of military operations with the American ambassador, partly to demonstrate to the Americans his willingness to cooperate, and partly to impress upon Harriman the rapid and powerful advance of the Soviet forces in Manchuria.

Harriman asked Stalin how he thought the atomic bomb would affect the Japanese. Stalin answered that "he thought the Japanese were at present looking for a pretext to replace the present government with one which would be qualified to undertake a surrender. The atomic bomb might give them this pretext." This is an important admission that Stalin took the atomic bomb seriously.

The discussion of the atomic bomb led to a startling conversation between Stalin and Harriman. Harriman observed that it was a good thing the United States, not Germany, had invented the atomic bomb. He then revealed that "the weapon of enormous destructive capacity" that the president had cryptically mentioned to Stalin at Potsdam was actually the atomic bomb. Without commenting on Truman's less than complete revelation about the atomic bomb, Stalin said: "The Soviet scientists said that it was a very difficult problem to work out," revealing that the Soviets were also involved in an atomic bomb project. He even referred to the German laboratory that had been working on the atomic project and had been seized by the Soviets. "England, too, had gotten nowhere with these researches," Stalin commented, "although they had excellent physicists." Harriman revealed that the British had "pooled their knowledge with us since 1941," and "Churchill deserved much of the credit for encouraging the development." Stalin kept a poker face, but he knew from his spies that the British had collaborated with the Americans. "It must have been very expensive," Stalin probed, to which Harriman replied, "it cost the United States two billion dollars."[38]

Harriman then shifted the topic of conversation to Sino-Soviet negotiations. He emphasized the importance of Dairen as an international open port, and asked Stalin to put in writing his verbal assurance supporting the Open Door policy. When Harriman presented the draft of the prepared text, Stalin read it carefully and said that it was satisfactory except for the last sentence in the first paragraph. He explained that in accordance with the Yalta Agreement, the Soviet Union should have a preeminent position in Dairen, which he understood to be a preferential position in the administration of the port. He explained that although Dairen would not be used as a Soviet naval base, the port would be included within the Soviet military zone, and that the Soviet government would have to be responsible for security in the city and the port. Harriman then notified Washington that Stalin was unlikely to endorse the U.S. position on Dairen as a free port.[39] The problem for the United States was that this issue was overtaken by military developments.

As Stalin had expected, Harriman never protested the fact that the Soviet Union entered the war without an agreement from the Chinese. Stalin's gamble had paid off.

Truman Reacts to Soviet Entry into the War

Within two hours after the first Soviet tanks crossed the Manchurian border, Truman and Byrnes learned of the Soviet invasion from Harriman's telegram, even before N. V. Novikov of the Soviet Embassy called the State Department at 2:45 P.M. on August 8. A few minutes after 3:00 Truman held an impromptu press conference. Although he entered the Press Room with a smile on his face, he quickly assumed a solemn expression and read a statement to reporters: "I have only a simple announcement to make. I can't hold a regular press conference today, but this announcement is so important I thought I would call you in. Russia has declared war on Japan." Then he added laconically: "That's all." This was the shortest While House press conference on record.[40]

This terse statement reveals the profound disappointment Truman must have felt over the news. He hinted at a sense of betrayal when he wrote in his memoirs that Stalin had assured him he would not join the war without an agreement with China.[41] Truman wanted to beat the Soviets in the race to induce Japan to surrender. He managed to use his ace, the atomic bomb, on Hiroshima, but the Soviets had snuck into the game nonetheless.

After Truman's short announcement, the secretary of state released a statement to the press. Byrnes welcomed the Soviet declaration of war against Japan, which he believed would "shorten the war and save . . . many lives." He further stated that at the Potsdam Conference, the president had conveyed to Stalin that Soviet participation in the war would be justified on the basis of Paragraph 5 of the Moscow Declaration of 1943 and Articles 103 and 106 of the proposed Charter of the United Nations. Clearly, Byrnes's statement was directed at the Soviet claim that Russia had been asked by the Allies to join the Potsdam Proclamation. Byrnes implied that this part of the Soviet declaration of war was not true. He even noted the contradiction between the Soviets' action and their commitment to the Neutrality Pact. Nevertheless, he stopped far short of assailing the Soviet declaration of war as a deception. Stalin's gamble worked. Senator Alexander Wiley of Wisconsin commented: "Apparently the atomic bomb which hit Hiroshima also blew 'Joey' off the fence." The *New York Times* reported: "Among the military and other official quarters there was no doubt that the devastating effects of the atomic bomb, as demonstrated in Hiroshima, had hastened Russia's entry." "Russia's declaration of war at this time," it continued to report, "came as a surprise to the Government from President Truman down."[42] The president was a disappointed man.

Why, given the knowledge that the Soviets had entered the war, didn't Truman order the suspension or postponement of the Nagasaki bomb? Fat Man, which was dropped on Nagasaki, was loaded onto a B-29 named *Bock's Car* at 10 P.M. on August 8. The bomber took off from Tinian, in the Northern Mariana Islands, at 3:47 on August 9. By then the Soviet-Japanese War was almost three hours old. When Truman held his press conference it was shortly after 3 P.M. on August 8 in Washington, and shortly after 4 A.M. on August 9 in Tinian. Therefore, *Bock's Car* had already left Tinian between the time Truman first received the news of the Soviet attack and the time when he held the press conference. When Truman made the announcement, the B-29 carrying the Nagasaki bomb was on its way to Japan. It dropped Fat Man on Nagasaki at 11:02.

Did Truman have time to recall *Bock's Car*? According to one expert, the Strategic Air Command's policy was to arm the bomb only after the flight was airborne. Thus, if the commander of *Bock's Car* were ordered to abort the mission, he would have had to jettison the bomb before landing.[43] But such technicalities were not the major issue. The existing documents reveal no indication that the decision to drop the second bomb was ever reconsidered. The decision to drop the bomb had been made on July 25, and no one thought it necessary to change the course because of the Soviet entry into the war.

Taken together, Truman's terse statement and Byrnes's press release indicate the displeasure the U.S. government felt at Soviet participation in the war. Once the Soviets were in the fight, they would pursue their own strategic interests. American policymakers now had to be concerned with the consequences of Soviet military conquests in Manchuria, Korea, and even North China. If Soviet action had any impact on American decisions, it reinforced the resolve of the U.S. government to continue the course it had thus far followed: to achieve Japan's surrender unilaterally. Now the outcome of the war would determine the influence and power of these emerging superpowers in the Far East.

Japan Reacts to Soviet Entry into the War

The whole purpose of the Far Eastern campaign was to ensure that Stalin secured the territories promised by the Yalta Agreement. The Soviets would make their move from three directions: the Transbaikal Army would come from the west and the First Far Eastern Army from the east, while the Second Far Eastern Army would thrust from the north, all in the direction of Changchun and Mukden. In August 1945, reinforced Soviet troops amounted to 1.5 million men against the shrinking Kwantung Army's 713,000 and 280,000 men in Korea, Sakhalin, and the Kurils.

At midnight Transbaikal time and 1 A.M. Khabarovsk time on August 9, Soviet tanks crossed the Manchurian border from all fronts. The main element of the western front, the 6th Guards Tank Army, led by Marshal Malinovskii, met with no resistance. The only enemy that slowed down its advance was the rugged terrain through the Gobi Desert and the Great Khingan range, and a shortage of fuel. On the third day of operations, Malinovskii ordered each corps to form advance detachments with a full fuel supply to speed up the advance.[44] (See Map 2.)

The First Far Eastern Front under Marshal Meretskov in the east met with more serious resistance. The major battle was fought in Mutanchiang, where fierce city fighting continued until August 16. While units of the 5th Army were engaging in house-to-house combat in the city, the 25th Army bypassed Mutanchiang and moved fast toward Kirin and Harbin to link up with the Transbaikal forces coming from the west. At the same time, a second thrust was made into Korea. Here, meeting with stiff resistance, the reinforced Soviet landing forces, assisted by the Pacific Fleet, managed to take Chongjin on August 16. Soviet troops advanced quickly only after the Japanese ceased hostilities. They then completed the occupation of Pyongyang and other major cities north of the thirty-eighth parallel.[45]

At 1 A.M. on August 9 (one hour later than Khabarovsk time) the General Headquarters of the Kwantung Army received alarming news that the Soviet Army had crossed the Soviet-Manchurian border in eastern

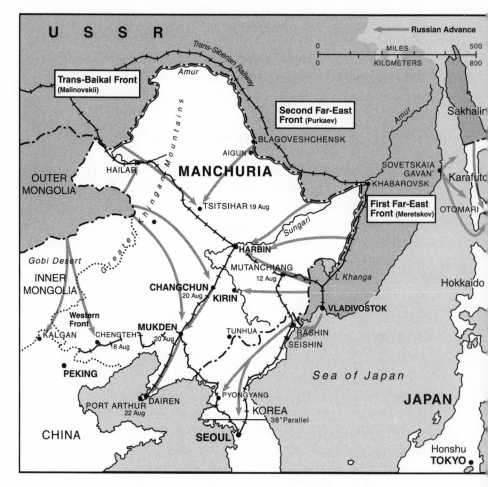

Map 2. August Storm: Soviet Attack on Manchuria, Korea, and Sakhalin. Adapted from Peter Young, ed., *Atlas of the Second World War* (N.Y.: G.P. Putnam's Sons, 1974), p. 168.

Manchuria. This news was followed by another report that Mutanchiang was being bombarded by air attacks. At 1:30 A.M., there was an air raid on a suburb of Changchun, the capital of Manchukuo. By 2 A.M., the Kwantung Army General Staff concluded that the Soviets had begun an all-out attack. But the Kwantung Army was instructed by the Imperial General Headquarters to limit action to self-defense. At 6 A.M., after receiving news of the Soviet declaration of war, the Imperial General Headquarters ordered the Kwantung Army to resist the invasion.[46] Only a few hours after the attack, the Kwantung Army decided to abandon the Manchurian capital.

It was around 1:30 in the morning on August 9, two and half hours after Soviet tanks had crossed the border, that the Domei News Agency intercepted a Moscow Radio broadcast of the Soviet declaration of war against Japan. Hasegawa of Domei News immediately relayed this information to Sakomizu and Togo. Awakened by this unexpected news, Sakomizu asked Hasegawa: "Is it really true? Can you verify the news?" When Hasegawa confirmed the accuracy of the broadcast, Sakomizu was overwhelmed by rage "as if all the blood in my body flowed backward." When Hasegawa told Togo, the thunderstruck foreign minister also asked if the news was accurate.[47]

Early on the morning of August 9, the top four officials in the Foreign Ministry (Togo, Matsumoto, Ando, and Shibusawa) gathered at Togo's residence. They immediately came to the conclusion that there was no alternative but to accept the Potsdam Proclamation. Given the strong hostility of Allied countries toward the emperor, they foresaw the difficulty that Japan might encounter should it insist on preservation of the imperial house as a condition for accepting the Potsdam Proclamation. Therefore, they agreed that the best policy would be to accept the Potsdam terms while unilaterally declaring that "the acceptance of the Potsdam Proclamation shall not have any influence on the position of the imperial house."[48] Thus the Gaimusho very quickly defined the *kokutai* narrowly as the preservation of the imperial house. They did not dare say it openly, but we surmise that what they really meant was that avoiding the trial and execution of the emperor should be a sufficient condition for surrender.

At dawn, Sakomizu drove to Suzuki's private residence to report the news that the Soviets had joined the war against Japan. The prime minister received the news silently, and then quietly told Sakomizu: "What we feared has finally come." It is interesting to recall that these same words were uttered by Sato after he heard that the Soviets had declared war. According to Suzuki's postwar memoirs, a vivid image of swarms of Soviet tanks crossing the border like water breaking through a dike immediately popped into his mind. Suzuki instantly concluded that "if we meet the Soviet advance as we are now, we will not be able to hold on for two months." He realized that at last the final chance to terminate the war had arrived.

Around 8 A.M. Togo arrived at Suzuki's residence and proposed that Japan accept the Potsdam Proclamation with one reservation regarding the imperial house. Sakomizu gave him two alternatives: either continue the war with an imperial declaration of war against the Soviet Union or terminate the war by accepting the Potsdam terms. At this moment the prime minister remained undecided. His judgment that Japan could not hold on for two months can be read as a statment that Japan still had the capacity to fight for two more months. After a long pause, he merely said that he would report to the emperor. Presumably, the prime minister wanted to know what Hirohito desired before making up his mind.[49]

Togo then went to meet Navy Minister Yonai, who accepted his decision to adhere to the Potsdam terms. Immediately after Togo left Yonai's office, he bumped into Prince Takamatsu, Hirohito's younger brother. The prince, too, saw no alternative but to accept the Potsdam terms. While Yonai and Prince Takamatsu agreed with Togo, however, it is unlikely that the details of the peace terms had been discussed and agreed upon. Konoe's adviser Hosokawa suggested to the prince that this was his opportunity to act: "You have to assume the premiership of the new cabinet and directly negotiate with the United States and Britain." The prince demurred and said: "Let Konoe take over." Using the prince's car, Hosokawa rushed to Konoe's residence in Ogikubo.[50]

While Togo was busy making the rounds to attain the consensus of the peace party, independent of Togo's efforts, Hirohito, too, had also come to the conclusion that it was time to terminate the war. At 9:55 A.M., he summoned Kido. "The Soviet Union declared war against us, and entered into a state of war as of today," Hirohito told Kido. "Because of this it is necessary to study and decide on the termination of the war." The emperor ordered Kido to consult the prime minister on this issue. Suzuki arrived at the palace at 10:10 A.M. Kido told the prime minister that the emperor's wish was to end the war by "taking advantage of the Potsdam Proclamation" and that the prime minister should make sure to convey this wish to the senior statesmen composed of former prime ministers.[51] It is not clear, however, what the emperor and Kido thought of the relationship between the acceptance of the Potsdam terms and the *kokutai*, but at this point they were probably content to leave the details of surrender to the Supreme War Council.

After he learned of the emperor's wish, Suzuki decided to convene the Supreme War Council immediately. The Big Six were summoned anew to assemble in the morning. In the meantime, Hosokawa drove to Konoe's home to inform him of the Soviet invasion. Konoe showed no sign of surprise at the news, and uttered: "This might be God's gift to control the army." Hosokawa and Konoe immediately went to see Kido at the imperial palace.[52]

The evidence is compelling that Soviet entry into the war had a strong impact on the peace party. Indeed, Soviet attack, not the Hiroshima bomb, convinced political leaders to end the war by accepting the Potsdam Proclamation.

But what about the military? The army's plan for a last-ditch defense was based on the premise that the Soviet Union would be kept neutral. The Army General Staff, it is true, had speculated that a Soviet attack might occur, but in the study it conducted in July it predicted that the Soviets would not likely launch a large-scale operation against Japan until February 1946.[53] On August 8, one day before the Soviet invasion, the Military Affairs Bureau produced a study outlining what Japan should do if the Soviets issued an ultimatum demanding Japan's total withdrawal from the continent. According to this plan, there were several alternatives: reject the Soviet demand and wage war against the Soviet Union, in addition to the United States and Britain; conclude peace with the United States and Britain immediately and concentrate on the war against the Soviet Union; accept the Soviet demand and seek Soviet neutrality while carrying out the war against the United States and Britain; or accept the Soviet demand and involve the Soviet Union in the Greater East Asian War. Of these alternatives, the army preferred to accept the Soviet demand, and either keep the Soviets neutral or, if possible, involve them in the war against the United States and Britain. The army recommended that if the Soviet Union entered the war, the Japanese should "strive to terminate the war with the Soviet Union as quickly as possible, and to continue the war against the United States, Britain, and China, while maintaining Soviet neutrality."[54] It bears emphasizing that right up to the moment of attack, the army not only did not expect a Soviet invasion, but also still believed that it could either keep the Soviets neutral or involve them in the war against the United States and Britain. The army leadership and the Kwantung Army were dominated by wishful thinking that the Soviet attack, while possible, would not happen.

When the Soviets began their large-scale attack, the Kwantung Army informed the Imperial General Headquarters by 5:30 A.M. that the Soviet action was an all-out invasion. This information caught the army by complete surprise. The Kwantung Army headquarters urgently requested instructions from the Imperial General Headquarters as to how to respond. But Major Shigeharu Asaeda, the staff member of the Imperial General Headquarters in charge of Soviet policy, at first refused to come to the phone, and when he finally took the call, he was evasive without giving definite instructions.[55]

Army Deputy Chief of Staff Kawabe was awakened in his bed at the

General Staff around 6 A.M. with the news that the intelligence division had intercepted a broadcast from Moscow and San Francisco that the Soviet Union had issued a declaration of war against Japan. Kawabe wrote down his first impressions of the news: "The Soviets have finally risen! My judgment has proven wrong."[56] Kawabe had been the main architect of the Ketsu-go strategy, and for that reason he had campaigned hard to secure Soviet neutrality through negotiations. The Soviet attack now destroyed the very foundation of his belief. The exclamation mark attached to this first sentence of Kawabe's diary speaks volumes about his shock.

In order to answer which event, the atomic bomb on Hiroshima or the Soviet attack, provided a bigger shock to Kawabe, one must compare the August 7 entry with the August 9 entry in his diary. In the entry for August 7, Kawabe wrote: "Having read various reports on the air raid by the new weapon on Hiroshima yesterday, the morning of the 6th, I received a serious jolt . . . With this development the military situation has progressed to such a point that it has become more and more difficult. We must be tenacious and fight on."[57] Kawabe admitted that he received "a serious jolt [*shigeki*]" from the reports on the atomic bombing of Hiroshima. Nevertheless, he avoided using the term "shock [*shogeki*]." Compared with this passage, his statement on August 9 that "the Soviets have risen" makes it clear that news of the Soviet attack was a greater shock than news of the atomic bomb.

Nevertheless, even after the Soviet invasion Kawabe was determined to continue the war. His elliptic memorandum singled out continuation of war against the United States as the major task, and suggested the establishment of a military dictatorship by proclaiming Martial Law and dismissing the current cabinet. As for the war in Manchuria, he suggested that Japan should completely abandon Manchuria and defend only southern Korea.[58]

When Kawabe presented his proposal to Umezu, the chief of staff did not express an opinion. Just before the Big Six meeting, Kawabe walked to the office of the army minister. There, he detected no change in Anami's countenance. After he listened to the deputy chief's recommendations, the army minister said that he understood Kawabe's view to represent that of the entire General Staff. Kawabe predicted that the impending Supreme War Council meeting would be a stormy one, and he asked the army minister to stand firm. Anami promised that he would defend his position "at the risk of his life." As he stood up and walked out of his office for the meeting, Anami broke into a broad smile and said, "If my view is not accepted, I will resign as army minister and request reassignment to a unit in China." The army minister's resignation would mean the collapse of the cabinet and the end of Japan's chance to terminate the war. Kawabe admired Anami's fighting spirit at this difficult moment. Anami also spoke of the need to study the establishment of a Martial Law government, indicating that he was receptive to Kawabe's idea.[59]

At 8 A.M., the Imperial General Headquarters held a strategic conference to discuss how to react to the Soviet invasion. According to Asaeda, the basic strategy the headquarters had followed before the Soviet invasion had been to deceive the Soviets into thinking that the Kwantung Army was strong. Now that the Soviet Union had attacked, the Kwantung Army would not last more than a few days or a few weeks at best. Thus, rather than declare war against the Soviet Union, as the Foreign Ministry and the Kwantung Army suggested, they should look to the future. The army still thought it possible to negotiate with the Soviet Union by exploiting the conflict between the Soviet Union and the Allies. Hence Asaeda drafted Continental Order 1374, instructing the Kwantung Army that though the Soviet Union had declared war against Japan, its military actions along the border were still small-scale. The Imperial General Headquarters ordered the Kwantung Army to make preparations for implementation of the operation against the Soviet Union. Although the army leadership knew full well that the attack constituted an all-out invasion, it attempted to restrain the Kwantung Army's military operations.[60]

Following Kawabe's proposal, the Military Affairs Bureau of the Army Ministry drafted a paper reaffirming the continuation of the war. The paper stated that the Japanese should practice self-defense against the Soviet military without declaring war. Meanwhile, the government would continue to negotiate with the Soviet Union to terminate the war and, further, would declare martial law. It is doubtful, however, that this document received the approval of Umezu and Anami.[61]

Fat Man Is Dropped on Nagasaki

The second atomic bomb was dropped on Nagasaki at 11:02 A.M. (Japan time) on August 9, killing 35,000 to 40,000 people. Truman announced on the radio: "Having found the bomb we have used it. We have used it against those who attacked us without warning at Pearl Harbor, against those who have starved and beaten and executed American prisoners of war, against those who have abandoned all pretense of obeying international laws of warfare."[62] Vengeance was a consistent theme in both his statements after Hiroshima and Nagasaki. One cannot help sensing, however, that a defensive tone had crept into this second statement.

Earlier, on August 7, Senator Richard Russell of Georgia had sent a telegram to the president, urging him to use more atomic bombs "to finish the job immediately." Truman disagreed with the Georgia senator. "I know that Japan is a terribly cruel and uncivilized nation in warfare," the president replied on the very day the Nagasaki bomb was dropped, "but I can't bring myself to believe that, because they are beasts, we should ourselves act in the same manner. For myself, I certainly regret the necessity of wiping out whole populations because of the 'pigheadedness' of the leaders of a nation and, for your information, I am not going to do it unless it is absolutely necessary." Then the president added: "It is my opinion that after the Russians enter into war the Japanese will very shortly fold up. My object is to save as many American lives as possible but I also have a humane feeling for the women and children in Japan." According to the diary of Secretary of Commerce Henry Wallace, at the cabinet meeting on August 10, Truman announced that he had given an order to stop further atomic bombing without his authorization: "He said the thought of wiping out another 100,000 people was too horrible. He didn't like the idea of killing . . . 'all these kids.'" Leahy also noted in his diary that "information from Japan" indicated that 80 percent of the city of Hiroshima had been destroyed and 100,000 people killed."[63]

It is not difficult to see that an important change had taken place in Truman between the time he celebrated the Hiroshima bomb and the time he wrote this letter. Despite his persistent claim that the atomic bombs were targeted at military installations, he knew that they had also killed "women and children," and that further use of the atomic bomb would violate "humane feelings." Truman had read the Magic Diplomatic Summary reporting that the atomic bomb on Hiroshima had killed 100,000 people.[64] This information must have had a sobering effect on the president. His order to halt the further use of the bomb without his express order was the first time he exerted his personal authority on decisions about the atomic bomb.

Nevertheless, this does not mean that Truman had completely ruled out further use of the bomb. In a postwar interview he was asked: "Were there any other bombs being prepared or ready for immediate follow-up?" Without hesitation Truman answered: "Yes. The other two cities on the list [Niigata and Kokura] would have been bombed."[65]

The Big Six in Stalemate

Meanwhile in Tokyo, shortly before 11 A.M. the Supreme War Council met in the basement of the imperial palace.[66] Suzuki opened the meeting by proposing that in view of the atomic bomb and the Soviet entry into the war, there was little choice but to terminate the war by accepting the terms of the Potsdam Proclamation. After the prime minister's opening remarks, an oppressive silence continued for several minutes, until Yonai spoke up: "There is no use in keeping silent. If we were to accept the Potsdam Proclamation, either we should accept the terms with no conditions attached or we should submit our conditions. If we were to attach conditions, the first should be the preservation of the *kokutai*. In addition, we might discuss the issues of punishment of war criminals, methods of disarmament, and stationing of the occupation forces in Japan." The loose agreement that Togo thought he had with Yonai had broken down. Instead of insisting on the preservation of the imperial house, as had the Foreign Ministry officials, Yonai added additional conditions that his closest adviser, Sokichi Takagi, had been discussing with a small but influential circle since June. Perhaps Yonai's position was not firmly established at this point, and he was simply laying the conditions on the table as the basis of discussion. In fact, throughout the meeting, Yonai kept silent.

Anami at first opposed the very idea of surrender. It was not known, he argued, if the United States would continue to use the atomic bomb, and the situation in Manchuria was uncertain. Anami's view, however, did not meet with the approval of the other members. Surrender was taken for granted, and what remained to be discussed were the conditions that should be attached to the acceptance of the Potsdam terms.[67] Togo argued that Japan should insist only on the preservation of the imperial house. Few noticed that Togo substituted the word "imperial house" for *kokutai*. All the participants agreed that Japan should insist upon the preservation of the *kokutai*, but they differed on the question of other conditions. Picking up Yonai's suggestion, Umezu and Anami argued that in addition to the preservation of the *kokutai*, Japan should also attach three other conditions: first, trials of war criminals should be entrusted to the Japanese; second, disarmament should be carried out by the Japanese, since in view of military tradition and education, implementation of disarmament by foreign power would cause resistance; and third, occupation of the Japanese homeland by the Allies should be avoided, and if not avoidable, Tokyo should not be occupied, and occupation should be as brief and limited in scope as possible.

At this point, the line between the war party and the peace party was not as clearly drawn as historians have argued. Although Suzuki and Yonai were leaning toward Togo's position, they did not raise any objections to insisting on three additional conditions. Toyoda thought it doubtful that Yonai completely supported Togo's one-condition proposal. Toyoda himself supported only two conditions, believing that the demand for non-occupation would be pointless.[68]

At 11:30 A.M., while the Big Six were engaged in a heated debate on what to do about the Potsdam terms, news of the second atomic bomb on Nagasaki was relayed to the Supreme War Council. The Nagasaki bomb, however, had little impact on the substance of the discussion. The official history of the Imperial General Headquarters notes: "There is no record in other materials that treated the effect [of the Nagasaki bomb] seriously." Describing the Big Six meeting on this crucial day, neither Togo nor Toyoda mentioned anything about the atomic bomb on Nagasaki.[69]

The Supreme War Council continued into the afternoon without coming to a consensus. While Suzuki and Yonai kept silent, Togo fought tenaciously for acceptance of the Potsdam terms with only one condition. To bring up three additional conditions would be tantamount to rejecting the ultimatum. He asked Umezu and Toyoda if the army and navy chiefs had any prospect of winning the war in the event the Allies rejected Japan's terms. The chiefs admitted that it would not be possible to achieve an ultimate victory, but insisted that they could inflict considerable damage on the enemy. When the chiefs said they were confident that they would be able to repulse the invading army in a homeland attack, Togo pointed out they would lose a substantial number of airplanes and other important weapons in the first battle, and the supply line would become precarious. If Japanese forces could inflict tremendous damage on the invading troops, the war party countered, it would break the enemy's morale and force it to terminate the war in terms favorable to Japan.

Togo's questioning penetrated deeply into the prerogatives of the military command, unthinkable only a week ago. The fact that Anami and

Soviet Ambassador Iakov Malik, third from right, with Molotov in the center. Malik sent Moscow valuable information on Japan's domestic conditions. In June Hirota negotiated with Malik to keep the Soviet Union out of the war. The Hirota-Malik negotiations were exploited by the Soviet Union to prolong the war. *(Rossiiskii gosudarstvennyi arkhiv kinofotodokumentov, Krasnogorsk)*

Mamoru Shigemitsu, Japan's foreign
minister under Hideki Tojo and
Kuniyoshi Koiso. As Kido's friend, he
played an important role in staging the
emperor's "sacred decision." As the
chief delegate of the Japanese government, he signed the surrender documents on the *Missouri* on September 2,
1945. *(Gaimusho Gaikoshiryokan)*

Prince Fumimaro Konoe. He was appointed the emperor's special envoy to
Moscow to terminate the war. While
the Japanese government's request to
send Prince Konoe was pending, the
Soviet government declared war against
Japan. *(Gaimusho Gaikoshiryokan)*

Army Minister General Korechika Anami, the most intransigent advocate for the continuation of war. He committed ritual *seppuku* in the early hours of August 15, after the emperor's acceptance of unconditional surrender. *(Kyodo tsushinsha)*

Army Chief of Staff General Yoshijiro Umezu, an advocate for continuation of the war. After the emperor's acceptance of the Potsdam terms, he quickly unified the Army high command to support the emperor's decision to surrender. *(National Archives)*

Navy Chief of Staff Admiral Soemu
Toyoda. Together with Anami and
Umezu, he was one of the three war
hawks in the cabinet. *(National Archives)*

Hisatsune Sakomizu, cabinet secretary
of the Suzuki cabinet. He worked behind the scenes for Japan's surrender.
(Kyodo tsushinsha)

Baron Kiichiro Hiranuma, president of the Privy Council. An important participant in the imperial conferences, he amended the condition that Japan attached to acceptance of the Potsdam terms, making it impossible for the United States to accept Japan's offer of peace. *(National Archives)*

General Shizuichi Tanaka, Oxford-educated commander of the Eastern Army. Tanaka adamantly opposed the coup engineered by staff officers on the night of August 14, and played a crucial role in suppressing it. Taking responsibility for the coup, he committed suicide on August 24.
(Kyodo tsushinsha)

"Little Boy," the atomic bomb that was dropped on Hiroshima on August 6, 1945. It was 28 inches in diameter, 120 inches long, and weighed 9,000 pounds. *(National Archives)*

"Fat Man," the atomic bomb that was dropped on Nagasaki on August 9, 1945. It was 60 inches in diameter, 120 inches long, and weighed 10,000 pounds. *(National Archives)*

Colonel Paul Tibbets, pilot of the *Enola Gay*, the plane that dropped the atomic bomb on Hiroshima, waves from his cockpit before takeoff, on August 6, 1945. *(National Archives)*

Truman eating lunch in the mess hall with the crew of the *Augusta*. It was on one such occasion that he received the news of the atomic bomb that had been dropped on Hiroshima on August 6, 1945. *(Harry S Truman Library)*

Soviet troops cross the Manchurian border on August 9, 1945, as part of Operation August Storm. *(Rossiiskii gosudarstvennyi arkhiv kinofotodokumentov, Krasnogorsk)*

Soviet landing operation in the Kurils. The Kuril operation began only after the emperor announced Japan's unconditional acceptance of the Potsdam Proclamation. *(Rossiiskii gosudarstvennyi arkhiv kinofotodokumentov, Krasnogorsk)*

Marshal Vasilevskii (left), commander of the Far Eastern Front. He led Operation August Storm against Japan. *(Rossiiskii gosudarstvennyi arkhiv kinofotodokumentov, Krasnogorsk)*

General Otozo Yamada, commander in chief of the Kwantung Army (seated at center), as he accepted the terms of cease-fire at Zharikovo. *(Rossiiskii gosudarstvennyi arkhiv kinofotodokumentov, Krasnogorsk)*

The emperor's "sacred decision" to accept the Potsdam terms with one condition at the first imperial conference, August 9–10. Four days later, at the second imperial conference, the emperor agreed to unconditional surrender. *(Suzuki Kantaro Memorial Museum)*

Truman announces Japan's surrender at the White House. *(Harry S Truman Library)*

The Japanese delegations headed by Chief Delegate Mamoru Shigemitsu stand on the U.S.S. *Missouri* before the surrender-signing ceremony on September 2, 1945. Members of the military delegation, headed by General Yoshijiro Umezu, representing the Imperial General Headquarters, were not allowed to bear swords. *(National Archives)*

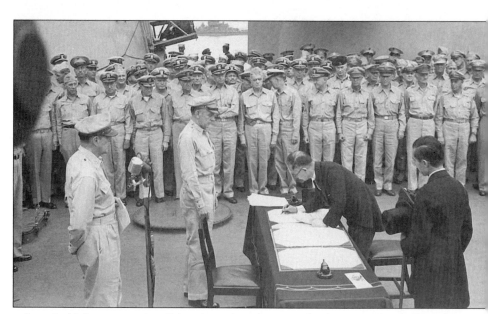

Japan's chief representative, Shigemitsu, signs the surrender documents on the *Missouri*. *(National Archives)*

Kuzma Derevianko, Soviet representative, signs the surrender documents, while General Douglas MacArthur looks on. *(Rossiiskii gosudarstvennyi arkhiv kinofotodoku-mentov, Krasnogorsk)*

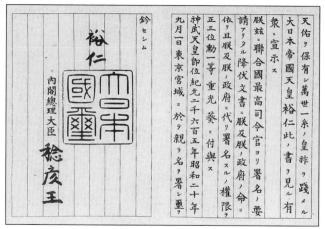

The surrender document signed by Emperor Hirohito with his official seal. *(National Archives)*

Stimson, General George Marshall, army Chief of Staff, and Truman show the surrender documents to the press. *(National Archives)*

Umezu responded without protest indicates a decline in the military's power. But Togo was the lone voice that strongly advocated acceptance of the Potsdam terms with one condition. When the Supreme War Council adjourned at 1 P.M., the Japanese leaders had decided to accept the Potsdam terms, but they had not reached any consensus about whether they should demand four conditions or one.

The Peace Party Plots a Conspiracy

A group of peace advocates outside the Big Six desperately sought a way out of this stalemate. At around the time the Supreme War Council adjourned, Prince Konoe drove up to the imperial palace to discuss the situation with Kido. At 1:30 P.M., Suzuki joined him to report on the Supreme War Council meeting. According to Kido, Suzuki said that the Big Six had "decided" to accept the Potsdam Proclamation by attaching the four conditions. What exactly Suzuki reported to Kido remains unclear. Richard Frank argues that the most likely explanation is that Suzuki simply reported the four-condition proposal as "the lowest common denominator of agreement within the Big Six."[70] Suzuki may have told Kido that the four-condition proposal gained the majority of the Big Six.

What is known for certain is that Kido at first approved acceptance of the Potsdam terms with four conditions. Konoe was aghast, convinced as he was that the four conditions would be promptly rejected by the Allies. Konoe and Hosokawa did not say, but they must have surmised that Hirohito himself supported that position. Rather than directly appealing to the emperor or working through Kido, the two men decided to recruit Prince Takamatsu to their position. Persuaded by Konoe's argument, Prince Takamatsu called Kido on the telephone and suggested that they should drop the three extra conditions. Kido told the prince, with obvious annoyance, that they had little choice but to accept the four conditions.[71]

Konoe's desperate maneuvers continued. In order to change the emperor's mind, he had to convince Kido first. At 3 P.M., while Hirohito was listening to Kido's report, Konoe met Shigemitsu at Kazan Hall, where he urged the former foreign minister to pressure Kido to persuade the emperor to cut the Gordian knot by making a "sacred decision [*seidan*]" to accept the Potsdam Proclamation with only one condition. He explained that Kido had been reluctant to take this position. Shigemitsu readily agreed with Konoe and drove to the imperial palace.

Kido received his old friend Shigemitsu at 4 P.M., but he did not hide his irritation at Shigemitsu's uninvited intervention. "You are all advocating a direct decision from the emperor," Kido complained. "But have you ever thought what trouble your opinion might cause His Majesty?" Kido's irritation must have stemmed from his knowledge that Hirohito himself supported the four conditions. Shigemitsu insisted. In order to break through the impregnable wall of the army, they had no alternative but to rely on the emperor's intervention. Shigemitsu's desperate plea finally convinced the emperor's trusted adviser. At 4:35 P.M., Kido had a long audience with the emperor. At 5:20 the marquis returned from the imperial library and reported back to Shigemitsu: "The emperor understands everything, and holds a firm resolution. You don't have to worry about it. Therefore, why don't we make all the arrangements through the cabinet to have an imperial conference where, after everyone expresses his view, the emperor is asked to express his decision?"[72] The scenario for the emperor's "sacred decision" was completed with Kido's approval. Shigemitsu then secretly sent Matsumoto to the cabinet to convey the emperor's decision to Togo.

In addition to the Konoe group, another circle was engaged in behind-the-scenes maneuvers to convince the emperor to intervene in the decision. Colonel Matsutani, who realized that it would be impossible to sway Anami, consulted Takagi and asked him what immediate measures should be taken. In the afternoon Takagi met Matsudaira at the House of Peers. There they decided to map out a scenario for the emperor's "sacred decision" that was similar to the one Kido had just approved. Matsudaira went to the imperial palace and petitioned Kido to remove all conditions from Japan's acceptance of the Potsdam terms.[73] Although the precise connection between the Konoe-Shigemitsu group and the Takagi-Matsutani-Matsudaira group cannot be established, it is almost certain that they were in contact through telephone and messengers and coordinated their activities.

Kido's talk with Hirohito in the inner sanctum of the imperial library between 4:35 and 5:20 on August 9 was perhaps one of the most crucial events that moved Japan decisively in the direction of surrender.[74] We still do not know what they discussed or what changed their minds. It is possible to speculate that Hirohito initially resisted relinquishing three additional conditions. Even more likely is the possibility that the emperor was reluctant to involve himself directly in the decision to terminate the war. What is clear is that they became convinced by Konoe and Shigemitsu's argument that the emperor's "sacred decision" to accept the Potsdam terms with one condition was the only way to save the *kokutai*. Foremost in their minds must have been the preservation of the imperial house.

We can speculate that at this crucial meeting they changed the Foreign Ministry's narrow definition of the *kokutai* from "the preservation of the imperial house" to a slightly broader definition, "the preservation of the emperor's status within the national laws." The former definition was the formula presented by Togo at the Big Six meeting that afternoon, but it was altered to the latter definition at the imperial conference convened later that night. The question is who changed this definition and where the change took place. Although there is no direct evidence, a process of elimination points to the crucial Kido-Hirohito meeting in late afternoon. Perhaps this was a concession Kido had to make to obtain the emperor's approval for the one-condition acceptance of the Potsdam terms.

In his attempt to persuade Kido to change his mind, Shigemitsu stressed the Soviet threat. In his postwar memoirs, he pointed out that Soviet forces were marching into Manchuria, South Sakhalin, and the Kurils, ready to invade Hokkaido. But on August 9, the Soviets had not initiated their operations on Sakhalin, not to speak of the Kurils. Nonetheless, Shigemitsu did not have to spell out in detail how the continuing Soviet expansion might jeopardize the position of the emperor.[75]

The deliberations of the Big Six were supposed to be secret, but as soon as the Supreme War Council adjourned, details of their discussions were leaked to their subordinates. Both those who stood for peace and those who were opposed to it gathered around their leaders to push for their respective causes. Matsumoto strongly urged Togo to stand firm for a one-condition proposal. In the meantime, Deputy Naval Chief Vice Admiral Takijiro Onishi, founder of the infamous kamikaze fighter planes, rushed to the Army Ministry and implored Anami not to give up the fight to continue the war, since he could not trust his own navy minister, Yonai.[76] Radical junior officers in the Army Ministry denounced army leaders for agreeing to accept the Potsdam terms even with four conditions attached.[77] Thus both camps attempted to fortify the respective positions of their leaders for the next round of discussion.

The emergency cabinet meeting began at 2:30 P.M., after Suzuki had returned from the imperial palace. Anami argued that the best guarantee for the preservation of the *kokutai* would be to maintain the armed forces intact, and that one-condition surrender would be tantamount to unconditional surrender without the military to back it up. Implied in this argument was the centrality of the emperor's prerogatives over the military command in the *kokutai*. After the atomic bomb and the Soviet entry into the war, victory would be unlikely, Anami conceded, but they always had a chance as long as they kept fighting for the honor of the Yamato race. While he remained silent during the Big Six meeting, Yonai took charge in challenging the army minister. The navy minister countered that aside from the atomic bombs and the Soviet entry into the war, the domestic condition made it impossible to continue the war. Japan could not win from a material or spiritual standpoint. The situation called for cold, rational judgment, not wishful thinking. It's a mystery why Yonai came to advocate the one-condition proposal at the cabinet meeting. Although documentary evidence is lacking, it might well be that he changed his mind under strong pressure from Takagi.[78]

Anami then shared the latest news about American possession of the atomic bombs, which he had obtained from the interrogation of an American prisoner named Lieutenant Marcus McDilda. During the interrogation McDilda had allegedly betrayed that the next atomic bomb target would be Tokyo. The war minister further revealed that the United States might still possess more than one hundred atomic bombs.[79] Shocking though it might be, this news did not seem to impress the cabinet ministers. It is not clear why Anami revealed this information. Just that morning, he had argued that they could not base future action on the assumption that Japan would be attacked by additional bombs. Now he was telling his colleagues that the enemy had more than one hundred atomic bombs, and that Tokyo might be the next target. Still, he insisted upon continuing the war. Anami's argument simply defied logic, contributing only to the erosion of his credibility. Each minister spoke, but no conclusion was reached. The first cabinet meeting adjourned at 5:30 P.M. without reaching any decision.

After the meeting, Matsumoto and Sakomizu both confirmed the necessity of moving toward the "sacred decision."[80] The pact between the two men was to serve as a driving force behind the push for Japan to accept surrender. In the meantime, Suzuki went to the palace to report what had happened at the first cabinet meeting. Kido told Suzuki that the emperor had consented to hold an imperial conference. This was the first time Kido gave Suzuki a clear signal that the emperor supported the one-condition proposal. The peace party had now formed a powerful coalition with the single aim of bringing the matter to an imperial conference, where the emperor's "sacred decision" would silence the opposition once and for all.[81]

The second cabinet meeting opened at 6 P.M. Togo explained the deliberations that had taken place at the Supreme War Council, depicting the equal division between the one-condition and four-condition proposals. Togo underscored his own opinion that there was no likelihood the Allies would accept three additional conditions, and he also stressed the importance of preserving "the imperial house." At this stage Togo still continued to define the *kokutai* as the preservation of the imperial house. Anami objected, stating that the majority view of the Supreme War Council was to submit four conditions and, if they were rejected, to continue the war. Each minister expressed his view for or against Togo's position. Only four ministers supported Anami's position. At 10 P.M., Suzuki cut off the endless discussion. Since cabinet decisions had to be endorsed with unanimity, this was tantamount to no decision at all. The prime minister announced that he would convene the Supreme War Council, and that he would report the results of the cabinet meeting to the emperor.[82] Suzuki was now following the scenario agreed upon with Kido.

Hirohito Makes the First "Sacred Decision"

At 10:50 P.M., Kido had an audience with the emperor that lasted three minutes. They must have reconfirmed the decision to hold an imperial conference at which the emperor would make a decision. Immediately after this meeting, Prime Minister Suzuki, accompanied by Foreign Minister Togo, came to the imperial palace to report the results of the cabinet meetings to the emperor. Suzuki then requested that the Supreme War Council be held with the emperor present, a request that was granted immediately. After Suzuki and Togo retired, Kido and the emperor had another meeting that lasted twelve minutes. Hirohito must have rehearsed what he would say at the end of the imperial conference.[83]

Calling an imperial conference required the signatures of the prime minister and both the army and the navy chiefs, but Sakomizu had already obtained the signatures of Toyoda and Umezu on the pretense that the conference might have to be convened within a moment's notice. The two chiefs signed the necessary forms but told Sakomizu to let them know in advance if a meeting was to be held. Sakomizu ignored that promise and submitted the necessary papers with the two chiefs' signatures without their permission. Sakomizu simply tricked the military.[84]

The announcement of the imperial conference sent shock waves through the military. Major General Masao Yoshizumi (army military affairs bureau chief), Zenshiro Hoshina (navy military affairs bureau chief), and other army and navy officers rushed to Sakomizu's office and accused him of double-dealing. Sakomizu calmed their anger by explaining that the imperial conference was a forum in which each member of the Supreme War Council could express his views in front of the emperor. Sakomizu tricked the military for the second time.[85] Once the imperial conference was convened, the game was over. The peace party had succeeded in its conspiracy to outwit the war party by recruiting the emperor as the major player in the script they had prepared.

Why was the war party so easily tricked by the peace party? It might be more accurate to say that Anami, Umezu, and Toyoda allowed themselves to be tricked. It is inconceivable that they did not know about the plot for the "sacred decision," and that the imperial conference would inevitably lead to a conclusion that they opposed. Their argument for the continuation of the war lacked conviction, but, as leaders of the military, they had to insist on it to control the officers below them. According to Toyoda, he supported Anami and Umezu because the isolation of the army might have led to revolt, and because he believed that Anami and Umezu also thought that accepting peace would be inevitable, although they took their strong stand under pressure from the radical officers.[86] Although neither Umezu nor Anami openly said so, we can surmise that they secretly hoped the "sacred decision" would relieve them of the onerous burden of arguing for the continuation of the war.

The imperial conference opened at 11:50 P.M. in a basement shelter in the imperial palace.[87] After Sakomizu read the text of the Potsdam Proclamation, Suzuki reported what had occurred at the Supreme War Council and the cabinet meetings, and then he presented two alternative proposals. Togo's one-condition proposal had been printed and laid on the table for each participant. It stated that Japan would "accept the Potsdam Proclamation on the understanding that it did not include any demand for a change in the status of the emperor under the national laws." Following Matsumoto's advice, Togo had advocated throughout the Big Six meeting and the cabinet meetings that the condition should be limited to the preservation of the imperial house. This position was changed to the "emperor's status within national laws," as proposed at the imperial conference.

This much broader definition of the emperor's status came close to the position advocated by Tatsukichi Minobe in his theory of the emperor as an organ of national laws. The writer of this proposal, however, was most likely referring to the Meiji Constitution when he spoke of "national laws." Given that the Meiji Constitution stipulated that the emperor had exclusive authority over the military command, the very cause of Japan's unbridled militarism, one can argue that this condition was contrary to the Americans' fundamental objective of eradicating sources of militarism. Nevertheless, this condition contained a narrow strip of common ground, though tenuous, with Stimson's notion of a "constitutional monarchy."

Togo and Yonai spoke in favor of Togo's proposal, which provoked Anami's indignant response. Anami expressed confidence in Japan's ability to inflict damage on the Americans in the expected homeland invasion, and he predicted that the acceptance of peace would lead to a civil war in Japan—a veiled threat insinuating that the army would revolt if Japan accepted defeat. Umezu supported Anami's proposal, though he lacked Anami's passionate indignation.

Suzuki then asked for Kiichiro Hiranuma's view, though it was Toyoda's turn to speak. The chairman of the Privy Council, who had been excluded from the preceding discussions but invited by the emperor with the expectation that he would support the peace party, asked about many things, beginning with the negotiations with the Soviet Union, the details of the Potsdam terms, the army's preparedness for air raids, especially against atomic bombs, and the morale of the people. To the annoyance of the prime minister, he took up an inordinate amount of time. But some of the questions he asked were pertinent. For instance, he asked Togo whether it was true, as the Soviet declaration stated, that the Japanese government had formally rejected the Potsdam Proclamation. Togo said that it was not true. Baron Hiranuma asked: "What, then, is the basis for their claim that we rejected the Potsdam Proclamation?" Togo simply replied: "They must have imagined that we did." To his question about the measures the army planned to take against atomic bombs, Umezu replied that the army was taking appropriate action, but that they would never surrender as a result of air raids. Hiranuma also expressed his concern that continuing the war would lead to domestic disturbances, a view with which the prime minister concurred. The baron even raised the question of the emperor's taking responsibility for the crisis.

After he expressed his support for the one-condition acceptance of the Potsdam terms, however, the baron proposed an amendment. Just as Hiranuma, champion of the ultra-nationalist movement, had taken charge of the attack on Minobe's emperor-organ theory, the chairman of the Privy Council argued that the imperial prerogatives of the emperor's rule originated not from any laws but from the national essence. Hence, the condition proposed by Togo should be changed to read: "on the understanding that the Allied Proclamation would not comprise any demand which would prejudice the prerogatives of His Majesty as a Sovereign Ruler [*Tenno no kokka tochi no taiken*]."[88]

Togo's original trick to define the *kokutai* narrowly as the preservation of the imperial house had been watered down, most likely at the Kido-Hirohito meeting, to "the preservation of the status of the emperor within the national laws." But Hiranuma succeeded in planting a time bomb by changing the definition of the *kokutai* even further from this watered-down version to the mythical essence that transcended the emperor, the imperial house, and any national laws. This was the affirmation of the emperor's theocratic power, unencumbered by any law, based on Shinto gods in antiquity, and totally incompatible with a constitutional monarchy. Although the condition originally proposed by Togo at the imperial conference could have narrow, though tenuous, common ground with Stimson's constitutional monarchy, Hiranuma's amendment removed any possibility that the United States would accept this condition.[89]

As the next chapter will show, this time bomb would nearly derail the surrender process in the coming days. Once Hiranuma let the cat out of the bag, it was impossible to put it back in. His understanding of the *kokutai* had been the prevailing orthodoxy since Minobe's emperor-organ theory was denounced in 1935. No one dared challenge it, and perhaps Suzuki and Yonai even agreed with this interpretation. For Togo, it was hard enough to fight for one condition, and he did not see any point in arguing against Hiranuma's amendment. After Hiranuma's long-winded intervention, Toyoda added his vote to include four conditions.

It was already past 2 A.M. Suzuki stood up and apologized for the lack of consensus despite the long deliberations. Ignoring Anami, who attempted to restrain him by calling, "Mr. Prime Minister!" Suzuki slowly walked in front of the emperor. He bowed deeply, then asked for the emperor's decision. Hirohito, still seated, leaned slightly forward and said: "Then I will express my opinion." There was a hush, and tension filled the room. The emperor then stated: "My opinion is the same as what the foreign minister said." His Majesty's "sacred decision" had been made. Hirohito then haltingly explained in his high-pitched voice why he supported the Potsdam Proclamation with one condition. Given the international and domestic situation, continuing the war would not only ruin Japan but also "bring unhappiness to mankind." Therefore, it would be necessary to "bear the unbearable." In a harsh indictment of the military, he pointed out the discrepancies between promises made by the military and the reality, exemplified by the lack of preparations for the defense of the Kanto Plain.[90] The game plan for Hirohito and the peace party was clear: they wanted to save the emperor and the imperial house by putting all the blame on the military.

After the emperor finished, Suzuki stood up and solemnly declared: "We have heard your august Thought." Hirohito left the room as everybody stood and bowed deeply. The Big Six, who remained in the shelter, immediately held a brief meeting of the Supreme War Council, and accepted the one-condition acceptance of the Potsdam terms with Hiranuma's amendment. Everyone, including three members of the war party, signed the document that approved the decision.[91]

In his postwar interview with his aide, Hirohito explained that there were two reasons for his decision. First, if he did not accept the Potsdam terms, "the Japanese race would perish and I would be unable to protect my loyal subjects [*sekishi*—children]." Second, "if the enemy landed near Ise Bay, both Ise and Atsuta Shrines would immediately come under their control. There would be no time to transfer the sacred regalia of the imperial family and no hope of protecting them. Under these circumstances, protection of the *kokutai* would be difficult." Historian Herbert Bix asserts that Hiranuma's right-wing Shinto notion of the *kokutai* was shared by the other participants at the imperial conference, and that this was the notion that Hirohito himself supported.[92] There is no question that Hirohito was concerned about his responsibility as the head of the Shinto religion. Nevertheless, in his statement he identifies the *kokutai* with highly personalized matters of the imperial house. Rather than clinging to absolute theocratic power, he was preoccupied with the household, which might be swept away unless he ended the war. This passage also gives a clue as to what Kido and Hirohito discussed at the crucial meeting between 4:35 and 5:10 on August 9. They were determined to save the institution of the emperor. But the price Kido had to pay for Hirohito's acceptance of the one-condition proposal was the dilution of the definition of the *kokutai* from the narrow preservation of the imperial house to the preservation of the emperor's status within the national laws. Hirohito and Kido knew that to save the institution of the emperor, they had to cut off the military as the sacrificial lamb.

It is difficult to speculate how Hirohito and Kido reacted to Hiranuma's amendment. One possibility, as Bix argues, is that they may have welcomed it. But it is also possible to argue that Hirohito was annoyed by Hiranuma's amendment, though he was not averse, at least at this point, to presenting this maximum demand to the Allies to see how they would react. What is clear is that Hirohito and Kido did not raise any objections to Hiranuma's amendment.

As the participants walked out of the shelter after the conference, Yoshizumi angrily confronted the prime minister about breaking his promise. Anami, walking side by side with Yoshizumi, restrained him: "Yoshizumi, that's enough." The army minister told Yoshizumi that he alone would take full responsibility for the army's acceptance of surrender, and that others should take no rash action.

At 3 A.M. the cabinet met for the third time, only to confirm the emperor's decision. Anami, however, staged a small coup against Suzuki. Seizing upon the condition attached to acceptance of the Potsdam Proclamation, Anami asked Suzuki and Yonai if they would support the continuation of war if the Allies refused to recognize "the prerogatives of the emperor as the sovereign ruler." Both Suzuki and Yonai had no choice but to reply that in that case they would support the continuation of the war.[93]

Umezu returned to the General Staff at 3 A.M. and told Kawabe about the emperor's decision. The emperor's distrust of the military came as a great shock to Umezu. In contrast to his entry of the previous day, the deputy chief of staff confessed in his diary: "All we have is the sentiment that we don't want to surrender, and we don't want to give up, even if we are killed."[94] The highest commanding officers of the army were coming around to accepting surrender.

CHAPTER 6

Japan Accepts
Unconditional Surrender

THE DAYS FOLLOWING August 11 were chaotic ones in Japan. As Takagi noted in his postwar memoirs, a movement to revolt gained momentum within the army, while war advocates in the navy desperately attempted to sabotage peace efforts. Suzuki failed to show any leadership and constantly turned to the emperor for direction. Moreover, "Anami, Umezu, and Toyoda were surrounded by war advocates, while senior statesmen watched the scene from a safe distance. Only a few men such as Yonai and Kido risked their lives to achieve peace."[1]

On the evening of August 9 officials from the Foreign Ministry prepared a draft text for the acceptance of the Potsdam Proclamation. Togo had instructed Matsumoto to prepare two drafts, one based on a single condition and another on four conditions, but Matsumoto defied this order, insisting that to prepare a draft with four conditions was tantamount to rejecting the Potsdam Proclamation. At 4 A.M. on August 10, Togo returned to the Foreign Ministry and told his subordinates about the emperor's sacred decision. Ministry officials racked their brains trying to translate Hiranuma's amendment, but finally settled on the words "prerogatives of His Majesty as a sovereign ruler." It was already past 6 A.M. when the draft was sent to the telegraph desk.[2]

On the morning of August 9, Malik had belatedly requested a meeting with Togo. Citing a busy schedule, Togo agreed to meet with him the next day. At that meeting the Soviet ambassador read the declaration of war. Togo responded with anger at the Soviets' betrayal. He explained that the Japanese government was waiting to hear Moscow's answer to the special mission before responding to the Potsdam Proclamation. Thus the statement in the declaration of war indicating that Japan had rejected the proclamation was an error. The Soviet decision to cut off diplomatic relations and enter the war without warning was "totally incomprehensible and regrettable." In response, Malik referred to Truman's statement, issued right after the Hiroshima bomb, in which the president noted that Japan had rejected the proclamation. Truman's distortion of fact was conveniently exploited by the Soviet Union to justify the violation of the Neutrality Pact.

Togo informed Malik that the Japanese government had decided to accept the Potsdam Proclamation with the one condition that imperial prerogatives be preserved, underscoring the importance of retaining the imperial house. He gave Malik the English translation of Japan's acceptance letter, and asked the Soviet ambassador to transmit it to his government as quickly as possible.[3] Togo clearly wanted to send the Allies a message that Japan's only concern was saving the emperor and the imperial house. This was not the intent of Hiranuma's amendment, but Togo twisted the amendment to suit his own objective.

Japanese reading the morning papers on August 11 must have had a hard time accepting that their government had decided to capitulate. In the official announcement, Director of Information Shimomura appealed to the people to weather the difficulties in order to preserve the kokutai. But he mentioned nothing about the acceptance of the Allied ultimatum. Moreover, the morning papers also printed the army minister's bellicose proclamation urging soldiers and officers to continue fighting, "even if we have to eat grass, chew dirt, and sleep in the field."[4]

Actually, the army minister's proclamation was given to the press without Anami's approval. Early on August 10, Anami returned to the Army Ministry and reported the emperor's sacred decision to all the senior officers. He declared, "Whether we should seek peace or keep fighting will depend on the enemy's answer. Whichever way we go, we must take united action under strict military discipline, and avoid any actions outside discipline." One officer defiantly stood up and asked a pointed question: "The minister said whichever way we choose. Are you then thinking about the possibility of surrender?" A chilling hush filled the room. It was a bold challenge from the staff officers who were determined to fight. Anami fired back that anyone who acted against the official policy must do so over his dead body.

This exchange was a harbinger of things to come. During the day on

August 11, the building that housed the Army Ministry and the General Staff was abuzz with unofficial meetings among junior officers. A plan for a coup was hatched in this highly charged atmosphere. Major Masao Inaba proposed to the military division chief that a proclamation be issued in the name of the army minister in order to maintain the morale of the officers and soldiers. Permission was granted, and Inaba drafted a call to continue the war that junior officers delivered to the media.[5]

News of the army minister's proclamation alarmed the peace party. But Togo refused to do anything, presumably out of fear that his intervention would have poured oil on the fire. Sakomizu, Yoshizumi, and Prince Konoe attempted to stop publication, but to no avail. Kido refused to intervene, citing concern that such a move might provoke the army to action. Anami, for his part, would not take action because, as he admitted, the army minister's statement expressed his own sentiment.[6] This episode indicates that Japan's surrender was still precarious. One false move could tip the balance, reverse the decision, and send Japan down the costly path of continuing the war. Anami's position was crucial in this balance, and he had not decided which side to take.

In order to prevent that reversal, Matsumoto and Hasegawa of Domei News decided to send the message of Japan's conditional acceptance of the Potsdam terms to the Allies as soon as possible. Since all news transmitted through short-wave radio was subject to military censorship, they surreptitiously sent the message through Morse code under the headline: "Japan Accepts Potsdam Proclamation." They managed to send the typed message three times before military censors got wind of the action and stopped it. Yoshizumi angrily protested. He feared that news of Japan's decision to end the war would affect the morale of the soldiers at the front. But within an hour, the United Press began to broadcast the news that Japan had accepted the Potsdam Proclamation. Truman learned of the decision at 7:33 A.M. (8:33 P.M. Japan time).[7] One shudders to think what might have happened had the United States picked up the army minister's bellicose statement before Domei's message. Thanks to Matsumoto and Hasegawa, Japan's acceptance of the Potsdam terms instantly became world news.

Truman Rejects Japan's Conditional Acceptance

At 7:30 in the morning on August 10, American radio monitors intercepted the message dispatched by Domei News. It was the news that Truman had anxiously been awaiting. Although it was not yet an official communication, Truman immediately called for Byrnes, Stimson, and Forrestal to come to his office at nine o'clock to discuss how to respond. The minute Stimson saw the text of the Japanese acceptance he realized that his fear had become reality. With the memory of his meetings at Potsdam with the president and Byrnes flashing through his mind, he hurried to the White House, where he found Truman, Byrnes, Forrestal, Leahy, and the president's aides already assembled.[8]

Historians are unanimous in the opinion that Byrnes played a decisive role in rejecting Japan's conditional acceptance of the Potsdam ultimatum. But one piece of evidence shedding light on Byrnes's thinking has been overlooked. Joseph Ballantine received the news of Japan's conditional surrender through short-wave radio at 7:30 A.M. Japan's insistence on imperial prerogatives instantly alarmed him. Ballantine rushed to the State Department to see Dooman and Grew, and told them: "We can't agree to that, because the prerogatives of the emperor include everything, and if you agree to that, you're going to have endless struggle with the Japanese." Ironically, it was the State Department's pro-emperor trio, Ballantine, Dooman, and Grew, who understood the significance of Hiranuma's amendment.

Byrnes, who was initially inclined to accept Japan's condition, had to be convinced that preservation of the imperial prerogatives demanded by Japan would be incompatible with America's basic objective in the war. Grew approached him twice, followed by Dooman and Ballantine, before Byrnes agreed that, despite the nation's war-weariness, they could not accept Japan's condition of surrender.[9]

Byrnes's willingness to make a deal with Japan despite its adherence to conditional surrender is not well known. His previous insistence on unconditional surrender and his subsequent reversion to that position make it difficult to believe that the secretary of state was inclined to approve Japan's conditional acceptance. Nevertheless, Ballantine's account cannot be dismissed as a total fabrication. Byrnes knew that Truman was becoming impatient about ending the war. Despite two atomic bombs, Japan had not surrendered, and the Soviets were advancing in Manchuria. He expected Stimson, Forrestal, and Leahy to insist on approval of Japan's answer. Nevertheless, if he had entertained the possibility of accepting Japan's answer for a flicker of a moment, it did not take him long to change his mind.[10]

The president opened the meeting by asking questions: Should they consider the message from Japan an acceptance of the Potsdam Proclamation? Could they allow the emperorship to continue and still manage to eliminate Japan's militarism? Should they even consider the Japanese acceptance given the significant condition attached to it? Byrnes said that he was troubled by the Japanese condition, and he expressed doubt about accepting it in light of some of the uncompromising public statements by Roosevelt and Truman. In his memoirs he gave a different reason: "While equally anxious to bring the war to an end, I had to disagree, pointing out that we had to get the assent of the British and Soviets; that we had their concurrence to the Potsdam Declaration [*sic*] with the words 'unconditional surrender,' and any retreat from these words now would cause much delay in securing their acquiescence."[11] If Byrnes made such an argument, it was simply an excuse to reject Japan's reply, since he knew that the British would accept Japan's condition. As for the Soviets, he did not see any reason to negotiate with them on this issue. It is puzzling that Byrnes did not forcefully present the most legitimate reason for rejecting Japan's demand: it violated the basic military objectives of the United States against Japan.

After Byrnes, Leahy spoke. He "took a good plain horse-sense position" that the retention of the emperor was minor compared with delaying a victory. The president then asked for Stimson's view. The secretary of war said that even if the question had not been raised by the Japanese, the United States would need to keep the emperor to ensure that the many scattered Japanese armies would surrender and "in order to save us from a score of bloody Iwo Jimas and Okinawas all over China and the New Netherlands." The Japanese armies would not recognize any authority but the emperor. Stimson's argument did not touch on the larger question of whether Japan's condition should be accepted in view of the U.S. objectives in the war. He also suggested that since "something like an armistice over the settlement of the question was inevitable, and . . . [since] it would be a humane thing and the thing that might effect the settlement, the bombing be stopped immediately." Forrestal supported Stimson's proposal to suspend bombing "heart and soul." According to the secretary of the navy, if the bombing were to continue, the United States "would have to bear the focus of the hatred by the Japanese, and the Russians or the British or the Chinese would not be the focus of hatred."[12]

Stimson, Forrestal, and Leahy argued for the immediate acceptance of Japan's reply. But Byrnes opposed the majority view. He argued: "at Potsdam the big-3 said 'unconditional surrender.' Then there was [no] atomic bomb and no Russia in the war. I cannot understand why now we should go further than we were willing to go at Potsdam when we had no atomic bomb, and Russia was not in the war." Accepting Japan's condition would lead to "the crucifixion of the President," he insisted.[13] Byrnes framed the question in raw political terms.

Stimson felt that the Soviet factor necessitated a flexible attitude. He recalls that in his view, "it was of great importance to get the homeland into our hands before the Russians could put in any substantial claim to occupy and help rule it." Byrnes also shared this concern.[14] Here was the chance to prevent an expansion of Soviet influence in Asia, and Byrnes, whom revisionist historians characterize as the most ardent anti-Soviet advocate, refused to take it.

Why did Byrnes reject Japan's conditional acceptance of the Potsdam terms? Certainly American public opinion against the emperor was one powerful motivation. But two other factors also influenced Byrnes's position. The first was his conviction that the United States should not allow Japan to dictate the terms of surrender. Byrnes was fully prepared to let the Japanese retain some form of the emperor system. But it would have to be the United States, not Japan, that should decide the matter. Byrnes was fully aware that the president shared this sentiment.

Second, Byrnes knew that allowing the imperial prerogatives was tantamount to accepting the emperor's unrestricted power, especially over military matters, making it impossible for the Allies to eradicate Japanese militarism. The difference between Byrnes, on the one hand, and Stimson, Forrestal, and Leahy, on the other, was actually not as significant as historians have claimed. Forrestal suggested a compromise: "we might in our reply indicate willingness to accept, yet define the terms of surrender in such a manner that the intents and purposes of the Potsdam Declaration would be clearly accomplished." Truman agreed, and he asked Byrnes to draft a reply.[15]

Byrnes prepared a draft reply with the help of Benjamin Cohen, Ballantine, and Dooman. Ballantine and Dooman strongly objected to the provision in Byrnes's draft requiring the emperor's signature on the surrender documents, but Byrnes vetoed their objection. In the meantime, Stimson discussed the issue with McCloy in the Pentagon. McCloy advocated clearly mentioning in the reply the intention to retain the monarchical system. But Stimson disagreed with McCloy and approved Byrnes's reply when he learned of its contents over the phone. Shortly before noon, Byrnes went back to the White House with a draft letter. Truman approved the document and ordered a cabinet meeting for two o'clock.[16]

At the meeting the president announced that he had received Japan's official acceptance from Sweden, and that Byrnes had drawn up a reply that he would send to Britain, China, and perhaps the Soviet Union for approval. He then read Byrnes's response. The major points of this draft were Articles 1 and 4. Article 1 stipulated: "From the moment of surrender the authority of the emperor and the Japanese Government to rule the state shall be subject to the Supreme Commander of the Allied Powers." Article 4 stated: "the ultimate form of government of Japan shall . . . be established by the freely expressed will of the Japanese people." These provisions did not rule out the possibility of retaining the emperor, but they remained silent on the fate of the emperor and the imperial house. The president said that he expected Britain and China to acquiesce promptly. But according to Forrestal, he "fiercely interjected" that he did not expect to hear from the Soviet Union. He said that if the Soviets failed to respond, the United States should act without them and proceed with the occupation of Japan. Stimson noted that "the Russians were in favor of delay so they could push as far into Manchuria as possible." Stimson's argument logically followed from his belief that the United States should accept Japan's reply. But Truman, too, noted, "it was to our interest that the Russians not push too far into Manchuria."[17] This is a puzzling statement that contradicted the Byrnes Note that he had just approved.

The Byrnes Note was sent to London, Chungking, and Moscow at 3:45 P.M. Washington time. Attlee and Bevin accepted the note with one modification: they did not think it wise to require the emperor to sign the surrender terms. To Ballantine's and Dooman's satisfaction, Byrnes had to accept the British amendment.[18] Chiang Kai-shek's reply arrived on the morning of August 11. In contrast to the British, Chiang Kai-shek concurred with the provision requiring the emperor to sign the surrender terms, but his opinion was conveniently ignored.

In an interview years later, Truman was asked, "Were there any representations made to the emperor that he would be retained?" Truman answered: "Yes, he was told that he would not be tried as a war criminal and that he would be retained as emperor." When asked who made that promise, Truman responded that it was presented "through regular channels."[19] Truman was wrong. The United States never communicated to Japan through "regular channels" that the emperor would not be tried as a war criminal or dethroned. Truman had somehow forgotten the central issue determining the fate of the war.

While Truman's cabinet was deliberating how to respond to Japan, McCloy began preparing a series of papers on Japan's surrender terms with George Lincoln, Colonel Bonesteel, and others. On August 11, the draft of Order Number 1 (to be issued by MacArthur), the Directive to the Supreme Commander of the Allied Powers (to be signed by the president), and the Instrument of Surrender were brought to the SWNCC meeting and approved.[20] The stage was set for the fierce end game between the United States and the Soviet Union.

The Emperor and American Public Opinion

It is the consensus among historians that Byrnes's motivation for rejecting Japan's condition stemmed from his concern that appeasement might cause a domestic backlash against the president. Public opinion surveys strongly support this assertion. The Gallup poll conducted on May 29 indicated that 33 percent of those polled demanded the emperor's execution, 17 percent a trial, 11 percent imprisonment, and 9 percent exile. Only 3 percent advocated his role as a puppet. Byrnes's comment that Truman's lenient treatment of the emperor would lead to the president's "crucifixion" has some validity. At the August 10 cabinet meeting, Truman referred to 170 telegrams he had received after the peace rumor on August 9, 153 of which supported unconditional surrender.[21]

Nevertheless, surveys are only one aspect of public opinion. Commentaries and editorials in leading newspapers and journals, though often overlooked by historians, also tend to influence policymakers' decisions. Opinions on the Japanese response were divided. William Shirer, Arthur Crock, and Drew Pearson argued for harsh terms that would not compromise unconditional surrender. William Shirer reasoned: "For the United Nations to support the imperial throne in Japan after the war is to strengthen an institution subversive of all the principles and aims for which this war is being fought." In contrast, Walter Lippmann argued that the retention of the emperor system would not be a sign of weakness, and was in fact compatible with the aims of the United States. Ernest Lindley, Lowell Mellett, Mark Sullivan, and Stanley Washburn similarly advocated specifying the terms of unconditional surrender and making it clear that the Japanese could retain a monarchical system.[22] Whereas the *New York Times* and the *New York Herald Tribune* generally supported harsh terms against the emperor, the *Washington Post* and the *Boston Globe* advocated soft peace.

Congressional pressure is another important aspect of domestic opinion. Congressman Charles A. Plumley (R-Vermont) wrote a letter to Byrnes: "Let the Japanese know unqualifiedly what unconditional surrender means. Let the dirty rats squeal." Senator Kenneth S. Wherry (R-Nebraska), meanwhile, campaigned to modify unconditional surrender in such a way as to let the Japanese retain the emperor. Senator Wallace H. White (R-Maine) stated that the terms of unconditional surrender should be clarified to exclude large-scale military occupation and abolition of the imperial institution. Senator Burton K. Wheeler (D-Montana) made a speech in the Senate on July 2 in which he urged Truman to clarify the terms of unconditional surrender and invited Grew to the Capitol to talk to a group of senators. Wheeler indicated that some of the senators were eager to speak, but Grew discouraged this out of fear that such action "might lead the Japanese to think we are cracking up."[23]

In the middle of July, Fred Burdick, editor of *Capitol Gist Service*, conducted a survey of congressional sentiment on unconditional surrender. According to this survey, Congress was virtually unanimous in favor of clarifying the terms for Japan. Although this survey did not directly address the issue of retention of the monarchy, many congressmen favored a statement similar to Wilson's Fourteen Points.[24] Immediately after the news of Japan's conditional acceptance of the Potsdam terms reached the Congress, the *New York Times* surveyed some members. Of eighteen senators and congressmen surveyed, ten were against the retention of the emperor and eight favored allowing Hirohito to remain on the throne.[25]

Thus public opinion was more fluid and murky than historians have argued. While the Gallup poll indicated overwhelming hostility toward the Japanese emperor, commentaries by columnists and editorials were evenly divided. Furthermore, letters to the editor also showed the division of views on this issue. Some letters strongly advocated softening unconditional surrender to bring American soldiers home sooner. This was the view that most worried military planners in the War Department. Recall that even in the Gallup poll, 23 percent had no opinion about the emperor. Combined with 4 percent for no action and 3 percent for a puppet role, 30 percent did not advocate harsh treatment of the emperor. Given the fickleness of public opinion, it was quite likely that when faced with an imminent invasion of Japan's homeland, a majority of Americans might then favor softening unconditional surrender to end the war.

Certainly, public opinion at home was a factor in Byrnes's and Truman's decision to reject Japan's conditional acceptance of the Potsdam terms. But Byrnes's oft-quoted statement that any softening of unconditional surrender would lead to "crucifixion of the president" is an exaggeration. It was not public opinion that dictated their course of action; rather, they selectively chose public opinion to justify their decision.

Moscow Responds to Japan's Reply

Moscow received the news of Japan's conditional acceptance of the Potsdam terms through Malik on the afternoon of August 10. The news also reached the Chinese delegation. The possibility that Japan's surrender might approach quickly gave both sides an incentive to conclude an agreement before the Pacific War was over. Neither side, however, was prepared to make concessions on fundamental issues. But with their troops quickly penetrating into Manchuria, the Soviets held a higher card.

As soon as the seventh session of the Sino-Soviet negotiations began, Stalin announced that Japan was about to surrender. But he added that the Japanese wanted to attach a condition to surrender, whereas the Allies wanted unconditional surrender. He demanded: "It is about time to sign the treaties." "We are ready to sign them before Japan's surrender," Soong agreed, "because [then] it would be easier to explain the agreement to the Chinese people." They then began discussing the remaining contentious issues. Stalin made a series of minor concessions, but they still disagreed on the administration of Dairen and the railroads, and the precise border between Outer Mongolia and Inner Mongolia.[26]

An important exchange took place over the issue of the Chinese Communists. In Article 1 of the draft of the Treaty of Friendship and Alliance, in which the Soviet Union pledged its support for the Nationalist government as the sole government of China, Stalin proposed the addition of a phrase: after the Soviet government was convinced that the Nationalist government would implement "national unity and democratization of China." This was Stalin's attempt to encourage the Nationalists to form a coalition government with the Communists. The Chinese delegation insisted on striking out this condition. "Don't you want to democratize China?" Stalin asked. Soong answered that the caveat constituted interference in China's domestic matters. Stalin explained: "If you continue to beat Communists, are we expected to support [the] Chinese government?

We do not interfere, but [it would be] hard for us to support morally when you fight Communists." Finally, Stalin gave up: "O.K. You see how many concessions we make. [The] Chinese Communists will curse us." Despite Stalin's major concession on this matter, however, they failed to come to an agreement. The Sino-Soviet Treaty remained an elusive goal. The seventh meeting ended with Stalin's ominous warning to Soong that they had better come to an agreement quickly or "the Communists will get into Manchuria."[27] The Chinese Communists were a powerful trump card in Stalin's hand.

Harriman was alarmed. He informed Byrnes that "the principal stumbling blocks appear to be Stalin's demand for joint ownership of the port facilities of Dairen and [his demand] for one Soviet manager for both railroads." Harriman did not think that the management of the railroads was sufficiently important to allow the negotiations to break down, but he warned: "our interests would be adversely affected if Soong agreed to give the Soviets joint ownership of the port facilities of Dairen, and the Yalta Agreement certainly does not envisage this." He urgently requested instructions from Washington.[28]

Harriman had other important business to attend to on that day. Late at night on August 10, Molotov summoned Harriman and Clark Kerr to his office to discuss Japan's surrender. Molotov informed the two ambassadors that the Soviet government had received information that the Japanese government was prepared to accept the Potsdam Proclamation with the understanding that doing so would not jeopardize the prerogatives of the emperor as the sovereign power. Molotov said that the Soviets were "skeptical" about this statement because it did not represent unconditional surrender. The Soviet Army had penetrated 170 kilometers into Manchuria, and its advance would continue. This was, as Molotov declared, the Soviet government's "concrete reply" to the Japanese request for conditional surrender.[29]

While Harriman and Clark Kerr were still meeting with Molotov, George Kennan, chargé d'affaires of the American Embassy in Moscow, burst into the room with the latest dispatch from Washington, requesting Moscow's agreement with the Byrnes Note. Harriman pressed Molotov for an immediate reply. Molotov promised to answer the following day, but Harriman insisted on receiving his answer before the night was out. At two o'clock in the morning Harriman and Clark Kerr were called back to Molotov's office. At that time they learned that the Soviets would accept the Byrnes Note, with the addition of the following passage: "The

Soviet Government also feels that, in case of an affirmative reply from the Japanese Government, the Allied Powers should reach an agreement on *the candidacy or candidacies* for representation of the Allied High Command to which the Japanese emperor and the Japanese Government are to be subordinated."[30]

This was the first in a series of conflicts between the United States and the Soviet Union over the occupation of Japan. The Byrnes Note stated: "From the moment of surrender the authority of the emperor and the Japanese Government to rule the state shall be subject to *the Supreme Commander of the Allied Powers*." The expression "supreme commander" was a well-chosen one. Forrestal wrote in his diary: "Both the President and the Secretary of State emphasized the fact that they had used the term 'Supreme Commander' rather than 'Supreme Command' so that it would be quite clear that the United States would run this particular business and avoid a situation of composite responsibility such as had plagued us in Germany."[31] Now the Soviet Union challenged this view by proposing that it share the position of supreme commander.

Harriman immediately dismissed the proposition as "utterly out of the question." The Soviet proposal would give veto power to the Soviet government in the choice of the supreme commander, a condition that he knew his government would reject. Molotov suggested that there might be two supreme commanders, perhaps Vasilevskii and MacArthur. This suggestion enraged Harriman. Undeterred, Molotov requested that, despite the ambassador's opinion of the proposal, he transmit it to his home government. Harriman promised to do so but reminded Molotov that "the United States had carried the main burden of the war in the Pacific on its shoulders for four years. It had therefore kept the Japanese off the Soviets' back. The Soviet Government had been in the war for two days. It was unthinkable that the Supreme Commander could be other than an American." Molotov heatedly replied that he did not wish to respond to the ambassador's statement, because doing so would compel him to make comparisons with the European war.

When Harriman returned to his office, Stalin's interpreter, Vladimir Pavlov, telephoned him to say that there had been a misunderstanding. The Soviet government only wished to be involved in "consultation," not "reaching an agreement," on the candidacies of the supreme commander. Thus Stalin suggested that the words "reach an agreement" be replaced by the word "consult." Harriman stood firm, even when the Soviets modified their proposal to "consult on the candidacy."[32] The Soviets backed down, but this was merely the beginning of the tug of war.

With approval from all three governments, the State Department sent the Byrnes Note to the Japanese government on the morning of August 11.

Japan's War Party Launches a Counterattack

The policymakers in Tokyo spent the entire day of August 11 anxiously awaiting an answer from the Allies on the conditional acceptance of the Potsdam Proclamation. Both the peace party and the war party made a series of moves anticipating the Allied reply. Sakomizu from the peace party secretly began working on a draft of the Imperial Rescript to be issued to the Japanese people.

In the meantime, Kido had come to the conclusion that in order to impose peace terms on Japan in the face of expected resistance from the military, the emperor would need to make an unprecedented radio broadcast. Hirohito agreed to record the rescript for the radio broadcast.[33] With the real voice of the emperor directly appealing to the Japanese subjects, and above all, to the soldiers and officers, the peace party planned to impose the imperial will on the country. If the war party wished to continue the war, they would have to prevent this broadcast. The battle for the phonographs assumed crucial importance for the fate of the nation and the war.

Tokyo received the official answer from the United States on August 12. Around 2 A.M. on August 12, the Byrnes Note was brought to Togo, Matsumoto, and Sakomizu. They were deeply disappointed that the Allies did not accept Japan's condition, but Matsumoto insisted that Japan had no choice but to accept the Byrnes Note. Around the same time, officials from the Foreign Ministry met to begin translating the note. Hoping that the military would rely on their translation, Shin'ichi Shibusawa (treaty division chief) and Takezo Shimoda (treaty division section chief), later joined by Matsumoto, intentionally translated the American reply in softer language. For instance, the statement "the Japanese government shall be subject to the supreme commander" was translated as "seigenka ni ari," or "the Japanese government shall be placed under the restriction of the supreme commander." Furthermore, "the ultimate form of government" was translated as "the definite form of the

Japanese government" to give the impression that the government would be under the emperor. But even Togo had a hard time believing the contorted explanation that the non-interference in Japan's domestic affairs implicit in the fourth section of the Byrnes Note would not contradict the *kokutai*.[34]

Around 5:30 A.M. Matsumoto, Shibusawa, and Ando drove down to see Togo at his house. They found the foreign minister in a state of depression. He was concerned about the backlash that the Byrnes Note was bound to provoke among the hard liners. He had barely succeeded in pushing through the one-condition acceptance. It was again Matsumoto who tried to encourage the dejected foreign minister to fight on. He insisted that if Japan did not accept the Byrnes Note there would be no peace at all. They talked for two hours, but Togo refused to commit himself to accepting the Byrnes Note. Matsumoto then left to meet with Sakomizu. The two men conspired to trick their bosses. Matsumoto went back to Togo's house and told the foreign minister that Suzuki had decided to accept the Allied reply, while Sakomizu told Suzuki that Togo had made up his mind to accept it. Togo finally agreed to accept the Byrnes Note.[35]

The army acted more swiftly than the Foreign Ministry had expected, producing a straight translation very quickly. In this version the first article was translated literally as "the emperor and the Japanese government shall be 'subject to' the Allied supreme commander"; and the fourth article as "the ultimate form of the Japanese government" shall be determined by the will of the Japanese people. The Military Affairs Section decided to reject the document in toto as grossly violating the *kokutai,* and informed Sakomizu and the Imperial Palace of its position.[36]

But the highest authority of the General Staff was much more sober in assessing the situation. According to Kawabe, the Byrnes Note was a document dictated by the complete victor to the complete loser. He added, however, that "although young officers are exercised by the document, more harm will be done than good to kick and struggle at this point." Kawabe noted that he sat in his office that day in a stupor. He listened as Lieutenant General Sumihisa Ikeda (director of the General Planning Bureau) assailed the knee-jerk reactions of the General Staff to the peace party's maneuvers. Kawabe did not disagree with Ikeda's opinion, but he felt that it was impossible to reverse the general currents for peace; moreover, the bid to attain peace originated from the emperor, whose authority was absolute and could not be questioned. To the suggestion that the government should try to get the Allies to accept three other conditions, Kawabe responded that it was a pipedream, and noted that such unrealistic thinking shared broadly by military officers had led to this tragedy. Kawabe blurted out in his diary: "Alas, we are defeated. The imperial state we have believed in has been ruined."[37] The high command was now permeated by a sense of defeat.

Umezu and Toyoda had to tread carefully between acceptance of the emperor's sacred decision and pressure from below to fight on. They submitted a joint petition to the emperor in which they argued that the Byrnes Note was tantamount to rendering Japan into a slave nation "subject to" the Allied commander. Acceptance of the note would allow the enemy to disarm the Imperial Army and Navy and to occupy Japan by stationing their own armed forces in the homeland. Moreover, this document would desecrate the dignity of the emperor, the very foundation of the *kokutai*. The emperor, however, reprimanded the chiefs for basing their hasty conclusion on information they had received from the broadcast and on a suspicious translation, rather than on the formal diplomatic document.[38] The emperor's mind was made up. If he had earlier allowed himself to be tempted by the desire to preserve his prerogatives, he was now fighting only to save himself and the imperial house. For this desperate struggle, he had to cut off his army and navy. Moreover, the lack of passion evident in Umezu and Toyoda's petition gave the impression that they were simply going through the motions to allay the dissatisfaction of radical officers.

In the meantime, the army General Staff prepared a document for the Supreme War Council meeting that would likely be convened to discuss Japan's reaction to the Byrnes Note. It stated that "the empire resolutely rejects the conditions in the enemy's reply on August 12, and exerts its utmost to achieve the goals of the Greater East Asian War, even at the risk of the extinction of the empire." Further, it stated the following three objectives: to "carry out vigorous and strong operations against the United States, Britain, and China, but not declaring war against the Soviet Union for the time being and attempting to improve the situation as much as possible"; to strengthen the domestic front in order to continue the war to the end and preserve the *kokutai;* and to renegotiate the conditions to end the war, while striving to separate the Soviet Union from the United States and Britain.[39] This document indicates that, as unrealistic as it might seem, the radical officers of the army General Staff continued to view the Soviet Union as the key to ensuring Japan's continuation of the war, and considered it possible to make a deal with Moscow and decouple the Soviet Union from the rest of the Allies. "Strengthening the domestic front" meant that the army was prepared to create a military dictatorship.

Radical staff officers continued to plan a coup. Lieutenant Colonel Takeshita, Anami's brother-in-law, plotted to use the Imperial Guard Division and units from the Eastern Military District to occupy the Imperial Palace and residences of the imperial family, arrest senior statesmen and cabinet ministers, seize the radio stations, navy and army ministries, and General Staffs, and "protect" important leaders, including the emperor. Typical of any coup concocted by army officers in the Showa era, this plan was heavy on action plans but extremely light on political programs.

Takeshita and a dozen other staff officers brought this plan to Kawabe. Kawabe did not approve the plan, but suggested instead that civilian terrorism be employed. The conspirators then brought the plan to Anami. Representing the group, Takeshita told his brother-in-law: "You should reject the Potsdam Proclamation. If you cannot stop it, then you should commit *seppuku*." Anami quietly listened to their view. He even commented on some weaknesses of the coup plan, as if he supported it. He gave his permission to mobilize the units of the Eastern Military District and the Imperial Guard Division. He did not approve or disapprove their plan, but his silence encouraged the hotheads to continue the plot.[40]

At 10:30 A.M., having made up his mind to accept the Byrnes Note, Foreign Minister Togo went to the prime minister's office to confer with Suzuki. Not knowing they had been tricked by Sakomizu and Matsumoto, the prime minister and the foreign minister concurred to accept the Allies' response. Togo then went to the Imperial Palace at 11 A.M. and had an audience with the emperor. This time Hirohito readily approved Togo's view. Hirohito was now asserting himself as a major proponent of peace. By noon, Suzuki, Togo, Kido, Yonai, and Hirohito had reached a consensus to push forward for peace by accepting the Byrnes Note.

No sooner had the consensus been formed than trouble came from two directions. The army minister went to see Suzuki and told him that the army was dead set against accepting the Byrnes Note; he reminded the prime minister of his pledge to support the continuation of the war if the Allies rejected the *kokutai*. But another blow came from an unexpected quarter. Hiranuma, who had supported the peace party at the imperial conference, opposed the acceptance of the Byrnes Note. As a believer in the mythical notion of the *kokutai,* he could not accept a situation in which the emperor would be subordinate to the supreme commander of the Allied powers. Furthermore, the condition that the form of the government be determined by the will of the people was antithetical to his belief. The *kokutai,* in his view, was not compatible with democracy. The coalition between Hiranuma and Anami, combined with the ominous possibility of a coup by the staff officers, considerably weakened Suzuki's resolve to accept the Byrnes Note.

The indefatigable Hiranuma then made a trip to the Imperial Palace, where he demanded to meet with Kido. Hiranuma's argument touched a sore spot with the Lord Keeper of the Privy Seal, whose job was not only to protect the current holder of the imperial seat but also to uphold the institution of the emperor itself. Disturbed by Hiranuma's argument, Kido reported his concerns to the emperor. Hirohito immediately responded that since the Byrnes Note referred to the "freely expressed will of the people," he did not see any problem. If the people still trusted the imperial house, as he thought they would, this condition could only make it stronger. Hiranuma's and Hirohito's views of the *kokutai* clashed. Whereas Hiranuma understood the *kokutai* to be the mythical source from which not only the emperor system but also the Japanese spiritual essence sprang, Hirohito now defined it narrowly as the preservation of the imperial house. Faced with the crisis, the emperor tenaciously clung to the preservation of his own household at all costs. Kido supported the emperor's view. He knew that it would defy logic to argue that the Byrnes Note did not contradict the preservation of the *kokutai,* but he would twist any logic in order to bring an end to the war and save the only things that mattered: the emperor and the imperial house.[41]

At 3 P.M. the emperor summoned his relatives to the palace. Thirteen princes from five houses attended. Convening an imperial household conference was unprecedented, an indication that the situation was becoming desperate. Seventy-one-year-old Prince Nashi, the empress's uncle, assured Hirohito that the princes would all cooperate with the emperor as a united body. Faced with a crisis in the imperial house, Hirohito's relatives circled the wagon. They came to accept the emperor's narrow definition of the *kokutai* in order to save the imperial household.[42]

While the emperor was meeting with his relatives, the cabinet was holding an emergency session. Togo employed a somewhat tortured logic and argued, without conviction, that the fourth provision in the Byrnes Note did not amount to interference in Japan's internal politics. Anami responded forcefully that accepting the Byrnes Note was tantamount to giving up the *kokutai*. The big surprise came in Suzuki's change of opinion. Not only did he raise objections to the Allies' rejection of Japan's sole condition, but he now began to voice opposition to disarmament by the Allies. If the Allies rejected these conditions, the prime minister argued, Japan would have no alternative but to continue the war. Yonai kept silent. Togo turned out to be the lone advocate for acceptance. The peace party was on the brink of defeat.

Togo, acting on advice from Matsumoto, managed to persuade his colleagues to postpone a decision until the Japanese government received the Allies' formal answer. Togo was shocked and angered by Suzuki's change of heart. He confided to Matsumoto his intention to resign. Matsumoto dissuaded the foreign minister from taking rash action, and asked him to wait until the government received the Allies' formal answer. Matsumoto then rushed to Suzuki's office and directly confronted him in an attempt to convince him to change his mind again. Suzuki demurred.

Encouraged by Matsumoto's pep talk, Togo went to the Imperial Palace at 6:30 P.M. to report to Kido what had transpired at the cabinet meeting. Kido assured Togo that the emperor's decision to accept the Byrnes Note was firm and unchanged. He promised to twist Suzuki's arm by conveying the emperor's position. At 9:30 P.M., Kido summoned the prime minister to the palace. Kido argued that they had no choice but to accept the Byrnes Note. Should Japan reject it, tens of millions of innocent people would suffer as a result of air raids and starvation. More important, there might be unrest. Suzuki finally accepted Kido's position.[43] Takagi met Yonai and urged the navy minister to act more decisively to accept the Byrnes Note. Yonai, for his part, summoned Toyoda and Onishi and severely reprimanded them for acting against the imperial wish. He was determined to contain any move for insubordination within the navy. Yonai confided to Takagi: "The atomic bombs and the Soviet entry into the war are, in a sense, God's gifts," since they provided an excuse to end the war. "The reason I have long been advocating the conclusion of the [war] . . . is my concern over the domestic situation. So it is rather fortunate that now we can end the war without bringing the domestic situation to the fore."[44]

Half an hour before Kido met with Suzuki, Anami paid a visit to Prince Mikasa, Hirohito's youngest brother, to ask him to intercede to change the emperor's mind. Prince Mikasa flatly rejected Anami's request.

Anami then told Hayashi that Prince Mikasa had accused the army of having consistently disregarded the emperor's wishes since the Manchurian Incident.[45] The imperial house had deserted the army. To save itself, it was now prepared to cut off an integral part of the emperor system.

At 6:30 P.M. the Foreign Ministry finally received the official text of the Byrnes Note, but, as Matsumoto had planned, they kept the news secret until the following morning to allow the peace party to form a new strategy. The General Staff meanwhile received numerous telegrams from commanders at the overseas fronts, urging it to stand firm to continue the war. The commander of the army in China, General Yasuji Okamura, dispatched a telegram: "We had anticipated Soviet participation in the war from the beginning . . . I am firmly convinced that it is time to exert all our efforts to fight to the end with the determination for all the army to die an honorable death without being distracted by the enemy's peace offensive and the domestic passive policy." Marshal Hisaichi Terauchi, commander of the Southern Army, also opposed the acceptance of peace: "If we now bend our will to complete our sacred war to the end and submit ourselves to the enemy's terms, who will guarantee the preservation of the *kokutai* and protection of the imperial land without military force? . . . Under no circumstances can the Southern Army accept the enemy's reply."[46] Strong pressure from the commanders of the armies in China and Burma confirmed the Army Ministry's fear that surrender would not be accepted by officers of the Imperial Army overseas. This was also what Stimson feared might happen.

The U.S. Waits for Japan's Answer

August 12 was a Sunday, but Truman worked in his office, waiting for Japan's reply to the Byrnes Note. It never came. He did, however, receive Stalin's final approval of the appointment of General Douglas MacArthur as the supreme commander for the Allied powers. But Truman continued to worry about the consequences of the Soviet advance in Manchuria. Some advisers recommended the urgent deployment of American troops in Manchuria and Korea. From Moscow Edwin Pauley, ambassador to the Allied Commission on Reparations, urged Truman to deploy American troops to "occupy quickly . . . much of the industrial areas of Korea and Manchuria." Harriman supported this recommendation. "While at Potsdam," he cabled, "General Marshall and Admiral King told me of the proposed landings in Korea and Dairen if the Japanese gave in prior to Soviet troops occupying these areas." Mindful of the on-going negotiations between Stalin and Soong, he suggested: "Considering the way Stalin is behaving in increasing his demands on Soong, I recom-mend that these landings be made to accept surrender of the Japanese troops at least on the Kwantung [Liaotung] Peninsula and in Korea. I cannot see that we are under any obligation to the Soviets to respect any zone of Soviet military operation."[47]

From Chungking, Ambassador Hurley and Lieutenant General Albert Wedemeyer, commander of the U.S. forces in China, sounded a tocsin, in-forming the president that Chu Teh, commanding general of the Chinese Communist forces, had broadcast an order that Japanese and Chinese puppet forces should surrender to the nearest anti-Japanese troops. Chu Teh also stressed that Communist forces should have the right to enter any city and control administration in any part of the territories occupied by Japan. Wedemeyer warned that a civil war was imminent. Both he and Hurley argued that the United States should take measures to ensure that all Japanese forces surrender to Nationalist forces, not to the Commu-nists.[48]

Thus the United States, concerned about Soviet expansion in Manchu-ria and Korea and collusion between Soviet forces and the Chinese Com-munists, began to consider countermeasures. On the afternoon of August 12, the Joint Chiefs of Staff brought the draft of the Instrument of Sur-render to Truman. Mindful of the recommendations he had received from Pauley, Harriman, and Hurley, Truman changed the draft to in-clude, after MacArthur's signature, the signatures of representatives of the four major powers.[49] He wanted to ensure that the American prerog-atives to occupy Japan as the predominant power should be sanctioned by the other allies.

Just the day before, Truman had decided, against the advice of Stimson and Forrestal, to continue bombing Japan. Barton Bernstein explains that Truman's policy was driven by domestic pressure. Most Americans were willing to prolong the war, Bernstein concludes, to secure the em-peror's removal. But Truman was motivated by more than a desire to sat-isfy the American public; he felt a strong need to bring Japan to its knees or, to put it more bluntly, to exact revenge. Between August 10 and Au-gust 14, more than 1,000 American bombers attacked Japanese cities, killing more than 15,000 Japanese.[50]

For the moment, he suspended the use of the atomic bomb, but he did not altogether rule out the use of a third bomb; he knew that the third bomb would not be ready until August 19. The War Department proceeded on the assumption that the third, fourth, and more bombs would be used against Japan. Altogether, seven bombs would be ready by the end of October. To General Hull, the question was whether the United States should "continue on dropping them every time one was made" or whether they should "pour them all on in a reasonably short time."[51]

Japan's Stalemate Continues

American incendiary bombs continued to rain on Japanese cities, but the Japanese government remained undecided. At 2:10 A.M. on August 13, the Foreign Ministry received a telegram from Minister Okamoto in Stockholm. The message contained editorials from newspapers in London with the information that the United States government had decided to include Article 4 of the Byrnes Note in order to retain the emperor's position, despite strenuous opposition within the United States as well as from the Soviet government. Negotiations with the United States on the position of the emperor, Matsumoto believed, would force Truman to take a definite position on a question that was intentionally left ambiguous. Matsumoto immediately sent a copy of this telegram to Suzuki and Kido. Matsumoto was certain that the emperor must have read it.[52]

In the meantime, Anami persistently worked for the rejection of the Byrnes Note. Early in the morning of August 13, he sought a meeting with Kido. Kido insisted that the Allies would not understand why the Japanese would reject terms that would actually be favorable to the imperial house. Should the emperor reject the Byrnes Note, the Allies would consider him "either stupid or mad." The emperor had made up his mind after long and careful deliberations, and all Japanese had to accept his decision.[53] Kido and Hirohito must have read Okamoto's telegram, and they must have come to the conclusion that the Byrnes Note would allow Japan to retain the imperial house, if not the *kokutai*, as Anami interpreted the document.

At 9 A.M. the Supreme War Council met in the basement shelter at the prime minister's official residence to discuss how to respond to the official Byrnes Note. At the request of the army, the director of the cabinet's legal division, Naoyoshi Murase, was also present. Murase agreed with the Foreign Ministry that acceptance of the Byrnes Note would not endanger the *kokutai*. Anami objected to this interpretation, insisting that acceptance would be tantamount to destroying the *kokutai*. The meeting was suspended when the two chiefs were suddenly called to report to the emperor at the Imperial Palace.

Hirohito summoned the chiefs to order suspension of all offensive military actions while Japan and the Allies were deciding the terms for ending the war. He wanted to make sure that the military would not take any unilateral actions to torpedo the negotiation process. Umezu answered that unless they were attacked, they would suspend all major operations.[54] Hirohito became increasingly assertive in his bid to terminate the war. By then rumors of a coup must have reached him, and he was most likely concerned that a large-scale uprising would spoil the chance for peace. Although neither Umezu nor Toyoda mentioned anything about the conversation, it is possible to speculate that Hirohito told the chiefs in no uncertain terms to do everything possible to prevent a coup. After this meeting, the tone of Umezu's and Toyoda's opposition to peace lost its sharp edge.

The meeting of the Supreme War Council resumed at 10:30, when the two chiefs returned. While Anami and Umezu continued to insist on demanding self-disarmament and non-occupation of the homeland, Toyoda did not support including these conditions. He did, however, support their argument that Articles 1 and 4 of the Byrnes Note would imperil "the prerogatives of the emperor as the sovereign." Therefore, he advocated at least proposing to the Allies that the "the emperor" be excluded from Article 1 as the entity to "be subject to the supreme commander of the Allied powers." Furthermore, he demanded a guarantee that the occupation force would not overrule the people's will to preserve the *kokutai*. The Allies might not accept these views, but it was worth presenting them.[55] Toyoda's argument indicates that, had the Byrnes Note included a provision clearly conveying the intention of the United States to retain the emperor, the war party's opposition would have weakened considerably.

The meeting ended in a stalemate. Togo argued that any amendment of the Byrnes Note would be tantamount to continuation of the war. Yonai and Suzuki did not say much, but they nonetheless supported Togo. At 2 P.M. Togo excused himself and drove to the Imperial Palace to report the hopeless stalemate of the Supreme War Council to the emperor. Hirohito reconfirmed his agreement with the foreign minister, and told him to convey his wish to the prime minister, presumably to make sure that Suzuki did not change his mind again.[56]

At 4 P.M. the cabinet meeting was reconvened. Suzuki went around the table and asked each minister's view. Twelve ministers out of fifteen supported Togo's position. Only three ministers, including Anami, opposed it. Finally, Suzuki spoke. He told the ministers the reasons for his change of mind: after reading the note many times, he had come to the conclusion that it would allow the possibility of preserving the emperor. Japan had no time to lose, Suzuki stated, and he would report to the emperor the views expressed by each minister. He would ask for the emperor's sacred decision.[57] The cabinet meeting adjourned at 7 P.M.

Anami hurried to Suzuki to ask him to wait two more days before holding the imperial conference. Suzuki refused: "Now is the time to act. I am sorry to say that there is no time to waste." In the prime minister's office a naval doctor named Gyota Kobayashi happened to be attending to the elderly prime minister. After Anami left the room, Kobayashi asked Suzuki: "If it is at all possible, why don't you wait for a few days?" Suzuki replied: "I can't do that. If we miss today, the Soviet Union will take not only Manchuria, Korea, Karafuto, but also Hokkaido. This would destroy the foundation of Japan. We must end the war when we can deal with the United States." Kobayashi said: "You know that Anami will commit suicide." "Yes, I know, and I am sorry," the prime minister replied.[58]

In the meantime, the coup plotters gathered in the basement of the Army Ministry to add the final touches to the coup plot. The two most radical leaders of the group were Lieutenant Colonel Jiro Shiizaki and Major Kenji Hatanaka of the Army Ministry's Military Bureau. Their superior officer, Colonel Okikatsu Arao, assumed leadership of the group. There is no question that Arao sympathized with the plotters, but his true intention remains unknown.[59]

Earlier in the afternoon, while the cabinet was meeting, the plotters had devised a public announcement: "The General Staff announced at 4 P.M. that the Imperial Army, having received an imperial order, began operations against the United States, Britain, the Soviet Union, and China." Sakomizu, who found out about the announcement from an *Asahi Shinbun* reporter, rushed to the cabinet meeting, but neither Anami nor Umezu had any knowledge of such an order. Umezu ordered this statement to be rescinded before it could be read on the radio at 4 P.M. Sakomizu later recalled that had this announcement been made public at such a delicate moment in the negotiating process, the Allies would have concluded that Japan had rejected the Byrnes Note.[60] It was a close call.

On the night of August 13, six coup plotters went to the army minister's official residence and showed Anami their detailed coup plan.
Anami listened to the young officers without committing himself one way
or the other. The men tried for two hours to recruit the army minister as
the head of the coup, but Anami refused to endorse the plot, though he
did not actively intervene to stop it. Anami's true attitude toward the
coup is difficult to ascertain. According to Takeshita, Anami told his
brother-in-law when the two were alone that night that he could not reveal his true intention to so many people, intimating his tacit approval of
the coup. Anami sent the junior officers home with the promise that he
would make his position known to Colonel Arao at midnight. When
Arao returned to the army minister's office at midnight, Anami told him
that the coup would not receive the people's support, and that it would
make the homeland defense more difficult. He told Arao that he would
reveal his position to the coup plotters after he consulted Umezu the following morning. Anami confided to Hayashi, who advised him to take
more decisive action to stop the coup, that he might be an unwitting
leader of an insurgency, much like the legendary Takamori Saigo, who
had led a coup in spite of himself against the Meiji government.[61]

The hot, muggy August night fell on Tokyo. Almost everyone in the
higher circles had difficulty sleeping, realizing that a momentous decision
would have to be made the following day.

Hirohito's Second Intervention

When Byrnes wrote his note to the Japanese government, he told Forrestal that he expected an answer within twenty-four hours.[62] Since the
Byrnes Note was sent, however, two days had passed without a word
from the Japanese. In the meantime, Soviet troops continued to march
deeply into Manchuria. By August 13 they were closing in from the west,
north, and east toward Changchun and Mukden. Clearly, the Byrnes
Note and Japan's delay in accepting it gave the Soviets a great opportunity to expand the territories under their control.

American patience was wearing thin. At 6:30 P.M. on August 13,
George Harrison telephoned McCloy to suggest that an ultimatum be issued to the Japanese government with the warning that Japan would
have to accept the Potsdam peace terms immediately; otherwise all negotiations, including the Potsdam Proclamation, would be off and the war

would go on more intensively.[63] McCloy's diary did not say what Harrison had in mind, but most certainly the new campaign against Japan would include the use of the next seven atomic bombs.

Moscow was emboldened by its military conquests. Chiang Kai-shek had urged the Chinese delegation to come to an agreement as quickly as possible by dropping the Mongolian border issue. The last negotiations began at midnight on August 14. Stalin made minor concessions on the control of Dairen and the railroads, but he demanded that the Chinese finance the cost of Soviet troops in Manchuria. Finally, they reached an agreement. At 3 A.M. on August 15, four hours after the Japanese government had cabled the Allies to accept the Potsdam Proclamation, they signed the Treaty of Friendship and Alliance between the USSR and the Chinese Republic.[64]

Early in the morning of August 14, Kido was awakened by his aide, who showed him a copy of the pamphlet dropped by B-29 that morning throughout Tokyo. This pamphlet provided the translated text of the emperor's August 10 acceptance letter and the Byrnes Note. Fearing that this information might provoke the military to action, Kido requested an audience with the emperor at 8:30, and proposed that Hirohito immediately convene a combined conference of the Supreme War Council and the cabinet, and impose his decision to accept the Potsdam terms unconditionally on the government. The emperor agreed, instructing Kido to proceed with this plan in consultation with the prime minister.[65]

The emperor's summoning not only the Big Six but also the entire cabinet to the imperial conference was unprecedented, but a conspiracy had already been secretly prepared by people acting behind the scenes. The real architects of this conspiracy were Sakomizu, Kase, Matsudaira, Matsutani, and Takagi. Suzuki had agreed with Sakomizu, and he went to the Imperial Palace to seek the emperor's permission for this idea. Kido agreed, and the emperor's order to convene the imperial conference at 10 A.M. at the Imperial Palace was issued to the participants as suggested by Sakomizu, without the signatures of the army and navy chiefs, which were required in order to convene an imperial conference. The military was outmaneuvered again.[66]

Altogether twenty-three participants who received the emperor's summons hurried to the Imperial Palace at 10 A.M., some without the necessary formal attire, still others borrowing neckties from their secretaries. Since the meeting room in the basement shelter was small and the participants were many, all the tables had been removed. Ministers, generals, and admirals, as well as the cabinet and the military secretaries, took their designated seats in the room and waited for the emperor in silence. At 10:50 A.M. Hirohito, clad in a formal marshal's uniform and white gloves, entered the room as the participants stood and took a deep bow. The prime minister then summarized what had transpired at the Supreme War Council and the cabinet meeting after the government had received the Byrnes Note, and stated that he regretted that the government had failed to come to a consensus. He therefore requested that the emperor listen to the minority's views and share his decision on this matter. Umezu, Toyoda, and Anami took turns expressing their by now familiar positions. Without bothering to ask Togo to present his view, Suzuki then asked the emperor for his decision without presenting the majority opinion; he was in a hurry.

The emperor spoke again. Despite the dissenting views, he stated, he had not changed his mind. He still considered it impossible to continue the war in light of the world situation as well as the domestic situation. As for doubts expressed about the future of the *kokutai,* he felt the enemy was approaching this question with favorable intentions. Because the confidence of the Japanese people was the most important thing, Hirohito concluded, he decided to accept the Byrnes Note, and he asked everyone present to respect his decision. It would be difficult for military officers and soldiers to lay down their arms and accept occupation, but in order to save the Japanese people and the nation, all had to bear the unbearable, tolerate the intolerable, and strive for the reconstruction of the nation.

Given that his subjects, especially the officers and soldiers of the military units, had remained uninformed about this decision, Hirohito noted that their shock might be great. In order to persuade them, the emperor was prepared to announce his decision on the radio. Looking straight at the army and navy ministers, he asked them to understand his wish and help convince the soldiers to accept his decision. He then instructed the government to prepare the Imperial Rescript for the termination of the war. Participants bowed their heads and wept as they listened to these words. Suzuki stood up. He thanked the emperor for his sacred decision and apologized for the cabinet's dereliction of duty, which had necessitated the emperor's intervention.[67]

The emperor had spoken to end the war. The question was how to impose his will on the nation.

Insurgents Seize the Imperial Palace

While the peace party was making a bold move to secure the emperor's support in ending the war, the coup plotters were working stealthily to take action before the emperor announced his decision to the nation. Until the emperor's second sacred decision, the army had shared the sentiment that the war should continue. But behind this consensus fissures of disagreement emerged. Some, like Umezu, secretly thought that Japan would be wise to accept the Potsdam Proclamation. Kawabe had conceded that Japan had lost the war. Others placed loyalty to the emperor above their personal convictions; still others conveniently used the emperor's decision as an excuse to justify a surrender that they could not openly advocate. Many young officers would have joined the coup, even if it contradicted the emperor's will, had the uprising been supported by the entire army. But their participation in the coup was contingent upon the support of the highest authorities of the army. Otherwise, they had no realistic possibility of success. Whatever their true feelings, the top army leaders had to tread carefully, given widespread sympathy for the plot and adamant opposition to surrender by commanding officers of the Japanese armies overseas.

On the night of August 14, the young officers staged a coup to stop Japan's acceptance of peace. The insurgency, led by two junior officers of the Army Ministry—Major Hatanaka and Lieutenant Colonel Shiizaki—aimed to occupy the Imperial Palace and establish martial law under Anami, with the help of the Eastern Army. But for the coup to be successful, it had to be sanctioned by the army minister (Anami) and the chief of staff (Umezu), as well as the commander of the Eastern Army (General Shizuichi Tanaka) and the commander of the Imperial Guard Division (Major General Takeshi Mori).[68]

The coup stumbled from the very beginning. At 7 A.M. Anami and Umezu arrived at the Army Ministry in Ichigaya Heights. Immediately Anami, accompanied by the leader of the coup plotters, Colonel Arao, went to Umezu's office and asked him what he thought about the plan. Umezu categorically refused to support the coup, effectively dooming the plot to disaster. Under Umezu's leadership, the army high command sought to stop the coup under the slogan, "Obey the Imperial Will without Fail." Umezu quickly gathered his senior staff to his side, leaving Anami without any organizational basis should he decide to support the coup.

And still Anami's true feelings about the coup remained ambiguous. He summoned the commander of the Eastern Army, General Tanaka, and asked him if the Eastern Army would support a military coup. Tanaka's chief of staff, Major General Tatsuhiko Takashima, told Anami: "It will require a legal document signed by you to do that." Tanaka kept silent on the coup, limiting himself to his task of maintaining order in the metropolitan district. There was disagreement between Tanaka and Takashima as to how to respond to the coup sanctioned by the army minister. General Tanaka was firmly committed to fulfilling the emperor's sacred decision, whereas Takashima might have followed Anami's order. The specter of a civil war hung over the army.[69]

Anami was determined to continue his fight for the rejection of the Potsdam Proclamation. The previous day, August 13, he had contacted three senior army offices, Marshals Shunroku Hata, Hajime Sugiyama, and Osami Nagano, and asked them to present a petition to the emperor to reject the Byrnes Note. At 10 A.M. on August 14, before the imperial conference, the men had an audience with the emperor. The emperor spoke before they could present their appeal: "The military situation has changed suddenly. The Soviet Union entered the war against us. Suicide attacks can't compete with the power of science. Therefore, there is no alternative but to accept the Potsdam terms." To the marshals' question of the preservation of the kokutai, the emperor responded that the enemy had guaranteed that the imperial house would be maintained. He ordered the marshals to obey his decision. Met with the emperor's unusually assertive intervention, Anami's final, desperate maneuver failed.[70]

In the meantime, Takeshita devised "The Second Plan for Deployment of Troops," which consisted of deploying the Imperial Guard Division to occupy the Imperial Palace, cut off communications with the outside, and close off all traffic in and out of the palace; and deploying the Eastern Army to occupy strategic points, "protect" important personages, and occupy the radio station until such time as the emperor changed his mind. Although the plotters were inspired by their burning passion to sacrifice their lives for the higher cause of the kokutai, they executed their plot miserably. They missed their chance to gain Anami's approval before the army minister left for the imperial conference. Once the emperor announced his decision to accept the Byrnes Note, it was too late for the plotters. When Anami returned to the Army Ministry, nearly twenty young officers rushed to his office eager to hear the news. Announcing the emperor's decision, Anami told the coup plotters to obey the imperial will. When asked why he had changed his mind, Anami answered: "The emperor told me, calling me Anami, that he understood my feelings. In tears he implored me to endure even though it is painful. I could no longer raise any objections." Anami then raised his voice and threatened: "Those who disobey must go over my dead body." Stunned silence was broken only by a sharp wailing. Major Hatanaka wept without restraint. The coup plotters realized that the game was over. Takeshita and Ida, who had been the main leaders of the plot up to this point, gave up, concluding that they had no prospect of success.

From the Army Ministry Anami went back to the cabinet meeting already in progress at the prime minister's residence. The cabinet decided that the emperor should record the Imperial Rescript on a phonograph; the message would then be broadcast over the radio throughout Japan and at the fronts. The Japanese policymakers could no longer be bothered with the myth that the emperor was a living God, and broke taboo by recording his human voice. The radio technicians of the Japan Broadcasting Company were ordered to report to the Imperial Palace with the recording equipment by 3 P.M.[71]

At 2:30 Chief of Staff Umezu read the announcement to all officers of the General Staff, ordering them to obey the emperor's decision. Fearing that the decision to surrender would provoke unrest among some officers, First Division Chief Lieutenant General Shuichi Miyazaki suggested that Kawabe urge the high command to pledge to respect the emperor's decision. Deputy Army Minister Tadakatsu Wakamatsu brought a piece of paper for Anami to sign. It stated: "The Imperial Army will act to the end in accordance with the emperor's sacred decision." By 2:40 P.M., Wakamatsu had collected the signatures of the army minister, the chief of staff, the director of military education, and two commanders of the two general armies as well as the commander of the Army Air Corps. From that moment, any action that violated the army minister's order would be treated as high treason. The major point of collective signatures was to prevent the loose cannon, Anami, from siding with the coup plotters.

At 3 P.M. Anami assembled all the members of the Army Ministry and read the announcement ordering all officers to respect the imperial will. Wakamatsu then introduced the order collectively signed by the highest officers of the army hierarchy to obey the emperor's sacred decision. The highest army leaders now began to use their authority to impose the decision to surrender on the entire army in the name of their supreme commander in chief, violating the age-old canon that there was no word "surrender" in the dictionary of the Japanese Imperial Army. The Army Ministry and the General Staff began burning documents. The Imperial Army began to administer its own death.

Not all officers attended the meeting convened by the war minister. Hatanaka and Shiizaki were conspicuously absent. Defying Anami's order, they went to the headquarters of the Imperial Guard Division and gained the support of a few staff officers to stage a coup. Hatanaka then drove to the Commanding Office of the Eastern Military District to recruit its commander, General Tanaka, to join the coup. But Tanaka violently denounced Hatanaka for defying the emperor's will. The coup was dealt another major blow.[72]

The cabinet meeting resumed at 4 P.M. Sakomizu at last presented a copy of the stenciled draft of the Imperial Rescript that he and other assistants had just finished writing. But the cabinet, engaged in endless debate over whether the emperor's decision required the approval of the Privy Council, took another recess. The clock was ticking, and still the Japanese government wasted precious time on this trivial legal procedure. Around this time, the Second Imperial Guard Regiment commanded by Colonel Toyojiro Haga entered the Imperial Palace to begin guard duty for the nights of August 14 and 15. The leaders of the conspiracy, Hatanaka and Shiizaki, slipped into the compound of the Imperial Palace without any trouble.

Within an hour the cabinet finally began discussing the text of the rescript. Anami offered an amendment: the phrase in Sakomizu's draft, "as the military situation is becoming unfavorable day by day," should be changed to "as the military situation does not develop in our favor." A heated argument ensued between Yonai, who argued that Japan was losing the war, and Anami, who disagreed. Anami was concerned with the effects of the rescript on the officers, especially in the armies overseas. To tell the officers of the Imperial Army to accept defeat and surrender would provoke them to action against the emperor's decision. He wished to give his men a graceful way out, a way to accept the unacceptable. The cabinet approved Anami's amendment.

The cabinet made three more amendments to the text, including Anami's proposal to add the expression, "having been able to preserve the *kokutai*." Anami knew that accepting the Byrnes Note meant destroying the *kokutai*, but if the officers and soldiers were to accept defeat, they would need to believe that the *kokutai* was preserved. The final text was approved at 7 P.M. and then sent to the ministry of the imperial household, where the imperial calligrapher wrote the original copy of the Imperial Rescript in the traditional brush and ink. In the precomputer age, the process was moving with excruciating slowness. In the meantime, the cabinet decided to broadcast the emperor's message at noon on the following day. At last, shortly after 8 P.M., the transcribed rescript was brought to the cabinet for its final approval. Suzuki then went to the palace to receive the emperor's stamp of approval. The Imperial Rescript was now complete. Prime Minister Suzuki wrote his name at the end of the original copy of the rescript around 10 P.M., followed by the signature of each cabinet member. When Anami's turn came up there was tension in the air, but the army minister calmly appended his signature.[73]

Around the same time, the coup plotters finally succeeded in convincing Colonel Haga, the commander of the Second Imperial Guard Regiment, to join the coup. To gain Haga's support, Hatanaka and Shiizaki concocted a story that the entire army was now supporting the insurgency. The rebels had made a major breakthrough; with Haga's consent, the very soldiers who were supposed to protect the emperor were suddenly transformed into rebel troops. (See Map 3.)

Hatanaka and Shiizaki then hurried back to the Army Ministry in search of Ida. In order to convince Commander Mori of the Imperial Guard Division, they needed a senior rank officer. Skeptical about the prospect of the coup, Ida nonetheless agreed to talk to Mori. Since no automobiles were available to them, they had to ride two rickety bicycles from Ichigaya to the headquarters of the Imperial Guard Division.[74]

At 11 P.M., Matsumoto finally received news that all the cabinet members had signed the Imperial Rescript. Instantly, the telegram containing the emperor's unconditional acceptance of the Potsdam terms was dispatched in Togo's name to Bern and Stockholm for transmittal to the four Allied governments.

Around the same time, Hirohito went to his office to record the Imperial Rescript. All the shutters in the building were tightly closed so that the light inside would not be noticed from outside. In addition to the radio technicians and the chamberlains, Director of Information Shimomura and his secretary had also assembled. The recording was over at 11:50 P.M. The two phonographs were put in bags and concealed in a safe in the empress's office.[75]

While the emperor was recording the rescript, the coup plotters gathered at the staff headquarters of the Imperial Guard Division, just north

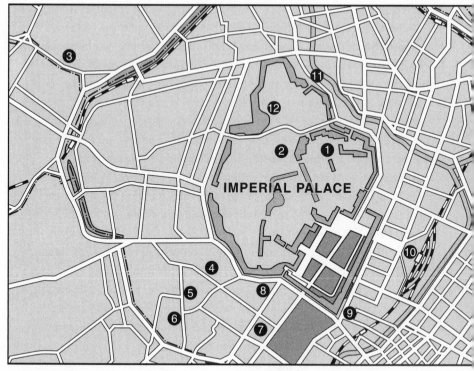

1. Imperial Palace
2. Ministry of Imperial Household
3. Army Ministry / General Staff
4. Army Minister's Residence
5. Diet
6. Prime Minister's Residence

7. Navy Ministry
8. Tokyo Metropolitan Police
9. Eastern Army Headquarters
10. Tokyo Station
11. Military Police Headquarters
12. Imperial Guard Division

Map 3. Central Tokyo around the Imperial Palace

from the Imperial Palace. Shiizaki and Ida were eager to obtain Mori's approval of the coup, but despite a long monologue the commander did not pledge his support. Met with his opposition to the coup, Hatanaka impulsively shot Mori to death.

The die was cast; the revolt had begun. In the name of the regimental commander he had just killed, Hatanaka forged an order to all seven Imperial Guard Regiments to "protect" the emperor, occupy the Imperial Palace, stop all traffic in and out of the palace, and cut off all communication to and from the palace. Battalion commanders began to execute this order efficiently.

Ida immediately drove to the headquarters of the Eastern Army to seek

their help in spreading the coup. But the Eastern Army not only adamantly rejected the coup but was also determined to crush it by force.
The coup faltered at the first step. Seeing the determination of Commander Tanaka, Ida finally gave up, and volunteered to appeal to the insurgents to surrender in order to avoid bloodshed. (See Map 3.)

Inside the Imperial Palace, however, the insurgents moved quickly by
closing all entrances, cutting off telephone lines, occupying the building
of the ministry of the imperial household, and arresting the radio technicians. Hatanaka and other ringleaders interrogated the radio technicians
and the court chamberlains to locate the phonographs, and looked for
Kido. The insurgent soldiers scurried around but could not find either the
phonographs or Kido.[76]

Around 1:30 A.M., Takeshita arrived at the army minister's official residence to ask for Anami's support for the coup. (See Map 3.) Takeshita
found Anami quietly drinking sake. Inviting Takeshita into the house, the
army minister told him: "I am going to commit *seppuku*. What do you
think?" Anami's brother-in-law answered: "I always thought that would
be your plan, and I have no intention to stop you." Forgetting his major
purpose of recruiting Anami to his cause, Takeshita joined him in drinking sake.

The coup quickly collapsed. The Eastern Army arrived at the headquarters of the Imperial Guard Division. Revealing that Mori's order was
a fake, Tanaka's forces restored order in the Imperial Palace. Shortly after
3 A.M., Ida drove to the headquarters of the insurgents and told Hatanaka to withdraw troops from the Imperial Palace to avoid bloodshed.
Finding out that he was deceived, Commander Haga told Hatanaka to
leave the palace compound immediately.

Anami was still enjoying his last sake and his final conversation with
his brother-in-law when Takeshita finally confided that the Imperial
Guard Division had revolted. Anami predicted that they would not succeed since the Eastern Army would not join them. When Anami was just
about to start the ritual of self-immolation, Ida arrived to report what
had transpired at the Imperial Palace. Inviting Ida in for a drink, Anami
continued the last banquet.[77]

Anami finally finished his sake, put on the white shirt that he had received from the emperor as a personal gift, then carefully folded his military uniform and placed it on the alcove. At 5:30 a general of the military police came to report on the revolt of the Imperial Guard Division.
Anami asked Takeshita to receive him, and told Ida to stand guard out-

side in the garden. Left alone, Anami sat quietly in the corridor facing the Imperial Palace. He violently thrust the unsheathed short sword into the left side of his abdomen, cut across to the right, and pulled up. When Takeshita returned, Anami was searching for his carotid artery with his left hand. He then placed the sword on the artery and pulled it quickly forward. Blood sprayed on the testament placed in front of him. Takeshita asked: "Do you want me to second?" "No need to help me. Leave me alone," were the war minister's last words. A few minutes later Anami was still breathing, though unconscious. Takeshita picked up the sword and cut Anami's artery. He laid the war minister on the tatami floor, placed the testament by his body, and covered the body with the uniform.

As Anami took his last breath, the Imperial Army also died. It was a calculated suicide, a ritual that was needed to bring to a close the inglorious history of the Imperial Army that had caused unprecedented calamities in the Showa era. Gone with Anami was also the fanatical concept of the *kokutai* for which he and like-minded military men had fought tenaciously by insisting on the continuation of the war.[78]

Morning had arrived. At 6 A.M. the emperor rose and was told that the Imperial Palace had been occupied by rebel soldiers. He told the chamberlains to assemble the soldiers in the courtyard: "I shall tell the soldiers directly how I feel in my heart." Hirohito had no idea that the rebel leaders saw the preservation of the imperial house as only a part of the *kokutai*. General Tanaka then walked to the Imperial Library. As the iron gate was opened, the morning sun penetrated into the library. Tanaka reported to the emperor that the coup had been completely put down. As the August sun rose high in the sky, the last drama of Imperial Japan, enacted in the Imperial Palace as center stage, was over.[79] This was the dawn of a new Japan, resurrected on the corpse of the Imperial Army, and with a new concept of a human emperor, no longer a living God.

Hirohito Broadcasts Surrender

At 7:21 A.M. on August 15 a radio announcer stated that the emperor would speak directly to the people at twelve o'clock, repeatedly urging everyone to listen to his message. The phonographs hidden in the safe were carefully delivered to the broadcasting center one hour before noon. At 12:00, all of Japan and the soldiers at the fronts gathered by the radio.

After *Kimigayo,* the national anthem, was played, the recorded voice of the emperor began to speak:

> After pondering deeply the general trends of the world and the actual conditions obtaining in Our Empire today, We have decided to effect a settlement of the present situation by resorting to an extraordinary measure. We have ordered Our Government to communicate to the Governments of the United States, Great Britain, China, and the Soviet Union that Our Empire accepts the provisions of their Joint Declaration.

Then the emperor gave a self-serving explanation for the war: "We declared war on America and Britain out of Our sincere desire to ensure Japan's self-preservation and the stabilization of East Asia, it being far from Our thought either to infringe upon the sovereignty of other nations or to embark upon territorial aggrandizement." But the war had lasted for four years, and the situation had developed "not necessarily to Japan's advantage." The emperor then obliquely referred to the atomic bombs: "Moreover, the enemy has begun to employ a new and most cruel bomb, the power of which to do damage is indeed incalculable, taking the toll of many innocent lives. Should We continue to fight, it would result not only in an ultimate collapse and obliteration of the Japanese nation, but also in the total extinction of human civilization." He then appealed to the soldiers to accept his decision, no matter how hard it might be. He appealed to his subjects: "Unite your total strength to be devoted to the construction for the future. Cultivate the ways of rectitude; foster nobility of spirit; and work with resolution so as ye may enhance the innate glory of the Imperial State and keep pace with the progress of the world."[80]

All Japanese listened to the emperor's voice. Although many did not understand the archaic words he used, they all knew that the emperor had decided to terminate the war. Many wept, but some were relieved.

Two men did not hear the emperor's voice. Shortly before the broadcast, Hatanaka and Shiizaki sat on the ground near Nijubashi, looking at the Imperial Palace. Hatanaka shot himself in the head with the same revolver he had used to kill Commander Mori. Shiizaki thrust a sword in his abdomen, then shot himself in the head with a revolver.

That afternoon, at 3:20, the Suzuki cabinet submitted its resignation.

Before doing so, it published its last message. Suzuki announced that the emperor's rescript to end the war had been issued. He mentioned the "new bomb" of unprecedented destructive power that changed the method of war, together with the Soviet entry into the war, as the two major factors leading to the decision to end the war. The task of the people now, Suzuki stressed, was to preserve the *kokutai*, and for this reason they should avoid internal conflict at any cost.[81] Although the emperor's acceptance of the Potsdam Proclamation deprived the concept of the *kokutai* of the essential ingredients that had prevailed as orthodoxy since 1935, Suzuki's message continued to perpetuate the myth that the *kokutai* was preserved.

At the imperial conference the emperor had offered to issue another rescript specifically addressed to the officers and soldiers so that they would lay down arms and surrender without resistance. It fell upon Sakomizu's assistant to write another historic document. For inexplicable reasons, the rescript was not issued until August 17. It explained:

> Now that the Soviet Union entered the war, to continue under the present conditions at home and abroad would only result in further useless damage and eventually endanger the very foundation of the empire's existence. Therefore, although the fighting spirit of the Imperial Navy and Army is still vigorous, I am going to make peace with the United States, Britain, the Soviet Union, and Chungking, in order to preserve our glorious *kokutai*.

He then expressed his sorrow for those officers and soldiers who had been killed during the war, and appealed to the men in uniform to act in accordance with his will, observing strict discipline.[82] It is important to note that while the Imperial Rescript of August 15 had an oblique reference to the atomic bomb without any mention of the Soviet entry into the war, his rescript to the officers and soldiers cited the Soviet entry as the most decisive reason for the termination of the war, with no reference to the atomic bomb. Furthermore, the emperor also emphasized that surrender was necessary to preserve the *kokutai*.

At 3 P.M. Washington time, Byrnes informed the president that he had received word that a coded message from Tokyo was being received in Bern. At 4:05 Byrnes called Bern and confirmed that Japan had surrendered. Byrnes called Bevin, Harriman, and Hurley, and arranged for the news to be announced simultaneously, at 7 P.M. Washington time, in four capitals. At 6 P.M. the charge d'affairs of the Swiss Embassy in Washington brought Japan's formal answer to Byrnes.

At 7 P.M., in front of a packed audience that included Mrs. Truman, current and former members of the cabinet, and White House correspondents, Truman read the statement announcing Japan's unconditional acceptance of the Potsdam Proclamation. Simultaneously, the president sent the following message to the Pentagon, which transmitted it to the field commanders: "The Government of Japan having on 14 August accepted the Allied Governments' demand for surrender, you are hereby directed to suspend offensive operations against Japanese Military and Naval forces insofar as is consistent with the safety of Allied forces in your area."

Truman wrote in his memoirs: "The guns were silenced. The war was over." But the guns were not silenced, and the war was not over. It was precisely Hirohito's acceptance of the Potsdam terms that prompted Stalin to step up military actions against Japan.[83]

CHAPTER 7

August Storm:
The Soviet-Japanese War
and the United States

THE REACTIONS of the United States and the Soviet Union to Japan's acceptance of the Potsdam Proclamation were poles apart. As soon as Truman received the news of Japan's unconditional surrender, he ordered American commanders in the Pacific and Western Pacific Areas to suspend offensive operations against Japanese forces. Marshal Vasilevskii ordered Soviet forces to "continue offensive operations against Japanese forces," since the emperor's statement on August 14 was merely a general declaration about unconditional surrender, not an order to Japan's armed forces to cease military action. "The armed forces of Japan can be considered capitulated," Vasilevskii explained, "only from the moment when the order is given by the Japanese emperor to cease military actions and lay down arms and when this order is in reality fulfilled."[1]

Soviet military actions troubled American policymakers. It was too late for Manchuria and southern Sakhalin, which they had already conceded to the Soviet Union, but four strategic areas still concerned them: Dairen, southern Korea, the Kurils, and North China. The challenge for American policymakers was to balance their primary task of implementing Japan's surrender with their concern over Soviet expansion.

Despite the emperor's declaration on August 15 that the war was over, Japanese armed forces had to receive a cease-fire order from the Imperial General Headquarters in order to stop fighting. For inexplicable reasons, the cease-fire order was not issued to the armed forces until August 17.

This delay gave the Soviet high command an excuse to continue hostilities in order to accomplish its major objectives in the Far Eastern campaign and physically seize all the territories promised at Yalta.

On August 15 the Imperial General Headquarters issued Continental General Order 1381, which directed all the armies abroad to "continue their current tasks until further ordered, but to stop offensive operations." Since no Kwantung Army units were engaged in offensive operations, this order amounted to a continuation of hostilities. On August 16, the Imperial General Headquarters issued another order, Continental Order 1382, commanding all armed forces to "immediately stop hostilities, but this does not prevent actions for self-defense when attacked by the enemy until the cease-fire negotiations are completed." This was also a meaningless order, since most of the units in the Kwantung Army were under attack from Soviet troops. It was not until August 18 that the Imperial General Headquarters issued Continental Order 1385 to "suspend all operational tasks and stop all hostilities."

The commanding staff of the Kwantung Army, including Commander in Chief General Otozo Yamada and Chief of Staff Lieutenant General Hikosaburo Hata, listened to the Imperial Rescript on August 15 at their headquarters in Changchun and awaited orders from the Imperial General Headquarters. Orders 1381 and 1382 were ambiguous as to whether they should continue resisting Soviet forces. They therefore held a staff meeting to discuss what measures they should take. Yamada and Hata knew the hopelessness of the situation and announced their decision to obey the emperor's wishes. After this staff meeting, at 10 P.M. on August 16, the Kwantung Army headquarters issued Order 106, directing all units to cease hostilities and surrender arms to local Soviet commanders.[2]

By August 15 Soviet forces were marching into the heart of the Manchurian plain, but major cities such as Harbin, Changchun, Kirin, and Mukden were still far from their reach. More important, Soviet forces needed to reach Dairen and Port Arthur, the prize possessions promised by the Yalta Agreement, before the American forces sent in the marines. They also needed to occupy northern Korea to cut off the escape route of the Kwantung Army from the Korean peninsula to Japan.

Soviet troops continued to move from three directions, from the northwest and west by the Transbaikal Front, from the east by the First Far Eastern Front, and from the north by the Second Far Eastern Front. By August 17 Soviet forces of the First Far Eastern Front were moving toward Harbin, Kirin, and Changchung.[3] (See Map 2.) The three days from

August 15 to August 17 represented the most crucial period for the Soviet operations; in that time Soviet forces needed to secure important strategic positions before reaching these cities. There was good reason Vasilevskii did not want to stop the offensive operation on August 15.

In the early morning of August 17, Yamada sent a telegraph message to the Soviet headquarters of the First Far Eastern Front, offering a cease-fire. Vasilevskii rejected this offer on the grounds that "not a word has been said about the capitulation of Japanese Armed Forces in Manchuria." Instead, he demanded that all hostilities against Soviet forces be stopped by noon on August 20, that all weapons be surrendered, and that all soldiers submit themselves as prisoners. On the same morning, Hata requested through the Soviet consulate office in Harbin that Soviet forces begin cease-fire negotiations. Hata requested an immediate meeting with Vasilevskii to work out the details of cease-fire and surrender of arms, but stated that he could wait only until August 19 to begin negotiations. This implied that unless a cease-fire agreement could be reached by August 19, the Kwantung Army would opt for desperate suicidal resistance. Furthermore, Hata noted that on August 16 the Americans had bombed several places in Korea. The Japanese were concerned that American airborne units might land on Korea. Hata stated that Japan would prefer to hand over Korea to the Soviets rather than to the Americans. Furthermore, he made the point that if the Soviet Red Army wished to advance into China, the Kwantung Army was prepared to welcome it.[4] Even at this stage, the Kwantung Army tried to make a deal with the Soviets in exchange for a cease-fire.

The Soviet side delayed its reply for two days. Finally, on August 19, Vasilevskii cabled Hata to fly to Zharikovo, the headquarters of the First Far Eastern Front. On the afternoon of August 19 Hata, accompanied by Colonel Ryuzo Seshima and Consul General Funao Miyakawa, flew to Zharikovo on a Soviet-supplied airplane. There they reached a cease-fire agreement with Vasilevskii. The major points were as follows: Japanese soldiers and officers were to surrender all power to Soviet military authorities after they were disarmed; Japanese officers would be allowed to bear swords and maintain their aides; and the Japanese armed forces were to guard the security of localities until the arrival of Soviet forces. The Japanese side considered this agreement generous under the circumstances, but in reality, the Soviets did not honor these provisions.[5]

Before the cease-fire negotiations, Vasilevskii had received Beria's instructions dated August 16 concerning the treatment of Japanese prisoners of war. This order stated that Japanese POWs should not be transported to the Soviet Union, but should instead be interned in prisoners' camps in local areas.[6] This policy was in conformity with Article 9 of the Potsdam Proclamation, which stipulated: "The Japanese military forces, after being completely disarmed, shall be permitted to return to their homes with the opportunity to lead peaceful and productive lives."

New archival evidence indicates that during the two days between Hata's offer for negotiations on August 17 and the conclusion of the cease-fire agreement on August 19, the Soviet high command attempted to recover as much territory as possible. On August 18, Soviet Chief of Staff General Ivanov ordered all units to disregard any Japanese offer for cease-fire unless the Japanese forces actually surrendered and laid down their arms. In accordance with this order, the Soviets rejected offers for cease-fire negotiations from Japanese emissaries, whom they often executed. On that day, the First Far Eastern Front flew a group of officers to Harbin, while rushing to the city units of motorcycle regiments as well as a mobile force from the First Red Banner Army. Similarly, a group of officers flew to Kirin. The Soviets were determined to capture these major cities before the Kwantung Army surrendered. Vasilevskii ordered the commanders at the Transbaikal Front and the First Far Eastern Front to form special mobile units "in order to occupy Changchun, Mukden, Kirin, and Harbin as quickly as possible." Soviet ground troops were to occupy Changchun by August 20, Mukden and Harbin by August 21, and Liaotung by August 28. Stalin was not happy with Vasilevskii's slow pace. Liaotung, especially Dairen, was Stalin's major concern, since he knew from Harriman that the Americans were keenly interested in securing it for themselves. He sent an order to Malinovskii, superceding Vasilevskii's order, to complete the occupation of Dairen and Port Arthur by August 22–23.[7]

The Red Army defeated the Kwantung Army, but this victory represented merely one part of Stalin's objective. The most important goal for Soviet forces was to capture the territory promised at Yalta—and if possible even more.

The Soviet Operation in Southern Sakhalin

Japanese Sakhalin, or Karafuto (southern Sakhalin, south of the 50th parallel), was defended by the 88th Division. Before the Soviet declaration of war, the Sakhalin military commanders expected an invasion to come from the United States. Thus they built fortifications on the eastern shore of the island. After the Soviet attack in Manchuria on August 9, the 88th Division hurriedly shifted its defense against a possible Soviet invasion from the north.[8]

Given the Soviets' numerical superiority, a Soviet victory in southern Sakhalin was only a matter of time, and since the United States had already conceded Sakhalin to the Soviet Union, there was little prospect that the operation would cause friction with the United States. But the Soviets had to hasten the Sakhalin operation, since their major objectives were not merely to occupy the southern part of the island, but also to concentrate Soviet forces at Maoka and Otomari, so that further operations could be launched against the northern part of Hokkaido and the southern Kurils.[9] (See Map 4.)

Late at night on August 10, after he became confident that the Manchurian campaign was proceeding successfully, Vasilevskii ordered Purkaev (commander of the Second Far Eastern Front) to deploy the 56th Rifle Corps in cooperation with the Pacific Fleet to invade southern Sakhalin the following morning and capture the island by August 22. At 9:35 A.M. on August 11 Soviet troops crossed the border into southern Sakhalin. Although the Japanese forces were hamstrung by the Imperial General Headquarters' strict order not to engage in offensive actions, the Japanese defenders entrenched in the Koton Fortified Region put up a strenuous defense against the invading Soviet forces. At noon on August 15, the Japanese heard the radio broadcast of the Imperial Rescript announcing the end of the war. The Imperial General Headquarters issued the order to stop offensive actions that night, and the next afternoon ordered an immediate cease-fire except for self-defense. Contrary to this order, however, the Fifth Area Army in Sapporo issued an order to the 88th Division to defend Karafuto to the last man, correctly predicting that the Soviets would assemble their troops in Otomari to prepare an operation against Hokkaido. Thus the 88th Division received two contradictory orders. Taking advantage of this confusion, Soviet forces continued offensive actions and finally overwhelmed the fierce Japanese resistance around Koton by the evening of August 17. On August 19, the Imperial General Headquarters ordered the Fifth Area Army to cease all hostilities and enter negotiations with the Soviet commanders. On August 20, the Fifth Area Army, rescinding the previous order, issued a new directive instructing commanders in local units to initiate negotiations with their Soviet counterparts for cease-fire and disarmament. Soviet troops moved

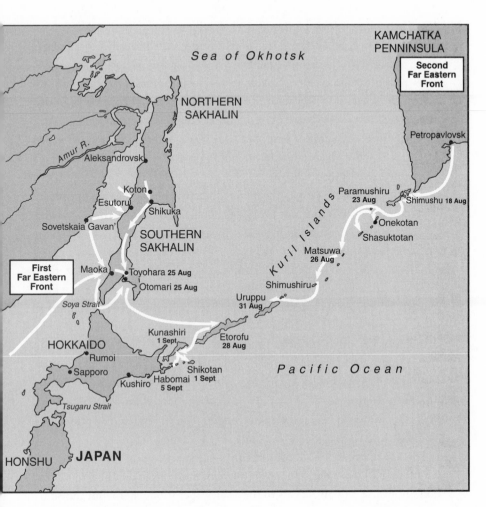

Map 4. Soviets' Kuril Operation

south and captured Toyohara on August 25, three days after the target date set by Vasilevskii.[10]

In contrast to the Soviet operation across the border, the occupation of the important ports of Maoka and Otomari had the distinct characteristics of a hastily implemented plan. The task of taking the ports was assigned to the landing units, Colonel S. E. Zakharov's 113th Rifle Brigade of the 16th Army of the Second Far Eastern Front and the Pacific Fleet under Captain A. I. Leonov. These hastily assembled units left Postovaia and Vanino on the night of August 18 to assault Maoka.[11]

As soon as the first Soviet units landed in Maoka on August 19, they immediately proceeded to shoot unarmed civilians waiting at the port to board ships bound for Hokkaido. The civilians ran in panic. The Soviet forces easily occupied the port by noon and then moved into the city, firing on civilians indiscriminately. Witnessing this situation, Japanese units began shooting at the Soviet forces, resulting in fierce crossfire between the Soviet and Japanese troops. But by 2 P.M. the city was under the control of Soviet forces. At 7:30 the commander of the Japanese defense units sent a team of emissaries for cease-fire negotiations, but before they reached the Soviet commanding post they were fired upon and all but one were shot to death.[12]

After occupying Maoka, the main objective of the Soviet operation was to occupy the important port of Otomari. Zakharov's troops moved on land toward Otomari along the railway. Captain Leonov received an order to organize a landing unit to occupy Otomari by the morning of August 24. As soon as Leonov's landing ships left Maoka, however, they encountered a violent storm on the night of August 23 and 24, which made it impossible to enter Soya Strait. They had no choice but to land at Honto, on the western shore of the island.[13] On August 24, after the storm had passed, Leonov's forces sailed to Otomari. On August 25, Soviet forces occupied Otomari from the land and from the sea. The capture of the port coincided with the 56th Rifle Corps' capture of Toyohara. On August 26, Japan's Fifth Area Army issued an order to all the Japanese forces in Sakhalin to surrender. The Sakhalin operation was over, but four days after the deadline set by Vasilevskii.

The United States had consistently held the position that the Soviet Union had a legitimate right to recover southern Sakhalin, and therefore it did not raise any objections to the Soviet operations there. But the Soviets were in a hurry to complete the occupation of southern Sakhalin, not for the sole purpose of seizing the island, but rather to prepare for the next stage of the operation: the Kurils and Hokkaido.

Stalin Orders the Kuril Operation

Although the Yalta Agreement stipulated that the Kurils would be "handed over" to the Soviet Union in return for Soviet participation in the war, a precise definition of the Kurils had not been given. At Potsdam, the U.S. and Soviet staffs had agreed that all of the Kurils with the exception of the four northernmost islands was an American zone of operation, though the Soviets had acquired a foothold in the Kurils by making the Sea of Okhotsk a zone of joint operations.[14] Thus, Stalin faced a difficult challenge: he had to occupy the islands as quickly as possible while carefully monitoring the American reaction. To achieve his goal, he used both skillful diplomacy and ruthless military action.

On the morning of August 15, Vladivostok time, which was still the evening of August 14, Moscow time, Vasilevskii gave orders to Purkaev and Admiral I. S. Iumashev to occupy the northern parts of the Kuril islands without waiting for reinforcement from other fronts. Whereas the Japanese considered the defense of the northernmost islands crucial to the defense of Hokkaido and mainland Japan, the Soviet leadership thought these islands would provide the USSR with an important entrance into the Pacific Ocean. Purkaev told front commanders: "Japan's capitulation is expected. Taking advantage of this favorable situation, it is necessary to seize Shimushu, Paramushiru, and Onekotan."[15]

Vasilevskii had most likely received an order from Stalin to initiate the Kuril operation. Washington had learned of Japan's acceptance of the Potsdam Proclamation at 8 P.M. Moscow time on August 14. Thus it is reasonable to assume that Stalin's order to initiate the Kuril operation was prompted by Japan's acceptance of the Potsdam terms.[16] The campaign in Manchuria, Korea, and southern Sakhalin had proceeded as expected, and in most cases faster than originally scheduled, but so far nothing had been done in the Kurils. Japan's impending capitulation must have convinced Stalin that he had to act immediately to occupy the Kurils before Japan's surrender. Vasilevskii's order to carry out the operation "without reinforcement from other fronts" indicated the haste with which this operation was implemented. Stalin was in a hurry.

Following Vasilevskii's order, Purkaev made only meager forces available for the operation—two regiments of the 101st Rifle Division, two or three naval infantry companies from the Pacific Fleet, and the ships and floating devices the local commander could scrape together in Petropavlovsk. The post-operation report of Major General A. R. Gnechko, commander of the Kamchatka Defense District, vividly described the lack of preparations for the occupation. The Kamchatka Defense District had only two days to prepare for the entire operation. They did not have enough ships, artillery, or weapons to carry out the landing operations. To compensate for the lack of preparations and equipment, they were to rely on an element of surprise by taking advantage of "the political situation" resulting from the impending Japanese capitulation. Gnechko's plan was to stage a surprise landing operation on the northeastern shore of Shimushu at 11 P.M. on August 16, dispatch the main force to Kataoka Naval Base on the south on the island, and occupy the entire island by 11 P.M. on August 17. The plan called for occupying Paramushiru and Onekotan using captured Shimushu as the base.[17] No further plan was made at this point.

Without knowing how the United States would act in the Kurils, Stalin had to be cautious. He ordered his military to occupy the two islands (Shimushu and Paramushiru) that clearly belonged to the Soviet zone of operation, and establish solid bases from which further operations could be launched. It is important to note that this first plan also envisaged the occupation of Onekotan, which fell within the American zone of operation, most likely to test the American reaction. If Stalin met with opposition from the Americans, he would retreat. If not, he would expand operations in the central and southern Kurils.

Gnechko and his commanding staff had numerous tasks to complete before leaving Petropavlovsk. They had to make detailed operational plans, mobilize the necessary forces into battle condition, transfer them to appropriate units, coordinate plans among various units, especially among the ground units, the naval units, and the air force, commandeer fishing trawlers and other vessels, convert them into military vessels, load the artillery, weapons, and communication gear, send written orders for all these actions, and obtain necessary information about enemy forces. And all these complicated preparations had to be made within thirty-six hours. It was an aberration of the usually careful planning of the rest of Operation August Storm. Naturally, many things went wrong. For instance, the Soviets first loaded on the ships the weapons and equipment they would need first at the landing, putting them at the bottom of the heavy load. When the operation began, they had to remove the piles on top to get to the necessary equipment at the bottom of the ship.[18] This was only one of many errors.

At 4 A.M. on August 17, two hours later than scheduled, a convoy of Soviet ships left Avacha Bay in Petropavlovsk. Led by the escort ship *Dzerzhinskii*, the convoy sailed stealthily and slowly in the thick fog from Petropavlovsk to Shimushu, for a distance of 170 sea miles, without using any lights for most of the way. This was the longest journey that any Soviet landing force had to make during the entire Second World War.[19] After the twenty-four-hour voyage, the first ship of the convoy approached Shimushu at 2 A.M. (midnight Japan time) on August 18. Two hours later, the rest of the ships lined up horizontally facing the landing zone. The battle of Shimushu was about to begin.

The Battle of Shimushu

At 2:15 A.M. (Japan time) on August 18, the Soviet forces launched a landing operation on Takeda Beach.[20] (See Map 5.) Premature firing from the Soviets provoked ferocious artillery fire from the two batteries installed at either end of the beach. It was not until 7 A.M. that the first Soviet echelon completed the landing. The Soviet units moved toward the two strategic points on Mt. Yotsumine but failed to take the hills owing to a lack of firepower. Commander Fusaki Tsutsumi of the 91st Division, still not knowing that he and his men were being attacked by the Soviets, ordered the 11th Tank Regiment and the 73rd Infantry Brigade to repulse the enemy. The tank regiment recklessly pursued the enemy without infantry support and became easy prey for Soviet antitank weapons. It was during this battle that Tsutsumi first learned that the enemy was the Soviets, not the Americans.

The second echelon of Soviet troops reached the shore at 9 A.M. The single radio that was saved from the landing was used to communicate

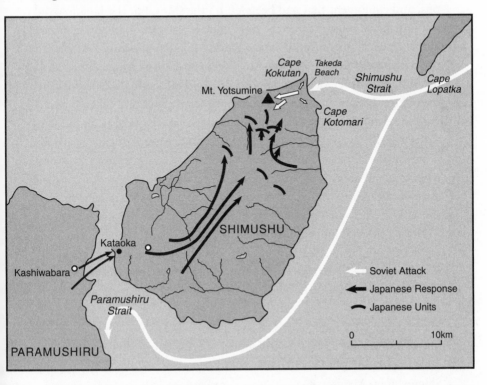

Map 5. Battle of Shimushu. Adapted from Nakayma Takashi, *1945nen natsu: saigono nissosen* (Tokyo: Kokusho kankokai, 1995), p. 186; and John J. Stephan, *The Kuril Islands: Russo-Japanese Frontier in the Pacific* (Oxford: Clarendon Press, 1974), p. 157.

with the artillery forces on Cape Lopatka and the warships on the bay, which began to pound the hills. Tsutsumi ordered the 74th Brigade in Paramushiru to join the defense of Shimushu. The major force of the 91st Division was assembled on Shimushu, marching to meet the invaders. Given their superiority of forces, it appeared only a matter of time before the Japanese defenders would repulse the Soviet forces.

But the conflict was decided off the battlefield. Japan's Fifth Area Army in Sapporo was panicked by what was happening on Shimushu. At a time when the Imperial General Headquarters was trying to secure the smooth surrender of all Japanese forces, a victory of the 91st Division against the Soviet forces would derail the entire process. Thus, around noon on August 18, the Fifth Area Army ordered Tsutsumi to stop fighting except in self-defense. Tsutsumi sent a team of ten emissaries to negotiate a cease-fire, but the Soviet fired on the emissaries, who were walking with a white flag. The Soviets began a counterattack and took the hills after two hours of hand-to-hand combat.

On August 19 Soviet forces began unloading the heavy artillery, weapons, and equipment that had been left on the ships, but the Japanese did not obstruct this operation. The Imperial General Headquarters, alarmed at the prospect of continued resistance from the Japanese forces, admonished the Fifth Area Army to stop any military action, even in self-defense, "on order of the emperor." Cease-fire negotiations were conducted on Takeda Beach that afternoon. On August 20, in accordance with the cease-fire agreement, the Soviet ships sailed toward Kataoka Bay to occupy the naval base, but the Japanese shore batteries began ferocious firing on the approaching ships in the excuse of self-defense. Tsutsumi soon received another strict order from the Fifth Area Army to cease all actions. On August 21, on a Soviet ship off Kashiwabara on Paramushiru, Tsutsumi and Gnechko signed the formal cease-fire agreement.[21]

The Battle of Shimushu demonstrates the fatal weaknesses in the Soviets' Kuril operation. Stalin was concerned that the war might end before he captured what he had been promised at Yalta. Despite the heroic actions of individual Soviet soldiers, the Soviet invasion was poorly planned and poorly executed. The lack of preparation, absence of a well-planned and well-coordinated strategy, shortage of ships, equipment, artillery, and weapons, and the numerical inferiority of soldiers made it almost impossible for Gnechko's forces to complete the mission to occupy Shimushu by August 18.

Gnechko's invading forces consisted of slightly more than 8,800 soldiers, whereas Japanese troops in Shimushu numbered 8,500—or 23,000 if the troops in Paramushiru are included. If we are to follow the general rule that the attacking side must have numerical superiority of three to one over the defender, we realize how reckless it was for the Soviets to attack the heavily fortified Shimushu with only equal forces.[22] The Soviet landing ships carried too heavy a load; they got stuck about 100 to 150 meters from the shore, where the depth was more than two meters. Soldiers jumped into the water carrying heavy equipment and weapons. All twenty-two radios except one were dipped in or dropped into the salt water and ruined. A more serious mistake was that, despite the strict order not to fire, someone from the invading ships began firing prematurely. If the Soviet forces scored a victory on Shimushu, it was largely because the Imperial General Headquarters did not want the 91st Division to win.

The Japanese were not given the opportunity to count the number of casualties at the Battle of Shimushu. According to Soviet sources, the Japanese suffered 1,018 and the Soviets 1,567 casualties. It was the last major battle in World War II. But these men did not die to end the war in the Pacific; the war had ended before the Battle of Shimushu. Why, then, was it necessary for Stalin to wage such a costly war when he could have gained possession of Shimushu simply by sending a military emissary to negotiate a cease-fire? In fact, had he done so, he might have succeeded in occupying the island much earlier, on August 18. Was this a miscalculation or just bad judgment rendered in a panic? Perhaps both, but there is also a third possibility. Stalin needed the blood of Soviet soldiers spilled on the battleground in order to justify his claim that the Soviet Union had earned the Kurils—all the Kurils—paid for with the blood of the sons of the motherland. In fact, the bloodshed was a down payment allowing him to take possession of the entire Kurils securely in his hands.

The high casualty figures in the Battle of Shimushu—despite the fact that the Japanese fought without the benefit of kamikaze pilots and human torpedoes, and that they were hamstrung by the superior command's pressure to conclude a cease-fire—provide a cautionary tale for the planners of the American operation, Olympic. When President Truman approved Olympic on June 18, Marshall had not expected the total Japanese forces in Kyushu to exceed 350,000 (four divisions) against a total of 766,700 American troops. By the time the Battle of Shimushu was waged, the Americans watched with horror as Japanese forces increased quickly in Kyushu, far exceeding Marshall's estimate to a total of 625,000 men and 14 field divisions. Whether American military planners closely watched the Battle of Shimushu is not known, but the resolute determination with which the Japanese fought the invading Soviet troops and the high casualty rate they inflicted on the enemy certainly gave credence to the boast of the Japanese military leaders that they could inflict significant damage on the invading American troops. Had Olympic been implemented, the result would have been an unprecedented bloodbath. As Richard Frank asserts: "the Japanese buildup on Kyushu was sufficient to threaten to make the cost of invasion unacceptable." The Battle of Shimushu validates this assertion.[23]

It is also important to note that Stalin was nervous about the American reaction to his Kuril operation. On August 18 the Imperial General Headquarters in Tokyo, having received the news of the attack on Shimushu, sent an urgent inquiry to MacArthur's headquarters in Manila: "Some of your forces landed on Shimushu Island. . . . Our forces are obliged to resort to arms for self-defense. Now that hostilities between both parties have been prohibited, it is earnestly desired that the hostile actions will be ceased." MacArthur's headquarters immediately transmitted this telegram to Moscow. Stavka was alarmed by this information, thinking that the Americans had landed on Shimushu in violation of the agreed-upon demarcation line. General Slavin asked Deane if this Allied landing reported by the Japanese Imperial General Headquarters was carried out by American troops. Moscow was relieved only when it received MacArthur's assurance that no Americans had landed on Shimushu.[24]

The United States Reacts to Soviet Actions

While reluctantly accepting MacArthur as the sole supreme commander of the Allied powers, Stalin had no intention of accepting his authority inside Soviet-occupied territories. On August 15 MacArthur transmitted his "instructions" through Deane in Moscow to the Soviet General Staff, demanding that the Soviet forces "discontinue further offensive action against the Japanese Forces" in the Soviet zone of operation. MacArthur's presumptuous order provoked an immediate reaction from Antonov. The following day Antonov reminded Deane: "Cessation or continuance of military operations of the Soviet Forces in the Far East against the Japanese Forces can be decided only by the Supreme Commander of the forces of the Soviet Union."[25]

The JCS was divided on the advisability of MacArthur's directive to Antonov. Assistant Chief of Staff Hull admitted that MacArthur had no authority over Soviet forces, and that his directive was sent merely as "information." Therefore, Antonov's reply that there had been "a misunder-standing" was correct. Admiral Charles Cooke, chief of the navy's Plans Division, argued, however: "there is no reason why he shouldn't request them to stop shooting Japs." Nevertheless, the JCS was not interested in causing a ruckus with the Soviets over this matter. Marshall directed MacArthur and Deane to inform the Soviets that MacArthur's original order was an error in transmission, and that it was meant for informa-tion only.[26] The Soviets barked, and the Americans retreated.

Despite this retreat, however, the Americans became concerned with the Soviet advance in the Kurils. The demarcation line agreed upon by military planners at Potsdam was still in effect even after the Soviets declared war against Japan. On the basis of this understanding, on Au-gust 13 the Joint Chiefs of Staff proposed instructing Nimitz that he should plan to receive the surrender of the Kurils south of the Onekotan Straits.[27] It was based on this understanding that on August 14 the Joint Chiefs of Staff prepared General Order Number 1, which, among other stipulations, designated to which military authority the Japanese troops were to surrender. The most important aspect of this order was Article 1-b, which stated: "The senior Japanese commanders and all ground, sea, air and auxiliary forces within Manchuria, Korea north of 38° north lati-tude and Karafuto shall surrender to the Commander in Chief of Soviet Forces in the Far East." The Kurils were conspicuously absent on the list of areas where the Japanese troops were to surrender to the Soviet forces.[28]

Recall that back in May Stimson had responded to Grew's inquiry about the possibility of reopening the Yalta terms by writing off the Kurils. Colonel Bonesteel had disagreed with Stimson. He had suggested that the United States should "go slow" in giving up all the Kurils to the Soviets, arguing: "Unless we kid ourselves we know damn well the only Asiatic enemy we are guarding against is Russia. Therefore why spend all the men and fortune we have to get security in the Pacific and then not make an effort to hold a base near the obvious springboard of the most possible route of attack on us?" In June and July, Bonesteel's recom-mendation had been incorporated into the JCS's decision to demand an American air base in one of the islands in any negotiations dealing with the disposition of the Kurils, and this had been the position adopted by Stimson at Potsdam.[29]

It is not clear what triggered the next move, but after the Soviets en-tered the war, the hard liners in the Operations Division revised this pol-icy and attempted to snatch the promised fruit of the Kurils from Soviet hands. Taking advantage of the understanding that the Kurils belonged exclusively to the American zone of operation, the hard liners in the Operation Division reversed the previous decision and excluded the Kurils from the Soviet occupation zone. According to Marc Gallichio, on the same day that General Order Number 1 was written, the Joint War Plans Committee recommended that U.S. forces be deployed to seize Matsuwa and Paramushiru in order to reinforce the U.S. position in negotiations over postwar airfield rights in the Kurils.[30] The occupation of Paramushiru in particular, which was clearly within the Soviet zone of operation, would have been perceived by the Soviets as a hostile action encroaching on their prerogatives.

Anticipating impending Soviet operations in the Kurils, these military planners pressured policymakers to seize at least some islands in the southern Kurils. According to Gallichio, "McCloy tried to persuade Secretary of State James Byrnes to agree to an American occupation of some of the Kurils." Byrnes was reluctant to accept this recommendation, noting, "we had agreed to give the Kuriles to the Russians and we couldn't go back on it."[31]

On August 12 the State-War-Navy Coordinating Committee met and discussed General Order Number 1. Assistant Secretary of State James Dunn commented that the State Department had no objections to the provisions of General Order Number 1, and thus saw no contradictions between the Yalta Agreement and the order. In the end, the SWNCC "agreed that Mr. Dunn would obtain further data as to commitments made as to the Kuriles prior to further consideration of the matter by the Committee." Colonel Bonesteel also attended this meeting, though he was not a regular member. Apparently the SWNCC was swayed by McCloy's argument. McCloy then requested that Admiral Gardner, assistant naval Chief of Staff, be told to "get out preliminary orders to Admiral Nimitz regarding this matter as well as the island that we want for an airbase."[32] That evening Dunn and McCloy met with Byrnes. After a heated exchange, Byrnes finally relented and "approved the operational line in the Kuriles for use by Admiral Nimitz as a surrender line." McCloy, undoubtedly supported by Bonesteel and Navy Secretary Forrestal, was a central figure in the push to take action and seize some islands, while the State Department resisted this pressure.

More than the Kurils, U.S. policymakers were concerned about Manchuria and Korea. At the night-long session of the SWNCC on August 10–11, Bonesteel and Major Dean Rusk were given the assignment of defining the American and Soviet occupation zones in Korea. McCloy instructed them "to have U.S. forces receive the surrender as far north as possible" within the limitations on their ability to reach the area. Using a small-scale wall map of the Far East, Bonesteel noted that the 38th parallel passed north of Seoul and divided Korea roughly in equal parts, though, according to Rusk, the 38th parallel was farther north than the U.S. forces could reach.[33] Given the casual and arbitrary manner in which the division of Korea was determined, the Americans had cause to be concerned about the Soviets' reaction.

On August 11, Truman issued a directive to Marshall and King to make advance arrangements to occupy Dairen and a port in Korea immediately following the surrender of Japan, "if the port should not at that time have been taken over by the forces of the Soviet government." Following this order, the navy began preparing an operational plan. Later that day Cooke questioned the wisdom of the draft proposal for General Order Number 1 with regard to Dairen. He complained to Hull that by conceding to the Soviets the areas north of the 38th parallel in Korea and all of Manchuria, General Order Number 1 was tantamount to inviting the Soviets to occupy these territories. Hull promised to call this to McCloy's attention.[34]

On August 15 Truman informed Attlee, Stalin, and Chiang Kai-shek that the United States intended to "use its naval and air power to expedite the surrender of Japanese forces in the coastal area of the Asiatic mainland in order to discourage continuation of local hostilities."[35] This message was to serve notice that, regardless of the boundary lines it had defined in General Order Number 1, the United States intended to take unilateral military action by air and sea in all the coastal areas in "the Asiatic mainland," which included China, Manchuria, and Korea. Although this message cast a wider net, the United States was especially interested in seizing Dairen and a coastal port in Korea.[36]

The new race was on, this time to see who would get to Dairen first. If both sides remained determined to capture the port, serious conflict would be inevitable, and a military confrontation could not be precluded.

Truman and Stalin Clash over General Order Number 1

On August 15 Truman sent General Order Number 1 to Stalin through Harriman. The next day Stalin sent his reply through Harriman as well as through Gromyko in Washington. He began in a feigned conciliatory tone, stressing that he "principally" accepted the contents of General Order Number 1 with the addition of two points. The first was "to include in the region of surrender of Japanese armed forces to Soviet troops *all the Kuril Islands*" in accordance with the Yalta Agreement. The second amendment was more audacious. Stalin demanded: "To include in the region of surrender of the Japanese armed forces to Soviet troops" the northern part of Hokkaido above the demarcation line between Kushiro and Rumoi. (See Map 4.) He then explained the reasons for the second amendment. During the Civil War of 1919–1922, Japan had held the entire Soviet Far East under its control. Thus if the Soviet Union failed to occupy some part of Japan proper, "Russian public opinion would be seriously offended."[37]

Stalin's demand for "*all* the Kuril islands" exceeded the provision of the Yalta Agreement, which pledged only "the Kuril islands" but failed to define precisely what they included. Stalin was also making a careful distinction between the Kurils and the northern part of Hokkaido. By referring to the latter as "Japan proper," Stalin implied that the Kurils were not. Implicit in his argument was that the Kurils legitimately belonged to Russia, and that they should be not "handed over," as the Yalta Agreement stipulated, but "returned" to their rightful owner.

Stalin revealed his intentions even more clearly in his August 17 directive to General Kuzma Derevianko, who was appointed Soviet military representative to General MacArthur's Allied headquarters in Manila. In this directive Stalin instructed Derevianko to present Soviet demands to include the Kurils and the northern part of Hokkaido from Kushiro to Rumoi in the Soviet occupation zone. In addition, Derevianko was to demand the creation of a Soviet occupation zone for stationing Soviet troops in Tokyo.[38]

Truman wrote a reply on August 17 and sent it to Stalin on August 18. He agreed "to modify General Order No. 1 to include all the Kurile Islands to the area to be surrendered to the Commander in Chief of the Soviet Forces in the Far East." While conceding this point, however, Truman demanded that the United States be granted "air base rights for land and sea aircraft" on one of the islands, preferably in the central group, "for military purposes and for commercial use." As for Stalin's demand to have an occupied zone in Hokkaido, Truman flatly rejected it: "it is my intention and arrangements have been made for the surrender of Japanese forces on all the islands of Japan proper, Hokkaido, Honshu, Shikoku, and Kyushu, to General MacArthur."[39]

Archives do not tell us what discussions went on within the American administration as to how to respond to Stalin's August 16 letter to Truman. Given the gravity of the question, we can assume that Stalin's message was discussed in the Operation Division of the War Department and the State-War-Navy Coordinating Committee. For reasons that are not clear, the OPD reversed the previous bellicose decision. Bringing the previous memoranda, written by Grew, Stimson, and Marshall, from the old files, which limited the scope of the demand over the Kurils to the request for an air base and landing rights, Lincoln proposed, though reluctantly, the acceptance of Stalin's demand over the Kurils. "At Yalta . . . the U.S. agreed to the Kuriles going to Russia," he stated begrudgingly. "There are no records available to the War Department indicating that there was any reservation to the agreement at Yalta on the Kuriles going to Russia. There are no records available to the War Department indicating that Mr. Hopkins discussed the matter of the Kuriles when he was in Moscow last May and June." The War Department should have raised objections then, Lincoln's argument implied, but did not; therefore, it had to accept the consequences. The War Department's change of heart was more than welcome by the State Department, and the final answer to Stalin was "prepared by State and Admiral Leahy."[40]

As for Hokkaido, Truman held firm: he was not going to give Stalin an inch. Nevertheless, the U.S. position on Hokkaido was not as firm as it seemed. In a study on the occupation, the War Department had entertained the possibility of dividing the zones of occupation in Japan, granting, in one variant, Hokkaido, and in another variant Hokkaido and Tohoku, to the Soviets.[41] Nevertheless, the study had remained an intellectual exercise of the military planners; when it was sent to Stimson, the secretary of war had taken a firm line to include Hokkaido within the U.S. zone of occupation. And this was the policy Truman adopted in his reply to Stalin. Nevertheless Stimson, who had left Washington for a well-deserved vacation, can hardly be considered a crucial player in Truman's decision. Although there is no documentary basis to support this supposition, Byrnes most likely exerted the most influence on Truman in his correspondence with Stalin.

Stalin's well-crafted letter put Truman in a position where he was unable to reject the first demand. The president categorically refused the demand for a slice of Hokkaido, but to also reject the first demand might cause Stalin to repudiate General Order No. 1 altogether. In such a case, there would have been no guarantee that the Soviets would stop at the

38th parallel in Korea, or cooperate in Manchuria. Moreover, the rejection of Stalin's demand for the Kurils would have meant U.S. military action in the Kurils, which might run the risk of developing into military confrontation with Soviet forces. No one thought that the control of the Kurils was so vital to American strategic interests that the United States should risk military confrontation with the Soviet Union. When Truman conceded on this point, the fate of the Kurils was sealed.

Truman's acceptance of Stalin's letter with the exception of the second amendment also meant that the president agreed to include the Liaotung Peninsula in the Soviet zone of occupation. This doomed the American attempt to capture Dairen. On August 18, Lincoln and Admiral Gardner had a telephone conversation in which they discussed the problem of the Dairen operation. According to Gardner, the navy had the capability of deploying forces into Dairen "any time we wanted to." The matter was not capability but intention. Lincoln said: "we really have no intention of putting a cruiser, naval vessels into Dairen at the present time for the purpose of . . . ," and then Gardner chimed in, "obstructing the Russians." They estimated that the Soviets would take Dairen by Monday, August 20. Gardner said: "We figure the Russians are going to beat us there anyhow, that putting ships in there isn't going to stop them from seizing the land and it's the land and the port facilities and all that sort of things that we're interested in." Lincoln agreed.[42] The U.S. operation to seize Dairen was dropped.

In contrast, Stalin moved quickly on Dairen. After Stalin received Truman's reply, Antonov ordered Vasilevskii on August 20 to "prepare and execute as quickly as possible an airborne operation for the occupation of Port Arthur and Dairen." On the same day, Vasilevskii reported to Stalin that he had given the order to the Transbaikal Front to make preparations to capture Port Arthur and Dairen by a surprise airborne assault.[43]

The United States, however, took a firm stand on Korea south of the 38th parallel. Even though Stalin had agreed with the demarcation line of Korea, the JCS was skeptical. A JCS memo stated, "There are unconfirmed reports that the Soviets are planning movements south of the 38° line." The Joint Chiefs of Staff thus asked how MacArthur and Nimitz would respond to this challenge. It is not known how the two men answered this inquiry, but as it turned out, the JCS's concerns had no foundation. The Soviets were not interested in crossing over the 38th parallel into the south. In fact, when they failed to challenge the 38th parallel as the demarcation line, Rusk was "somewhat surprised."[44] The Americans stood firm only in areas into which the Soviets had no intention of moving.

Stalin's Order to Occupy Hokkaido and the Southern Kurils

Historians tend to treat Stalin's demand for the northern half of Hokkaido as a bargaining ploy.[45] But Stalin was dead serious about the Hokkaido operation. Shortly before or immediately after he wrote his August 16 letter to Truman, he ordered Vasilevskii to implement the Hokkaido and southern Kuril operation. On August 18 Vasilevskii in turn ordered the commander of the First Far Eastern Front "to occupy the northern half of Hokkaido from Kushiro to Rumoi and the southern part of the Kuril Islands" by September 1. For this operation three divisions of the 87th Rifle Corps would be deployed: two divisions for the Hokkaido operation, and one division for the southern Kuril operation. After Hokkaido was occupied, the operational headquarters was to be established there.[46] At this point Stalin considered Hokkaido the major part of this operation.

On August 20 Antonov sent a telegram to Vasilevskii, instructing the commander of the Far Eastern Front "to prepare the operation for Hokkaido and the southern Kurils, but to initiate this operation only by special order of the Stavka, [and] . . . to concentrate Ksenofontov's 87th Rifle Corps on the southern part of Sakhalin Island and prepare it for an operation *either* for Hokkaido *or* for the southern Kuril islands."[47] After Stalin received Truman's August 18 letter, he began to equivocate by shifting from *both* the Hokkaido *and* the southern Kuril operation to *either* the Hokkaido operation *or* the southern Kuril operation. He also made sure that the operations were strictly under the control of the highest military authority headed by himself.

On August 21, having received Stalin's second order, Vasilevskii issued a directive to begin "immediately and no later than August 21" the landing operation of the 87th Rifle Corps on Maoka, and to assemble the rifle corps onto Otomari and Toyohira for the operations in Hokkaido and the southern Kurils. The commanders of the First and Second Far Eastern Fronts, the Pacific Fleet, and the air force were ordered to launch an airborne operation in the port and the city of Rumoi and to make the air base available by August 23 for the occupation of the northern part of Hokkaido. Furthermore, Iumashev was ordered to send at least two infantry divisions in two or three echelons to Hokkaido. Finally, Vasilevskii reminded all commanders that he would personally give the order to begin the landing operation for Hokkaido, but that the preparations for this operation should be completed by August 23.[48] (See Map 4.)

But on August 22, something happened to change Stalin's mind.

Stalin Responds to Truman's Message

On August 22 Stalin sent a letter in response to Truman's August 18 message. In the first paragraph, Stalin expressed his great disappointment with Truman's rejection of his demand. "I have to say," Stalin wrote, "that my colleagues and I did not expect such an answer." Further on in his message, he vehemently rejected Truman's request for an air base and landing rights on one of the Kuril islands. First, there was no such decision made either at Yalta or at Potsdam. Second, such a demand would humiliate the Soviet Union. In his view, "demands of such a nature are usually laid before either a conquered state, or such an allied state which is in no position to defend with its own means certain parts of its territory and, in view of this, expresses readiness to grant its ally an appropriate base." He did not consider the Soviet Union to be such a state. Third, he did not understand the motivation behind Truman's request.[49]

In contrast to Stalin's August 16 message, this telegram was striking in its angry tone. Why was Stalin angrier in this message than in his reply to Truman's earlier message? Was he really upset or was this anger merely a bargaining tactic? It was most likely both. Stalin did not feel grateful to Truman in the least for including the Kurils in the Soviet zone of occupation, as he thought the area rightfully belonged to the Soviet Union. But he was offended by Truman's rejection of his modest proposal to have a slice of Hokkaido. The tone of this message was also part of his calculated strategy. Through his anger he wanted to convey a clear warning that Truman was risking good relations with the Soviet Union. By rejecting the American air base and landing rights in a most strident tone, Stalin attempted to make it impossible for Truman to disagree that the Kurils were inherent Soviet territory.

Why did it take Stalin four full days to answer Truman's message? In contrast, he had promptly responded to Truman's August 15 message the following day. This delay was most likely connected with military preparations. As mentioned, the decision to implement the Hokkaido and southern Kuril operation was made between August 16 and August 17.

Even after he received Truman's letter, he let his military proceed with the plan to invade Hokkaido. He was weighing the pros and cons of going ahead with the Hokkaido invasion plan. That explains why he did not reply to Truman until August 22.

Stalin did not accept Truman's exclusion of the Soviet Union from Hokkaido. Nevertheless, he did not pursue his demand any further. By stating that he "understood" the president's refusal, he was retreating from his ambition over Hokkaido, while leaving the possibility of a Soviet operation there slightly open.

This was the first sign of retreat. Although we do not know exactly what happened, something must have led Stalin to change his mind about the Hokkaido operation. It could be that he had received an intelligence report indicating the determination of the United States to hold on to mainland Japan, including Hokkaido. Or perhaps, on the basis of detailed information he had received from General Deane on American military activities, he may have thought it too risky to implement the Hokkaido operation. Or maybe he came to learn that his secret plan to invade Hokkaido was leaked to the United States, and he feared the U.S. reaction. In fact, on August 21, a U.S. naval liaison officer in Vladivostok reported to the Navy Department that "a reliable source has indicated . . . that the Soviets are planning to land forces on Hokkaido and southern Karafuto [Kurils]."[50] Or Stalin realized, perhaps on Molotov's advice, that the Hokkaido operation, which clearly violated the Yalta Agreement, would weaken his claim over the Kurils, which was based on that same agreement.

The Kurils now assumed center stage. Moreover, suspension of the Hokkaido operation determined the fate of the Japanese POWs captured in Manchuria, Korea, Sakhalin, and the Kurils. On August 23, the Soviet State Defense Committee (GKO) adopted the notorious resolution GKO 9898, "On reception, placement, and use of labor of 500,000 Japanese prisoners of war." On the basis of this resolution, the Military Council of the Acting Army in the Far East was entrusted with selecting 500,000 Japanese POWs physically fit for hard labor in the severe conditions of the Soviet Far East and Siberia. In the following months 640,000 POWs were sent to labor camps in various parts of the Soviet Union, despite Beria's August 16 instruction to the Far Eastern commanders not to send Japanese POWs to the Soviet Union. The change in policy was most likely connected with the suspension of the Hokkaido operation, a main objective of which was to dragoon the Japanese prisoners for reconstruction and development in the Far East and Siberia. With Hokkaido no longer a goal, Stalin was forced to seek other sources of labor. Hence, in violation of the Potsdam Proclamation, he decided to use the Japanese POWs for hard labor.[51]

On August 24 the Japanese Imperial General Headquarters sent an urgent message to MacArthur in Manila: "According to a Moscow broadcast, it is reported that the Soviet Union is about to send Airborne Troops to Hokkaido."[52] By August 24, therefore, the United States was well aware of Soviet preparations to invade Hokkaido. The next day, Truman wrote a strongly worded reply to Stalin's August 22 message.

It was now time to retreat. General Ivanov, chief of staff of the Far Eastern Front, sent the order to all commanders: "In order to avoid creating conflict and misunderstanding in relations with the Allies you are categorically prohibited from sending whatever ships and airplanes in the direction of Hokkaido Island." Stalin instructed Derevianko to drop the demand for the occupation of Hokkaido and the creation of a Soviet occupation zone in Tokyo. On August 25, Antonov told Deane that landing on Hokkaido was not part of the Soviet General Staff's plans.[53] What he omitted was that it had been the central part of its plan until a few days before.

U.S. Chiefs React to the Soviet Kurils Operation

On the morning of August 23, Cooke and Hull had a telephone conversation about the situation in the Kurils. Both men were skeptical about the prospect of Stalin's agreeing to Truman's request for landing rights. They discussed the idea of turning the islands of Etorofu and Kunashiri into an international trusteeship, but neither Cooke nor Hull thought that the Kurils were an important issue. According to Cooke, "Our people over here can't get very much stirred up about it." To this Hull answered, "Well, I can't personally."[54]

After the president received Stalin's August 22 message, Assistant Secretary of State Dunn called the War Department and intimated that "the feeling on the higher levels of the State Department was that this matter should be dropped unless there were good reason why the military should secure such rights for the period of occupation." "The higher levels of the State Department" could be none other than Byrnes. Byrnes was the decisive player on this issue. Though often regarded by revisionist historians as an ardent advocate for a tough stance against the Soviet Union, Byrnes favored a conciliatory position on this issue.[55]

Shortly after 5 P.M., Cooke and Hull had another telephone conversation in which they agreed that the issue of landing rights on the Kurils was not worth fighting for. Hull said that he understood the Russians' refusal to agree to the U.S. request. In Cooke's view, when the Russians said that they wanted the Kurils, the United States should have said: "You can occupy the Kuriles, but we'll count Etorofu and those two islands right next to Hokkaido as adjacent islands." The Russians would have had a hard time disputing the logic of the U.S. claim at that point. Hull, for his part, blamed the State Department for having "muffed this whole thing." It failed to take up the issue when opportunities were available during Hopkins's visit to Moscow and at Potsdam. Hull admitted, "I don't blame them [the Russians] a damn bit for not liking it. As a matter of fact, I don't think personally it's too important." Cooke concurred: "I don't either . . . We're not much interested."[56]

Finally, on August 24 Hull wrote to McCloy: "in view of Marshal Stalin's present stand, it is felt that U.S. interests in an air base in the Kuriles are insufficient to justify taking issue in the matter." Although rights of transit and refueling for military aircraft at an air base in the central Kurils would be desirable, Hull felt that "the Army Air Forces do not desire to press the matter to the point of political involvement. Neither the requirements of our occupation forces or of our redeployment justify a persistent attitude on our part." Lincoln agreed, and on August 24 he told the Operation Division "that in view of all circumstances we shouldn't press the matter further at this time."[57] Now the Kuril case was closed. The United States would not lift a finger when the Soviets seized the islands.

Vyshinskii's Mysterious Inquiry

The United States, more than anything else, feared that the Soviet occupation of Manchuria might lead to the collusion of Soviet forces with Chinese Communists. On August 19, Harriman wrote in an unsent memo to Byrnes that Stalin might be engaged in "covert encouragement of Yenan and [the] Mongolian People's Republic to resist actively Chiang and [the] US," and establish an "independent and friendly regime in Manchuria and Korea occupied by the Soviet forces." Byrnes shared

Harriman's concerns. On August 23, the secretary of state instructed Harriman to see Molotov and convey the message that he intended to enforce General Order No. 1, which stipulated that the Japanese forces were to surrender to Chiang Kai-shek alone. Byrnes proposed to issue a joint statement signed by the U.S. and Soviet governments reaffirming the Nationalists as the sole authority in China.[58]

Despite American apprehension, however, Stalin was not interested in interfering in China's domestic conflict. Faithful to the Sino-Soviet Treaty of Alliance and Friendship he had just concluded with T. V. Soong, he recognized the Nationalist Government as China's sole legitimate government. On August 18, Stalin had already instructed his commanders in Manchuria to allow the Chinese to raise the Nationalist flag under the administration appointed by Chiang Kai-shek, and not to interfere with the efforts of the Nationalists to restore order. The same order, however, directed all commanders to consider all stockpiles of food, fuel, weapons, automobiles, and other properties seized by Soviet forces the trophies of the Soviet Army and not to transfer them to the Chinese.[59] As far as Stalin was concerned, China was not ripe for revolution, and therefore could be exploited to Soviet advantage.

Byrnes's proposal to issue a joint statement with the Soviet Union with regard to China invited a mysterious response from the Soviet Foreign Ministry. On August 25, Deputy Foreign Minister Andrei Vyshinskii wrote to Harriman on Molotov's behalf that as long as Byrnes's proposal was concerned with the publication of General Order No. 1, he wanted to clarify that the Kuril Islands were included in the area where Japanese forces were to surrender to Soviet forces, as Stalin's letter on August 16 had requested.[60]

Vyshinskii's letter baffled the Americans. Harriman immediately replied to Vyshinskii, reminding him that on August 19 Deane had informed Antonov in a letter that Truman had accepted Stalin's proposed amendment. Deane had further told General Slavin orally about the change in General Order No. 1, Harriman continued, and the Japanese government had been notified about this change on August 20. On Harriman's instruction, Deane went to see Antonov on Saturday night, August 25, and reminded Antonov and Slavin that the text of General Order No. 1 that he had handed to them included the surrender of the Kurils to the Soviet commander. Both Harriman and Deane thought that the General Staff had made a major gaffe by failing to inform the Foreign Ministry about the amendment to General Order No. 1. According to Deane,

"Antonov was taken by surprise, and I could see that Slavin was about to die of mortification. I tried to cover him with his chief by suggesting that in view of the mass of material that was being translated I could easily understand how this correction had escaped their notice."[61]

But it was Harriman and Deane who were fooled. Recently opened Stalin papers contain Harriman's letter to Molotov, dated August 18 and received by Molotov on August 19, which clearly stated Truman's acceptance of Stalin's proposed amendment to include the Kurils in the Soviet occupation zone.[62] As the Soviets used to say, this mistake was "not by accident"; rather, it was an important part of a well-crafted diplomatic strategy. It is unthinkable that Molotov, who was the main conduit, together with Harriman, of the Truman-Stalin correspondence, did not know of this important change in General Order No. 1. Exploiting Byrnes's inquiry about the possibility of a joint statement on China, Stalin used Vyshinskii to double-check if the amendment still stood, to make sure that the Americans would not deploy troops in any part of the Kurils. The Americans reconfirmed the amendment. Having thus satisfied this requirement, Stalin finally issued the order to implement the southern Kuril operation, confident that the Americans would not react strongly. What concerned him now was the date of completion of this operation, since he did not know when the Americans were planning to hold the official surrender ceremony.

The Americans Prepare for Japan's Surrender

Whereas the Soviets were moving fast to consume the territories under their control, the United States was slow in moving into Japan. General Douglas MacArthur, now appointed the supreme commander for the Allied powers, was more concerned with the question of how to stage his dramatic entry into Japan than he was with the extra square miles the Soviets might gain. The general ordered the Japanese government to send their sixteen-man delegation to Manila to discuss the surrender. The Japanese delegation arrived in Manila on August 19.[63]

In Manila, after being shown the surrender document, the Japanese were aghast: the Japanese version of the document that the emperor was supposed to sign began: "I, the emperor of Japan," using the first-person pronoun *watakushi*. The Japanese emperor referred to himself only with the word *chin* (the equivalent of the royal "We"). In response to protest from the Japanese delegation, Colonel Sidney Mashbir changed the word to *chin*. After Mashbir explained this change to the general, MacArthur put his arm around Mashbir's shoulder and said: "Mashbir, you handled that exactly right. I have no desire whatever to debase him in the eyes of his own people." The emperor and the peace party, who had hastened to end the war hoping that the Americans would deal with the emperor more generously than the Soviets, gambled on the right horse after all. In the meantime, MacArthur's advance party, headed by Colonel Charles Tench, arrived in Tokyo on Tuesday, August 28.[64] By then Stalin's southern Kuril operation was in full swing. While MacArthur moved at a snail's pace, carefully planning a dramatic entry into Japan, the Soviets were frantically engaged in a mopping up operation to conquer the remaining Kuril islands.

On August 26 Antonov made three amendments to the draft of the Instrument of Surrender prepared by the United States. The first two amendments were to ensure a free hand for Soviet forces within their occupation zone, irrespective of the policy of the supreme commander of the Allied powers. Antonov's third amendment was to demand the Soviet right to determine the status of the emperor.[65] Stalin had his own plan with regard to the prisoners and the industrial assets in the Soviet-occupied territories, and he was going to go ahead with this plan unencumbered by U.S. policies. As for the amendment on the status of the emperor, Antonov stated that initially the authority of the emperor would be subject to the sole authority of the supreme commander for the Allied powers, but that it might later be desirable to set up an Allied organization to control the government of Japan similar to that which existed in Germany. This was another attempt by the Soviet government to insinuate itself into the decision-making body that would determine the occupation of Japan. If Hirohito and the peace party had feared the consequence of expanded Soviet influence over the status of the emperor, here again their fear was justified.

On August 27, at his meeting with Harriman, Stalin asked the ambassador when the act of surrender would take place. Harriman told him that the American naval forces should be in the outer bay of Yokohama Harbor that morning. From there they would go to Tokyo Bay to sign the surrender documents on September 2. This was the first time that Stalin learned the precise date of Japan's surrender. This information gave him a definite deadline by which to complete the Kuril operation. Having received Antonov's proposed amendments for the Instrument of Surrender document, MacArthur, supported by the War Department, directed

Deane to reject them on the grounds that any amendments at this late stage would complicate the already complex arrangements.[66]

Truman and Stalin Continue to Spar

Truman was not pleased with Stalin's August 22 message. After receiving the letter, the White House sent a message to Harriman: "At the present time the President is not disposed to reply."[67] He did not write a reply until August 25, and the message was not delivered to Stalin until August 27. Hull-Cook telephone conversations on August 22 indicate that Stalin's angry reply was discussed at the highest level of the administration. Although there is no record as to how the president prepared his reply, Byrnes is the most likely candidate to have had a decisive influence on Truman on this matter. It is not known, however, why Truman waited to deliver his reply until August 27. These five days turned out to be crucial for Stalin's Kuril operations.

Truman began his response with Stalin's rejection of his request for landing rights on the Kurils. He explained that he had brought up the idea to help "the cooperative action in connection with the carrying out of the Japanese surrender terms as [a U.S. airfield] would afford another route for air connection with the United States for emergency use during the period of occupation of Japan." He also did not hesitate to suggest using the landing facilities for commercial purposes. Then Truman launched a counterattack:

> You evidently misunderstood my message because you refer to it as a demand usually laid before a conquered state or an allied state unable to defend parts of its territory. *I was not speaking about any territory of the Soviet Republic. I was speaking of the Kurile Islands, Japanese territory, disposition of which must be made at a peace settlement.*[68]

This was the strongest statement to date from Truman with regard to the Kurils. The president did not consider the Kurils to be inherent territory of the Soviet Union, as Stalin had suggested in his previous message; on the contrary, he took the position that the Kurils were Japanese territory, and, though he admitted that his predecessor had agreed to support Soviet claims to the islands, he asserted that their disposition would have to be determined by a peace settlement. This message must have confirmed

Stalin's suspicion that the United States was backing away from the commitment made at Yalta, and it made him even more determined to seize all the islands before the official termination of the war.

Stalin realized that his August 22 message might have backfired, triggering Truman to reconsider the entire Kuril issue. Now it was necessary to back off. He sent a reply to Truman on August 30. He said that he was glad that "the "misunderstanding that slipped into our correspondence" had cleared away. He explained that he was "not in the least offended" by Truman's proposal, but merely "experienced a state of perplexity" because of the misunderstanding. "I, of course, agree with your proposal," Stalin continued, "to secure for the United States the right of landing on our aerodromes on one of the Kuril Islands in emergency cases in the period of occupation of Japan." He would consent also to provide an airfield for landing commercial planes. But in return, he expected the United States to provide an American airfield for Soviet commercial planes on one of the Aleutian Islands. He explained: "It is the case that the present aviation route from Siberia across Canada to the United States of America does not satisfy us because of its long stretch. We prefer a shorter route from the Kuril Islands through the Aleutian Islands, as an intermediate point, to Seattle." Stalin thus appeared to satisfy Truman's demand. But the crafty dictator was in his element when he demanded reciprocity, throwing the very argument made by the Americans back at them, fully aware that there existed no Soviet commercial airline flying overseas through the Pacific at the time.[69]

The timing of this response is also important. Stalin received Truman's message on August 27 but waited until August 30 to send his reply. Those three days were crucial for the Soviet operation in the Kurils. Stalin wanted to make sure that he seized most of the islands before he sent his answer.

Stalin Orders the Southern Kuril Operations

On August 19, while Soviet forces were still engaged in the battle at Shimushu, the Pacific Fleet Command sent a coded telegram, most likely under instructions from Moscow, to the Petropavlovsk Naval Base Command Post ordering occupation of the northern Kuril islands as far as Shimushiru. Gnechko's first task after the occupation of Shimushu was to occupy Paramushiru and Onekotan. The occupation of Paramushiru was completed on the night of August 23 and 24. But Gnechko did not have an accurate map, and therefore he did not have accurate information as to which beaches in the northern Kurils were appropriate for landing. Nor did he have any information as to what Japanese forces existed on those islands. Gnechko divided the landing units and ships at his disposal into two groups, each accompanied by a Japanese officer.[70]

The first group "occupied" Onekotan on August 25, Shashikotan on August 26, and Harumukotan on August 27, capturing a small number of Japanese soldiers stationed on these islands. The group returned to Kataoka Bay on August 28. (See Map 4.) The second group sailed on the *Dzerzhinskii* from Kataoka Bay on August 24 and reached Matsua, where the Japanese staff officer Major Mitsuru Suizu persuaded the commander of the Japanese defense forces stationed on this island to surrender. The main landing units occupied Matsua on August 27. On the same day, the forward group on the *Dzerzhinskii* moved to Shimushiru. Despite Suizu's assurance that no Japanese soldiers were stationed there, the Soviet commander forged a report stating that the Japanese soldiers had slipped away.[71] The assignment given to Gnechko—to occupy the Kuril islands up to Shimushiru—was completed. The Kuril operation, as it was conceived in the beginning, was over.

The suspension of the Hokkaido operation on August 22 meant a shift in emphasis in the southern Kuril operation. On August 23, Vasilevskii ordered Iumashev to dispatch the main divisions of the 87th Rifle Corps from Sakhalin to Kunashiri and Etorofu, avoiding Hokkaido. Following Vasilevskii's order, the General Staff of the Pacific Fleet had ordered the commander of the Northern Pacific Fleet "to dispatch two minesweepers with a marine company each to Etorofu and Kunashiri, and to accept the surrender of Japanese forces, if they encountered no resistance." This task was entrusted to Leonov, who was at that time commanding his units to move from Maoka to Otomari in a violent storm. Unable to sail through the Soya Strait, Leonov landed on Honto, and reached Otomari only on August 25. As soon as he arrived at Otomari, he received another order from the Pacific Fleet Chief of Staff Admiral A. S. Frolov to "prepare a landing operation for the occupation of Etorofu," and "for fulfillment of this task to use a . . . minesweeper from Maoka with a group commanded by Captain . . . Chicherin." This hasty order provoked a protest from local commanders as well as the Northern Pacific Fleet. Vice Admiral V. A. Andreev reminded Frolov that the Otomari operation had not been completed. He noted that given the conditions of the ships in Maoka and the incompletion of the occupation of Otomari, there was no way to finish the reconnaissance operation in the southern Kurils.[72]

On August 25 the Pacific Fleet headquarters, presumably under orders from the Kremlin, issued a directive to the 87th Rifle Corps in Maoka to occupy the southern Kurils and an airborne operation to seize the airfield on Etorofu. The Kremlin was determined to have physical possession of the southern Kurils before the imminent formal surrender of Japan. This order also expanded the area of the operation not merely to Etorofu and Kunashiri but also to Shikotan and the Habomai islands.[73]

This order also called for extending the operation in the central Kurils. Previously, the operation in the northern and central Kurils was designed to occupy the islands up to Shimushiru, but this order expanded the task further south to Uruppu. (See Map 4.) Responsibility for this operation, which was given to the Kamchatka District Command under Gnechko, was separated from the southern Kuril operation, which was to be implemented by the 87th Rifle Corps from Sakhalin.[74]

The seizure of Uruppu demonstrated a lack of preparation on the part of the occupying forces. The reconnaissance units circled the island for four days from August 26 to August 30, unable to find a suitable landing spot; nor could they find accurate information as to where Japanese forces were located on the island. The provisions supplied to the units ran out. The transport ship *Volkhov,* which was supposed to send the units to Uruppu, ran up on the rocks and was stranded near Harumukotan. The two battalions, which were intended for deployment on Uruppu, were ordered to land on Harumukotan. Thus the "occupation" of Harumukotan, where no Japanese forces were stationed, was completed with unusually large occupying forces. On Uruppu itself, the reconnaissance force did not locate the Japanese forces until August 30. Finally, when the second reconnaissance force reached the shore, the Japanese emissary appeared with a white flag. All along, the Japanese forces had been waiting for the arrival of Soviet forces with the intention of surrendering. Finally, on August 31, the Japanese surrendered themselves and their weapons in an orderly fashion.[75]

Major Suizu, who accompanied the Soviet reconnaissance force on the *Dzerzhinskii,* noticed a change in behavior on the part of the Soviet forces when they approached Uruppu. In the operation as far as Shimushiru, the Soviet forces had sailed in the Okhotsk, never venturing into the Pacific Ocean. Now that they neared Uruppu, they ventured into the

Pacific Ocean for the first time. But they stayed away from the island and made no preparations to land. When Suizu asked Commander R. B. Voronov why they were waiting, Voronov answered that they were waiting because the Americans might be on the island. Suddenly a siren sounded on the ship, followed by the sounds of artillery fire. After everything had returned to normal half an hour later, Suizu asked again Voronov what the commotion was all about. Voronov replied that an American plane had approached, and they had responded. Suizu expected the *Dzerzhinskii* to sail farther down to the southern Kurils, but soon the ship sailed north. Curious Suizu again asked Voronov why they were going back. Voronov replied: "The southern Kurils are in the Americans' jurisdiction. We will not go in there."[76] But that was only on August 27, and Voronov was still acting on previous instructions, not knowing that the Kremlin had decided to occupy the southern Kurils.

Local commanders did not understand why the Kremlin was so eager to implement the southern Kuril operation. On August 26, Leonov received an order to conduct a reconnaissance operation on Kunashiri and Etorofu. But this order appeared to Andreev and Leonov a reckless adventure. The majority of ships lacked machine oil, having already used it all. Marine infantry units were scattered in various parts of Otomari to defend strategic positions. There was an acute shortage of food. No information about Etorofu and Kunashiri was available.[77]

But Andreev and Leonov did not understand the big picture. Stalin was racing against time. On August 27 Leonov received another urgent order to sweep mines en route from Otomari to the southern Kurils, and to organize a reconnaissance mission to Etorofu and Kunashiri. Leonov still resisted what seemed to him a reckless order. The Northern Pacific Fleet had ordered Leonov to send one minesweeper each to Kunashiri and Etorofu, with one company on each minesweeper. Citing the information he had received that there were 13,500 soldiers on the islands, Leonov wanted to amend the order by sending two minesweepers first to Etorofu, and then on to Kunashiri if there was no resistance. It was not until 12:50 on August 27 that two minesweepers left Otomari: No. 589, under the command of Lieutenant Captain Brunshtein, with a company of the 113th Rifle Battalion consisting of 176 soldiers, and No. 590, with another company (166 soldiers) of the same battalion.[78] Things were not moving as fast as the Kremlin had wished.

On August 28, the Military Council of the Pacific Fleet decided to expand the southern Kuril operation further. It instructed the commander of the Northern Pacific Fleet to send a large contingent of reinforcements to Etorofu and Kunashiri, to solve all the problems associated with the occupation of the islands by consulting the commander of the 87th Rifle Corps, and to complete the operation by September 2.[79] The most important part of this order was the date of completion. On that date, Japan was to sign the formal surrender document on the *Missouri* in Tokyo Bay. Stalin had to occupy the islands before September 2.

Several hours before Leonov received this order, Minesweepers No. 589 and No. 590 reached Rubetsu Bay in Etorofu in thick fog. The company on ship 589 landed on the island first, while the forces on ship 590 took a position to protect the landing unit. At this point, the Japanese emissaries arrived and told Brunshtein that their forces were ready to surrender. The Japanese forces, 6,000 soldiers and officers, peacefully surrendered. The first question that Soviet soldiers asked on Etorofu was: "Are there any American soldiers on the island?"[80]

Leonov's delay in discharging the order must have angered higher authorities. At 5:25 P.M. on August 30, Vasilevskii ordered Leonov to immediately send one company from Etorofu to Kunashiri to seize the island, while maintaining one company on Etorofu. This order was conveyed to Brunshtein, who responded that it would be impossible to land on Kunashiri before September 1. The Pacific Fleet headquarters, presumably under orders from impatient Moscow, ordered Brunshtein to speed up the operation as quickly as possible, and organized another landing unit at Otomari. On August 31, Minesweeper No. 590 with a landing unit of 100 soldiers left Rubetsu Bay in Etorofu, while two ships transporting a landing unit of 216 soldiers under Lieutenant Vinichenko sailed from Otomari. It was not until September 1 that the two groups met at the mouth of Furukamappu Bay in Kunashiri and began landing on the island. As soon as the Soviet units appeared, they met the Japanese military emissaries, who told Vinichenko that all 1,250 Japanese troops were ready to surrender. The occupation of Kunashiri was completed within several hours on September 1.[81]

The occupation of Kunashiri did not mean that the southern Kuril operation was over. The Soviets were interested in acquiring more prizes: Shikotan and the Habomai group. The Soviets called the group the Small Kuril chain, but the islands were an extension of Hokkaido and clearly belonged to the American occupation zone. In order to occupy Shikotan, Lieutenant Vostrikov organized a landing unit on board two ships, which left Otomari on August 31 and arrived at Shakotan Bay in Shikotan on

September 1. The Japanese defense unit, consisting of 4,800 men, surrendered without any resistance. Here, too, the first question the Soviet soldiers asked the Japanese was, "Are there any Americans on the island?"[82]

Thus, before Japan formally surrendered on September 2, the Soviets managed to occupy Etorofu (August 28), Kunashiri (September 1), and Shikotan (September 1). The occupation of the Hobomai group had not been completed yet, however. In order to launch an operation for the Habomai islands, the Pacific Fleet headquarters decided to use Kunashiri as its base. A large landing force under Captain Chicherin boarded two ships, the *Vsevold Sibirtsev* (632 soldiers) and the *Novosibirsk* (1,847 soldiers). The ships left Otomari on September 1 and sailed into Furukamappu Bay on September 3. Another landing unit under Captain Uspenskii with 1,300 soldiers also arrived in Furukamappu Bay on September 4. But by the time these forces arrived in Kunashiri, the war was already over.[83]

Japan Signs the Surrender Documents

Shortly after 2:00 in the afternoon on August 30, MacArthur finally made a dramatic entry into Japan.[84] On Sunday, September 2, American officers, flanked by an Allied delegation, were on board the USS *Missouri,* anchored in Tokyo Bay, waiting for the arrival of the eleven-man Japanese delegation headed by Shigemitsu, foreign minister of the newly formed cabinet of Prince Higashikuni, and Chief of Staff Umezu. At 8:55 A.M. Tokyo time the Japanese delegation arrived at the *Missouri.* Once the Japanese were led to the quarterdeck and their designated positions, MacArthur, accompanied by Admiral Chester Nimitz, commander of the Pacific Fleet, and Admiral William Halsey, commander of the U.S. Third Fleet, on either side, briskly walked in and stood facing the Japanese. Then he announced: "We are gathered here, representative of the major warring powers, to conclude a solemn agreement whereby peace may be restored."

Shigemitsu and Umezu signed two sets of three surrender documents, one set bound in leather for the Allies, and the other canvas-bound for the Japanese. Representing the Allied powers, MacArthur signed the documents, and the rest of the Allied representatives followed. Derevianko signed after Nimitz. Then China, Britain, Austria, Canada, France, Holland, and New Zealand appended their signatures. The ceremony was over in eighteen minutes. The Pacific War was over at last, marking the final end of World War II. At 9:25 A.M. Tokyo time (10:25 P.M. Washington time), MacArthur rose and announced: "These proceedings are now closed."

After MacArthur's speech, the radio broadcast switched to the White House, and Truman spoke to the nation. "My fellow Americans," the president began, "the thoughts and hopes of all America—indeed of all the civilized world—are centered tonight on the battleship *Missouri*. There on that small piece of American soil anchored in Tokyo Harbor, the Japanese have just officially laid down their arms. They have signed terms of unconditional surrender." Thus the cherished goal that he had emphasized since April 16 was finally realized.

"Four years ago the thoughts and fears of the whole civilized world were centered on another piece of American soil—Pearl Harbor," the president continued. "We shall not forget Pearl Harbor." The imposition of "unconditional surrender" to avenge Pearl Harbor—the theme that ran through Truman's policy toward Japan—again resurfaced in this speech.

He invoked Almighty God, spoke about those who had been killed, those who had fought on the battlefields and at the rear, President Roosevelt, the Allies, and concluded: "As the President of the United States, I proclaim Sunday, September 2, 1945, to be V-J Day—the day of formal surrender by Japan. . . . It is a day which we Americans shall always remember as a day of retribution—as we remember that other day, the day of infamy."[85]

Truman was not the only one to read a statement on that day. Stalin also read a victory speech. "Comrades," he began, "today, on September 2, the government and the military representatives of Japan signed the document of unconditional surrender." He then equated German and Japanese fascism to justify his war against Japan. He went on: "Japanese aggression inflicted damage not only on our allies, China, the United States, and Great Britain. It brought serious damage to us also. Therefore, we have our own account to settle with Japan." He reminded the Soviet citizens of the tsarist past: "As is well known, in February 1904, when the negotiations between Japan and Russia were still going on, Japan, taking advantage of the weakness of the tsarist government, unexpectedly and treacherously, without a declaration of war—attacked our country." Implied in this statement was a justification for the Soviet attack on Japan while negotiations were ongoing; Japan, after all, had done the same thing before. Stalin's words also implied that the Soviet government issued a declaration of war before its invasion of Manchuria. Then, Stalin compared Japan's treachery in the Russo-Japanese War to Japan's attack on Pearl Harbor.[86] This part of the speech was clearly intended to justify the Soviet violation of the Neutrality Pact. Stalin apparently decided that it would be better not to dwell too much on the reasons for the Soviet entry into the war, since it was a delicate issue that might provoke a comparison to Hitler's surprise attack in violation of the Nazi-Soviet Non-Aggression Pact. Thus, he mentioned neither the Neutrality Pact nor the Yalta Agreement.

"As is well known, in the war with Japan," Stalin continued with regard to the Russo-Japanese War, "Russia suffered a defeat. Japan exploited the defeat of tsarist Russia by seizing from Russia southern Sakhalin and gaining a firm foothold on the Kuril Islands, whereby it shut us in by blocking the passage to the ocean as well as to the ports of Kamchatka and Chukotka." Here, Stalin cleverly falsified a historical fact. The Japanese had not acquired the Kurils as a result of the Russo-Japanese War. The Shimoda Treaty in 1855 had divided the Kurils into the Russian islands north of the Uruppu and the Japanese islands south of Etorofu; then in 1875, as a result of the St. Petersburg Treaty, Russia gained southern Sakhalin in exchange for the northern Kurils. What Japan gained as a result of the Russo-Japanese War was southern Sakhalin. The southern Kurils (the islands the Japanese now call the "Northern Territories") had never been part of Russian or Soviet territory, while the northern Kurils had been legally and legitimately acquired by Japan rather than taken by "force and greed."[87] This historical falsification was necessary to convince the Soviet citizens of the sacrifice of their country and to justify the acquisition of a slice of inherent Japanese territory in the eyes of world public opinion.

Stalin then moved on to list Japan's acts of aggression against the Soviet Union: Siberian intervention (1918), Lake Khasan (1938), and Khalkin Gol, or Nomonhan (1939). Although these attacks were repulsed by Soviet armed forces, "the Russian defeat in the Russo-Japanese War left a painful memory in the consciousness of the Russian people. It left a black mark on our history." He then made the famous remarks, "We, the old generation, have waited for forty years to remove this mark. This day has finally come. Today, Japan has accepted its defeat and signed the document of its unconditional surrender." One cannot help recognizing the uncanny similarities between Stalin's speech and Truman's.

But this crudely chauvinistic statement, alien to Marxist-Leninist principles, was merely an introduction to the most important point of Stalin's message:

> This means that southern Sakhalin and the Kurils will be transferred to the Soviet Union and from now on will serve not as a means to isolate the Soviet Union from the Pacific Ocean, not as a base for Japanese attack on our Far East, but as the means to connect the Soviet Union with the ocean and as a base to defend the country from Japanese aggression.[88]

This statement underscored the primary motivation behind Stalin's entire Far Eastern operation. More than anything else, he was driven by geopolitical interests. Ideology or revolutionary zeal played little part in this campaign.

Stalin's message was a well-crafted effort to justify the violation of the Neutrality Pact, the occupation of the Kurils, and the war against Japan. It became the foundation on which the Soviet government and official Soviet historians viewed Soviet actions in the war against Japan.

The Kuril Operation Continues

The guns were silenced, as MacArthur said at the surrender ceremony on September 2. But the war was not yet over. The Soviets stealthily continued the Kuril operation even after the Japanese signed the official surrender papers. The operation for the Habomai Islands was given directly to Captain Chicherin by the Pacific Fleet headquarters on September 2, and Chicherin's superior officer, Leonov, was not informed of this decision until much later that day. Chicherin decided to divide the forces made available to him into two groups: the first group was to occupy the islands of Suisho, Yuri, and Akiyuri on one minesweeper, and the second group was to take the islands of Taraku, Shibotsu, and Harukari. Leonov reported to the General Staff of the Pacific Fleet and the Northern Pacific Fleet: "Connection with Chicherin is bad. The radio operators on the frigate are poor. As a result, I could not explain to him that what is needed on 2 September 1945 is not action, but a plan." The Habomai operation was too dangerous to be left to the local commander, since there was a good chance that the Americans might be there already. On September 4 Leonov noted: "After my report Cheremisov ordered

Zakharov not to occupy the islands until he received the order from the front."[89] Clearly, the Pacific Fleet headquarters wanted to keep the operation under its strict control, lest it should cause military conflict with the Americans.

Chicherin did not receive these orders owing to the poor radio connections with Leonov. Thinking that he had an order to occupy the Habomai islands, Chicherin left Furukamappu in Kunashiri with the two groups on the morning of September 3, and arrived at the first Habomai islands around 4 A.M. the following day. After reconnaissance, they discovered that no mines were laid, and there were no signs of resistance from the Japanese forces. By 7 P.M. on September 3, the two groups landed on each assigned island. All the Japanese soldiers and officers, including the largest contingent of 420 on Shibotsu and 92 on Taraku, surrendered without incident. By 7 P.M. on September 5, the surrender of the soldiers and weapons on all the Habomai islands was completed. The islands thus serendipitously fell into Soviet hands. Only after the Habomai operation was over did the staff of the Pacific Fleet approve Chicherin's actions.[90] The Pacific War was finally over three days after Japan formally surrendered.

In the end, Stalin succeeded in capturing all the Kurils, including the Habomai group, which he had not expected to acquire. He succeeded, not because the military operations were executed brilliantly; in fact, Soviet military operations in the Kurils were marred by haste, lack of preparations, equipment, and information, and poor communications. If the Soviet operations succeeded, it was mainly because the Japanese were prepared to surrender, and the Americans were not much interested in the Kurils. On the whole, both sides were satisfied, because the Yalta limit was more or less observed.

CONCLUSION

Assessing the Roads Not Taken

T HE END OF THE Pacific War was marked by the intense drama of
two races: the first between Stalin and Truman to see who could
force Japan to surrender and on what terms; and the second between the
peace party and the war party in Japan on the question of whether to end
the war and on what conditions. To the very end, the two races were in-
extricably linked. But what if things had been different? Would the outcome have changed if the key players had taken alternative paths? Below
I explore some counterfactual suppositions to shed light on major issues
that determined the outcome of the war.

*What if Truman had accepted a provision in the Potsdam
ultimatum allowing the Japanese to retain a constitutional
monarchy?*
This alternative was supported by Stimson, Grew, Forrestal, Leahy,
McCloy, and possibly Marshall. Churchill also favored this provision,
and it was part of Stimson's original draft of the Potsdam Proclamation.
Undoubtedly, a promise to retain the monarchy would have strengthened
the peace party's receptivity of the Potsdam ultimatum. It would have
led to intense discussion much earlier among Japanese policymakers on
whether or not to accept the Potsdam terms, and it would have considerably diminished Japan's reliance on Moscow's mediation.

Nevertheless, the inclusion of this provision would not have immediately led to Japan's surrender, since those who adhered to the mythical

notion of the *kokutai* would have strenuously opposed the acceptance of the Potsdam terms, even if it meant the preservation of the monarchy. Certainly, the three war hawks in the Big Six would have objected on the grounds that the Potsdam Proclamation would spell the end of the armed forces. But peace advocates could have accused the war party of endangering the future of the imperial house by insisting on additional conditions. Thus, the inclusion of this provision would have hastened Japan's surrender, though it is doubtful that Japan would have capitulated before the atomic bomb was dropped on Hiroshima and the Soviet Union entered the war. The possibility of accepting the Potsdam terms might have been raised immediately after the atomic bombing on Hiroshima. This provision might have tipped the balance in favor of the peace party after the Soviet invasion, thus speeding up the termination of the war.

Why, then, didn't Truman accept this provision? One explanation was that he was concerned with how the public would react to a policy of appeasement. Domestic public opinion polls indicated an overwhelmingly negative sentiment against the emperor, and inevitably Archibald McLeish, Dean Acheson, and others would have raised strident voices of protest. Byrnes had warned that a compromise with the emperor would lead to the crucifixion of the president.

But would it have? Although public opinion polls were overwhelmingly against the emperor, newspaper commentaries were evenly split between those who advocated the abolition of the emperor system and those who argued that the preservation of the monarchical system could be compatible with eradication of Japanese militarism. Truman could have justified his decision on two powerful grounds. First, he could have argued that ending the war earlier would save the lives of American soldiers. Second, he could have explained that this decision was necessary to prevent Soviet expansion in Asia, though he would have had to present this argument carefully so as not to provoke a strong reaction from the Soviet Union.

Truman's refusal to include this provision was motivated not only by his concern with domestic repercussions but also by his own deep conviction that America should avenge the humiliation of Pearl Harbor. Anything short of unconditional surrender was not acceptable to Truman. The buck indeed stopped at the president. Thus, as long as Truman firmly held to his conviction, this counterfactual supposition was not a real alternative.

But the story does not end here. Another important, hidden reason motivated Truman's decision not to include this provision. Truman knew that the unconditional surrender demand without any promise to preserve a constitutional monarchy would be rejected by the Japanese. He needed Japan's refusal to justify the use of the atomic bomb. Thus so long as he was committed to using the atomic bomb, he could not include the provision promising a constitutional monarchy.

What if Truman had asked Stalin to sign the Potsdam
Proclamation without a promise of a constitutional monarchy?
In this case, Japanese policymakers would have realized that their last hope to terminate the war through Moscow's mediation was dashed. They would have been forced to confront squarely the issue of whether to accept the Potsdam surrender terms. The ambiguity of the emperor's position, however, still remained, and therefore the division among policymakers was inevitable, making it likely that neither the cabinet nor the Big Six would have been able to resolve the differences.

Japan's delay in giving the Allies a definite reply would surely have led to the dropping of the atomic bombs and Soviet participation in the war. Would Japan have surrendered after the first atomic bomb? The absence of a promise to preserve the monarchical system in the Potsdam terms would have prevented the peace party, including Hirohito and Kido, from acting decisively to accept surrender. Ultimately, the Soviet invasion of Manchuria would still have provided the coup de grace.

What if Truman had invited Stalin to sign the Potsdam
Proclamation and included the promise to allow the Japanese
to maintain a constitutional monarchy?
This would have forced Japanese policymakers to confront the issue of whether to accept the Potsdam terms. Undoubtedly, the army would have insisted, if not on the continuation of the war, at least on attaching three additional conditions to the Potsdam Proclamation in order to ensure its own survival. But the promise of preserving the monarchical system might have prompted members of the peace party to intercede to end the war before the first atomic bomb, although there is no guarantee that their argument would have silenced the war party. The most crucial issue here is how the emperor would have reacted to the Potsdam terms had they contained the promise of a constitutional monarchy and been signed by Stalin in addition to Truman, Churchill, and Chiang Kai-shek. Undoubtedly, he would have been more disposed to the Potsdam terms, but the promise of a constitutional monarchy alone might not have induced

the emperor to hasten to accept the ultimatum. A shock was needed. It is difficult to say if the Hiroshima bomb alone was sufficient, or whether the combination of the Hiroshima bomb and Soviet entry into the war was needed to convince the emperor to accept surrender. Either way, surrender would have come earlier than it did, thus shortening the war by several days.

Nevertheless, these counterfactual suppositions were not in the ream of possibility, since Truman and Byrnes would never have accepted them, for the reasons stated in the first counterfactual. The atomic bomb provided them with the solution to previously unsolvable dilemmas. Once the solution was found to square the circle, Truman and Byrnes never deviated from their objectives. An alternative was available, but they chose not to take it.

This counterfactual was dubious for another reason. If Stalin had been asked to join the ultimatum, he would never have agreed to promise a constitutional monarchy. Stalin's most important objective in the Pacific War was to join the conflict. The promise of a constitutional monarchy might have hastened Japan's surrender before the Soviet tanks crossed the Manchurian border—a disaster he would have avoided at all costs. This was why Stalin's own version of the joint ultimatum included the unconditional surrender demand. Had Stalin been invited to join the ultimatum that included the provision allowing Japan to retain a constitutional monarchy, he would have fought tooth and nail to scratch that provision. Ironically, both Stalin and Truman had vested interests in keeping unconditional surrender for different reasons.

What if Hiranuma had not made an amendment at the imperial conference on August 10, and the Japanese government had proposed accepting the Potsdam Proclamation "with the understanding that it did not include any demand for a change in the status of the emperor under the national law"?
Hiranuma's amendment was an egregious mistake. Although the three war hawks in the Big Six attached three additional conditions to acceptance, they lacked the intellectual acumen to connect their misgivings to the fundamental core of the *kokutai* debate. Without Hiranuma's amendment the emperor would have supported the one-conditional acceptance of the Potsdam terms as formulated at the first imperial conference; this condition was compatible, albeit narrowly, with a constitutional monarchy that Stimson, Leahy, Forrestal, and Grew would have accepted. If we believe Ballantine, Byrnes and Truman might have accepted the provi-

sion. But Hiranuma's amendment made it impossible for the American policymakers to accept this condition without compromising the fundamental objectives of the war.

On the other hand, given Truman's deep feelings against the emperor, even the original one condition—retention of the emperor's status in the national laws—or even the Foreign Ministry's original formula (the preservation of the imperial house) might have been rejected by Truman and Byrnes. Nevertheless, either formula might have been accepted by Grew, Dooman, and Ballantine, and would have strengthened the position advocated by Stimson, Leahy, Forrestal, and McCloy that Japan's first reply should be accepted.

What if the Byrnes Note had contained a clear indication that the United States would allow the Japanese to retain a constitutional monarchy with the current dynasty?

The rejection of Japan's conditional acceptance of the Potsdam terms as amended by Hiranuma was not incompatible with the promise of a constitutional monarchy. The lack of this promise triggered the war party's backlash and endangered the peace party's chances of ending the war early. Had the Byrnes Note included the guarantee of a constitutional monarchy under the current dynasty, Suzuki would not have temporarily defected to the war party, and Yonai would not have remained silent on August 12. War advocates would have opposed the Byrnes Note as incompatible with the *kokutai*. Nevertheless, a promise to preserve the monarchy would have taken the wind out of their sails, especially, given that the emperor would have more actively intervened for the acceptance of the Byrnes Note. Stalin would have opposed the Byrnes Note if it included the provision for a constitutional monarchy, but Truman was prepared to attain Japan's surrender without the Soviet Union anyway. This scenario thus might have resulted in Japan's surrender on August 12 or 13 instead of August 14.

Without the atomic bombs and without the Soviet entry into the war, would Japan have surrendered before November 1, the day Operation Olympic was scheduled to begin?

The *United States Strategic Bombing Survey*, published in 1946, concluded that Japan would have surrendered before November 1 without the atomic bombs and without Soviet entry into the war. This conclusion has become the foundation on which revisionist historians have constructed their argument that the atomic bombs were not necessary for Japan's surrender.[1] Since Barton Bernstein has persuasively demonstrated in his critique of the *Survey* that its conclusion is not supported by its own evidence, I need not dwell on this supposition.[2] The main objective of the study's principal author, Paul Nitze, was to prove that conventional bombings, coupled with the naval blockade, would have induced Japan to surrender before November 1. But Nitze's conclusion was repeatedly contradicted by the evidence provided in the *Survey* itself. For instance, to the question, "How much longer do you think the war might have continued had the atomic bomb not been dropped?" Prince Konoe answered: "Probably it would have lasted all this year." Bernstein introduced numerous other testimonies by Toyoda, Kido, Suzuki, Hiranuma, Sakomizu, and others to contradict the *Survey*'s conclusion. As Bernstein asserts, the *Survey* is "an unreliable guide."[3]

The Japanese leaders knew that Japan was losing the war. But defeat and surrender are not synonymous. Surrender is a political act. Without the twin shocks of the atomic bombs and Soviet entry into the war, the Japanese would never have accepted surrender in August.

Would Japan have surrendered before November 1 on the basis of Soviet entry alone, without the atomic bomb?

Japanese historian Asada Sadao contends that without the atomic bombs but with Soviet entry into the war, "there was a possibility that Japan would not have surrendered before November 1."[4] To Asada the shock value was crucial. Whereas the Japanese anticipated Soviet entry into the war, Asada argues, the atomic bombs came as a complete shock. By contrast, Bernstein states: "In view of the great impact of Soviet entry . . . in a situation of heavy conventional bombing and a strangling blockade, it does seem quite probable—indeed, far more likely than not—that Japan would have surrendered before November without the use of the A-bomb but after Soviet intervention in the war. In that sense . . . there may have been a serious 'missed opportunity' in 1945 to avoid the costly invasion of Kyushu without dropping the atomic bomb by awaiting Soviet entry."[5]

The importance to Japan of Soviet neutrality is crucial in this context. Japan relied on Soviet neutrality both militarily and diplomatically. Diplomatically, Japan pinned its last hope on Moscow's mediation for the termination of the war. Once the Soviets entered the war, Japan was forced to make a decision on the Potsdam terms. Militarily as well, Japan's Ketsu-go strategy was predicated on Soviet neutrality; indeed, it was for this reason that the Military Affairs Bureau of the Army Ministry constantly overruled the intelligence section's warning that a Soviet invasion might be imminent. Manchuria was not written off, as Asada claims; rather, the military was confident that Japan could keep the Soviets neutral, at least for a while. When the Soviets invaded Manchuria, the military was taken by complete surprise. Despite the bravado that the war must continue, the Soviet invasion undermined the confidence of the army, punching a fatal hole in its strategic plan. The military's insistence on the continuation of war lost its rationale.

More important, however, were the political implications of the Soviet expansion in the Far East. Without Japan's surrender, it is reasonable to assume that the Soviets would have completed the occupation of Manchuria, southern Sakhalin, the entire Kurils, and possibly half of Korea by the beginning of September. Inevitably, the Soviet invasion of Hokkaido would have been raised as a pressing issue to be settled between the United States and the Soviet Union. The United States might have resisted the Soviet operation against Hokkaido, but given the Soviets' military strength, and given the enormous casualty figures the American high command had estimated for Olympic, the United States might have conceded the division of Hokkaido as Stalin had envisaged. Even if the United States succeeded in resisting Stalin's pressure, Soviet military conquests in the rest of the Far East might have led Truman to concede some degree of Soviet participation in Japan's postwar occupation. Whatever the United States might or might not have done regarding the Soviet operation in Hokkaido or the postwar occupation of Japan, Japanese leaders were well aware of the danger of allowing Soviet expansion to continue beyond Manchuria, Korea, Sakhalin, and the Kurils. It was for this reason that the Japanese policymakers came together at the last moment to surrender under the Potsdam terms, that the military's insistence on continuing the war collapsed, and that the military accepted surrender relatively easily. Japan's decision to surrender was above all a political decision, not a military one. Therefore, even without the atomic bombs, the war most likely would have ended shortly after Soviet entry into the war—before November 1.

Would Japan have surrendered before November 1 on the basis of the atomic bomb alone, without the Soviet entry into the war?

The two bombs alone would most likely not have prompted the Japanese to surrender, so long as they still had hope that Moscow would mediate peace. The Hiroshima bombing did not significantly change Japan's policy, though it did inject a sense of urgency into the peace party's initiative to end the war. Without the Soviet entry into the war, it is not likely that the Nagasaki bomb would have changed the situation. Anami's warning that the United States might have 100 atomic bombs and that the next target might be Tokyo had no discernible impact on the debate. Even after the Nagasaki bomb, Japan would most likely have still waited for Moscow's answer to the Konoe mission.

The most likely scenario would have been that while waiting for the answer from Moscow, Japan would have been shocked by the Soviet invasion in Manchuria sometime in the middle of August, and would have sued for peace on the Potsdam terms. In this case, then, we would have debated endlessly whether the two atomic bombs preceding the Soviet invasion or the Soviet entry would have had a more decisive impact on Japan's decision to surrender, although in this case, too, clearly Soviet entry would have had a more decisive impact.

Richard Frank, who argues that the atomic bombings had a greater impact on Japan's decision to surrender than Soviet involvement in the war, relies exclusively on contemporary sources and discounts postwar testimonies. He emphasizes especially the importance of Hirohito's statement at the first imperial conference, the Imperial Rescript on August 15, and Suzuki's statements made during cabinet meetings.[6] This methodology, though admirable, does not support Frank's conclusion. Hirohito's reference to the atomic bomb at the imperial conference comes from Takeshita's diary, which must be based on hearsay. None of the participants who actually attended the imperial conference remembers the emperor's referring to the atomic bomb. The Imperial Rescript on August 15 does refer to the use of the "cruel new bomb" as one of the reasons for the termination of the war, with no mention of Soviet entry into the war. But during his meeting with the three marshals on August 14, the emperor referred to both the atomic bomb and Soviet entry into the war as the decisive reasons for ending the war. Moreover, the Imperial Rescript to the Soldiers and Officers issued on August 17 refers to Soviet entry as the major reason for ending the war and makes no reference to the atomic bomb. In contemporary records from August 6 to August 15 two sources (the Imperial Rescript on August 15 and Suzuki's statement at the August 13 cabinet meeting) refer only to the impact of the atomic bomb, three sources only to Soviet entry (Konoe on August 9, Suzuki's statement to his doctor on August 13, and the Imperial Rescript to Soldiers and Officers on August 17), and seven sources both to the atomic bomb and Soviet involvement.[7] Contemporary evidence does not support Frank's contention.

Without Soviet participation in the war in the middle of August, the United States would have faced the question of whether to use the third bomb sometime after August 19, and then the fourth bomb in the beginning of September, most likely on Kokura and Niigata. It is hard to say how many atomic bombs it would have taken to convince Japanese policymakers to abandon their approach to Moscow. It is possible to argue, though impossible to prove, that the Japanese military would still have argued for the continuation of the war after a third or even a fourth bomb.

Could Japan have withstood the attacks of seven atomic bombs before November 1? Would Truman and Stimson have had the resolve to use seven atomic bombs in succession? What would have been the impact of these bombs on Japanese public opinion? Would the continued use of the bombs have solidified or eroded the resolve of the Japanese to fight on? Would it have hopelessly alienated the Japanese from the United States to the point that it would be difficult to impose the American occupation on Japan? Would it have encouraged the Japanese to welcome the Soviet occupation instead? These are the questions we cannot answer with certainty.

On the basis of available evidence, however, it is clear that the two atomic bombs on Hiroshima and Nagasaki alone were not decisive in inducing Japan to surrender. Despite their destructive power, the atomic bombs were not sufficient to change the direction of Japanese diplomacy. The Soviet invasion was. Without the Soviet entry into the war, the Japanese would have continued to fight until numerous atomic bombs, a successful allied invasion of the home islands, or continued aerial bombardments, combined with a naval blockade, rendered them incapable of doing so.

Legacies

The Bomb in American Memory

After the war was over, each nation began constructing its own story about how the war ended. Americans still cling to the myth that the atomic bombs dropped on Hiroshima and Nagasaki provided the knockout punch to the Japanese government. The decision to use the bomb saved not only American soldiers but also the Japanese, according to this narrative. The myth serves to justify Truman's decision and ease the collective American conscience. To this extent, it is important to American national identity. But as this book demonstrates, this myth cannot be supported by historical facts. Evidence makes clear that there were alternatives to the use of the bomb, alternatives that the Truman administration for reasons of its own declined to pursue. And it is here, in the evidence of roads not taken, that the question of moral responsibility comes to the fore. Until his death, Truman continually came back to this question and repeatedly justified his decision, inventing a fiction that he himself later came to believe. That he spoke so often to justify his actions shows how much his decision to use the bomb haunted him.

On August 10 the Japanese government sent a letter of protest through the Swiss legation to the United States government. This letter declared the American use of the atomic bombs to be a violation of Articles 22 and 23 of the Hague Convention Respecting the Laws and Customs of War on Land, which prohibited the use of cruel weapons. It declared "in the name of the Japanese Imperial Government as well as in the name of humanity and civilization" that "the use of the atomic bombs, which surpass the indiscriminate cruelty of any other existing weapons and projectiles," was a crime against humanity, and demanded that "the further use of such inhumane weapons be immediately ceased."[8] Needless to say, Truman did not respond to this letter. After Japan accepted the American occupation and became an important ally of the United States, the Japanese government has never raised any protest about the American use of the atomic bombs. The August 10 letter remains the only, and now forgotten, protest lodged by the Japanese government against the use of the atomic bomb.[9]

To be sure, the Japanese government was guilty of its own atrocities in violation of the laws governing the conduct of war. The Nanking Massacre of 1937, biological experiments conducted by the infamous Unit 731, the Bataan March, and the numerous instances of cruel treatment of POWs represent only a few examples of Japanese atrocities. Nevertheless, the moral lapses of the Japanese do not excuse those of the United States and the Allies. After all, morality by definition is an absolute rather than a relative standard. The forgotten letter that the Japanese government sent to the United States government on August 10 deserves serious consideration. Justifying Hiroshima and Nagasaki by making a historically unsustainable argument that the atomic bombs ended the war is no longer tenable. Our self-image as Americans is tested by how we can come to terms with the decision to drop the bomb. Although much of what revisionist historians argue is faulty and based on tendentious use of sources, they nonetheless deserve credit for raising an important moral issue that challenges the standard American narrative of Hiroshima and Nagasaki.

The Stalinist Past

Soviet historians, and patriotic Russian historians after the collapse of the Soviet Union, justify the Soviet violation of the Neutrality Pact by arguing that it brought the Pacific War to a close, thus ending the suffering of the oppressed people of Asia and the useless sacrifices of the Japanese themselves. But this book shows that Stalin's policy was motivated by expansionist geopolitical designs. The Soviet leader pursued his imperialistic policy with Machiavellian ruthlessness, deviousness, and cunning. In the end he managed to enter the war and occupy those territories to which he felt entitled. Although he briefly flirted with the idea of invading Hokkaido, and did violate the provision of the Yalta Agreement to secure a treaty with the Chinese as the prerequisite for entry into the war, Stalin by and large respected the Yalta limit. But by occupying the southern Kurils, which had never belonged to Russia until the last days of August and the beginning of September 1945, he created an intractable territorial dispute known as "the Northern Territories question" that has prevented rapprochement between Russia and Japan to this day. The Russian government and the majority of Russians even now continue to cling to the myth that the occupation of the southern Kurils was Russia's justifiable act of repossessing its lost territory.

Stalin's decisions in the Pacific War are but one of many entries in the ledger of his brutal regime. Although his imperialism was not the worst of his crimes compared with the Great Purge and collectivization, it represented part and parcel of the Stalin regime. Certainly, his conniving against the Japanese and the blatant land-grabbing that he engaged in during the closing weeks of the war are nothing to praise. Although the crimes committed by Stalin have been exposed and the new Russia is making valiant strides by shedding itself of the remnants of the Stalinist past, the Russians, with the exception of a few courageous historians, have not squarely faced the historical fact that Stalin's policy toward Japan in the waning months of the Pacific War was an example of the leader's expansionistic foreign policy. Unless the Russians come to this realization, the process of cleansing themselves of the Stalinist past will never be completed.

The Mythology of Victimization and the Role of Hirohito

It took the Japanese a little while to realize that what happened to the Kurils during the confused period between August 15 and September 5 amounted to annexation of Japan's inherent territory, an act that violated the Atlantic Charter and the Cairo Declaration. But the humiliation the Japanese suffered in the four-week Soviet-Japanese War was not entirely a result of the Soviet occupation of the Kurils. The Soviet occupation of the Kurils represented the last of many wrongs that the Soviets perpetrated on the Japanese, beginning with the violation of the Neutrality Pact, the invasion of Manchuria, Korea, southern Sakhalin, and the deportation and imprisonment of more than 640,000 prisoners of war. The "Northern Territories question" that the Japanese have demanded be resolved in the postwar period before any rapprochement with the Soviet Union (and Russia after 1991) is a mere symbol of their deep-seated resentment of and hostility toward the Russians who betrayed Japan when it desperately needed their help in ending the war.

Together with the Soviet war against Japan, Hiroshima and Nagasaki have instilled in the Japanese a sense of victimization. What Gilbert Rozman calls the Hiroshima syndrome and the Northern Territories syndrome are an inverted form of nationalism.[10] As such they have prevented the Japanese from coming to terms with their own culpability in causing the war in Asia. Before August 14, 1945, the Japanese leaders had ample opportunities to surrender, for instance, at the German capitulation, the fall of Okinawa, the issuance of the Potsdam Proclamation, the atomic bomb on Hiroshima, and Soviet entry into the war. Few in Japan have condemned the policymakers who delayed Japan's surrender. Had the Japanese government accepted the Potsdam Proclamation unconditionally immediately after it was issued, as Sato and Matsumoto argued, the atomic bombs would not have been used, and the war would have ended before the Soviets entered the conflict. Japanese policymakers who were in the position to make decisions—not only the militant advocates of war but also those who belonged to the peace party, including Suzuki, Togo, Kido, and Hirohito himself—must bear the responsibility for the war's destructive end more than the American president and the Soviet dictator.

In postwar Japan, Hirohito has been portrayed as the savior of the Japanese people and the nation for his "sacred decisions" to end the war. Indeed, without the emperor's personal intervention, Japan would not have surrendered. The cabinet and the Big Six were hopelessly divided, unable to make a decision. Only the emperor broke the stalemate. His determination and leadership at the two imperial conferences and his steadfast support for the termination of the war after the decisive meeting with Kido on August 9 were crucial factors leading to Japan's surrender.

This does not mean, however, that the emperor was, in Asada's words, "Japan's foremost peace advocate, increasingly articulate and urgent in expressing his wish for peace."[11] He was, as all other Japanese leaders at that time, still pinning his hope on Moscow's mediation, rejecting the unconditional surrender demanded by the Potsdam Proclamation until the Soviet entry into the war. After the Soviets joined the fight, he finally changed his mind to accept the Potsdam terms. In Japan it has been taboo to question the motivation that led Hirohito to accept surrender. But the findings of this book call for a reexamination of his role in the ending of the Pacific War. His delay in accepting the Allied terms ensured the use of the bomb and Soviet entry into the war.

Although Hirohito's initiative after August 9 should be noted, his motivation for ending the war was not as noble as the "sacred decision" myth would have us believe. His primary concern was above all the preservation of the imperial house. He even flirted with the idea of clinging to his political role. Despite the myth that he said he did not care what happened to him personally, it is likely that he was also in fact deeply concerned about the safety of his family and his own security. At the crucial imperial conference of August 10, Hiranuma did not mince words in asking Hirohito to take responsibility for the tragedy that had befallen Japan. As Konoe, some of the emperor's own relatives, and Grew, the most ardent supporter of the Japanese monarchy, argued, Hirohito should have abdicated at the end of the war to make a clean break with the Showa period that marked anything but what "Showa" meant: enlightened peace. His continuing reign made Japan's culpability in the war ambiguous and contributed to the nation's inability to come to terms with the past.

Thus this is a story with no heroes but no real villains, either—just men. The ending of the Pacific War was in the last analysis a human drama whose dynamics were determined by the very human characteristics of those involved: ambition, fear, vanity, anger, and prejudice. With each successive decision, the number of remaining alternatives steadily diminished, constraining ever further the possibilities, until the dropping of the bomb and the destruction of the Japanese state became all but inevitable. The Pacific War could very well have ended differently had the men involved made different choices. But they did not.

So they left it for us to live with the legacies of the war. The question is, Do we have the courage to overcome them?

ABBREVIATIONS
NOTES
ACKNOWLEDGMENTS
INDEX

Abbreviations

ABC	America, Britain, China
AVP RF	Arkhiv vneshnei politiki Rossiiskoi federatsii
BKSS	*Boeikenshujo senshishitsu*
CCS	Combined Chiefs of Staff
DBPO	Rohan Butler and M.E. Pelly, eds., *Documents on British Policy Overseas,* series I, vol. I, *The Conference at Potsdam, July–August 1945* (London: Her Majesty's Stationery Office, 1984)
DHTP	Dennis Merrill, ed., *Documentary History of the Truman Presidency,* vol. 1, *The Decision to Drop the Atomic Bomb on Japan* (Bethesda, Md.: University Publications of America, 1995)
Entry of the Soviet Union	U.S. Department of Defense, *The Entry of the Soviet Union into the War against Japan: Military Plans, 1941–1945* (Washington, D.C.: U.S. Government Printing Office, 1955)
Forrestal Diary	James Forrestal Diary, Mudd Library, Princeton University
FRUS: 1945	U.S. Department of State, *Foreign Relations of the United States, Diplomatic Papers, 1945:* vol. 5, *Europe* (Washington, D.C.: U.S. Government Printing Office, 1967); vol. 6, *The British Commonwealth, the Far East* (Washington, D.C.: U.S. Government Printing Office, 1969)
FRUS: Potsdam	U.S. Department of State, *Foreign Relations of the United States, Diplomatic Papers: Conference of Berlin (The Potsdam Conference), 1945,* 2 vols. (Washington, D.C.: U.S. Government Printing Office, 1960)
FRUS: Yalta	U.S. Department of State, *Foreign Relations of the United States, Dipomatic Papers: The Conferences at Malta and Yalta, 1945* (Washington, D.C.: U.S. Government Printing Office, 1955)
G-2	Intelligence Division, U.S. Army General Staff
Grew Papers	Joseph C. Grew Papers, Houghton Library, Harvard University
Harriman Papers	W. Averell Harriman Papers, Library of Congress
HSTL	Harry S. Truman Library
JCS	Joint Chiefs of Staff
JIC	Joint Intelligence Committee

JSSC	Joint Strategic Survey Committee
McCloy Diary	John J. McCloy Diary, Amherst Library
MHDC	Miscellaneous Historical Documents Collection, Harry S. Truman Library
NA	National Archives
OPD	Operation Division, U.S. Army General Staff
OSW	Office of the Secretary of War
PSF	President's Secretary's File, Harry S. Truman Library
PSIS	Pacific Strategic Intelligence Section
RG	Record Group, National Archives
RGASPI	Rossikii gosudarstvennyi arkhiv sotsiali'no-politicheskoi istorii
RKO	V S. Miasnikov, ed., *Russko-Sovetsko-Kitaiskie otnosheniia v XX veke: Dokumenty i materially, 1937–1945*, Book 2, 1945 g. (Moscow: Pamiatniki istoricheskoi mysli, 2000).
SAO	Ministerstvo inostrannykh del SSSR, *Sovietsko-amerikanskie otnosheniia vo vremia Velikoi otechestvennoi voiny 1941–1945: Dokumenty I materially,* 2 vols. (Moscow: Politizdat, 1984)
Shusen shiroku	Gaimusho, ed., *Shusen shiroku,* 6 vols. (Tokyo: Hokuyosha, 1977)
SMOF	Staff Member and Office File, Harry S. Truman Library
SRH	Special Research History. Records of National Security Agency/Central Security Service, Studies in Cryptograph, 1917–1972, Box 23, RG 457, NA
SRS	Filing system for "Magic" Diplomatic Summary, Records of National Security Agency, Magic Files, Box 18, RG 457, NA
Stimson Diary	Henry Stimson Diary, Sterling Library, Yale University
SWNCC	State-War-Navy Coordinating Committee
Takagi nikki	Ito Takashi, ed., *Takagi Sokichi: Nikki to joho,* 2 vols. (Tokyo: Misuzu shobo, 2000)
VO	V. N. Vartanov et al., *Velikaia otechestvennanaia: Sovietsko-iaponskaia voina 1945 goda; istoriia voenno-politicheskogo protivoborstva dbukh derzhav v 30-40-e gody: Dokumanty i materially,* vol. 7, pt. 1 (Moscow: Terra-Terra, 1997); vol. 7, pt. 2 (Moscow: Terra-Terra, 2000)
WDGS	War Department General Staff
WHCF	White House Central File, Harry S. Truman Library

Notes

INTRODUCTION

1. Robert J. C. Butow, *Japan's Decision to Surrender* (Stanford: Stanford University Press, 1954). Other notable scholarly works in English include Leon V. Sigal, *Fighting to a Finish* (Ithaca: Cornell University Press, 1988); Richard Frank, *Downfall: The End of the Imperial Japanese Empire* (New York: Random House, 1999); Robert A. Pape, "Why Japan Surrendered," *International Security*, 18, no. 2 (1993): 154–201; Forrest E. Morgan, *Compellence and the Strategic Culture of Imperial Japan: Implication for Coercive Diplomacy in the Twenty-First Century* (Westport: Praeger, 2003). See also two journalistic books: Lester Brooks, *Behind Japan's Surrender: The Secret Struggle That Ended an Empire* (New York: McGraw Hill, 1968); and William Craig, *The Fall of Japan* (New York: Dial Press, 1967). None of these works adequately treats the Soviet factor in Japan's decision to surrender. The only attempt in English to evalaute the Soviet factor is Yukiko Koshiro, "Eurasian Eclipse: Japan's Endgame in World War II," *American Historical Review*, 109, no. 2 (2004): 417–444. Koshiro, however, does not use Russian-language sources.

2. B. N. Slavinskii, *Sovetskaia okkupatsiia Kuril'skikh ostrov (avgust–sentiabr' 1945 goda): dokumental'noe issledovanie* (Moscow: TOO "Lotos," 1993); *Pakt o neitralitete mezhdu SSSR i Iaponiei: diplomaticheskaia istoriia, 1941–1945 gg.* (Moscow: TOO "Novina," 1995); *Ialtinskaia konferentsiia i problema "severnykh territorii"* (Moscow: TOO "Novina," 1996); *SSSR i Iaponiia—na puti k voine: diplomaticheskaia istoriia, 1937–1945 gg.* (Moscow: ZAO "Iaponia segodnia," 1999).

3. See Dale M. Hellegers, *We, the Japanese People: World War II and the Origins of the Japanese Constitution*, vol. 1, Washington (Stanford: Stanford University Press, 2001), pp. 233–241.

4. See Maruyama Masao, *Gendai seiji no shiso to kodo* (Tokyo: Miraisha, 1956), vol. 1, pp. 7–24.

5. Suzuki Masayuki, ed., *Kindai no tenno: Kindai nihon no kiseki,* vol. 7 (Tokyo: Yoshikawa kobunkan, 1993), pp. 189–202.

6. A detailed historiographical discussion on the atomic bomb and Soviet entry into the war is outside the scope of this book. For this debate, see Barton Bernstein, "The Struggle over History: Defining the Hiroshima Narrative," in Philipo Nobile, ed., *Judgment at the Smithsonian* (New York: Marvolowe and Co., 1995), pp. 127–256; J. Samuel Walker, "Recent Literature on Truman's Atomic Bomb Decision: A Search for Middle Ground," *Diplomatic History* (forthcoming).

1. TRIANGULAR RELATIONS AND THE PACIFIC WAR

1. George Alexander Lensen, *The Strange Neutrality* (Tallahassee: The Diplomatic Press, 1972), p. 19; Nishi Haruhiko, "Sono hino Matsuoka," Appendix to Nihon kokusai seijigakkai, Taiheiyo senso gen'in kenkyubu, ed., *Taiheiyo senso eno michi: Kaisen gaikoshi,* vol. 5, *Sangoku domei, Nisso churitsu joyaku* (Tokyo: Asahi shinbunsha, 1987), pp. 1–3.

2. Jonathan Haslam, *The Soviet Union and the Threat from the East, 1933–41* (Pittsburgh: University of Pittsburgh Press, 1992), p. 1.

3. For U.S.–Japanese relations during the interwar period, see Akira Iriye, *The Origins of the Second World War in Asia and the Pacific* (London: Longman, 1987); Japanese trans., *Taiheiyo senso no kigen* (Tokyo: Tokyo daigaku shuppankai, 1991). See also Nihon kokusai gakkai, *Taiheiyo senso eno michi,* 8 vols., plus a supplementary volume (Tokyo: Asahi shinbunsha, 1963). For Soviet-Japanese relations, see Haslam, *The Soviet Union and the Threat from the East.*

4. B. N. Slavinskii, *Pakt o neitralitete mezhdu SSSR i Iaponiei: diplomaticheskaia istoriia, 1941–1945 gg.* (Moscow: TOO Novina, 1995), pp. 66–135.

5. See Lensen, *Strange Neutrality,* p. 278; Slavinskii, *Pakt,* pp. 102–104.

6. Ozawa Haruko, "Beiso kankei to nihon," in Miwa Kimitada and Tobe Ryoichi, eds., *Nihon no kiro to Matsuoka gaiko* (Tokyo: Nansosha, 1993), pp. 65–66; Akira Iriye, *Pearl Harbor and the Coming of the Pacific War: A Brief History with Documents and Essays* (New York: Befford/St. Martin's, 1999), pp. 6–8; also see Iriye, *The Origins of the Second World War in Asia and the Pacific.*

7. Robert E. Sherwood, *Roosevelt and Hopkins: An Intimate History* (New York: Harper Brothers, 1948), pp. 323–348.

8. Hosoya Chihiro, "Sangoku domei to Nisso churitsu joyaku," *Taiheiyo senso eno michi,* vol. 5, p. 312.

9. Lensen, *Strange Neutrality,* pp. 24–25; Slavinskii, *Pakt,* pp. 120–121. For the Liaison Conferences, see Sanbo honbu, *Sugiyama Memo,* vol. 1 (Tokyo: Hara shobo, 1989), pp. 225–227, 240–253. After the outbreak of World War II in Europe, the Japanese decision-making process became highly centralized. The cabinet became less important, while the Liaison Conference, consisting of the army and navy chiefs of staff, army and navy ministers, the prime minister, the foreign minister, and a few important ministers, became the highest decision-making body.

10. Gaimusho, *Nihon gaiko nenpyo narabini shuyo bunsho,* vol. 2 (Tokyo: Hara shobo, 1966), pp. 531–532; Sanbo Honbu, *Sugiyama Memo,* vol. 1, p. 260; Hosoya, "Sangoku domei," pp. 315–321; Lensen, *Strange Neutrality,* pp. 26–27; Nishi Haruhiko, *Nisso kokko mondai, 1917–1945* (Tokyo: Kashima kenkyujo, 1960), p. 231.

11. Hosoya, "Sangoku domei," pp. 321–323; N. M. Pegov, "Stalin on War with Japan, October 1941," *Soviet Studies in History,* 24, no. 3 (1985–1986): 33–36. For Sorge's reports, see VO, Documents 148–152, 154, 157–162, 164–166, 168, 170, 172, and 174.

12. Sherwood, *Roosevelt and Hopkins,* pp. 349–365.

13. David M. Kennedy, *Freedom from Fear: The American People in Depres-*

sion and War, 1929–1945 (New York: Oxford University Press, 1999), pp. 516–522.

14. John R. Deane, *The Strange Alliance: The Story of Our Efforts at Wartime Co-operation with Russia* (New York: Viking Press, 1946); Ernest R. May, "The United States, the Soviet Union, and the Far Eastern War, 1941–1945," *Pacific Historical Review,* 24 (1955): 154; John Stephan, *Kuril Islands: Russo-Japanese Frontier in the Pacific* (Oxford: Clarendon Press, 1974), p. 144. For further details of Soviet-Japanese relations during the war, see Lensen, *Strange Neutrality,* pp. 35–77; Slavinskii, *Pakt,* pp. 174–175, 301–303.

15. *SAO,* pp. 144, 145. For Stalin-Eden meeting, see O. A. Rzheshevskii, "Vizit A. Idena v Moskvu v dekabre 1941 g. i peregovora s I. V. Stalinym i V. M. Molotovym: Iz arkhiva prezidenta RF," *Novaia i noveishaia istoriia,* no. 3 (1994): 105, 118. For Lozovskii'e memorandum, see Document 1, "Zaniat'sia podgotovka budushchego mira," *Istochnik: Dokumenty russkoi istorii: Vestnik arkhiva prezidenta Rossiiskoi Federatsii,* no. 4 (1995): 114–115. Also see Yokote Shinji, "Dainijitaisenki no soren no tainichi seisaku, 1941–1944," Keio daigaku hogaku kenkyukai, *Hogaku kenkyu,* 71, no. 1 (1998): 206.

16. Hayashi Shigeru, "Taiso kosaku no tenkai," Nihon gaiko gakkai, *Taiheiyo senso shuketsuron* (Tokyo: Tokyo daigaku shuppankai, 1958), pp. 189–190, 195–196.

17. Morishima Goro, "Kuno suru chuso taishikan," in Morishima Yasuhiko, *Showa no doran to Morishima Goro no shogai* (Tokyo: Ashi shobo, 1975), p. 164; Lensen, *Strange Neutrality,* pp. 108–109.

18. Gaimusho, ed., *Shusen shiroku,* 5 vols. (Tokyo: Hokuyosha, 1977), vol. 1, pp. 73–94; Nishihara Masao, *Shusen no keii* (typewritten report prepared by Nishihara), vol. 1, BKSS, p. 9.

19. "Tokushi haken kosho (Gaimusho chosho, Nis'so' gaiko kosho kiroku no bu)," Gaimusho, *Shusen shiroku,* vol. 1, pp. 100–102; Hayashi, "Taiso kosaku," pp. 202–205.

20. Morishima, "Kuno suru chuso taishikan," pp. 172–173, 175–177; Lensen, *Strange Neutrality,* 61–73, 78–104.

21. Brian L. Villa, "The U.S. Army, Unconditional Surrender, and the Potsdam Proclamation," *Journal of American History,* vol. 63 (June 1976): 70. For the process by which Roosevelt came to adopt the term, see Iokibe Makoto, *Beikoku no nihon senryo seisaku,* 2 vols. (Tokyo: Chuokoronsha, 1985), vol. 1, pp. 84–91; Dale M. Hellegers, *We, the Japanese People: World War II and the Origins of the Japanese Constitution,* vol. 1 (Stanford: Stanford University Press, 2001), pp. 1–33.

22. Iokibe, *Beikoku no nihon senryo seisaku,* vol. 1, pp. 110–128.

23. The following description is based on ibid., pp. 178–282; vol. 2, pp. 4–140.

24. Waldo H. Heinrichs, Jr., *American Ambassador: Joseph C. Grew and the Development of the United States Diplomatic Tradition* (Boston: Little, Brown, and Co., 1966), pp. 364–369.

25. Cordell Hull, *The Memoirs of Cordell Hull,* vol. 2 (New York: Macmillan, 1948), pp. 1113, 1309–1310; *Entry of the Soviet Union,* p. 22; Charles E. Bohlen, *Witness to History, 1929–1969* (New York: Norton, 1973),

p. 128; Nihon hoso kyokai [NHK] Nisso Purojekuto, *Korega soren no tainichi gaiko da: Hiroku, Hopporyodo kosho* (Tokyo: NHK, 1991), pp. 15–17.

26. W. Averell Harriman and Elie Abel, *Special Envoy to Churchill and Stalin, 1941–1946* (New York: Random House, 1975), p. 237.

27. Slavinskii, *SSSR i Iaponia*, pp. 327–328; S. M. Shtemenko, *The Soviet General Staff at War: 1941–1945*, 2 vols. (Moscow: Progress, 1981), vol. 2, p. 405; May, "The United States, the Soviet Union, and the Far Eastern War," pp. 164–165.

28. Aleksei Kirichenko, "Hakkutsu: KGB himitsu bunsho: Sutarin shunen no tainichi sansen, sore wa shino tetsudokara hajimatta," *This Is Yomiuri*, December 1992, pp. 236–243.

29. Lensen, *Strange Neutrality*, p. 53.

30. Bohlen, *Witness to History*, p. 195; *Entry of the Soviet Union*, p. 24; Memorandum, 12 Jan. 45, Papers of George M. Elsey, HSTL; Iokibe, *Beikoku no nihon senryo seisaku*, vol. 2, pp. 76–79.

31. Document no. 5, "Zaniat'sia podgotovkoi," *Istochnik*, no. 4 (1995): 124–125, 133–134. Also see Yokote, "Dainijitaisenki no soren no tainichi seisaku," pp. 216–218.

32. AVP RF, f. 06, op. 6, pap. 58, d. 803a, ll. 204–258. For the analysis of the Malik Report, see Yokote, "Dainijitaisenki no soren no tainichi seisaku," pp. 222–225; Slavinskii, *Pakt*, pp. 239–244; Jonathan Haslam, "Soren no tainichi gaiko to sansen," in Hosoya Chihiro, Irie Akira, Goto Kan'ichi, and Hatano Sumio, eds., *Taiheiyosenso no shuketsu* (Tokyo: Kashiwa shobo, 1997), pp. 74–81.

33. AVP RF, f. 06, op. 6, pap. 58, d. 803a, ll. 213–215, 218–219, 223–225.

34. Ibid., ll. 230–240. Lozovskii criticized Malik's report for lacking class analysis; ibid., ll. 259–262.

35. G. N. Sevost'ianov, "Iaponia 1945 g. v otsenke sovetskikh diplomatov, novye arkhivnye materialy," *Novaia i noveishaia istoriia*, no. 6 (1995): 37; A. Vasilevskii, *Delo vsei zhizni* (Moscow: Iza-vo politicheskoi literatury, 1975), pp. 552–553; Shtemenko, *The Soviet General Staff at War*, vol. 1, p. 406; S. Shtemenko, "Iz istorii razgroma Kvantunskoi armii," *Voenno-istoricheskii zhurnal*, no. 4 (1967): 55.

36. John Ray Skates, *The Invasion of Japan: Alternative to the Bomb* (Columbia: University of South Carolina Press, 1994), pp. 33–59.

37. Ray S. Cline, *Washington Command Post: The Operations Division* (Washington, D.C.: Office of the Chief of Military History, U.S. Department of the Army, 1951), pp. 337–339; Douglas J. MacEachin, *The Final Months of the War with Japan: Signal Intelligence, U.S. Invasion Planning, and the A-Bomb Decision* (Washington D.C.: Center for the Study of Intelligence, 1998), pp. 1–2.

38. *Entry of the Soviet Union*, pp. 30–32.

39. Gaimusho, *Shusen shiroku*, vol. 1, pp. 131–175; Koketsu Atsushi, *Nihon kaigun no shusen kosaku* (Tokyo: Chuko shinsho, 1996), pp. 149–156.

40. *Takagi nikki*, vol. 2, pp. 765, 823; Matsudaira Yasumasa chinjutsuroku, p. 593, BKSS; Matsutani Makoto, "Watashino shusen memo (2)," *Kokubo*, September 1982, pp. 98–100.

41. "Taiso gaiko shisaku ni kansuru ken (an)," Gaimusho, *Shusen shiroku,* vol. 1, pp. 248–252; Nishihara, *Shusen no keii,* vol. 1, pp. 19–20.

42. "Nisso gaiko kosho kiroku (Gaimusho chosho)," *Shusen shiroku,* vol. 1, pp. 152–154; Morishima, "Kuno suru chuso taishikan," pp. 180–184.

43. *Takagi nikki,* vol. 2, pp. 771–779.

44. Harriman to Roosevelt, 23 Sept. 45, Harriman Papers, Moscow Files, 19–24 Sept. 44, Library of Congress; also see *Entry of the Soviet Union,* pp. 34–35.

45. Harriman to the President, Eyes Only Cable, 15 Oct. 44, Harriman Papers, Moscow Files, 15–16 Oct. 44; "Summary of Conclusions of the Meeting Held at the Kremlin, October 15, 1944," Harriman Papers, Moscow Files, 17–20 Oct. 44.

46. "Conversation, the Far Eastern Theater," 15 Oct. 44, Harriman Papers, Moscow Files, 15–16 Oct. 44.

47. "Interpretative Report on Developments in Soviet Policy Based on the Soviet Press for the Period, October 15–December 31, 1944," Harriman Papers, Moscow Files, 13 Oct. 44. As for Japan's reactions to Stalin's speech, see *Takagi nikki,* vol. 2, p. 781.

48. *Entry of the Soviet Union,* pp. 39–41.

49. "Conversation: MILEPOST," 14 Dec. 44, Harriman Papers, Moscow Files, 8–14 Dec. 44; Harriman to the President, 15 Dec. 44, Harriman Papers, Moscow Files, 15–20 Dec. 44.

50. AVP RF, f. 06, op. 7, pap. 55, d. 898, ll. 1–2; Slavinskii, *Pakt,* 261–263; Sevost'ianov, "Iaponia 1945 g.," pp. 35–36.

51. A. A. Gromyko, *Pamiatnoe,* 2 vols. (Moscow: Politizdat, 1988), vol. 1, p. 189; Andrei Gromyko, *Memoirs* (New York: Doubleday, 1989), p. 89.

52. For the Blakeslee memorandum, see *FRUS: The Conferences at Malta and Yalta, 1945,* pp. 379–383. Sevost'ianov found a copy of the Blakeslee recommendation in Russia's presidential archive. Sevost'ianov, "Iaponia 1945 g.," p. 34.

53. Harriman's Note, 10 Feb. 45, Harriman Papers, Moscow Files, Conferences, Library of Congress. See also three attachments, Stalin's original draft, Harriman's amendments, and the final agreement, ibid. Also Harriman and Abel, *Special Envoy,* pp. 398–399; Fiona Hill, "A Disagreement between Allies: The United Kingdom, the United States, and the Soviet-Japanese Territorial Dispute, 1945–1956," *Journal of Northeast Asian Studies,* 14, no. 3 (1995): 11.

54. *FRUS: Malta/Yalta,* p. 984.

55. Harriman and Abel, *Special Envoy,* p. 399.

56. Ibid., pp. 399–400. The old Japan hands in the State Department, such as Grew and Eugene Dooman, did not know the contents of the Yalta Agreement. When they later learned of them, they were shocked. They considered Roosevelt's concessions to Stalin a sell-out of vital U.S. strategic interests. Even Charles Bohlen, who translated for Roosevelt, wrote that the president was ignorant of the history of Sakhalin and the Kurils, believing that the Kurils had been seized by Japan. Bohlen, *Witness to History,* p. 197. As historian Marc Gallichio writes, however, "Roosevelt sought to satisfy Russian security interests in Northeast Asia as part of his larger

Soviet policy. Intent on building a working relationship with Stalin that would survive after the war, Roosevelt saw no reason to quarrel over the Kuriles." Marc Gallichio, "The Kuriles Controversy: U.S. Diplomacy in the Soviet-Japanese Border Dispute, 1941–1956," *Pacific Historical Review,* 60, no. 1 (1991): 76–77. Japanese historian Iokibe Makoto suggests a different, tantalizing hypothesis: that Roosevelt was engaged in a Machiavellian maneuver to create a possible source of territorial conflict in the postwar relationship between Japan and the Soviet Union. Iokibe, *Beikoku no nihon senryo seisaku,* vol. 2, pp. 87–94.

57. *FRUS: Malta/Yalta,* p. 826; Iokibe, *Beikoku no nihon senryo seisaku,* vol. 2, pp. 131–133.
58. Vasilevskii, *Delo vsei zhizni,* pp. 554–555.
59. "Konoe ko no josobun," Gaimusho, *Shusen shiroku,* vol. 2, pp. 42–49.
60. "Sekai josei handan," 15 Feb. 45, Sanbo honbu shozo, *Haisen no kiroku* (Tokyo: Hara shobo, 1989), pp. 230–232; Nishihara, *Shusen no keii,* vol. 1, pp. 21–22; Hattori Takushiro, *Daitoasenso zenshi* (Tokyo: Hara shobo, 1965), p. 809.
61. AVP RF, f. 06, 1945 g., op. 7, pap. 2, d. 29, ll. 109–113; Slavinskii, *Pakt,* pp. 257–260.
62. *Takagi nikki,* vol. 2, pp. 823–829.
63. *Entry of the Soviet Union,* pp. 50–52.
64. Deane, *Strange Alliance,* pp. 152–162; Minutes of the Meetings of the Combined Planning Group from 26 Jan. 45 through 13 March 45, OPD, 336TS, Sec. VIII, Box 145, RG 165, NA.
65. "Military Use of the Atomic Bomb," George Lincoln Papers, West Point, MHDC #746, donated by Robert Ferrell, Box 30, HSTL; Martin Sherwin, *A World Destroyed: Hiroshima and the Origins of the Arms Race* (New York: Vintage Books, 1987), pp. 111, 133, 284.
66. Churchill to Roosevelt, 12 April 45, Naval Aide Communication File, Churchill to Truman, HSTL.
67. Arnold A. Offner, *Another Such Victory: President Truman and the Cold War, 1945–1953* (Stanford: Stanford University Press, 2002), pp. 28–30.
68. Draft, Navy Cable, 29 Dec. 44, Harriman Papers, Moscow Files, 28–31 Dec. 44.
69. Unsent memorandum, 10 April 45, Harriman Papers, Moscow Files, 10–13 April 45.
70. Memorandum of Conference with the President, 31 Dec. 44, Stimson Papers, Reel 128, Sterling Library, Yale University; Sherwin, *A World Destroyed,* p. 134.

2. STALIN, TRUMAN, AND HIROHITO

1. Hattori Takushiro, *Daitoasenso zenshi* (Tokyo: Hara shobo, 1965), p. 803; Tanaka Nobumasa, *Dokyumento Showa Tenno,* vol. 5, *Haisen,* pt. 2 (Tokyo: Ryokufu shuppan, 1988), pp. 30–33, 37–38; Herbert P. Bix, *Hirohito and the Making of Modern Japan* (New York: Harper Collins, 2000),

pp. 484–486; Dale M. Hellegers, *We, the Japanese People: World War II and the Origins of the Japanese Constitution,* vol. 1 (Stanford: Stanford University Press, 2001), pp. 27–28.

2. "Priem Iaponskogo posla Sato," 5 April 45, Iz dnevnika V. I. Molotova, AVP RF, f. 06, op. 7, pap. 2, d. 30, l. 32; f. Sekretareiat V. M. Molotova, op. 7, por. 28, pap. 2, l. 3. For the English translation from the Japanese, see SRH-071, Abrogation of the Soviet-Japanese Neutrality Pact: PSIS 400–8, 23 April 45, Records of National Security Agency/Central Security Service, Studies on Cryptograph 1917–1972, Box 23, RG 457, NA. This is a summary based on the Magic Intercepts. Hereafter archival reference is omitted. See also B. N. Slavinskii, *Pakt o neitralitete mezhdu SSSR i Iaponiei: diplomaticheskaia istoriia, 1941–1945 gg.* (Moscow: TOO "Novina," 1995), pp. 265–267.

3. Document 212, *SAO,* vol. 2, pp. 347–348.

4. Dnevnik Malika, 22 March 45, AVP RF, f. Molotova, op. 7, pap. 54, d. 891, ll. 201–202. Also see Document 195 (report of the Tokyo *rezidentura*), *VO,* vol. 7, pt. 1, pp. 207–208.

5. Documents 312 and 313, *VO,* vol. 7, pt. 1, pp. 330–332.

6. Kurihara Ken and Hatano Sumio, *Shusen kosaku no kiroku,* 2 vols. (Tokyo: Kodansha, 1986), vol. 2, pp. 15–25; Suzuki Kantaro, *Shusen no hyojo* (Tokyo: Rodo bunkasha 1946), p. 9; Takagi Sokichi, *Shusen oboegaki* (Tokyo: Kobundo, 1948), pp. 22–23; Sakomizu Hisatsune, *Shusen no shinso* (Tokyo: Dotoku kagaku kenkyujo, 1955), p. 29. For the process of forming the Suzuki cabinet, see *Takagi nikki,* vol. 2, pp. 834–837, 840–842, 848; also see Kurihara and Hatano, *Shusen kosaku,* vol. 2, pp. 33–37, 39–44; Tanaka, *Dokyumento Showa Tenno,* vol. 5, *Haisen,* pt. 2, pp. 100–101. For the army's conditions see Gunjishigaku, ed., *Daihonei Rikugunbu sensoshidohan, Kimitsu senso Nisshi* (Tokyo: Kinseisha, 1998), vol. 2, p. 697 (hereafter *Kimitsu senso Nisshi*).

7. Kurihara and Hatano, *Shusen kosaku,* vol. 2, pp. 45–46; "Togo Shigenori chinjutsuroku (3)," ibid., pp. 47–48; Tanaka, *Dokyumento Showa Tenno,* vol. 5, *Haisen,* pt. 2, pp. 104–105.

8. Suzuki, *Shusen no hyojo,* p. 19; Tanaka, *Dokyumento Showa Tenno,* vol. 5, *Haisen,* pt. 2, pp. 107–108.

9. Robert H. Ferrell, ed., *Off the Record: The Private Papers of Harry S. Truman* (New York: Harper and Row), pp. 14–15; David McCullough, *Truman* (New York: Simon and Schuster, 1992), pp. 341–342, 345–348.

10. McCullough, *Truman,* p. 353.

11. John J. McCloy Diary, 20 July 45, John J. McCloy Papers, Amherst College.

12. Fleet Admiral William D. Leahy, *I Was There: The Personal Story of the Chief of Staff to Presidents Roosevelt and Truman Based on His Notes and Diaries Made at the Time* (New York: Whittlessy House, McGraw-Hill Book Company, 1950), pp. 347–348; William Leahy Diary, 13 April 45, p. 56, Library of Congress; Harry S. Truman, *Memoirs,* vol. 1, *Year of Decisions* (Garden City, N.Y.: Doubleday, 1955), p. 10; Ferrell, *Off the Record,* p. 17; Arnold A. Offner, *Another Such Victory: President Truman and the Cold War, 1945–1953* (Stanford: Stanford University Press, 2002),

pp. 23–24; David Robertson, *Sly and Able: A Political Biography of James F. Byrnes* (New York: W. W. Norton, 1998), p. 390.

13. McCullough, *Truman*, p. 359.

14. Hurley to Stettinius, 17 April 45, Department of State, Incoming Telegram, Truman Papers, HSTL. For a version claiming that Truman and Byrnes did not see a copy of the Yalta Agreement, see Robert L. Messer, *The End of an Alliance: James F. Byrnes, Roosevelt, Truman, and the Origins of the Cold War* (Chapel Hill: University of North Carolina Press, 1982), pp. 79–80, 97–100. For the meeting with Soong, see Truman, *Memoirs*, vol. 1, p. 66.

15. Douglas J. MacEachin, *The Final Months of the War with Japan: Signal Intelligence, U.S. Invasion Planning, and the A-Bomb Decision* (Washington, D.C.: Center for the Study of Intelligence, 1998), pp. 2–3.

16. Iokibe, *Beikoku no hihon senryo seisaku*, vol. 2, pp. 41–44.

17. Waldo H. Heinrichs, Jr., *American Ambassador: Joseph C. Grew and the Development of the United States Diplomatic Tradition* (Boston: Little, Brown, and Co., 1966), p. 370. See Grew's letter to Randal Gould, editor of *The Shanghai Evening Post and Mercury*, 14 April 45, Grew Papers, Houghton Library, Harvard University; also quoted in Len Giovannitti and Fred Freed, *The Decision to Drop the Bomb* (New York: Coward-McCann, 1965), p. 71.

18. Ellis M. Zacharias, "We Did Not Need to Drop the A-Bomb," *Look*, vol. 14 (May 23, 1950), pp. 31–35. For Zacharias, see Hellegers, *We, the Japanese People*, vol. 1, pp. 72–78. For Japan's peace maneuvers through Bagge, see J. C. Butow, *Japan's Decision to Surrender* (Stanford: Stanford University Press, 1954), pp. 54–57; Kurihara and Hatano, *Shusen kosaku*, vol. 2, pp. 257–272. For Malik's contact with Bagge, see G. N. Sevost'ianov, "Iaponia 1945 g. otsenke sovetskikh diplomatov, novye arkhivnye materialy," *Novaia i noveishaia istoriia*, no. 6 (1995), p. 39.

19. Brian L. Villa, "The U.S. Army, Unconditional Surrender, and the Potsdam Proclamation," *Journal of American History*, 63 (1976): 80–81; JIC 266/1.18, "Military Use of the Atomic Bombs," Lincoln Papers, pp. 16–17; Hellegers, *We, the Japanese People*, vol. 1, p. 30.

20. John R. Deane, *The Strange Alliance: The Story of Our Efforts at Wartime Co-operation with Russia* (New York: Viking Press, 1946), p. 265; Hellegers, *We, the Japanese People*, vol. 1, pp. 41–45, 47, 48; Present Policy-JCS 1313/2, OPD 336TS, Case 132, Box 144 RG 165, NA; "History of the U.S. Mission in Moscow, Part I," p. 59, and "History of the U.S. Mission in Moscow, Part II," p. 194, OPD 336TS, Section VIII, RG 165, NA; Appendix C, 3, "Appendix to Brigadier General G. A. Lincoln's Memo," OPD, 336TS, Case 132, Box 144, RG 165, NA.

21. Deane, *Strange Alliance*, p. 166; Hellegers, *We, the Japanese People*, vol. 1, p. 46.

22. Hellegers, *We, the Japanese People*, vol. 1, pp. 29–31, 32.

23. "Iaponskaia pechat' o denonsatsii Iapono-Sovetkogo Pakta o Neitralitete," Dnevnik Malika, 13 April 45, AVP RF, f. Molotova, op. 7, pap. 54, d. 891, ll. 234–235, 244.

24. "Beseda s Togo," 20 April 45, Dnevnik Malika, AVP RF, f. Molotova, op. 7, pap. 54, d. 891, ll. 264–265; Document 295, *VO*, vol. 7, pt. 1, p. 302.

25. "Vybody," Dnevnik Malika, AVP RF, f. Molotova, op. 7, pap. 54, d. 891, l. 267.

26. Document 196, *VO*, vol. 7, pt. 1, p. 208.

27. Harriman to Truman, Paraphrase of Navy Cable, 14 April 45, Harriman Papers, Moscow Files, 14–16 April 45, Library of Congress; Harriman to Stettinius, Paraphrase of Embassy's Telegram, No. 1163, 14 April 1945, Harriman Papers, Moscow Files, 14–16 April 45. Stalin-Harriman conversation is also in Document 219, *SAO*, vol. 2, pp. 356–359. Harriman's versions in his telegrams were slightly different from the Soviet version. In the latter, Harriman first suggested Molotov's trip to the United States, and Stalin asked if Truman's policy toward Japan might become more conciliatory than Roosevelt's.

28. Gromyko to Molotov, 21 April 45, *SAO*, vol. 2, pp. 364–366.

29. Boeicho Boeikenshujo Senshishitsu, *Kantogun (2), Kantokuen, Shusenji no taiso sen* [hereafter *Kantogun (2)*] (Tokyo: Asagumo shinbunsha, 1974), p. 325.

30. *Kantogun (2)*, pp. 331–332; Edward J. Drea, "Missing Intentions: Japanese Intelligence and the Soviet Invasion of Manchuria, 1945," *Military Affairs*, vol. 48, issue 2 (April 1984), p. 68.

31. Tanemura Suetaka, *Daihonei kimitsu nisshi* (Tokyo: Fuyosha, 1995), p. 269.

32. Kawabe Torashiro, *Jicho nisshi,* quoted in Kurihara and Hatano, *Shusen kosaku,* vol. 2, p. 57.

33. Tanemura Taisa, Gokuhi [Top Secret], "Kongo no tai'so' shisaku ni taisuru iken," 29 April 45, BKSS; also Sanbo honbu, *Haisen no kiroku* (Tokyo: Hara shobo, 1989), pp. 343–352. For a shortened version, see Kurihara and Hatano, *Shusen kosaku,* vol. 2, pp. 61–66.

34. Morishima, "Kuno suru chuso taishikan," in Morishima Yasuhiko, *Showa no doran to Morishima Goro no shogai* (Tokyo: Ashi shobo, 1975), pp. 196–197; *Hirota Koki* (Tokyo: Hirota Koki denki kankokai, 1966), pp. 355–356. For Morishima's view, see *Takagi nikki,* 14 Apr 45, vol. 2, p. 843.

35. Melvyn Leffler, *A Preponderance of Power: National Security, the Truman Administration, and the Cold War* (Stanford: Stanford University Press, 1992), p. 30.

36. Elsey to Admiral Brown, 16 April 45, Papers of William Ridgon, Box 1, HSTL; Offner, *Another Such Victory,* pp. 24–30; Truman to Churchill, 13 April 45, Papers of Harry S. Truman, White House Map Room File 1945, Outgoing Messages, Top Secret File, Secret and Confidential File, London Files, Messages to the Prime Minister from the President, Box 2, Set II, HSTL; Truman to Harriman, 16 April 1945, White House Central File, Confidential File, Box 36, HSTL.

37. Harriman to Stettinius, 6 April 45, *FRUS: 1945,* vol. 5, pp. 821–824; John Lewis Gaddis, *The United States and the Origins of the Cold War* (New York: Columbia University Press, 1972), p. 201; Forrestal Diary, 20 April 45, Mudd Library, Princeton University.

38. Department of State, Memorandum of Conversation, 20 April 45, Participants: The President, the Secretary of State, Mr. Grew, Ambassador Harriman, and Mr. Bohlen, Papers of Harry S. Truman, PSF, HSTL; also in

FRUS: 1945, vol. 5, pp. 232–233; W. Averell Harriman and Elie Abel, *Special Envoy to Churchill and Stalin, 1941–1946* (New York: Random House, 1975), pp. 448–449.

39. Leahy, *I Was There,* pp. 349–350.

40. Department of State, Memorandum of Conversation, 22 April 45, Truman papers, PSF, HSTL; Document 226, *SAO,* vol. 2, pp. 367–369; Truman, *Memoirs,* vol. 1, pp. 75–76.

41. Stimson Diary, 23 April 45; Leahy Diary, 23 April 45; Memorandum of meeting at the White House, 2:00 P.M., April 23, Truman Papers, PSF, HSTL.

42. Stimson Diary, 23 April 45; Memorandum of meeting at the White House, 2:00 P.M., April 23, Truman Papers, PSF, HSTL; Walter Mills, ed., *The Forrestal Diaries* (New York: Viking Press, 1951), pp. 50–51; Harriman and Abel, *Special Envoy,* pp. 451–453; Leahy, *I Was There,* p. 351. Stimson's Diary for 23 April 45, contradicts Truman's statement from Memorandum of meeting at the White House, 2:00 P.M., April 23. *FRUS:* vol. 5, pp. 252–255, is based on the memorandum, and this version is supported by the Forrestal diary.

43. Leahy Diary, 23 April 45.

44. Department of State, Memorandum of Conversation: The President, the Secretary of State, Mr. Molotov, Ambassador Harriman, Ambassador Gromyko, Admiral Leahy, Mr. Pavlov, and Mr. Bohlen, 23 April 45, Truman Papers, PSF, HSTL; Harriman and Abel, *Special Envoy,* pp. 452–453; Truman, *Memoirs,* vol. 1, p. 82. The last part of the conversations between Truman and Molotov comes from Truman, *Memoirs,* vol. 1, p. 82, and Harriman and Abel, *Special Envoy,* p. 452, but Bohlen's record does not include this heated exchange.

45. Harriman and Abel, *Special Envoy,* pp. 452–453.

46. A. A. Gromyko, *Pamiatnoe,* 2 vols. (Moscow: Politizdat, 1988), vol. 1, pp. 212–213. The translation of Gromyko's memoirs, Andrei Gromyko, *Memoirs* (New York: Doubleday, 1989), does not include this portion. *SAO* does not include the record of the Truman-Molotov meeting on April 23, though it includes the record of the meeting on April 22.

47. Stalin to Truman, 24 April 45, quoted in Truman, *Memoirs,* vol. 1, pp. 85–86.

48. Stimson Diary, 23 and 24 April 45; Gar Alperovitz, *The Decision to Drop the Atomic Bomb and the Architecture of an American Myth* (New York: Knopf, 1995), p. 130, quoting from "White House Correspondence," Box 15, Stimson Safe File, Entry 74A, RG 107, NA.

49. Stimson Diary, 25 April 1945; Memorandum discussed with the president, April 25, 1945, in Stimson Diary, pp. 70–72; also see "The Atomic Bomb," Papers of Eben A. Ayers, Subject File, Box 5, Atomic Bomb [3 of 4], HSTL.

50. Alperovitz, *The Decision to Drop the Atomic Bomb,* p. 133, quoting Memorandum for the Secretary of War, Atomic Fission Bombs, from Leslie R. Groves, 23 April 45, pp. 6–17, Military Reference Branch, NA; Robert B. Norris, *Racing for the Bomb: General Leslie R. Groves, the Manhattan Project's Indispensable Man* (South Royalton, Vt.: Steerforth Press, 2002), pp. 375–376.

51. Barton Bernstein, "The Atomic Bombings Reconsidered," *Foreign Affairs,* 74, no. 1 (1995): 140–141; Norris, *Racing for the Bomb,* pp. 380–381.

52. *DHTP,* 9–11; Bernstein, "The Atomic Bomb Reconsidered," p. 142; Richard Frank, *Downfall: The End of the Imperial Japanese Empire* (N.Y.: Random House, 1999), 256–257; Norris, *Racing for the Bomb,* pp. 386–387; Naka Akira, *Mokusatsu* (Tokyo: NHK Books, 2000), vol. 2, p. 16.

53. "Doku kuppuku no baai ni okeru sochi yoko," 30 April 45, Supreme War Leadership Council Decision No. 25, Sanbo honbu, *Haisen no kiroku,* pp. 254–255; "5-gatsu 3-kka, Suzuki shusho dan," *Shusen shiroku,* vol. 2, pp. 228–229; "Suzuki naikaku soridaijin dan," Sanbo honbu, *Haisen no kiroku,* p. 256; "5-gatsu 6-ka, Togo gaiso no kishadan eno genmei," *Shusen shiroku,* vol. 2, pp. 229–230, 233; "Teikoka seifu seimei," *Shusen shiroku,* vol. 2, p. 233; Sanbo honbu, *Haisen no kiroku,* p. 255.

54. Tanaka, *Dokumento Showa Tenno,* vol. 5, *Haisen,* pt. 2, p. 217; "Konoe koshaku dan," *Takagi nikki,* 13 May 45, vol. 2, p. 855.

55. *Takagi nikki,* 24 May 45, vol. 2, p. 855; Tatsumi Kineo [psyd. Takagi Sokichi], "Shusen oboegaki, 3," *Sekai,* May 1946, quoted in *Shusen shiroku,* vol. 2, pp. 241–242.

56. The Committee of Three, designed to coordinate the policies of the State, War, and Navy Departments through weekly Tuesday meetings of the three secretaries, was revived in December 1944 at Stimson's initiative. The meeting was held in Stimson's office at the Pentagon.

57. Mills, ed., *Forrestal Diaries,* 1 May 45, pp. 52–53; Forrestal Diary, 1 May 45, p. 323; Iokibe, *Beikoku no nihon senryo seisaku,* vol. 2, pp. 148–149; Grew's memorandum to Leahy, 3 May 45, Grew Papers; Memorandum for the President, 6 May 45, from William D. Leahy, File 125, Box 19 (U.S. Joint Chiefs of Staff), Chairman's file, Admiral Leahy, 1942–1948, RG 218, NA, quoted in Alperovitz, *The Decision to Drop the Atomic Bomb,* p. 677. Strangely, Stimson did not mention a word about unconditional surrender in his diary entries between May 1 and May 8.

58. Department of State, Government Press, Foreign Service, Radio Bulletin, No. 110, 8 May 45, White House, "VE Day Address," Clippings, Grew Papers; Truman, *Memoirs,* vol. 1, p. 207.

59. Truman, *Memoirs,* vol. 1, pp. 207–208; Hatano Sumio, "'Mujoken kofuku' to nihon," Keio daigaku hogaku kenkyukai, *Hogaku kenkyu,* 73, no. 1 (1990): 307. For Zacharias's message, see Hellegers, *We, the Japanese People,* vol. 1, pp. 77–78.

60. Hatano, "'Mujoken kofuku' to nihon," p. 306.

61. "Reaktsiia Iaponii na kapituliatsiiu Germanii," Dnevnik Malika, AVP RF, f. Molotova, op. 7, pap. 54, d. 891, ll. 278–279, 292–293.

62. *Shusen shiroku,* vol. 2, pp. 246–267; "Togo shigenori chinjutsuroku (4)," Kurihara and Hatano, *Shusen kosaku,* vol. 2, pp. 69–70: Nishihara, *Shusen no keii,* vol. 1, p. 33; "Togo gaiso uchiwa," *Takagi nikki,* 19 May 45, vol. 2, p. 865; Matsutani Makoto, *Daitoa senso shushu no shinso,* pp. 138–139; Takagi, *Shusen oboegaki,* pp. 32–33; Togo, *Jidai no ichimen,* pp. 330–331; Sakomizu, *Kikanju ka no shusho kantei,* pp. 160–161.

63. "Togo Shigenori chinjutsuroku (4)," Kurihara and Hatano, *Shusen kosaku,* vol. 2, pp. 71–76; "Oikawa Koshiro chinjutsuroku," Kurihara and

Hatano, *Shusen kosaku,* vol. 2, pp. 77–80; Tanaka, *Dokyumento Showa Tenno,* vol. 5, *Haisen,* pt. 2, pp. 229–230; *Tagaki nikki,* 22 June 45, vol. 2, p. 889.

64. *Shusen shiroku,* vol. 2, pp. 249–253, 258–259; Kurihara and Hatano, *Shusen kosaku,* vol. 2, pp. 81–82; Nishihara, *Shusen no keii,* vol. 1, pp. 39–40; Tanaka, *Dokyumento Showa Tenno,* vol. 5, *Haisen,* pt. 2, pp. 231–232; "Yonai daijin dan," *Takagi nikki,* 22 May 45, vol. 2, p. 868.

65. Sigal, *Fighting to a Finish,* p. 54. For Japan's various peace overtures, see Butow, *Japan's Decision to Surrender,* pp. 103–111; also Sigal, *Fighting to a Finish,* pp. 54–64; Kurihara and Hatano, *Shusen kosaku,* vol. 2, pp. 257–317.

66. *Takagi nikki,* 22 May 45, vol. 2, pp. 868–869.

67. George C. Herring, Jr., *Aid to Russia, 1941–1946: Strategy, Diplomacy, the Origins of the Cold War* (New York: Columbia University Press, 1973), p. 205; Offner, *Another Such Victory,* pp. 44–46; Hellegers, *We, the Japanese People,* vol. 1, pp. 53–56.

68. Herring, *Aid to Russia,* p. 201; Hellegers, *We, the Japanese People,* vol. 1, p. 55; Harriman and Abel, *Special Envoy,* pp. 459–460.

69. Novikov to Molotov, 12–13 May 45, *SAO,* vol. 2, pp. 388–391. For Novikov's protest, see Grew's Telephone Memorandum of Conversation with Novikov, Grew Papers.

70. Harriman and Abel, *Special Envoy;* Hellegers, *We, the Japanese People,* vol. 1, p. 55.

71. Joseph Davies Diary, 27 and 30 April 45, Joseph E. Davies Papers, Chronological File, Co. No. 16, File 13–20 April 45, File 22–29 April 45, Library of Congress; Davies Journal, 30 April, 13 May, 45, Davies MSS, quoted in Herring, *Aid to Russia,* p. 215.

72. Forrestal Diary, 11 May 45, p. 333; Memorandum of Conversation, Stettinius, McCloy, Harriman, Grew, U.S. Policy in the Far East, 12 May 45, Grew Papers.

73. Grew to Stimson, 12 May 45, quoted in Joseph C. Grew, *Turbulent Era: A Diplomatic Record of Forty Years, 1904–1945* (Boston: Houghton Mifflin, 1952), pp. 1455–1457.

74. Stimson Diary, 13 May 45, pp. 123–124, 14 May 45, p. 126. Navy's response was ambiguous. On May 18, Forrestal met with King, who said he would prefer not to let the Soviets have Port Arthur, but he would support American national policy to create a strong China. In any case, to King the Yalta Agreement was not particularly important. Forrestal Diary, 18 May 45, p. 340.

75. Stimson Diary, 8 May 45, p. 106, 15 May 45, pp. 128, 129. Stimson told Forrestal and Grew about S-1 on May 8. Grew, however, does not clearly state how he reacted to this information in his memoirs.

76. Grew, *Turbulent Era,* pp. 1462–1464.

77. Hoover to Stimson, 15 May 45, Office of Secretary of War, Stimson Safe File, Japan (After 7 Dec. 41), RG 107, NA, quoted in Hellegers, *We, the Japanese People,* vol. 1, p. 102.

78. Memorandum for Assistant Chief of Staff, OPD, from Clayton Bissell, 15 May 45, ABC, Historical Draft Documents–Jap Surrender 1945, RG 165, NA.

79. Helleger, *We, the Japanese People,* vol. 1, pp. 102–103.

80. Memorandum for the Chief of Staff from McCloy, 20 May 45, Memorandum for the Assistant Secretary, War Department General Staff (WDGS), 28 May 45, ABC, Historical Draft Documents–JAP Surrender 1945, RG 165, NA. For McCloy's thinking and his influence on Stimson, see Hellegers, *We, the Japanese People,* vol. 1, pp. 83–85.

81. Grew, *Turbulent Era,* pp. 1458–1459; OPD, 336TS (Section III), RG 165, NA; also see "Operational Arrangements to be Made with USSR in Event They Decide to Come into the War against Japan," Part I, Item 4, OPD, Exec File #5, Item #21a, RG 165, NA.

82. Shimomura Kainan, *Shusenki* (Tokyo: Kamakura bunko, 1948), p. 31.

83. Eugene H. Dooman, "Memoir of Eugene H. Dooman: American Foreign Service, 1912–1945," Oral History Project, Butler Library, Columbia University, pp. 142–143; also see "Memoir of Eugene H. Dooman," pp. 13–14, Eugene Dooman Papers, Hoover Institution; Grew Diary, 25 May 45, in "Miscellaneous," Dooman Papers, Hoover Institution; Dooman's NBC interview with Freed, Dooman Papers, p. 4. See also Hellegers, *We, the Japanese People,* vol. 1, p. 91.

84. Quoted in Leon Giovanitti and Fred Freed, *Decision to Drop the Bomb* (New York: Coward-McCann 1965), pp. 92–93 (emphasis added).

85. Dooman's NBC interview with Freed, Dooman Papers, p. 4; Dooman, "American Foreign Service," p. 14; also see Iokibe, *Beikoku no nihon senryo seisaku,* vol. 2, pp. 166–167; Hellegers, *We, the Japanese People,* vol. 1, p. 93.

86. Memorandum of Conversation, by the Acting Secretary of State, 28 May 45, *FRUS: 1945,* vol. 6, pp. 545–547; Grew, *Turbulent Era,* pp. 1428–1431; Dooman, NBC interview with Freed, p. 5, Dooman Papers; Memorandum of Conversation with the President, 28 May 45, Grew Papers.

87. Grew, *Turbulent Era,* vol. 2, p. 1434; Stimson Diary, May 29, 1945; Forrestal Diary, 29 May 45, p. 349.

88. The best account of the Hopkins-Stalin conference is "Hopkins-Stalin Conference: Record of Conversations between Harry L. Hopkins and Marshal Stalin in Moscow," 26 May–6 June 1945, Papers of HST, Staff Member and Office File, Naval Aide to the President Files, 1945–1953, Subject File, Box 12, "Hopkins-Stalin Conference in Moscow," HSTL. The Hopkins-Stalin conversations are also contained in *FRUS: Potsdam,* vol. 1, pp. 21–62, but this record is incomplete, lacking a portion of the fourth and the entire fifth conversations. For the Russian version, see Documents 258, 260, *SAO,* vol. 2, pp. 397–403, 404–411.

89. Document 260, *SAO,* vol. 2, p. 406. The Russian version better conveys Stalin's talk than the American version, "Hopkins-Stalin Conference, Third Meeting," p. 3; *FRUS: Potsdam,* vol. 1, pp. 43–44. The American version, however, makes it clear that it was Stalin, not Hopkins, who initially raised the question of unconditional surrender. Part of the conversation is omitted in the Russian version; see "Hopkins-Stalin Conference, Third Meeting," p. 4; *FRUS: Potsdam,* vol. 1, p. 44.

90. Hopkins to Truman, Paraphrase of Navy Cable, 30 May 45, "Hopkins-Stalin Conference."

91. "Hopkins-Stalin Conference, Third Meeting," p. 7; *FRUS: Potsdam,* vol. 1;

p. 47. According to the American version, "Mr. Hopkins said he thought at the next meeting of the three heads of Government all these matters should be discussed." But the Russian version is more specific, stating: "Hopkins said that at the next meeting Marshal Stalin and Truman can discuss possible proposals for Japanese capitulation and also plans of occupation of Japan, and other urgent matters." Document 260, *SAO*, vol. 2, p. 407.

92. "Hopkins-Stalin Conference, Third Meeting," pp. 6, 8; *FRUS: Potsdam*, vol. 1, p. 46.

93. Harriman to Truman, 8 June 1945, *FRUS: Potsdam*, vol. 1, p. 62.

94. S. P. Ivanov, "Strategicheskoe rukovodstvo vooruzhennoi bor'by v khode kampaniia Sovetskikh Vooruzhennykh Sil na Dal'nem Vostoke," Institute voennoi istorii Ministerstva oborony SSSR, Institut Dal'nego Vostoka Akademii Nauk SSSR, Institut Vostokovedeniia Akademii Nauk SSSR, *Razgrom iaponskogo militarizma vo vtoroi mirovoi voine* (Moscow: Voennoe izdatel'stvo, 1986), pp. 69–70.

95. M. Zakharov, "Kampaniia sovetskikh vooruzhennykh sil na Dal'nem Vostoke," *Voenno-istoricheskii zhurnal*, no. 9 (September 1960), p. 5.

96. David Glantz, *August Storm: The Soviet 1945 Strategic Offensive in Manchuria, Leavenworth Papers*, No. 7 (February 1983), pp. 1–2; A. Vasilevskii, *Delo vsei zhizni* (Moscow: Iza-vo politicheskoi literatury, 1975), pp. 559–560; Edward J. Drea, "Missing Intentions: Japanese Intelligence and the Soviet Invasion of Manchuria, 1945," *Military Affairs*, 48, issue 2 (1984): 67.

97. "Hopkins-Stalin Conference, Third Meeting," p. 2.

98. Dnevnik Malika, 20 May 45, AVP RF, f. Molotova, op. 7, pap. 54, d. 891, ll. 300–301; also see the intelligence report, Document 203, 18 May 45, *VO*, vol. 7, pt. 1, pp. 213–214.

99. Dnevnik Malika, 25 May 45, AVP RF, f. Molotova, op. 7, pap. 54, d. 891, l. 314; also see the intelligence report that must have been based on the same source, Document 205, 23 May 45, *VO*, vol. 7, pt. 1, p. 215. This information more or less corresponded to the position advocated by Colonel Tanemura, indicating that someone close to the Foreign Ministry—most likely Yasuatsu Tanakamaru, CEO of the Roryo Suisan Kumiai, who was often used by Togo as an unofficial liaison with the Soviet Embassy—had revealed how far Japan was willing to go to seek Soviet mediation for peace.

100. Dnevnik Malika, 30 May 45, AVP RF, f. Molotova, op. 7, pap. 54, d. 891, ll. 325–328.

3. DECISIONS FOR WAR AND PEACE

1. Stimson Diary, 31 May 45, "Notes of the Interim Committee Meeting," 31 May 45, Harrison-Bundy Files Relating to the Development of the Atomic Bomb, 1942–1946, p. 11, Miscellaneous Historical Documents Collection, Item #661–179, HSTL; *DHTP*, 23, 31–33; Richard Rhodes, *The Making of the Atomic Bomb* (New York: Simon and Schuster, 1986), pp. 642–647; James F. Byrnes, *All in One Lifetime* (New York: Harper and Brothers,

1958), p. 285; Martin Sherwin, *A World Destroyed: Hiroshima and the Origins of the Arms Race* (New York: Vintage Books, 1987), pp. 202–207; Robert B. Norris, *Racing for the Bomb: General Leslie R. Groves, the Manhattan Project's Indispensable Man* (South Royalton, Vt.: Steerforth Press, 2002), pp. 390–391. Stimson had to excuse himself from the meeting to attend a White House ceremony, so he missed Byrnes's talk.

2. "Notes of the Interim Committee Meeting," 31 May 45, 1 June 45; *DHTP*, pp. 46–47; Byrnes, *All in One Lifetime*, p. 285; David Robertson, *Sly and Able: A Political Biography of James F. Byrnes* (New York: W. W. Norton, 1998), p. 409; Sherwood, *A World Destroyed*, p. 209; Barton Bernstein, "The Atomic Bombings Reconsidered," *Foreign Affairs*, 74, no. 1 (1995): 144. For the account of the lunchtime discussion, see Robertson, *Sly and Able*, pp. 407–409; Sherwood, *A World Destroyed*, 207–208; Rhodes, *The Making of the Atomic Bomb*, 647–648; Norris, *Racing for the Bomb*, pp. 391–392. Only Ralph Bard, undersecretary of the navy, dissented, and he sent his dissenting view to Stimson on June 27.

3. Sherwin, *A World Destroyed*, p. 209; Stimson Diary, 6 June 45; Memorandum of Conference with the President, 6 June 45, Stimson Papers, Reel 118, Sterling Library, Yale University.

4. Memorandum of Conference with the President, 6 June 45, Stimson Papers.

5. Magic Diplomatic Summary, SRS-1684, 31 May 45; SRS 1685, 1 June 45, A1–A6.

6. Magic Diplomatic Summary, SRS-1688, 4 June 45, p. 2; "Russo-Japanese Relations (June, 1945)," PSIS 400-IS, 2 July 45, SRH-179, p. 5.

7. *Hirota Koki* (Tokyo: Hirota Koki denki kankokai, 1966), p. 359.

8. AVP RF, f. 0146 (fond Referentura po Iaponii), op. 29, p. 269, d. 4, ll. 261–265. For the abbreviated version of this conversation, see "Ia A. Malik—v NKID SSSR," 7 June 45, "Za kulisami Tikhookeanskoi bitvy," *Vestnik MIDa SSSR*, 15 Oct. 1990, pp. 46–47. For the Japanese version, see *Hakone Kaidanroku, Nihon gaimusho kiroku*. Gaimusho, ed., *Gaiko shiryo: Nis'so' gaiko kosho kiroku no bu* (Tokyo: Gaimusho, 1946), pp. 148–154, is merely a brief summary of the Malik-Hirota talks. Malik's diary in the Russian Foreign Ministry archive is the most detailed account of the conversations in June. Malik's diary is also translated into Japanese [hereafter *Malik Documents (Japanese)*]. That Hirota's approach to Malik was initiated by the Foreign Ministry, and Togo in particular, is confirmed by a Foreign Ministry official, Ogata Shoji, in Gaimusho, ed., *Shusen shiroku*, 5 vols. (Tokyo: Hokuyosha, 1977), vol. 3, p. 17. Also see *Hakone Kaidanroku*, 2 and 3 June; George Alexander Lensen, *The Strange Neutrality* (Tallahassee: The Diplomatic Press, 1972), pp. 135–136; *Hirota Koki*, pp. 361–362; Hatano Sumio, "Hirota-Malik kaidan to senji nisso kankei," *Gunji shigaku*, 29, no. 4 (March 1994): 4–26.

9. AVP RF, f. 0146, op. 29, pap. 269, d. 4, ll. 265–293; AVP RF, f. Molotova, op. 7, pap. 54, d. 891, Dnevnik Malika, ll. 339, 346; "Za kulisami," pp. 47–48; *Hakone Kaidanroku*, 3 June, pp. 2–8, 10–24; *Malik Documents (Japanese)*, pp. 1–10; *Hirota Koki*, pp. 362–364.

10. AVP RF, f. 0146, op. 29, pap. 269, d. 4, ll. 273–276; AVP RF, f. Molotova, op. 7, pap. 54, d. 891, Dnevnik Malika, ll. 346–348; "Za kulisami,"

pp. 48–49; *Malik Documents (Japanese)*, pp. 10–11; Hatano, "Hirota-Malik kaidan," pp. 18–19.

11. "Za kulisami," pp. 48–49.

12. Sato to Togo, 8 June 45, Kurihara Ken and Hatano Sumio, *Shusen kosaku no kiroku*, 2 vols. (Tokyo: Kodansha, 1986), vol. 2, pp. 115–119; Sato to Togo, 8 June 45, quoted in *Hirota Koki*, p. 358; Magic Diplomatic Summary, SRS-1695, 11 June 45, pp. 2–3; SRH-079, 2 July 45, p. 6.

13. "Kongo torubeki senso shido no Kihon taiko," "Sekai josei handan," and "Kokuryoku no genjo," Sanbo honbu, *Haisen no kiroku* (Tokyo: Hara shubo, 1989), pp. 265–270; also see Robert Butow, *Japan's Decision to Surrender* (Stanford: Stanford University Press, 1954), pp. 92–102; Leon V. Sigal, *Fighting to a Finish* (Ithaca: Cornell University Press, 1988), pp. 64–69; *Shusen shiroku*, vol. 3, pp. 19–62; Kurihara and Hatano, *Shusen kosaku*, vol. 2, pp. 137–178. The documents had been brought to Kido prior to the meeting by Matsudaira, who had obtained them from Takagi. Matsudaira pointed out the discrepancies between the analysis of the current situation and the conclusion, and suggested that the emperor would summon the Big Six later to have them explain these discrepancies. Matsudaira's idea became the basis of Kido's subsequent maneuverings. See "Matsudaita Yasumasa kojutsu yoshi," *Shusen shiroku*, vol. 3, pp. 90–91.

14. "Sekai josei handan," Sanbo honbu, *Haisen no kiroku*, p. 267; also *Shusen shiroku*, vol. 3, pp. 30–31.

15. Iio Kenji, *Jiketsu: Mori Konoe shidancho zansatu jiken* (Tokyo: Shueisha, 1982), p. 8.

16. "Togo gaiso dan," "Gozenkaigi gaiyo," *Takagi nikki*, 7 June 45, vol. 2, pp. 877, 879; "Hoshina Zenshiro chinjutsuroku, 1," *Shusen shiroku*, vol. 3, pp. 159–160.

17. *Shusen shiroku*, vol. 3, pp. 69–87; Kurihara and Hatano, *Shusen kosaku*, vol. 2, pp. 178–188; *Hirota Koki*, p. 364.

18. Memorandum of Conversation with Truman and Soong, 9 June 45, Grew Papers, Houghton Library, Harvard University; Grew's Memorandum of Conversation, the President, T. V. Soong, Grew, Bohlen, 14 June 45, Grew Papers.

19. "McCloy on the A-Bomb," Appendix, James Reston, *Deadline: A Memoir* (New York: Random House, 1991), p. 495.

20. Hoover to President Truman, "Memorandum on Ending the Japanese War," OPD ABC 387, Japan (15 Feb. 45), Sec. 1-B, RG 165, NA, quoted in Dale M. Hellegers, *We, the Japanese People: World War II and the Origins of the Japanese Constitution* (Stanford: Stanford University Press, 2001), vol. 1, p. 96 (summary of Hoover's letter can be found in General Handy to General Hull, "Memorandum on Ending the Japanese War," Records of the U.S. Joint Chiefs of Staff, JCS Historic Office, Dr. Edward P. Lilly Papers, Box 7, RG 218, NA); Walter Mills, ed., *Forrestal Diaries* (New York: Viking Press, 1951), 12 June 45, pp. 68–69; Forrestal Diary, 12 June 45, p. 364; Hellegers, *We, the Japanese People*, vol. 1, p. 104; Truman to Stimson, 9 June 45, OPD, ABC 387, Sec. 4-A, RG 165, NA. Stimson did not mention anything about unconditional surrender in his diary. Stimson Diary, 12 June 45. Stimson quoted in Hellegers, *We, the Japanese People*, vol. 1, p. 97.

21. Mills, ed., *Forrestal Diaries,* p. 69.

22. Grew to Rosenman, 16 June 45, Letters, 1945, Grew Papers; also in Office of Secretary of War, Stimson's Safe File, "Japan (After 7 Dec. 41)," RG 107, NA; Joseph C. Grew, *Turbulent Era: A Diplomatic Record of Forty Years, 1904–1945* (Boston: Houghton Mifflin, 1952), pp. 1435–1436; Grew to President Truman, 13 June 45, Office of Secretary of War, Stimson Safe File, "Japan (After 7 Dec. 41)," RG 107, NA.

23. Grew, *Turbulent Era,* p. 1437. Truman invited Grew to come to the White House meeting to discuss the military plan for the invasion of Japan. Grew intened to go to the meeting with Dooman, but, met with Truman's rejection of his proposal to revise unconditional surrender on the morning of June 18, Grew must have concluded that there was no point in attending the military conference. Memorandum of Conversation with the President, 15 June 45, 18 June 45, General Record of Department of State, 1945–49, Central Decimal File, from 740.00119PW/1-145 to 740.00119PW/7-3145, RG 59, NA. See also, Hellegers, *We, the Japanese People,* vol. 1, pp. 98–99.

24. Molotov to Malik, 15 June 45, "Za kulisami," p. 49. See also a photocopy of Molotov's telegram to Malik, 15 June 45, ibid., p. 50.

25. Matsuura Masataka, "Munakata Hisataka to mo hitotsuno shusen kosaku, 1," *UP,* 291, no. 1 (1997): 16–17; *Takagi nikki,* 8 June 45, 15 June 45, vol. 2, pp. 881–882, 886–887; *Showa Tenno dokuhakuroku* (Tokyo: Bungei shunju, 1991), p. 122.

26. *Kido nikki* (Tokyo: Tokyo daigaku shuppankai, 1966), vol. 2, pp. 1208–1210; *Shusen shiroku,* vol. 3, pp. 91–94; Tanaka Nobumasa, *Dokyumento Showa Tenno,* vol. 5, *Haisen,* pt. 2 (Tokyo: Ryokufu shuppan, 1988), pp. 287–288; Matsuura, "Munakata Hisataka, 1," pp. 17–18; Nishihara Masao, *Shusen no keii,* BKSS, vol. 1, pp. 49–50; "Kido kojutsusho," *Shusen shiroku,* vol. 3, p. 94.

27. "Matsudaira hishokan kojutsu," *Takagi nikki,* 14 June 45, vol. 2, pp. 885–886; *Showa Tenno dokuhakuroku,* pp. 116–118.

28. Nishihara, *Shusen no keii,* vol. 1, pp. 50–51; Tanaka, *Dokyumento Showa Tenno,* vol. 5, *Haisen,* pt. 2, pp. 291–295.

29. *Shusen shiroku,* vol. 3, pp. 94–98; Tanaka, *Dokyumento Showa Tenno,* vol. 5, *Haisen,* pt. 2, pp. 297–298.

30. "Togo Gaiso kojutsu hikki, 'Shusen ni saishite,'" Sept. 45, *Shusen shiroku,* vol. 3, p. 101; Kase Toshikazu, "Potsudamu sengen judakumade," *Sekai,* Aug. 46, quoted in *Shusen shiroku,* vol. 3, pp. 104–105; "Togo Gaiso shuki 'Shusen gaiko,'" *Kaizo,* Nov. 45, *Shusen shiroku,* vol. 3, p. 102; Tanaka, *Dokyumento Showa Tenno,* vol. 5, *Haisen,* pt. 2, pp. 299–301. For Malik's observation of this situation, see AVP RF, f. Molotova, op. 7, pap. 54, d. 891, Dnevnik Malika, ll. 360–363.

31. Memo, Ad. Leahy to JCS, 14 June 45, in *Entry of the Soviet Union,* p. 76; Douglas J. MacEachin, *The Final Months of the War with Japan: Signal Intelligence, U.S. Invasion Planning, and the A-Bomb Decision* (Washington, D.C.: Center for the Study of Intelligence, 1998), p. 11.

32. Hellegers, *We, the Japanese People,* vol. 1, p. 105.

33. "McCloy on the A-Bomb," pp. 495–496.

34. "Minutes of Meeting Held at the White House on Monday, 18 June 1945,

at 1530," pp. 3, 5, 17, MHDC #736, HSTL; *Entry of the Soviet Union,* pp. 78–79, 84, 85; Ernest J. King, *Fleet Admiral King: A Naval Record* (New York: W. W. Norton, 1952), pp. 605–607.

35. "Minutes of the Meeting Held at the White House," pp. 3–6; *Entry of the Soviet Union,* pp. 79–81; Leahy Diary, 18 June 45, p. 98. For the casualty issue, see MacEachin, *The Final Months,* pp. 11–14; Hellegers, *We, the Japanese People,* vol. 1, pp. 106–108. For McCloy's view see "McCloy on the A-Bomb," p. 497.

36. Leahy Diary, 18 June 45, p. 99; *Entry of the Soviet Union,* pp. 83–84.

37. "McCloy on the A-Bomb," pp. 497–499. See also Forrestal's account of McCloy's statement, Mills, ed., *Forrestal Diaries,* 8 March 47, pp. 70–71; Forrestal Diary, 18 June 45, p. 370.

38. "McCloy on the A-Bomb," p. 499; McCloy to Clark Clifford, 17 Sept. 84, and attachment, "President Truman and the Atomic Bomb," Harry S. Truman Centennial Collection, HSTL.

39. "Yonai shuki," *Takagi nikki,* 22 June 45, vol. 2, pp. 890–891; "Yonai kaigun daijin chokuwa," *Takagi nikki,* 23 June 45, vol. 2, pp. 891–892; "Yonai kaiso tono mendan yoshi," *Takagi nikki,* 25 June 45, p. 894; "Togo Shigenori chinjutsuroku," Kurihara and Hatano, *Shusen kosaku,* vol. 2, pp. 203–207; Toyoda Soemu, "Ayamararetaru gozenkaigi no shinso," *Bessatsu Bungei Shunju* (Jan. 50), pp. 45–50; "Takagi hiroku (shoroku)"; "Kido kokyosho"; "Togo Gaiso kojutsu hikki, 'Shusen ni saishite,'" Sept. 45, *Shusen shiroku,* vol. 3, pp. 116–117; Tatsum Kineo, "Shusen oboegaki, 3," *Sekai,* May 46, in *Shusen shiroku,* 3: 111–120; Sakomizu Hitsatsune, *Shusen no shinso* (Tokyo: Dotoku kagaku kenkyujo, 1955), p. 36.

40. "Konoe Ko chokuwa," *Takagi nikki,* 26 June 45, vol. 2, pp. 894–895; Tanemura Suetaka, *Daihonei kimitsu nisshi* (Tokyo: Fuyo shobo, 1995), p. 286.

41. *Hakone Kaidanroku,* pp. 23–25; *Hirota Koki,* p. 365; Lensen, *Strange Neutrality,* p. 137.

42. Morishima, "Kuno suru chuso taishikan," in Morishima Yasuhiko, *Showa no doran to Morishima Goro no shogai* (Tokyo: Ashi shobo, 1975), pp. 198–199; Lensen, *Strange Neutrality,* pp. 140–141.

43. AVP RF, f. 0146, op. 29, pap. 269, d. 4, ll. 463–469. See also "Za kulisami," pp. 49–52; *Hakone Kaidanroku,* pp. 27–39; *Malik Documents (Japanese),* 24 June, pp. 1–11; *Hirota Koki,* pp. 365–367.

44. SRH-079, 2 July 45, p. 9; *Gaiko shiryo: Nis'so' gaiko kosho kiroku no bu,* pp. 151–154, in *Shusen shiroku,* vol. 3, pp. 124–126.

45. AVP RF, f. Molotova, op. 7, por. 891, pap. 54, Zapis' besed posla SSSR s Koki Hirota v Iapnoii, ll. 422–423 (the text in Japanese); *Hirota Koki,* pp. 367–368; Lensen, *Strange Neutrality,* pp. 141–142; *Gaiko shiryo: Nis'so' gaiko kosho kiroku no bu,* pp. 151–154; "Za kulisami," p. 52.

46. Molotov to Malik, 8 July 45, "Za kulisami," p. 53.

47. Malik to Molotov, 13 July 45, "Za kulisami," p. 53; Lensen, *Strange Neutrality,* p. 143.

48. Kase Toshikazu shuki, "Shusen kinenbi o mukaete," *Yomiuri shinbun,* 14 Aug. 49, quoted in *Shusen shiroku,* vol. 3, p. 17; Kase Toshikazu, "Potsudamu sengen judaku made," *Sekai,* Aug. 46, quoted in *Shusen shiroku,* vol.

3, pp. 102–103; Sato Naotake, *Kaiko 80-nen* (Tokyo: Jiji tsushinsa, 1968), p. 489; Hatano, "Hirota-Mariku kaidan," p. 15.

49. "Togo gaiso kojutsuki, 'Shusen ni saishite,'" Sept. 45, in *Shusen shiroku*, vol. 3, p. 117.

50. Stimson Diary, 19 June 45; Forrestal Diary, 19 June 45, p. 372. Actually, Forrestal did not attend this meeting. This diary entry must be based on reports given by his aide, Major Correa.

51. Minutes of Meeting of the Committee of Three, 26 June 45, Stimson's Draft Proposal for Japan, Formerly Security Classified Correspondence of John J. McCloy, 1941–45, Office of Secretary of War, Assistant Secretary of War, RG 107, NA; First draft memorandum for the president (undated), "Proposed Program for Japan," Office of Secretary of War, Stimson Safe File, "Japan (After 7 Dec. 41)," RG 107, NA; Mills, ed., *Forrestal Diaries*, 26 June 45, pp. 71–72; Forrestal Diary, 26 June 45, p. 376; "Minutes of a Meeting of the Committee of Three," *FRUS: Potsdam*, vol. 1, p. 887.

52. Memorandum for the President, "Proposed Program for Japan," 27 June 45, Records of the U.S. JCS, JCS Historic Office, Lilly Papers on Psychological Warfare, Box 7, RG 218, NA.

53. Ballantine's Memorandum to Grew, 27 June 45, and Ballantine's Draft of Proposed Statement, General Record of Departmnt of State, 1945–49, Central File, from 740.00119PW/1-145 to 740.00119PW/7.3145, RG 59, NA; Ballantine's (State Department) draft as revised 28 June, "Draft of Proposed Statement," Records of the U.S. JCS, JCS Historic Office, Lilly Papers on Psychological Warfare, Box 7, RG 218, NA; G. A. Lincoln, Memorandum for General Hull, 28 June 45, ABC, Historical Draft Documents—JAP Surrender, 1945, RG 165, NA; "Allied War Aims in Japan," ABC, Historical Draft Documents—JAP Surrender, 1945, RG 165, NA. For the subcommittee's discussion see also Hellegers, *We, the Japanese People*, vol. 1, pp. 113–116.

54. J. McC[loy], "Memo for Record, Subject: Demand for Japanese Surrender," 29 June 45, ABC, Historical Draft Documents—JAP Surrender, 1945, RG 165, NA; George A. Lincoln, "Memorandum, for General Hull, Subject: Demand for Japanese Surrender," OPD, ABC, Historical Draft Documents—JAP Surrender, 1945, RG 165, NA; also in Records of the Office of the Secretary of War, Stimson Safe File, White House Cable, Box 15, RG 107, NA; Records of the U.S. JCS, JCS Historic Office, Lilly Papers on Psychological Warfare, Box 7, RG 218, NA.

55. G. A. L[incoln], "Memorandum for General Hull, Subject: Timing of Proposed Demand for Japanese Surrender," 29 June 45, ABC, Historical Draft Documents—JAP Surrender, 1945, RG 165, NA; also in Office of Secretary of War, Stimson's Safe File, "Japan (After 7 Dec. 41)," Box 8, RG 107, NA; also in Records of the U.S. JCS, JCS Historic Office, Lilly Papers on Psychological Warfare, Box 7, RG 218, NA.

56. John J. McCloy, "Memorandum for Colonel Stimson," 29 June 45, ABC, Historical Draft Documents—JAP Surrender, 1945, RG 165, NA. The short form sent by McCloy most likely consisted of the seven points included in Stimson's memorandum to the president on July 2.

57. McCloy, "Memorandum for Colonel Stimson," 29 June 45.

58. G. A. L[incoln], "Memorandum for General Hull, Subject: Demand for Japanese Surrender." Hellegers's interview with Bonesteel, quoted in Hellegers, *We, the Japanese People,* vol. 1, p. 114.
59. For different interpretations, see Gar Alperovitz, *The Decision to Use the Atomic Bomb* (New York: Vintage Books, 1996), p. 78; Richard Frank, *Downfall: The End of the Imperial Japanese Empire* (New York: Random House, 1999), pp. 215–219.
60. S. M. Shtemenko, *The Soviet General Staff at War: 1941–1945,* 2 vols. (Moscow: Progress, 1981), vol. 1, p. 423; A. Vasilevskii, *Delo vsei zhizni* (Moscow: Izd-vo politicheskoi literatury, 1975), p. 563.
61. B. N. Slavinskii, *Sovetskaia okkupatsiia Kuril'skikh ostrov (avgust-sentiabr' 1945 goda): dokumental'noe issledovanie* (Moscow: TOO "Lotos," 1993), pp. 126–127; B. N. Slavinskii, *Pakt o neitralitete mezhdu SSSR i Iaponiei: diplomaticheskaia istoriia, 1941–1945 gg.* (Moscow: TOO "Novina," 1995), pp. 305–306; *Izvestiia,* 28 July 92. The record of this decisive meeting has not been made public.
62. Documents 314, 315, 316, *VO,* vol. 7, pt. 1, pp. 332–336; also see three identical directives, nos. 11112, 11113, 11114, in the Volkogonov Papers, Reel 4, Library of Congress.
63. S. M. Shtemenko, *General'nyi shtab v gody voiny* (Moscow: Voenizdat, 1985), vol. 1, p. 390; Shtemenko, "Iz istorii razgroma Kvantunskoi armii," *Voenno-istoricheskii zhurnal,* no. 4 (1967), p. 66; Shtemenko, *The Soviet General Staff,* vol. 1, pp. 422, 423–424; Vasilevskii, *Delo vsei zhizni,* p. 564. Vasilevskii dates his arrival at Chita as June 5, but he must have meant July 5. As for Korea, Moscow and Washington had not reached any concrete plan except for their general agreement on trusteeship. It appears that both believed that the other side would take military action in Korea, and that the forthcoming Potsdam Conference would determine the precise demarcation of the other's zone of operation. See Bruce Cumings, *The Origins of the Korean War,* vol. 1, *Liberation and the Emergence of Separate Regimes, 1945–1947* (Princeton: Princeton University Press, 1981), pp. 101–107.
64. Stimson to the President, 2 July 45, *FRUS: Potsdam,* vol. 1, pp. 891–892; also in ABC, Historical Draft Documents—JAP Surrender, 1945, RG 165, NA.
65. Ibid., p. 892. The "elements" were complete destruction of the military and militarism; limitation of Japanese sovereignty to the country's main islands; disavowal of any intention to exterminate the Japanese as a race or destroy them as a nation; permission for the Japanese to maintain the economy in order to continue a reasonable standard of living; and withdrawal of allies after the establishment of a peacefully inclined government. This must be the short list that the Operation Division had prepared and that McCloy had sent to Stimson on June 29.
66. Stimson, "[Enclosure 2] Proclamation by the Heads of State," *FRUS: Potsdam,* vol. 1, p. 893; *DHTP,* pp. 103–105; "Draft: Proclamation by the Heads of State," ABC, Historical Draft Documents—JAP Surrender, 1945, RG 165, NA. This draft has the following handwritten remarks in the right-hand corner: "Bonesteel draft (to rev McCloy 29 June)."
67. Stimson "[Enclosure 2] Proclamation by the Heads of State," *FRUS: Pots-*

dam, vol. 1, p. 894; *DHTP,* p. 105. In Bonesteel's draft, Stimson's paragraph 13 is placed in paragraph 14.

68. "Proclamation by the Heads of State," "United States Delegation Working Paper: Draft Proclamation by the Heads of State," *FRUS: Potsdam,* vol. 1, pp. 893–894, 897–899.

69. Dean Acheson, *Present at the Creation* (New York: Norton, 1969), p. 112; MacLeish to the Secretary of State, 6 July 45, *FRUS: Potsdam,* vol. 2, pp. 895–897.

70. Mills, ed., *Forrestal Diaries,* pp. 73–74.

71. "Minutes of the 133rd Meeting of the Secretary's Staff Committee," *FRUS: Potsdam,* vol. 1, pp. 900–901.

72. James Byrnes, *Speaking Frankly* (New York: Harper and Brothers, 1947), pp. 204–205; Walter Brown Diary, 6 July 45 (CFM) Conferences 2–1, Potsdam, Folder 602, James F. Byrnes Papers, Clemson University. Hull's memo was sent by Grew to Byrnes on July 16. *FRUS: Potsdam,* vol. 2, p. 1267; Cordell Hull, *The Memoirs of Cordell Hull,* vol. 2 (New York: Macmillan, 1948), pp. 1593–1594.

73. Togo's July 5 message to Sato, SRH-084, p. 6; "Japan-Peace Negotiations (Japan thru Russia)," 2 July to 16 Aug. 45, Folder 571, James F. Byrnes Papers, Clemson University. Togo's June 30 message to Sato, Magic Diplomatic Summary, SRS-1723; SRH-084, p. 3.

74. Sato questioned the wisdom of meeting Molotov before his departure for Berlin and suggested continuing negotiations through the Hirota-Malik channel. But Togo sent another "extremely urgent" telegram instructing Sato to meet Molotov. Magic Diplomatic Summary, SRS-1724, 10 July 45; SRH-084, p. 7; Magic Diplomatic Summary, SRS-1727, 13 July 45; SRH-085, p. 3; Sato to Togo, 12 July 45, SRH-085, pp. 3–4.

75. "Yonai daijin chokuwa," *Takagi nikki,* 9 July 45, vol. 2, p. 904; Matsudaira Yasumasa shinjutsusho, BKSS.

76. *Kido Koichi nikkii,* 7 July 45, vol. 2, p. 1215; *Shusen shiroku,* vol. 3, p. 139; *Takagi nikki,* 14 July 45, vol. 2, p. 911; Hosokawa Morisada, *Joho Tenno ni tassezu: Hosokawa Nikki* (Tokyo: Isobe shobo, 1953), vol. 2, pp. 400, 402; Kurihara and Hatano, *Shusen kosaku,* vol. 2, pp. 225–226; *Shusen shiroku,* vol. 3, pp. 135–142, 147–149.

77. "Yonai Kaiso chokuwa," *Takagi nikki,* 12 July 45, vol. 2, p. 909.

78. Togo Shigenori, *Jidai no ichimen* (Tokyo: Hara shobo, 1989), pp. 342–343.

79. "Yonai kaiso chokuwa," *Takagi nikki,* 14 July 45, vol. 2, pp. 909–911; *Takagi nikki,* 20 July 45, vol. 2, pp. 916–917; "Togo chinjutsuroku," Kurihara and Hatano, *Shusen kosaku,* vol. 2, p. 235; *Shusen shiroku,* vol. 3, pp. 130–131; "Konoe ko shuki, Ushinawareshi seiji," pp. 152–153, quoted in *Shusen shiroku,* vol. 3, pp. 142–143.

80. "Taiso koshoan yoshi," *Takagi nikki,* 5 July 45, vol. 2, p. 903.

81. "Taiso kunreian kosshi," *Takagi nikki,* 17 July 45, vol. 2, pp. 921–922.

82. "Japan-Peace Negotiations," Folder 571, James Byrnes Papers; Magic Diplomatic Summary, SRS-1726, 11 July 45; SRH-084, pp. 8–9; original Japanese telegram, Togo to Sato, 11 July 45, *Shusen shiroku,* vol. 3, pp. 165–166.

83. Sato to Togo, 12 July 45, Diplomatic Summary, SRS-1728, 14 July 45; Diplomatic Summary, SRS-1729, 15 July 45; SRH-085, pp. 5–6.

84. Magic Diplomatic Summary, SRS-1727, 13 July 45; SRH-084, pp. 9–10; original Japanese telegram, Togo to Sato, 12 July 45, *Shusen shiroku*, vol. 3, p. 167; AVP RF, f. Molotova, op. 7, por. 889, pap. 54, ll. 19, 20.

85. Hatano, "Hirota-Malik kaidan," p. 20.

86. Magic Diplomatic Summary, SRS-1729, 15 July 45; SRH-085, pp. 7–8; original Japanese telegram from Sato to Togo, No. 1385, *Shusen shiroku*, vol. 3, pp. 169–170. For the Soviet version of the Lozovskii-Sato meeting, see AVP RF, f. Molotova, op. 7, por. 897, pap. 54, O priezde Konoe, nach. 14 VII—Okonch. 6, VIII, Iz dnevnika S. A. Lozovskogo, 14 iulia 1945 goda, ll. 1–3. The only difference between Sato's and Lozovskii's version of the meeting is that Lozovskii said the delegation would leave either late at night or early in the morning.

87. Magic Diplomatic Summary, SRS-1729, 15 July 45; SRH-085, pp. 8–9; original Japanese telegram from Sato to Togo, No. 1386, 13 July 45, *Shusen shiroku*, vol. 3, p. 171.

88. SRH-085, p. 10; Sato to Togo, 14 July 45, *Shusen shiroku*, vol. 3, p. 172.

89. SRH-085, pp. 10–11.

90. Ibid., pp. 12–13; Togo to Sato, No. 913, 17 July 45, *Shusen shiroku*, vol. 3, pp. 175–176.

91. SRH-084, pp. 9–10.

92. John Weckerling, Memorandum for the Deputy Chief of Staff, 12 July 45 and 13 July 45, OPD, Exec. File, #17, Box 98, item #13, RG 165, NA; also Reel 109, item 2518, Marshall Library. On the basis of the naval intelligence analysis, Alperovitz concludes that Japan was on the verge of surrendering. Richard Frank, citing Weckerling's assessment at face value, argues that the United States was justified by not taking Japan's peace overtures seriously, since Japan's request for Moscow's mediation hardly represented a serious effort to terminate the war "on terms acceptable to the United States." Frank, *Downfall*, pp. 223–228.

93. "Notes Taken at Sino-Soviet Conference, Moscow 1945 (hereafter Hoo Notes)," 2 July 45, pp. 1–11, Victor Hoo Papers, Box 6, Hoover Institution; "Zapis' vtoroi besedy," *RKO*, pp. 73–82.

94. Chiang Kai-shek's telegram to T. V. Soong, reprinted in *RKO*, pp. 102–104; see also Odd Arne Westad, *Cold War Revolution: Soviet-American Rivalry and the Origins of the Chinese Civil War* (New York: Columbia University Press, 1993), pp. 40–41.

95. Hoo Notes, 9 July 45, pp. 16–23; "Zapis' chetvertoi besedy," *RKO*, pp. 105–111.

96. Hoo Notes, 11 July 45, pp. 31–37; 12 July 45, pp. 38–40; "Zapis' piatoi besedy," *RKO*, pp. 124–131; "Zapis' shestoi besedy," *RKO*, pp. 134–137.

4. POTSDAM: THE TURNING POINT

1. For the Potsdam Conference, see Herbert Feis, *Between War and Peace: The Potsdam Conference* (Princeton: Princeton University Press, 1960); Charles L. Mee, Jr., *Meeting at Potsdam* (New York: M. Evans and Company, 1975); Stanley Weintraub, *The Last Great Victory: The End of*

World War II, July/August 1945 (New York: Truman Talley Books, 1995); Naka Akira, *Mokusatsu: Potsudamu sengen no shinjitsu to nihon no unmei*, 2 vols. (Tokyo: NHK Books, 2000). For documents of the Potsdam Conference, see *FRUS: Potsdam*; Ministerstvo inostrannykh del SSSR, *Sovetskii Soiuz na mezhdunarodnykh konferentsiiakh perioda Velikoi otechestvennoi voiny, 1941–1945 gg.*, vol. VI, *Berlinskaia (Potsdamskaia) Konferentsiia rukovoditelei trekh soiuznykh derzhav—SSSR, SShA i Velkobritanii (17 iulia-2 avgusta 1945 g.): Sbornik dokumentov* (Moscow: Izd-vo politicheskoi literatury, 1980) (hereafter *Potsdamskaia konferentsiia*).

2. Robert H. Ferrell, ed., *Dear Bess: The Letters from Harry to Bess Truman, 1910–1959* (New York: W. W. Norton, 1983), p. 517; Harry S. Truman, *Memoirs*, vol. 1, *Year of Decisions* (Garden City, N.Y.: Doubleday, 1955), p. 334; Mee, *Meeting at Potsdam*, p. 5; Leahy Diary, 7 July 1945, Library of Congress; "Potsdam Diary," Stimson Papers, Reel 12, Sterling Library, Yale University. Charles (Chip) Bohlen, a specialist on Russia, was on board the *Augusta*, but he was never invited to conferences with Truman. In fact, Byrnes abolished Bohlen's job as liaison between the White House and the State Department. Charles E. Bohlen, *Witness to History, 1929–1969* (New York: Norton, 1973), p. 225.

3. "Arkhiv: Gornichnykh predsavit' k nagradam," *Kommersant Vlast'*, 18 July 2000, pp. 52–53.

4. David McCullough, *Truman* (New York: Simon and Schuster, 1992), pp. 407–408. Quartered in the Little White House with Truman were Byrnes, Leahy, Press Secretary Charles Ross, Charles Bohlen, and Truman's close aides. Truman, *Memoirs*, vol. 1, pp. 339–340. See also McCloy Diary, 15 July 45.

5. "Arkhiv," *Kommersant Vlast'*, 18 July 2000, pp. 53–54. The NKVD operative whose mission was to install secret listening devices was Beria's son, Sergo Beria. Truman did not seem to suspect that the Soviets had installed listening devices in the Little White House. He writes: "The house had been stripped of its furnishings during the war but had been refurnished by the Russians." Truman, *Memoirs*, vol. 1, p. 339.

6. The precise date of attack is still clouded in mystery. According to Deputy Chief of Staff S. M. Shtemenko, it was originally set for some time between August 20 and August 25. S. M. Shtemenko, *General'nyi shtab v gody voiny* (Moscow: Voenizdat, 1985), vol. 1, p. 390; Shtemenko, "Iz istorii razgroma Kvantunskoi armii," *Voenno-istoricheskii zhurnal*, no. 4 (1967): 66. According to Vasilevskii, on July 16 Stalin called him from Potsdam and asked him to move up the date of attack by ten days, to August 1. A. Vasilevskii, "Final," *Voenno-istoricheskii zhurnal*, no. 6 (1967): 85. This means that some time between June 27 and July 16, the date of attack was changed to August 11. This is the interpretation David Holloway takes. David Holloway, "Jockeying for Position in the Postwar World: Soviet Entry into the War with Japan in August 1945." Tsuyoshi Hasegawa, ed., *The End of the Pacific War: Sixty Years Later* (forthcoming). But in his memoirs published in 1975, Vasilevskii dropped the reference to August 1. A. Vasilevskii, *Delo vsei zhizni* (Moscow: Izd-vo politicheskoi literatury, 1975), p. 570. In his conversation with Truman on August 17, Stalin stated that

the Soviet Union would be ready to enter the war by August 15, but he also said later in the conversation that the Soviet Union would join the war in mid-August. At the joint military conference held on July 24, General Aleksei Antonov told the Americans that the Soviet Union would join the war in the second half of August, indicating that the Soviet General Staff had not changed the original date of attack set for August 20–25. From these pieces of evidence and other circumstantial evidence that I will discuss in Chapter 5, I take the view that the original date of attack, August 20–25, did not change until the Potsdam Conference was nearly over.

7. Richard Frank, *Downfall: The End of the Imperial Japanese Empire* (New York: Random House, 1999), pp. 240–241, 413; James F. Byrnes, *All in One Lifetime* (New York: Harper and Brothers, 1958), p. 292; Japan, Peace Negotiations, 2 July to 16 Aug. 45, Folder 571, James Byrnes Papers, Clemson University.

8. Stimson Diary, 16 July 45; McCloy Diary, 16 and 17 July 45; Walter Mills, ed., *Forrestal Diaries* (New York: Viking Press, 1951), p. 74; Forrestal Diary, 13 July 45, p. 398, Mudd Library, Princeton University.

9. Stimson to Truman, 16 July 45, *FRUS: Potsdam,* vol. 2, pp. 1266–1267; Stimson to Byrnes, 16 July 45, *FRUS: Potsdam,* vol. 2, p. 1265; also Stimson Papers, Reel 113.

10. Stimson Diary, 17 July 45; also quoted in *FRUS: Potsdam,* vol. 2, p. 1266.

11. James F. Byrnes, *Speaking Frankly* (New York: Harper and Brothers, 1947), pp. 211–212.

12. Harrison to Stimson, *FRUS: Potsdam,* vol. 2, p. 1360; "Potsdam Diary," Stimson Papers, Reel 128; Robert B. Norris, *Racing for the Bomb: General Leslie R. Groves, the Manhattan Project's Indispensable Man* (South Royalton, Vt.: Steerforth Press, 2002), p. 406; Stimson Diary, 16 July 45; Stimson's letter to his wife, 18 July 45, Stimson Papers, Reel 113, Sterling Library, Yale University.

13. Davies Diary, 16 July 45, Davies Papers, No. 18, Chronological File, 16 July 45, Library of Congress; Robert H. Ferrell, ed., *Off the Record: The Private Papers of Harry S. Truman* (New York: Harper and Row), p. 53; Truman, *Memoirs,* vol. 1, p. 342; *DHTP,* pp. 117–118.

14. For the Stalin-Truman meeting on July 17, see "Bohlen Notes," *FRUS: Potsdam,* vol. 2, pp. 43–46; "Appendix D: Bohlen Post-Conference Memoranda on Two Truman-Stalin Meetings at the Berlin Conference," *FRUS: Potsdam,* vol. 2, pp. 1582–1587; for the Soviet version of the meeting, see Document No. 2, *Potsdamskaia konferentsiia,* pp. 41–43. Truman's statements from Ferrell, ed., *Off the Record,* p. 53; "Bohlen Notes," *FRUS: Potsdam,* vol. 2, p. 1584; *DHTP,* pp. 117–118. For the Soviet version see *Potsdamskaia konferentsiia,* p. 43. According to the Bohlen Notes, Stalin referred to the Soviet entry into the war against Japan twice. First, he said that "the Soviets would be ready for such entry by the middle of August." *FRUS: Potsdam,* vol. 2, p. 1585. But later he said that "the Soviets would be ready in mid-August." Ibid., p. 1586.

15. Ferrell, ed., *Off the Record,* p. 53; Truman Diary, 17 July 45, original, Papers of Harry S. Truman, PSF, Roosevelt, Eleanor (folder 2)-S, Box 322, Ross, Mr. and Mrs. Charles G., PSF-Personal, 17 July 45, HSTL; Truman, *Memoirs,* vol. 1, p. 411; Ferrell, ed., *Dear Bess,* p. 519.

16. McCullough, *Truman,* p. 419; Frank, *Downfall,* p. 243; "Appendix D:

Bohlen Post-Conference Memoranda," *FRUS: Potsdam,* vol. 2, p. 1586; Walter Brown Diary, 16 July 45, Folder 602, also in Folder 54 (1), James F. Byrnes Papers, Clemson University.

17. Truman, *Memoirs,* vol. 1, p. 417 (emphasis added); see also Gar Alperovitz, *The Decision to Use the Atomic Bomb* (New York: Vintage Books, 1996), p. 241.

18. Truman, *Memoirs,* vol. 1, p. 350; Harrison to Stimson, 17 July 45, *FRUS: Potsdam,* vol. 2, pp. 1360–1361; Stimson Diary, 17 July 45; McCloy Diary, 17 July 45.

19. Stimson Diary, 18 July 45; Winston S. Churchill, *The Second World War: Triumph and Tragedy* (Boston: Houghton Mifflin Co. 1953), pp. 638–639, 640; "Summarized Note of Churchill's Conversation with Truman," 18 July 45, *DBPO,* pp. 367–368.

20. "Record of Private Talk between Churchill and Stalin," 17 July 45, *DBPO,* p. 348; Document 181, *DBPO,* pp. 369–370; John Ehrman, *Grand Strategy,* vol. 6, *October 1944–August 1945* (London: Her Majesty's Stationery Office, 1956), pp. 302–303; *FRUS: Potsdam,* vol. 2, p. 81.

21. "Bohlen Memorandum, March 28, 1960," *FRUS: Potsdam,* vol. 2, pp. 1587–1588; Bohlen, *Witness to History,* p. 236; Ferrell, ed., *Off the Record,* p. 53.

22. Walter Brown Diary, 18 July 45, Folder 602, 18 July 45, Folder 54 (1), James F. Byrnes Papers, Clemson University.

23. Magic Diplomatic Summary, No. SRS-1734, 20 July 45; SRH-086, p. 1; Sato to Togo, 19 July 45, in *Shusen shiroku,* 5 vols., vol. 3, p. 177; AVP RF, f. Molotova, op. 7, por. 889, pap. 54, l. 23; f. 7, op. 7, por. 897, pap. 54, l. 7; f. 7, op. 10, pap. 39, d. 542, ll. 2–4; Sato to Togo, 19 July 45, *Shusen shiroku,* vol. 3, pp. 177–178; Sato to Togo, 20 July 45, Magic Diplomatic Summary, SRS-1736, 22 July 45; SRH-086, pp. 1, 3–5; *Shusen shiroku,* vol. 3, pp. 197–202.

24. For Togo's two dispatches to Sato, see Magic Diplomatic Summary, SRS-1736, 22 July 45; SRH-086, pp. 2–3; Togo to Sato, 21 July 45, *Shusen shiroku,* vol. 3, pp. 179, 180–181. For Sato's dispatch to Togo see SRH-086, p. 6; Sato to Togo, 25 July 45, *Shusen shiroku,* vol. 3, pp. 181–183.

25. AVP RF, f. Molotova, op. 7, por. 897, pap. 54, ll. 10–11; Magic Diplomatic Summary, SRS 1740, 26 July 45, pp. 5–7; Magic Diplomatic Summary, SRS-1741, 27 July 45, pp. 3–9; SRH-086, pp. 7–8; Togo to Sato, 25 July 45, *Shusen shiroku,* vol. 3, pp. 185–187. For Lozovskii's questions to Sato, see Magic Diplomatic Summary, SRS-1741, 27 July 45, pp. 6–7.

26. SRH-086, pp. 7–8; Togo to Sato, 25 July 45, *Shusen shiroku,* vol. 3, pp. 185–187.

27. Sato to Togo, 21 July 45, *Shusen shiroku,* vol. 3, p. 179.

28. "Meeting of the Combined Chiefs of Staff, Monday, July 16, 1945," *FRUS: Potsdam,* vol. 2, p. 36; "Combined Chiefs of Staff Minutes [16 July 45]," *FRUS: Potsdam,* vol. 2, p. 37; Document No. 172, "Minute from General Sir H. Ismay to Mr. Churchill," *DBPO,* p. 347.

29. Brian Villa, "The U.S. Army, Unconditional Surrender, and the Potsdam Proclamation," *Journal of American History,* 63 (June 1976): 69.

30. Enclosure "A," Report by the Joint Strategic Survey Committee, Military Aspects of Unconditional Surrender Formula for Japan, Reference: J.C.S,

334 Notes to Pages 146–153

1275 Series, Records of the Office of the Secretary of War, Stimson Safe
File, RG 107, NA.

31. H. A. Craig's Memorandum for General Handy, 13 July 45, Records of the
Office of the Secretary of War, Stimson Safe File, RG 107, NA.

32. "Meeting of the Joint Chiefs of Staff, Tuesday, July 17, 1945," *FRUS:
Potsdam,* vol. 2, pp. 39–40; "Meeting of the Joint Chiefs of Staff, Wednesday, July 18, 1945, 10 A.M.," *FRUS: Potsdam,* vol. 2, p. 64; "Joint Chiefs
of Staff to the President, 18 July 1945," *FRUS: Potsdam,* vol. 2, p. 1269;
OPD Exec File #17, Item 21A, Box 99, RG 165, NA.

33. Groves to Stimson, Washington, 18 July 1945, *FRUS: Potsdam,* vol. 2,
pp. 1361–1363, 1368.

34. Stimson Diary, 21 July 45; McCloy Diary, 23 July 45. Describing in two
pages various eyewitnesses' accounts of Truman's change in behavior after
Groves's report, Alperovitz never asks whether Stalin and the Soviet side
also noticed this change. See Alperovitz, *The Decision to Drop the Atomic
Bomb,* pp. 258–261.

35. Harrison to Stimson, 21 July 45, *FRUS: Potsdam,* vol. 2, p. 1372; Stimson
to Harrison, 21 July 45, *FRUS: Potsdam,* vol. 2, p. 1372. Also see Stimson
Diary, 21 July 45.

36. Harrison to Stimson, 21 July 45, *FRUS: Potsdam,* vol. 2, p. 1372. For Truman's reaction to the timetable, see Stimson Diary, 22 July 45; also quoted
in *FRUS: Potsdam,* vol. 2, p. 1373; H. H. Arnold, *Global Mission* (New
York: Harper and Brothers, 1949), pp. 588–589.

37. Stimson Diary, 23 July 45; Stimson to Harrison, 23 July 45, Harrison to
Stimson, 23 July 45, *FRUS: Potsdam,* vol. 2, pp. 1373, 1374.

38. Stimson Diary, 24 July 45; Stimson also quoted in *FRUS: Potsdam,* vol. 2,
p. 1373; Harrison to Stimson (Doc. 1311), 23 July 45, Harrison to Stimson
(Doc. 1312), 23 July 45, *FRUS: Potsdam,* vol. 2, p. 1374.

39. Stimson Diary, 23 July 45.

40. For Spaatz's request for a written order, see Alperovitz, *The Decision to
Use the Atomic Bomb,* pp. 344–345. The document was largely prepared
by Groves. It arrived at Babelsberg on the evening of July 24 and was sent
back by Marshall six hours later. Forrest C. Pogue, *Marshall, Organizer of
Victory, 1943–1945* (New York: Viking Press, 1973), p. 21. See Richard
Rhodes, *The Making of the Atomic Bomb* (New York: Simon and Schuster,
1986), p. 691; Colonel Pasco's telegram to Marshall, 24 July 45, War De-
partment Classified Center, Outgoing Message, File 5B, Directives,
Memos, etc., RG 77, NA; Rhodes's account comes from WAR 37683,
MED 5E. A copy of Handy's order can be found in PSF-General File,
Atomic Bomb, Box 96, HSTL; *DHTP,* p. 513; W. F. Craven and J. L. Cate,
eds., *The Army Air Forces in World War II,* vol. 5, *The Pacific: Matterhorn
to Nagasaki, June 1944 to August 1945* (Washington, D.C.: Office of Air
Force History, 1953), photograph between pp. 696–697.

41. Truman, *Memoirs,* vol. 1, p. 421. Truman dates Handy's order as July 24,
but the copy in the Truman Library and the National Archives is dated July
25.

42. Stimson Diary, 23 July 45, also quoted in *FRUS: Potsdam,* vol. 2, p. 1324.

43. Stimson Diary, 23 July 45, p. 37. This part is not included in *FRUS:
Potsdam.*

44. Stimson Diary, 24 July 45. On the basis of his meticulous analysis of Ultra intercepts, postwar statements and interrogations of Japanese military leaders, and Japanese-language sources, Richard Frank makes a convincing argument that in view of the massive reinforcements in Kyushu in the Ketsu-go strategy in anticipation of the American invasion, which far exceeded the original estimation of the American military planners, Operation Olympic became untenable. From this analysis, Frank concludes that "once American leaders learned of the odds facing Olympic, there is no prospect that any other consideration could have stayed the use of atomic weapons," and "it is inconceivable that any American who could have been president in the summer of 1945 would have failed to use nuclear weapons in the face of this evidence." Frank, *Downfall,* p. 343; Frank, "Ketsu Go: Japanese Political and Military Strategy in 1945," in Hasegawa, ed., *The End of the Pacific War.* There is no evidence to show either that Truman, Stimson, and Byrnes were aware of this information or that this factor played an important role in their decision to drop the bomb.

45. Truman, *Memoirs,* vol. 1, p. 416. The impressions of Byrnes, Leahy, and Churchill are recorded in "Truman-Stalin Conversation, Tuesday, July 24, 1945, 7:30 P.M.," *FRUS: Potsdam,* vol. 2, pp. 378–379. See also Bohlen, *Witness to History,* p. 237.

46. "Bomb-Spies," Papers of Eben A. Ayers, Subject File, Box 5, "Atom Bomb" [1 of 4], HSTL. This information comes from an article by Michael Amrine in *Reporter* magazine, 5 Jan 54.

47. Vladimir Chikov and Gary Kern, *Okhota za atomnoi bomboi: Dos'e KGB No. 13676* (Moscow: Veche, 2001), pp. 251–252; Andrei Gromyko, *Memoirs* (New York: Doubleday, 1989), p. 110. That Stalin immediately understood that Truman was talking about the atomic bomb is also confirmed by Georgii Zhukov and Molotov. See G. K. Zhukov, *Vospominania i razmyshleniia,* vol. 3 (Moscow: Novosti, 1992), p. 336; F. Chuev, *Sto sorok besed c Molotovym* (Moscow: Terra-Terra, 1991), p. 81.

48. "Tripartite Military Meeting, Tuesday, July 24, 1945, 2:30 P.M.," *FRUS: Potsdam,* vol. 2, pp. 345–346.

49. B. N. Slavinskii, *Pakt o neitralitete mezhdu SSSR i Iaponiei: diplomaticheskaia istoriia, 1941–1945 gg.* (Moscow: TOO "Novina," 1995); p. 293.

50. Although the document is often referred to as the "Potsdam Declaration," the State Department officially called this document "Potsdam Proclamation," as distinguied from "Potsdam Declaration," which was the Allied policy statement relating to Europe. See J. C. Butow, *Japan's Decision to Surrender* (Stanford: Stanford University Press, 1954), p. 133, n. 61.

51. Byrnes, *All in One Lifetime,* p. 296. Byrnes writes that the Potsdam ultimatum did declare that "the ultimate form of their government should be left to the Japanese people." This was included in the Byrnes Note of August 11, but not in the Potsdam Proclamation. Dooman, "American Foreign Service," p. 23, Dooman Papers, Hoover Institution. For British suggestions for revision, see "Proposal by the British Delegation, No. 1245," *FRUS: Potsdam,* vol. 2, p. 1277; Document No. 221, "Minutes from Mr. Eden to Mr. Churchill," 21 July 45, *DBPO,* p. 514; Document 231, "Min-

ute from Mr. Rowan to Sir E. Bridges," 23 July 45, *DBPO*, pp. 550–551; Hosoya Chihiro, *Nihon gaiko no zahyo* (Tokyo: Chuokoronsha, 1979), pp. 155–160.

52. Stimson Diary, 24 July 45; also *FRUS: Potsdam*, vol. 2, p. 1272.

53. Walter Brown Diary, Tuesday, 24 July 45, Folder 54 (1), Folder 602, James Byrnes Papers. A copy of the Magic intercepts was kept in the Byrnes Papers, indicating that the secretary of state had received a copy. See Folder 571, James Byrnes Papers.

54. David Robertson, *Sly and Able: A Political Biography of James F. Byrnes* (New York: W. W. Norton, 1998), p. 431; Byrnes, *All in One Lifetime*, p. 308; Mills, ed., *Forrestal Diaries*, 24 July 45, p. 76.

55. Robertson, *Sly and Able*, p. 435; Walter Brown Diary, 24 July 45, Folder 602, James Byrnes Papers; Mills, ed., *Forrestal Diaries*, p. 78; Byrnes, *All in One Lifetime*, p. 297.

56. Walter Brown Diary, Thursday, 26 July 45, Folder 602, James Byrnes Papers, Clemson University.

57. David McCullough's interview with Elsey in David McCullough, *Truman* (New York: Simon and Schuster, 1992), p. 442. Eugene Dooman states: "Now, if I had seen the telegram, I must assume that the President also had seen this intercept; that he knew perfectly well that the Japanese were trying to get Prince Konoye to come to Moscow; and that he was to be their messenger to bring about Japan's surrender. He knew that perfectly well." Columbia University Oral History Project, Eugene Dooman, Butler Library, pp. 166–167.

58. Farrell, ed., *Off the Record*, pp. 56–57; Papers of Harry S. Truman, PSF, Roosevelt, Eleanor (folder 2), S, Box 322, Ross, Mr. and Mrs. Charles, G, PSF-Personal, HSTL; *DHTP*, 155, 156; Arnold, *Global Mission*, p. 589.

59. Truman to Hurley, 24 July 1945, Truman to Churchill, 25 July 45, Churchill to Truman, 25 July 1945, *FRUS: Potsdam*, vol. 2, pp. 1278–1279; Truman, *Memoirs*, vol. 1, pp. 387, 390; Hurley to Truman and Byrnes, 25 July 45, The White House Map Room to Hurley, 25 July 45, Hurley to Truman and Byrnes, 26 July 45, *FRUS: Potsdam*, vol. 2, pp. 1278, 1281, 1282–1283. Truman explained to Joseph Davies that "he had to do it in a hurry and did not have time to advise the Soviet Union." Davies Diary, 27 July 45, No. 19, Chronological file, 25 July 45, 27–28 July 45, Library of Congress. For the full text of the Potsdam Proclamation, see Document 1382, *FRUS: Potsdam*, vol. 2, pp. 1474–1476.

60. Ayers to Ross, Washington, 27 July 45, *FRUS: Potsdam*, vol. 2, p. 1290. No original copy of the Proclamation was kept. The copy that was kept at the Byrnes Papers at Clemson University has Truman's signature, but Churchill's and Chiang Kai-shek's signatures were handwritten by Truman. "Atomic Bomb 1945, Proclamation by the Heads of Government," Folder 596 (1), James F Byrnes Papers. Also see Robert H. Ferrell, ed., *Truman in the White House: The Diary of Eben A. Ayers* (Columbia: University of Missouri Press, 1991), p. 55.

61. Byrnes, *Speaking Frankly*, p. 207. Also see Walter Brown Diary, 26 July, Folder 602, James F. Byrnes Papers, Clemson University.

62. AVP RF, f. 0639, op. 1, d. 77, l. 9. This document was first introduced by Viacheslav P. Safronov, *SSSR, SShA i Iaponiia agressiia na Dal'nem vostoke*

i Tikhom Okeane, 1931–1945 gg. (Moscow: Institut rossiiskoi istorii, 2001), pp. 331–332.

63. "Byrnes-Molotov Meeting, Friday, July 27, 1945, 6 P.M.," Bohlen Notes, *FRUS: Potsdam,* vol. 2, pp. 449–450; Byrnes, *Speaking Frankly,* p. 207; Byrnes, *All in One Lifetime,* p. 297; also see Walter Brown Diary, 26 July 45, Folder 602, James F. Byrnes Papers, Clemson University. For the Soviet version of the Molotov-Byrnes meeting, see Document 22, *Potsdamskaia konferentsiia,* p. 218.

64. "Tenth Plenary Meeting, Saturday, July 28, 1945," Thompson Minutes, *FRUS: Potsdam,* vol. 2, p. 460; Document 23, *Potsdamskaia konferentsiia,* p. 222; G. N. Sevost'ianov, "Iaponia 1945 g. v otsenke sovetskikh diplomatov, novye arkhivnye materially," *Novaia i noveishaia istoriia,* no. 6 (1995): 49; Truman, *Memoirs,* vol. 1, p. 396.

65. Truman-Molotov meeting, 29 July 45, *FRUS: Potsdam,* vol. 2, p. 476; Byrnes, *Speaking Frankly,* pp. 207–208; Byrnes, *All in One Lifetime,* pp. 297–298; Leahy Diary, 29 July 45, p. 133; Butow, *Japan's Decision to Surrender,* pp. 156–157. Molotov's request for the Allied invitation to the Soviet government to join the war is excluded from the Soviet version of the minutes of the Potsdam Conference. See *Potsdamskaia konferentsiia,* pp. 234–243.

66. Truman, *Memoirs,* vol. 1, pp. 402–404; Byrnes, *Speaking Frankly,* p. 208.

67. "Shiraki Taisa Hokoku," *Takagi nikki,* 26 July 45, vol. 2, pp. 918–919.

68. Tanaka Nobumasa, *Dokyumento Showa Tenno,* vol. 5, *Haisen* (Tokyo: Ryokufu shuppan, 1988), pt. 2, pp. 413–414; *Takagi nikki,* 26 July 45, vol. 2, p. 919; Matsumoto Shun'ichi shuki, "Shusen Oboegaki," March 1946, in *Shusen shiroku,* vol. 4, p. 15; Kashima heiwa kenkyujo, *Nihon gaikoshi,* vol. 25 (Tokyo: Kashima kenkyujo, 1972), pp. 197, 198, quoted in Tanaka, *Dokyumento Showa Tenno,* vol. 5, *Haisen,* pt. 2, pp. 419–420.

69. Matsumoto Shun'ichi shuki, "Shusen Oboegaki," pp. 15–16; Togo chinjutsusho, pp. 321, 323, BKSS.

70. *Shusen shiroku,* vol. 4, p. 4; Togo, *Jidai no ichimen,* p. 354; Fujita Hisanori, *Jijucho no kaiso* (Tokyo: Kodansha, 1986), p. 122; *Kido Koichi nikki, Tokyo saibanki,* p. 432.

71. *Shusen shiroku,* vol. 4, pp. 4–5; "Togo gaiso kokyo sho," *Shusen shiroku,* vol. 4, pp. 14–15.

72. Shimomura Kainan, *Shusenki* (Tokyo: Kamakura bunko, 1948), pp. 88–89; Shimomura Kainan, *Shusen hishi* (Tokyo: Dainihon yubenkai kodansha, 1950), pp. 67–68.

73. Shimomura, *Shusenki,* p. 89; Shimomura, *Shusen hishi,* pp. 68; *Yomiuri hochi,* 28 July 45; *Asahi shinbun,* 28 July 45.

74. Sakomizu, *Kikanju ka no shusho kantei* (Tokyo: Kobunsha, 1965), pp. 230–231; *Yomiuri hochi,* 30 July 45; Suzuki Kantaro, *Shusen no hyojo* (Tokyo: Rodo no bunkasha, 1946), p. 32; "7 gatsu 30 nichi zuke shinbun kiji," *Shusen shiroku,* vol. 4, p. 19; Shimomura, *Shusenki,* p. 90; Shimomura, *Shusen hishi,* p. 69.

75. Nihon hoso kyokai, ed., *20 seiki hososhi* (Tokyo: Nihon hoso kyokai, 2001), vol. 2, p. 186; Naka, *Mokusatsu,* vol. 2, pp. 121–122.

76. Naka, *Mokusatsu,* vol. 2, pp. 127, 128–131; Togo, *Jidai no ichimen,* pp. 354–355.

77. Truman, *Memoirs,* vol. 1, pp. 396–397. It should be pointed out that Truman's memoirs were written by a group of ghost writers who collected pertinent documents and interviewed key persons, including Truman himself. This explains discrepancies that appear throughout the memoirs. But Truman's indifference to these discrepancies calls into question his grasp of the issues that confronted his administration during these crucial days.

78. Truman, *Memoirs,* vol. 1, p. 421. Also, in his interview in preparation for his memoirs he stated: "We sent an ultimatum to Japan through Sweden or Switzerland . . . and received a refusal of our suggestions in that ultimatum. And the bomb was dropped." Truman, A Statement, Memoirs: Foreign Policy, Atomic Bomb, Post-Presidential Memoirs, Truman Papers, HSTL.

79. Truman, *Memoirs,* vol. 1, p. 422; Dooman, Oral History Project, p. 166.

80. Magic Diplomatic Summary, SRS 1743, 29 July 45, pp. 5–6; Sato to Togo, 28 July 45, *Shusen shiroku,* vol 4, p. 27; Togo to Sato, 28 July 45, *Shusen shiroku,* vol. 4, p. 30; SRH-088, p. 3.

81. Magic Diplomatic Summary, SRS 1744, 30 July 45, pp. 2–6; Sato to Togo, 28 July 45, *Shusen shiroku,* vol. 4, pp. 28–29.

82. Magic Diplomatic Summary, SRS 1746, 1 Aug. 45, pp. 3–4; SRH-088, p. 4; Sato to Togo, 30 July 45, *Shusen shiroku,* vol. 4, pp. 31–32.

83. SRH-088, pp. 5–6; Kase to Togo, 30 July 45, *Shusen shiroku,* vol. 4, pp. 35–37; Shimomura, *Shusenki,* p. 94.

84. Magic Diplomatic Summary, SRS 1745, 31 July 45, pp. 2–5; SRH-088, p. 6; Sato to Togo, No. 1484, 30 July 45, *Shusen shiroku,* vol. 4, pp. 32–34. For the Soviet version of this meeting, see Iz dnevnika S. A. Lozovskogo, 31 July 45 g., AVP RF, f. V. M. Molotova, op. 7, por. 897, pap. 54, ll. 21–22.

85. Magic Diplomatic Summary, SRS 1747, 2 Aug. 45, pp. 1–3; SRH-088, pp. 7, 16.

86. The Byrnes Papers contain a summary of the Magic intercepts of Togo's telegram to Sato on July 28, and Sato's telegrams to Togo on July 30 and August 3, but for some reason Togo's August 3 dispatch is missing. Japan, Peace Negotiations, Folder 571, James Byrnes Papers, Clemson University.

87. Alperovitz, *The Decision to Drop the Atomic Bomb,* p. 268. His source is Herbert Feis, "Talk with Former Secretary of State, James F. Byrnes (c. November 25, 1957) about His Experience at the Potsdam Conference," in Feis, *Between War and Peace,* and Churchill's statement to Eden reported by Ehrman, *Grand Strategy,* vol. 4, p. 292.

88. See Odd Arne Westad, *Cold War and Revolution: Soviet-American Rivalry and the Origins of the Chinese Civil War, 1944* (New York: Columbia University Press, 1993), p. 48; Truman to Hurley, 23 July 45, White House Map Room File 1945, HSTL; Byrnes to Hurley, 28 July 45, White House Map Room File, Outgoing Messages, HSTL; Petrov-Hurley conversation, 23 July 45, *RKO,* pp. 144–145.

89. Petrov-Chiang Kai-shek conversation, 28 July 45, *RKO,* p. 149.

90. Memorandum for the Secretary, 28 July 45, Harriman Papers, Moscow Files, 28–31 July 45, Library of Congress.

91. Stimson to Truman, 30 July 45, *FRUS: Potsdam,* vol. 2, p. 1374; McCullough, *Truman,* p. 448; Naka, *Mokusatsu,* vol. 2, p. 157. For Tru-

man's penciled answer, see Stimson to HST, 30 July 45, Urgent, George M. Elsey Papers, Box 71, Japan Surrender, HSTL; *DHTP*, p. 175.

92. Later Truman claimed that he had issued the order to drop the bomb on the way home from Potsdam, in the middle of the Atlantic, in response to Professor James Cate, official historian for the air force. For Truman's attempts to falsify the events leading to his decision to drop the bomb, see Alperovitz, *The Decision to Drop the Atomic Bomb*, pp. 543–546; Barton J. Bernstein, "Writing, Righting, or Wronging the Historical Record: President Truman's Letter on His Atomic Bomb Decision," *Diplomatic History*, 16, no. 1 (1992): 167–173. Truman's letter to Cate in Craven and Cate, eds. *The Army Air Forces in World War II*, vol. 5, opposite p. 713.

5. THE ATOMIC BOMBS

1. For the ambiguities on the precise date of attack set by Stalin and the Soviet General Staff prior to the Potsdam Conference, see Chap. 4, n. 6

2. Document 318, Stalin's and Antonov's Order, No. 11120, 30 July 45, *VO*, vol. 7, pt. 1, p. 336; Dmitrii A. Volkogonov Papers, Microfilm Reels 5, Library of Congress.

3. Document 321, Vasil'ev and Ivanov to Stalin, 3 August 45, *VO*, vol. 7, pt. 1, pp. 337–338; S. Shtemenko, "Iz istorii razgroma Kantunskoi armii," *Voenno-istoricheskii zhurnal*, no. 5 (1967): 54.

4. *VO*, vol. 7, pt. 1, p. 322; Document 325, Vasilevskii to Commander of the Transbaikal Front, 7 Aug 45, *VO*, vol. 7, pt. 1, p. 341.

5. RGASPI, f. 558, op. 1, d. 416, ll. 660b–67. Antonov's name never appears in Stalin's appointment log, indicating that Stalin had another means of communicating with the General Staff.

6. "Atomic Bomb—Army Preparations," Papers of Eben A. Ayers, Subject File Box 5, Atom Bomb [1 of 4], HSTL; Richard Rhodes, *The Making of the Atomic Bomb* (New York: Simon and Schuster, 1986), pp. 680, 700.

7. Rhodes, *The Making of the Atomic Bomb*, pp. 701–710; Also see Robert B. Norris, *Racing for the Bomb: General Leslie R. Groves, the Manhattan Project's Indispensable Man* (South Royalton, Vt.: Steerforth Press, 2002), p. 417.

8. Midorikawa Toru, *Hiroshima Nagasaki no genbaku saigai* (Tokyo: Iwanami shoten, 1979), p. 274; also see Rhodes, *The Making of the Atomic Bomb*, pp. 713–734. According to Midorikawa, the population of Hiroshima was 350,000, including 20,000 Koreans (p. 266).

9. Harry S. Truman, *Memoirs*, vol. 1, *Year of Decisions* (Garden City, N.Y.: Doubleday, 1955), p. 421; Rigdon's book, "White House Sailor," Papers of Eben A. Ayers, Subject File Box 5, Atom Bomb [1 of 4], HSTL; "Aboard U.S.S. *Augusta* with President Truman, August 6 (UP)," Rigden Papers, HSTL; Truman, *Memoirs*, vol. 1, p. 422.

10. Statement read by President Truman aboard U.S.S. *Augusta*, 6 Aug. 45, Papers of Harry S. Truman, PSF, General File A-Ato, Atomic Bomb, HSTL.

11. Papers of Eben A. Ayers, Subject File Box 5, Atom Bomb [1 of 4], HSTL.

The figure of 323,000 to 333,000 is given by Rhodes, *The Making of the Atomic Bomb,* p. 713, and Richard Frank, *Downfall: The End of the Imperial Japanese Empire* (New York: Random House, 1999), pp. 263, 287. Japanese sources give higher figures: Hattori Takushiro, *Daitoasenso zenshi* (Tokyo: Hara shobo, 1965), gives 343,000 (p. 921); and Midorikawa, *Hiroshima Nagasaki no genbaku saigai,* gives 350,000 (pp. 265–266).

12. SRH-088, pp. 7, 16; "Memorandum for the President, Office of Strategic Services, August 1945," Papers of Harry S. Truman, SMOF: Rose A. Conway Files, HSTL. Frank argues that an important factor in Truman's decision to drop the bomb was the information that the JCS had received from the Joint War Plans Committee, which reported the "massive Japanese buildup" in Kyushu on the basis of the information it obtained from the Ultra decrypt, and recommended the reconsideration of alternatives to Olympic. This report was forwarded to the JCS "on the day the first atomic bomb was dropped" (Frank, *Downfall,* p. 273). This information may explain why Truman did not intervene to stop the atomic bombing on Nagasaki, but it does not explain why he decided to drop the bomb on Hiroshima.

13. For Japan's preparations for the expected American invasion, see Frank's detailed analysis in *Downfall,* Chapter 11.

14. Like all presidential statements on important occasions, Truman's statement had been carefully prepared by his assistants, in this case, by Stimson beginning as early as February. The examination of these drafts leaves one with the nagging suspicion that the atomic bomb, once conceived as a means to induce Japan's surrender, became the end in itself to which all else became subordinated.

15. Nihon hoso kyokai, *20 seiki hososhi* (Tokyo: Nihon hoso kyokai, 2001), vol. 1, p. 182; Hattori, *Daitoasenso zenshi,* pp. 921–922; Sakomizu Hisatsune, *Kikanju ka no shusho kantei* (Tokyo: Kobunsha, 1964), p. 341; Shimomura Kainan, *Shusenki* (Tokyo: Kamakura bunko, 1948), p. 97; "Kawabe Torsshiro chinjutsuroku," Kurihara and Hatano, *Shusen kosaku,* vol. 2, pp. 342–343. For the Japanese Army's atomic project, see Frank, *Downfall,* p. 253.

16. *Anami Korechika nikki,* 7 Aug. 45, BKSS.

17. Arisue Seizo, *Arisue kikancho no shuki* (Tokyo: Fuyo shobo, 1987), pp. 26–37; "Genbaku hantei no keii—Nishina Yoshio chinjutsuroku," Kurihara and Hatano, *Shusen kosaku,* vol. 2, pp. 344–345; Hosokawa Morisada, *Joho Tenno ni tassezu: Hosokawa nikki* (Tokyo: Isobe shobo, 1953), 8 Aug. 45, pp. 413–414.

18. Togo to Sato, 7 Aug 45, in *Shusen shiroku,* vol. 4, p. 77; Sato to Togo, 7 Aug 45, *Shusen shiroku,* vol. 4, pp. 77–78.

19. Togo Shigenori, *Jidai no ichimen* (Tokyo: Hara shobo, 1989), pp. 355–356.

20. *Takagi nikki,* 8 Aug 45, vol. 2, pp. 923–924; Toyoda Soemu, "Ayamarareta gozenkaidgi," *Bungei shunju,* no. 1 (1950): 52–53.

21. See *Pravda,* 7 and 8 Aug. 45; RGASPI, f. 558, op. 1, d. 416, l. 650b.

22. Memorandum of Conversation between Harriman and Molotov, August 7, 1945, Harriman Papers, Moscow Files, 5–9 Aug. 45, Library of Congress.

23. MO TsVMA, f. 129, d. 25324, Istoricheskii zhurnal shtaba TOF, Telegram No. 11122 from Stalin and Antonov, 8 Aug. 45, l. 1. See Document 325,

Vasilevskii to Malinovskii, 7 Aug. 45, Document 326, Vasilevskii to Meretskov, 7 Aug. 45, Document 327, Vasilevskii to Iumashev, 8 Aug. 45, and Document 328, Vasilevskii to Purkaev, 8 Aug. 45, *VO,* vol. 7, pt. 2, pp. 341–343.

24. Sato to Togo, 7 Aug. 45, *Shusen shiroku,* vol. 4, pp. 77–78; Magic Diplomatic Summary, SRS 1753, 8 Aug. 45. Magic Diplomatic Summary states that Sato dispatched this telegram "presumably before he had received Togo's message." Neither Yuhashi, Sato, nor Morishima mentions anything about Togo's telegram. Sato Naotake, *Kaiko 80-nen* (Tokyo: Jiji tsushinsha, 1963), pp. 497–498; Yuhashi Shigeto, *Senji nisso kosho shoshi, 1941nen-1945nen* (Tokyo: Kasumigaseki shuppan, 1974), p. 217; Morishima, "Kunosuru chuso taishikan," p. 209. It may well be that Togo's last telegram never reached the Japanese Embassy in Moscow.

25. The editors of VO explain that the time of attack was changed by forty-eight hours because the Soviet leaders wanted to have the maximum surprise effect on the enemy, preparations for the attack were completed by August 5, and Stalin had made a verbal commitment to initiate attack three months after the German surrender. Significantly, the editors, still under the ideological spell of Soviet historiography, fail to mention the most crucial factor: the atomic bomb on Hiroshima. It was the Hiroshima bomb that prompted Stalin to order the attack earlier than originally planned. *VO,* vol. 7, pt. 2, p. 322.

26. RGASPI, f. 558, op. 1, d. 416, l. 67. In addition to these individuals, he must have carried on telephone conversations with Antonov and Vasilevskii.

27. W. Averell Harriman and Elie Abel, *Special Envoy to Churchill and Stalin, 1941–1946* (New York: Random House, 1975), p. 494; Harriman's Memorandum to Byrnes, 31 July 45, Harriman Papers, Moscow Files, 28–31 July 45; Byrnes to Harriman, 5 Aug. 45, White House Map Room File 1945, Outgoing Messages, Box 2, Set II, Outgoing Messages, Top Secret File, 1945, August-November Map Room, HSTL.

28. Memorandum from Harriman to Truman and Byrnes, Paraphrase of Navy Cable, 7 Aug. 45, Harriman Papers, Moscow Files, 5–9 Aug. 45.

29. RGASPI, f. 558, op. 1, d. 416, l.67; Soong to Harriman, handwritten note, Harriman Papers, Moscow Files, 5–9 Aug. 45.

30. For the detailed minutes, see Hoo Notes, 7 Aug. 45, pp. 41–56, Victor Hoo Papers, Box 6, Hoover Institution Archive, and Document 693, *RKO,* pp. 156–161. See also a useful list of major disagreements prepared by the Far Eastern Division of the People's Commissariat of Foreign Affairs, Document 692, *RKO,* pp. 154–156. Hoo included Dairen in the concessions, but the Soviet version does not refer to Dairen. Hoo Notes, p. 44; also see Document 693, *RKO,* pp. 158–159.

31. Sakomizu, *Kikanju ka no shusho kantei* (Tokyo: Kobunsha, 1965), pp. 245–246.

32. For Sato's meeting with Molotov, see "Priem Posla Iaponii Naotake Sato v 17 chas 00 min, 8 avgusta 1945 g.," "Ob Ob"iavlenii voina Iaponii SSSR," Iz dnevnika V. I. Molotova, AVP RF, f. Molotova, op. 7, por., No. 904, pap. 55, ll. 1–7; Sato, *Kaiko 80-nen,* pp. 498–500; Gaimusho, ed., *Gaiko shiryo: Nis'so' gaiko kosho kiroku no bu* (Gaikoshiryokan, n.d.), pp. 162–

163. The most detailed description is Molotov's account in the Russian Foreign Ministry archive, cited first in this note.

33. This translation is taken from Telegram from Harriman to the President, and Secretaries of State, War, and Navy, Declaration of War, 8 Aug. 45, Harriman Papers, Moscow Files, 5–9 Aug. 45. This seems to be the earliest English translation. For the Russian original, see *Izvestiia*, 9 Aug. 45, "Priem Posla Iaponii Naotake Sato," Iz dnevnika Molotova, l. 2, l.7; Document 694, *RKO*, pp. 161–162. For the Japanese translation of the declaration of war, see Sato, *Kaiso 80-nen*, p. 498; *Gaiko shiryo: Nis'so' gaiko kosho kiroku no bu*, pp. 162–163; "Soren no tainichi sensen hukoku," in Shigeta Hiroshi and Suezawa Shoji, eds., *Nisso kihon bunsho, shiryoshu* (Tokyo: Sekai no ugokisha, 1988), pp. 48–49.

34. Malik did not contact Togo until late in the morning of August 9. By that time, Soviet tanks had penetrated deep into Manchuria. For the Molotov-Sato meeting see "Iz dnevnika Molotova," ll. 3–4. For a less detailed account, see "Nis'so' gaiko kosho kiroku," p. 83; Yuhashi, *Senji nisso kosho shoshi*, p. 218.

35. "Iz dnevnika Molotova," ll. 5–6.

36. Sato, *Kaiko 80-nen*, p. 499; Yuhashi, *Senji nisso kosho shoshi*, p. 219.

37. Harriman to the President and Secretaries of State, War, and Navy, signed by Deane, Operational Priority, "Declaration of War," 8 Aug. 45, Harriman Papers, Moscow Files, 5–9 Aug. 45; Harriman to Byrnes, 9 Aug. 45, White House Map Room File, Top Secret Incoming Messages 1945, HSTL.

38. "Far Eastern War and General Situation," 8 Aug. 45, Harriman Papers, Moscow Files, 5–9 Aug. 45

39. Harriman to Truman and Byrnes, Paraphrase of Navy Cable, 8 Aug. 45, Harriman Papers, Moscow Files, 5–9 Aug. 45.

40. Truman, *Memoirs*, vol. 1, p. 425; "Declaration of War on Japan by the Soviet Union," Harriman Papers, Moscow Files, 5–9 Aug. 45; Edward T. Folliardy, *Washington Post*, 9 Aug. 45; Felix Belair, *New York Times*, 9 Aug. 45.

41. Truman, *Memoirs*, vol. 1, p. 425.

42. "Declaration of War on Japan by the Soviet Union," Harriman Papers, Moscow Files, 5–9 Aug. 45; *New York Herald Tribune*, 9 Aug. 45; *Washington Post*, 9 Aug. 45; *New York Times*, 9 Aug. 45.

43. I am grateful to Richard Frank for calling my attention to the take-off procedures adopted by the 509th Group. For the Nagasaki mission, see Norris, *Racing for the Bomb*, pp. 421–424.

44. For the Soviet campaign in Manchuria, see David M. Glantz, *August Storm: The Soviet 1945 Strategic Offensive in Manchuria, Leavenworth Papers*, No. 7 (February 1983).

45. Ibid.

46. Yomiuri shinbunsha, *Showashi no tenno* (Tokyo: Yomiuri shinbunsha, 1985), vol. 5, pp. 183–184.

47. Sakomizu, *Kikanju ka no shusho kantei*, p. 246; Sakomizu Hisatsune, *Nihon teikoku saigono 4-kagetsu* (Tokyo: Oriento shobo, 1973), p. 188; Hasegawa Saiji, "Hokai no zenya," *Fujin Koron*, August 1947, in *Shusen shiroku*, vol. 4, p. 84.

48. Matsumoto Shun'ichi shuki, "Shusen oboegaki," March 1946, *Shusen shiroku,* vol. 4, p. 85.
49. Suzuki Kantaro, *Shusen no hyojo* (Tokyo: Rodo no bunkasha, 1946), pp. 35–35; Sakomizu, *Kikanju ka no shusho kantei,* p. 255; Sakomizu, *Nihon teikoku saigono 4-kagetsu,* pp. 188–189; Suzuki Hajime, ed., *Suzuki Kantaro jiden* (Tokyo: Jiji tsushinsha, 1964), p. 245; Matsutani Makoto, "Watashino shusen memo," *Kokubo,* August-October 1947, p. 431.
50. Togo, *Jidai no ichimen,* p. 359; "Togo chinjutsuroku," Kurihara and Hatano, *Shusen kosaku,* vol. 2, p. 359; *Hosokawa nikki,* vol. 2, p. 415.
51. *Kido nikki,* vol. 2, p. 1223; "Kido kojutsusho," *Shusen shiroku,* vol. 4, p. 102; Tanaka Nobumasa, *Dokyumento Showa Tenno,* vol. 5, *Haisen,* pt. 2 (Tokyo: Ryokufu shuppan, 1988), pp. 473–474.
52. The meeting was not the one Sakomizu had planned to have the previous night; it was called anew after the Soviet invasion. Suzuki, *Shusen no hyojo,* p. 35; Toyoda Soemu, *Saigono teikoku kaigun* (Tokyo: Sekai no nihonsha, 1950), p. 206. Konoe quote is in *Hosokawa nikki,* vol. 2, p. 415.
53. BKSS, *Senshi sosho: Kantogun (2), Kantokuen, Shusenji no taiso sen* (Tokyo: Asagumo shinbunsha, 1974), p. 330.
54. "Soren no tainichi saigo tsucho ni taishite torubeki sochi no kenkyu," Nishihara Masao, *Shusen no keii,* BKSS, vol. 1, pp. 104–108. The Kwantung Army's chief of staff, General Hata Hikosaburo, recalled that the Kwantung Army had believed it could count on Soviet neutrality until the spring of the following year. Quoted in BKSS, *Senshi sosho: Daihonei rikugunbu* (10) (Tokyo: Asagumo shinbunsha, 1975), p. 427.
55. Yomiuri shinbunsha, *Showashi no Tenno* (Tokyo: Yomiuri shinbunsha, 1968), vol. 5, pp. 184–185.
56. Kawabe Torashiro sanbo jicho nisshi, 26 July–2 Sept. 45, Chuo, sensoshido, juyokokusakubunsho 1206, BKSS, p. 155; Kawabe Torashiro, "Sanbo jicho no nikki," in *Kawabe Torashiro kaisoroku* (Mainichi shinbunsha, 1979), p. 253; see also the quotes from Kawabe's diary in *Daihonei rikugunbu* (10), p. 430; Document No. 196, in Kurihara and Hatano, *Shusen kosaku,* vol. 2, p. 364. Kawabe's diary is redacted in the published version. It must be compared with the original manuscript in BKSS.
57. Sanbo jicho nisshi, BKSS, p. 153; Kawabe, "Sanbo jicho no nikki," p. 252; also quoted in *Daihonei rikugunbu* (10), p. 420.
58. Sanbo jicho nisshi, BKSS, p. 158; Kawabe, "Sanbo jicho no nikki," p. 253; *Daihonei rikugunbu* (10), p. 430.
59. Sanbo jicho nisshi, BKSS, p. 158; Kawabe, "Sanbo jicho no nikki," p. 253; *Kawabe Torashiro Kaisoroku,* pp. 156–157; *Daihonei rikugunbu* (10), p. 430. Based on the last source cited, Frank argues: "Anami set War Ministry officers to work implementing martial law" (Frank, *Downfall,* p. 289). Anami's reaction was tacit approval, but he did not order an implementation of martial law. See also *Ikeda Sumihisa Shuki,* 9 Aug. 45, BKSS.
60. Asaeda's testimony in *Showashi no Tenno,* vol. 5, pp. 187–188. Although Umezu did not attend, Kawabe and Shuichi Miyazaki (the first division

chief) did attend. Frank argues that the extent of the Soviet invasion was not reported to the Imperial General Headquarters, but the Kwantung Army headquarters and the Imperial General Headquarters were connected by direct telephone line, and therefore the Imperial General Headquarters was fully informed of the extent of the Soviet action. Frank argues that twenty-four hours after the Soviet invasion "the Kwantung Army had yet to even detect the 'swarms' of Soviet soldiers on the march from the west." Frank, *Downfall*, p. 347. This account is contradicted by the Kwantung Army staff officers Kyo Suzuki (Intelligence) and Teigo Kusachi (Operations), who recalled that by 5:30 the Kwantung Army had concluded that the Soviet invasion was an all-out, massive attack along the border. This information was relayed to the Imperial General Headquarters in Tokyo, an assessment confirmed by Asaeda's testimony. See *Showashi no Tenno*, vol. 5, pp. 183–186.

61. Takeshita Masahiko, "Kimitsu sakusen nikki: Takeshita nikki," in Gunji shigakukai, *Kimitsu senso nisshi*, vol. 2 (Tokyo: Kinseisha, 1998) [hereafter Takeshita, "Kimitsu sakusen nikki," its handwritten original in BKSS]; Nishihara, *Shusen no keii*, vol. 1, pp. 113–114. According to *Showashi no Tenno*, vol. 5, p. 188, the meeting attended by Anami, Umezu, bureau chiefs, and division chiefs was held at 9:00 A.M. and adopted this document. Anami and Umezu were to bring the document to the Supreme War Council, have it adopted by the cabinet and the imperial conference, and announce it at 5:00 P.M. But Umezu and Anami failed to present this document at the Supreme War Council (*Showashi no Tenno*, vol. 5, pp. 188–189). Nishihara mentions nothing about such a meeting, and writes that the document never went higher than the bureau chief.

62. Cyril Clemens, ed., *Truman Speaks* (New York: Columbia University Press, 1960), p. 69.

63. Telegram, Senator Richard Russell to Truman, 7 Aug. 45, Papers of Harry S. Truman, Official File, Box 196 Misc. (1946), HSTL; Truman to Russell, 9 Aug. 45, ibid.; *DHTR*, pp. 210, 211–212; John Morton Blum, ed., *The Price of Vision: The Diary of Henry A. Wallace, 1942–1946* [hereafter *Wallace Diary*] (Boston: Houghton Mifflin Company, 1973), p. 474; Leahy Diary, 9 Aug. 45, p. 140, Library of Congress.

64. SRS-507, Magic Far East Summary, 9 Aug. 45, p. 5, cited by Frank, *Downfall*, pp. 302, 427.

65. Post-Presidential memoirs, 89a, Truman Papers, HSTL.

66. The account of the Supreme War Council meeting on August 9 is based on Toyoda Soemu, *Saigono teikoku kaigun*, pp. 206–210; "Togo gaisho kojutsu hikki," *Shusen shiroku*, vol. 4, pp. 110–112; "Togo Shigenori chinjutsuroku," Kurihara and Hatano, *Shusen kosaku*, vol. 2, pp. 370–373; "Toyoda Soemu Chinjutsuroku," Kurihara and Hatano, *Shusen kosaku*, vol. 2, pp. 375–378; Toyoda, "Ayamarareta gozenkaigi," p. 53.

67. Frank identifies Toyoda as the one who made this argument (Frank, *Downfall*, p. 290), but it was Anami who made this point. See Toyoda, *Saigono teikoku kaigun*, p. 207; Toyoda, "Ayamarareta gozenkaigi no shinso," p. 53.

68. For an interpretation that draws a clear division between the two sides, see J. C. Butow, *Japan's Decision to Surrender* (Stanford: Stanford University

Press, 1954), pp. 160–161; Sadao Asada, "The Shock of the Atomic Bomb and Japan's Decision to Surrender: A Reconsideration," *Pacific Historical Review,* 67, no. 4 (1998): 493. For the details of the Big Six meeting, see Nishihara, *Shusen no keii,* vol. 1, p. 117; Toyoda, *Saigono teikoku kaigun,* pp. 207–209; Toyoda chinjutsuroku, BKSS; Toyoda, "Ayamarareta gozenkaigi," pp. 53–54.

69. *Daihonei rikugunbu* (10), p. 443; Togo, *Jidai no ichimen,* pp. 356–358; Toyoda, *Saigo no teikoku kaigun,* p. 207; Togo chinjutsuroku, BKSS; Toyoda, "Ayamarareta gozenkaigi," p. 54.

70. *Kido Koichi nikki,* vol. 2, p. 1223; Frank, *Downfall,* p. 291. Takagi and Hosokawa also support the contention that the Supreme War Council decided to attach four conditions. *Takagi nikki,* 9 Aug. 45, vol. 2, p. 925; *Hosokawa nikki,* vol. 2, pp. 415–416.

71. *Hosokawa nikki,* pp. 414, 420, 421; *Kido Koichi nikki,* vol. 2, p. 1223. Discounting Kido's postwar statement that his diary entry was in error, Frank persuasively argues that Kido and Hirohito were not disposed to accept unconditional surrender. Frank, *Downfall,* pp. 291–292.

72. Ito Takashi and Watanabe Ikuo, eds., *Shigemitsu Mamokru shuki* (Tokyo: Chuokoronsha, 1986), pp. 523–524; Shigemitsu bunsho, "Heiwa no tankyu, sono 3," quoted in *Shusen shiroku,* vol. 4, p. 135; *Kido Koichi nikki,* vol. 2, p. 1223.

73. Takagi Sokichi, *Shusen oboegaki* (Tokyo: Kobundo, 1953), p. 53; *Takagi nikki,* 9 Aug. 45, vol. 2, p. 925. In addition, Kase also contacted Kido and recommended the emperor's sacred decision. Kase Toshikazu, "Potsudamu sengen judaku made," *Sekai,* August 1946, quoted in *Shusen shiroku,* vol. 4, p. 133.

74. The importance of the Kido-Hirohito conversation has been ignored by historians, with the exception of Frank. See Frank, *Downfall,* p. 291.

75. Shigemitsu Mamoru, *Showa no doran,* 2 vols. (Tokyo: Chuokoronsha, 1952), vol. 2, p. 286.

76. Matsumoto Shun'ichi shuki, "Shusen oboegaki," *Shusen shiroku,* vol. 4, p. 112. For Onishi's visit to Yonai, see Takeshita, "Kimitsu sakusen nikki," p. 754; *Daihonei rikugunbu* (10), p. 437; Nishihara, *Shusen no keii,* vol. 1, p. 119.

77. Takeshita, "Kimitsu sakusen nikki," p. 752. Colonel Matsutani, who wished to persuade Anami to accept the one-condition proposal, gave up his efforts after seeing the army minister surrounded by radical officers pressuring him to stand firm for the continuation of the war. Takagi, *Shusen oboegaki,* p. 53.

78. The best account for the cabinet meetings is Shimomura, *Shusenki,* pp. 118–120. Also see Nishihara, *Shusen no keii,* vol. 1, pp. 121–125, 126–129; *Ikeda shuki,* 9 Aug. 45. Takagi's diary and notes do not have any record of his meeting with Yonai on August 9, but clearly he obtained the information about the Supreme War Council deliberations from Yonai. He also mentions that Matsutani was dispatched to the Army Ministry to persuade Anami. If so, it is reasonable to assume that Takagi also went to the Navy Ministry to confer with Yonai. At 3:30 Takagi and Matsutani met to exchange information. *Takagi nikki,* vol. 2, p. 995.

79. Shimomura, *Shusenki,* pp. 118–120; Shimomura Kainan, *Shusen hishi* (To-

kyo: Dainihon yabenkai kodansha, 1950), pp. 79–83; Nishihara, *Shusen no keii*, vol. 1, p. 123. For McDilda's testimony, see Frank, *Downfall*, pp. 290, 423; William Craig, *The Fall of Japan* (New York: Dial Press, 1967), pp. 490–491.

80. Matsumoto, "Shusen oboegaki," quoted in *Shusen shiroku*, vol. 4, pp. 127–128.

81. Tanaka, *Dokymento Showa Tenno*, vol. 5, pt. 2, pp. 485, 491.

82. Shimomura, *Shusenki*, pp. 121–128; Shimomura, *Shusen hishi*, pp. 83–88; Takeshita, "Kimitsu sakusen nikki," pp. 752, 754. Those who supported Anami were Toji Yasui (state minister), Hiromasa Matsuzaka (justice minister), Tadahiko Okada (minister of welfare), and Genji Abe (minister of internal affairs).

83. *Kido Koichi nikki*, vol. 2, p. 1223.

84. Sakomizu, *Kikanju ka no shusho kantei*, pp. 259–260; Toyoda, *Saigo no teikoku kaigun*, p. 210.

85. Sakomizu, *Kikanju ka no shusho kantei*, pp. 260–261.

86. "Toyoda Soemu chinjutsuroku," Kurihara and Hatano, *Shusen kosaku*, vol. 2, pp. 377–378.

87. For the imperial conference, the best account is "Hoshina memo," in Hoshina Zenshiro, *Daitoasenso hishi: Ushinawareta wahei kosaku: Hoshina Zenshiro kaisoroku* (Tokyo: Hara shobo, 1975), pp. 139–147. Hoshina memo is quoted in *Shusen shiroku*, vol. 4, pp. 147–155; see also Togo Gaiso kojutsu hikki, "Shusen ni saishite," September 1945, *Shusen shiroku*, vol. 4, pp. 138–139; Sakomizu Hisatsune, "Kofukuji no shinso," *Jiyu kokumin*, February Special Issue, 1946, in *Shusen shiroku*, vol. 4, pp. 139–142; Toyoda, *Saigono teikoku kaigun*, pp. 210–213; Shimomura, *Shusen hishi*, p. 105; Sakomizu, *Kikanju ka no shusho kantei*, pp. 261–269; Togo, *Jidai no ichimen*, pp. 359–360. In addition to the Big Six, Kiichiro Hiranuma (chairman of the Privy Council), Sakomizu, Ikeda (General Planning Agency director), Yoshizumi (army military affairs chief), Hoshina (navy military affairs chief), and Hasunuma (grand chamberlain) attended.

88. The translation is from Butow, *Japan's Decision to Surrender*, p. 173.

89. Herbert P. Bix, *Hirohito and the Making of Modern Japan* (New York: Harper Collins, 2000), pp. 517–518.

90. Hirohito's words are reproduced in Butow, *Japan's Decision to Surrender*, pp. 175–176. Relying on *Daihonei rikugunbu* (10), which exclusively uses Takeshita's *Kimitsu sakusen nisshi*, Frank stresses that the emperor refers to the atomic bomb(s). Frank, *Downfall*, p. 296. The reference to the atomic bomb appears only in *Kimitsu sakusen nisshi*, which is based on what Anami told his brother-in-law. None of the participants (Suzuki, Togo, Toyoda, Sakomizu, or Hoshina) recalls that Hirohito referred to the atomic bombs in his speech.

91. Sakomizu, *Kikanju ka no shusho kantei*, pp. 268–269.

92. Hirohito quoted in Terasaki Hidenari and Mariko Terasaki Miller, eds., *Showa tenno dokuhakuroku* (Tokyo: Bungei shunju, 1991), p. 126. See also Bix, *Hirohito*, pp. 517–518.

93. Takeshita, "Kimitsu sakusen nisshi," p. 753; also quoted in *Daihonei rikugunbu* (10), p. 450.

94. Sanbo jicho nisshi, BKSS, p 101; Kawabe, "Sanbo jicho no nikki," p. 255; *Kawabe Torashiro Kaisoroku*, p. 158.

6. JAPAN ACCEPTS UNCONDITIONAL SURRENDER

1. Takagi Sokichi, *Shusen oboegaki* (Tokyo: Kobundo, 1948), p. 56.
2. Matsumoto Shun'ichi, "Shusen oboegaki," in *Shusen shiroku*, vol. 4, pp. 158–159; "Sangoku sengen judaka no ken," *Shusen shiroku*, vol. 4, pp. 159–160; Nishihara Masao, *Shusen no keii* (typewritten manuscript, BKSS), vol. 1, p. 141. The letter of acceptance received by Truman was slightly different in wording from the original. Harry S. Truman, *Memoirs,* vol. 1, *Year of Decisions* (Garden City, N.Y.: Doubleday, 1955), p. 427.
3. Togo, *Jidai no ichimen* (Tokyo: Hara shobo, 1989), p. 361; "Togo gaimudaijin-Mariku taishi kaidanroku," *Shusen shiroku*, vol. 4, pp. 86–90; Gaimusho, ed., *Gaiko shiryo: Nis'so' gaiko kosho kiroku no bu* (Tokyo: Gaimusho, 1946), pp. 164–166; Matsumoto, "Shusen oboegaki," *Shusen shiroku,* vol. 4, p. 85.
4. "Johokyoku sosai dan," *Shusen shiroku*, vol. 4, p. 174; "Rikugun daijin fukoku," *Shusen shiroku*, vol. 4, pp. 174–175; Kurihara Ken and Hatano Sumio, *Shusen kosaku no kiroku* (Tokyo: Kodansha, 1986), vol. 2, p. 423.
5. Hayashi Saburo, "Shusen goro no Anami san," *Sekai*, Aug. 1946, p. 164; Nishihara, *Shusen no keii*, vol. 1, pp. 139–140, 151–153; Takeshita Masahiko, "Kimitsu sakusen nikki," Gunjishigakkai, ed., *Daihonei rikugunbu senso shidohan: Kimitsu senso nisshi* (Tokyo: Kinseisha, 1998), vol. 2, pp. 753, 756–757; Hando Toshikazu, *Nihon no ichiban nagai hi*, ed. Oya Soichi (Tokyo: Kadokawa bunko, 1976), p. 31; BKSS, *Senshi sosho: Daihonei rikugunbu* (10) (Tokyo: Asagamo shinbunsha, 1975), pp. 454–456.
6. Shimomura, *Shusen hishi* (Tokyo: Kodansha, 1950), pp. 97–98; Hayashi, "Shusen goro no Anami san," p. 165; Ando Yoshiro shuki, "Shusen oboegaki," in *Shusen shiroku*, vol. 4, pp. 176–177; *Daihonei rikugunbu* (10), p. 456; *Kido Koichi nikki* (Tokyo: Tokyo daigaku shuppankai, 1966), vol. 2, p. 1224 (hereafter *Kido nikki*); Hosokawa Morisada, *Joho Tenno ni tassezu: Hosokawa nikki* (Tokyo: Isobe shobo, 1953), vol. 2, p. 419.
7. Ota Saburo shuki, "Potsudamu sengen judaku kaigai hoso," *Shusen shiroku*, vol. 4, pp. 181–182; Hasegawa Saiji dan, "Hokai no zenya," *Fujin koron*, Aug. 1947, in *Shusen shiroku*, vol. 4, pp. 183–184; "Shusen to hoso," Nihon hosokyokai hososhi, ed., *Nihon hososhi*, 2 vols. (Tokyo: Nihon hoso kyokai, 1965), vol. 2, pp. 647–648; Nihon hoso kyokai, *20 seiki hososhi* (Tokyo: Nihon hoso kyokai, 2001), vol. 2, p. 188.
8. Stimson did not say in his diary how he received the first news of Japan's conditional acceptance of the Potsdam Proclamation, but in his diary Forrestal revealed his source as the Magic decrypt. Stimson Diary, 10 Aug. 45; Forrestal Diary, 10 Aug. 45, p. 427, Mudd Library, Princeton University.
9. Joseph Ballantine, 28 April 61, p. 63, Oral History Project, Butler Library,

Columbia University; Joseph Ballantine, Diary, pp. 264–265, Joseph
Ballantine Papers, Box 1, Hoover Institution. Ballantine's account is not
corroborated by Grew and Dooman, though Dooman supports his contention that they participated in drafting the Byrnes Note. Transcript of the
NBC Interview with Dooman, Roll 2, pp. 15–16, Dooman Papers, Atomic
Bomb, Box 2, Hoover Institution. Ballantine's time sequence is fuzzy, merg-
ing what must have been two meetings, before and after Truman's crucial
meeting with his top advisers, into one.

10. For a different interpretation of the role of Ballantine and Dooman, see
Dale M. Hellegers, *We, the Japanese People: World War II and the Origins
of the Japanese Constitution,* vol. 1 (Stanford: Stanford University Press,
2001), p. 358.

11. Truman, *Memoirs,* vol. 1, p. 428; James F. Byrnes, *All in One Lifetime*
(New York: Harper and Brothers, 1958), p. 305. Whether Byrnes actually
gave this reason at the meeting is questionable, since Truman was quite
prepared to seek the end of the war without the Soviets' approval.

12. Stimson Diary, 10 Aug. 45; Forrestal Diary, 10 Aug. 45, Mudd Library,
Princeton University, p. 428.

13. Walter Brown Diary, 10 Aug. 45, Potsdam Folder 602, Clemson University.

14. Stimson Diary, 10 Aug. 45, pp. 74–75; James F. Byrnes, *Speaking Frankly*
(New York: Harper and Brothers, 1947), p. 208.

15. Stimson Diary, 10 Aug. 45; Forrestal Diary, 10 Aug. 45, Mudd Library,
Princeton University, pp. 428–430; Truman, *Memoirs,* vol. 1, p. 428.

16. Ballantine, p. 63, Oral History Project, Butler Library, Columbia University; Ballantine, Diary, p. 265, Box 1, Hoover Institution; Transcript of
NBC interview with Eugene Dooman, Roll 2, pp. 11–16; Stimson Diary,
10 Aug. 45; McCloy Diary, 11 Aug. 45. Hellegers treats Dooman's testimony with suspicion (Hellegers, *We, the Japanese People,* vol. 1, p. 358).
See also Truman, *Memoirs,* vol. 1, p. 428. After the cabinet meeting, Truman met with Congressman Mike Mansfield and Senator Warren Mag-
nuson separately to tell them about Japan's clever maneuver to retain the
emperor, and about his intention to make no concessions on unconditional
surrender. See Hellegers, *We, the Japanese People,* vol. 1, p. 151. This episode shows Truman's deep conviction on unconditional surrender.

17. Truman, *Memoirs,* vol. 1, p. 429; Forrestal Diary, 10 Aug. 45, Mudd Library, Princeton University, p. 430; John Morton Blum, *The Price of Vision: The Diary of Henry A. Wallace, 1942–1946* (Boston: Houghton Mifflin Co., 1973), 10 Aug. 45, p. 474 (hereafter *Wallace Diary*).

18. Transcript of the NBC Interview with Dooman, Roll 2, pp. 15–16.

19. Truman, A Statement, Memoirs: Foreign Policy, Atomic Bomb, Post-Presidential Memoirs, HSTL.

20. McCloy Diary, Friday, 10 Aug. 45; State-War-Navy Coordinating Committee, Minutes of the 20th Meeting, 11 Aug. 45, Xerox 1597, Marshall
Library. As for McCloy's activities, see McCloy Diary, Saturday, 11 Aug.
45.

21. Barton Bernstein, "The Perils and Politics of Surrender: Ending the War
with Japan and Avoiding the Third Atomic Bomb," *Pacific Historical Review,* 46, no. 1 (1977), 5; Bernstein, "The Atomic Bombings Reconsidered," *Foreign Affairs,* 74, no. 1 (1995), 149; Leon V. Sigal, *Fighting to a*

Finish (Ithaca: Cornell University Press, 1988), pp. 95, 246, 250; *Wallace Diary,* 10 Aug. 45, p. 474.

22. William Shirer, "What to Do with Japan," 9 July 45, source unknown, from clippings in Grew Papers, Houghton Library, Harvard University. See also the similar argument by Barner Noves, *Washington Post,* 12 July 45, Grew's clippings, Grew Papers. Walter Lippman, "Today and Tomorrow," *Washington Post,* 12 July 45; Stanley Washburn, *Washington Post,* 8 July 45; Mark Sullivan, *Washington Post,* 12 July 45; Ernest Lindley, *Washington Post,* 16 July 45, 13 Aug. 45; Lowell Mellett, *Washington Post,* 16 July 45.

23. Plumley quoted in Bernstein, "Perils and Politics of Surrender," pp. 5–6; Wherry in *Washington Post,* 4 July 45, and *New York Times,* 24 July 45; White in Ernest Lindley, "Japanese Surrender," *Washington Post,* 23 July 45; telephone memorandum of conversation between Grew and Wheeler, 2 July 45, Grew Papers, Houghton Library, Harvard University.

24. Fred Burdick to President Truman, 14 July 45, encl. copy of *Capitol Gist Service,* vol. 8, no. 25, Truman Papers, OF 190 Misc., 1945, Box 662, HSTL; see also Hellegers, *We, the Japanese People,* vol. 1, p. 320.

25. C. P. Trussel, "Many Congressmen Are Hostile to Any Leniency to Hirohito," *New York Times,* 11 Aug. 45.

26. Document 699, *RKO,* pp. 164–169; Victor Hoo Papers, Hoover Institution Archive, pp. 48–56.

27. Stalin quotes from Hoo Papers, p. 52; also see Document 699, *RKO,* p. 167. Harriman to Truman and Byrnes, Paraphrase of Navy Cable, 11 Aug. 45, to Washington, Harriman Papers, Moscow Files, 10–12 Aug. 45.

28. Harriman to Truman and Byrnes, Paraphrase of Navy Cable, 11 Aug. 45, Harriman Papers, Moscow Files, 11–12 Aug. 45.

29. W. Averell Harriman and Elie Abel, *Special Envoy to Churchill and Stalin, 1941–1946* (New York: Random House, 1975), p. 499; "Japanese Surrender Negotiations," 10 Aug. 45, Harriman Papers, Moscow Files, 10–12 Aug. 45.

30. Harriman and Abel, *Special Envoy,* p. 499; Harriman to Molotov, 11 Aug. 45, Moscow Files, 10–12 Aug. 45, Harriman Papers, Molotov to Harriman, 11 Aug. 45, ibid. (emphasis added).

31. Forrestal Diary, 10 Aug. 45, p. 429, Mudd Library, Princeton University; *Stimson Diary,* 10 Aug. 45, p. 75.

32. "Japanese Surrender Negotiations," 10 Aug. 45, Harriman Papers, Moscow Files, 10–12 Aug. 45; John R. Deane, *The Strange Alliance: The Story of Our Efforts at Wartime Co-operation with Russia* (New York: Viking Press, 1946), pp. 278–279; Robert Pickens Meiklejohn, "World War Diary at London and Moscow, March 10, 1941–February 14, 1946," vol. 2, pp. 724–745, Harriman Papers.

33. Sakomizu, *Kikanju ka no shusho kantei* (Tokyo: Kobunsha, 1965), pp. 294–296; *Kido nikki,* vol. 2, p. 1224; *Shusen shiroku,* vol. 4, pp. 187–189.

34. Matsumoto Shun'ichi, "Shusen oboegaki," *Shusen shiroku,* vol. 4, pp. 204–205; Shusen shiroku, vol. 4, pp. 201–202; Matsumoto Shun'ichi, "Shusen oboegaki," *Shusen shiroku,* vol. 4, pp. 204–205; Matsumoto Shun'ichi, *Shusenji no kaiso jakkan ni tsuite,* BKSS; Nishihara, *Shuen no keii,* vol. 1, pp. 164–167.

35. Matsumoto Shun'ichi, "Shusen oboegaki," pp. 204–205; Matsumoto Shun'ichi, *Shusenji kaiso;* Shibusawa Shin'ichi shuki, "Shusen tsuho ni tsuite," *Shusen shiroku,* vol. 4, pp. 206–207.

36. For the translation and interpretation given by the Military Affairs Bureau, see Sanbo honbu, *Haisen no kiroku,* pp. 286–287. See also *Daihonei rikugunbu* (10), pp. 474–475; Nishihara, *Shusen no keii,* vol. 1, pp. 168–173.

37. Kawabe Torashiro, *Sanbo jicho nisshi,* 26 July–2 Sept. 45, 11 Aug. 45, p. 164, BKSS; partially quoted in *Daihonei rikugunbu* (10), p. 475; Kawabe Torashiro, "Sanbo jicho no nikki," in Kawabe Torashiro, *Kawabe Torashiro Kaisoroku* (Tokyo: Mainichi shinbunsha, 1979), p. 255. Many in the military did not share Kawabe's pessimism. Vice Admiral Matome Ugaki of the Fifth Naval Air Force Command in Kyushu received a confidential telegram from the naval General Staff stressing that the war was to continue, with the warning that they should not be misled by rumors to the contrary. Ugaki Matome, *Sensoroku* (Tokyo: Hara shobo, 1996), p. 549.

38. *Daihonei rikugunbu* (10), pp. 476–477; Sanbo honbu, *Haisen no kiroku,* p. 288; "Ryo socho no joso," Kurihara and Hatano, *Shusen kosaku,* vol. 2, pp. 441–442; Nishihara, *Shusen no keii,* vol. 1, pp. 174–176; Kawabe, *Jicho nisshi,* BKSS, Aug. 45, pp. 171–172; also partially quoted in *Daihonei rikugunbu* (10), p. 477; "Jicho no nikki," p. 257.

39. *Daihonei rikugunbu* (10), pp. 477–478; "Banzu kaito to rikugun," Kurihara and Hatano, *Shusen kosaku,* vol. 2, pp. 437–438; Nishihara, *Shusen no keii,* vol. 1, pp. 191–192.

40. Takeshita, "Kimitsu sakusen nikki," pp. 757–758; Nishihara, *Shusen no keii,* vol. 1, pp. 186–188; *Daihonei rikugunbu* (10), p. 479; Sanbo honbu, *Haisen no kiroku,* pp. 366–367; Hayashi, "Shusen goro no Anami san," p. 165.

41. Hayashi, "Shusen gorono Anami san," p. 165; Hiranuma chinjutsusho, 26 Dec. 49, BKSS; "Kido Koichi chinjutsusho (2)," Kurihara and Hatano, *Shusen kosaku,* vol. 2, pp. 432–434.

42. Terasaki Hidenari and Mariko Terasaki Miller, eds., *Showa tenno dokuhakuroku* (Tokyo: Bungei shunju, 1991), p. 129; Tanaka, *Dokyumento Showa Tenno,* vol. 5, pt. 2, p. 541, quoting *Higashikuni nikki,* p. 200. Also see *Kido nikki,* vol. 2, p. 1225; Higashikuni no miya, *Watashino kiroku* (Tokyo: Toho shobo, 1947), pp. 101, 104, quoted in *Shusen shiroku,* vol. 4, pp. 244–245. Hirohito said that Prince Asaka questioned if the emperor would continue the war if the *kokutai* were not assured, to which Hirohito answered he would. This indicates that there was some dissension and criticism against Hirohito even at the conference of the imperial household.

43. Shimomura, *Shusenki,* pp. 134–138; *Shusen shiroku,* vol. 4, pp. 224–225; "Togo Shigenori chinjutsuroku (12)," Kurihara and Hatano, *Shusen kosaku,* vol. 2, pp. 450–453; "Togo gaiso kojutsu hikki: 'Shusen ni saishite,'" *Shusen shiroku,* vol. 4, pp. 226–228; *Ikeda shuki,* 12 Aug. 45, BKSS; Nishihara, *Shusen no keii,* vol. 1, pp. 180–182; Matsumoto Shun'ichi, *Shusenji no kaiso;* Togo gaisho shuki, "Shusen gaiko," *Kaizo,* Nov. 1950, p. 140; Matsumoto Shun'ichi, "Shusen oboegaki," pp. 231–232; "Matsudaira Yasumasa kojutsu yoshi," *Shusen shiroku,* vol. 4, p 232; "Kido kojutsusho (sokkiroku)," in *Shusen shiroku,* vol. 4, p. 229; *Kido*

nikki, vol. 2, p. 1225; "Kido to Baanzu kaito," Kurihara and Hatano, *Shusen kosaku*, vol. 2, p. 455.

44. "Yonai kaiso chokuwa," *Takagi nikki*, 12 Aug. 45, vol. 2, p. 927; Takagi Sokichi, *Kaigun Taisho Yonai Mitsumasa oboegaki* (Tokyo: Kojinsha, 1978), pp. 153–154.

45. Hayashi, "Shusen gorono Anami san," p. 166.

46. Kase to Togo, 11 Aug., in *Shusen shiroku*, vol. 5, pp. 5–7; Matsumoto, *Shusenji no kaiso*, BKSS; *Daihonei rikugunbu* (10), pp. 480–481; Nishihara, *Shusen no keii*, vol. 1, pp. 195–199.

47. Truman, *Memoirs*, vol. 1, pp. 433–434.

48. Wedemeyer to Hull, CM-IN-12388, 12 Aug. 45, Incoming Classified Message (Army Staff), Plans and Operations Division, "ABC" File, 1942–48, 387 Japan, Box 506, Sec. 3, RG 319 NA, Xerox 2380, Marshall Library. On August 15, the JCS planned the deployment of American troops in Dairen, but on August 18, informed by the JCS that it would take at least several days to prepare U.S. troops to land on Dairen, while Soviet troops were expected to reach it by the following day, Byrnes decided to cancel the occupation. Ibid.

49. Truman, *Memoirs*, vol. 1, p. 435.

50. Forrestal Diary, 10 Aug. 45, Mudd Library, Princeton University, pp. 429–430; Bernstein, "Perils and Politics," pp. 12–14; Bernstein, "The Atomic Bombings Reconsidered," p. 148.

51. Hull and Seeman telephone conversation, 13 Aug. 45, Verofax 1691, Item 2598, Marshall Library.

52. Okamoto to Togo, 12 Aug. 45, *Shusen shiroku*, vol. 5, pp. 9–10; Matsumoto Shun'ichi, "Shusen oboegaki," *Shusen shiroku*, vol. 5, pp. 10–11; "Matsumoto Shun'ichi shuki," Kurihara and Hatano, *Shusen kosaku*, vol. 2, p. 461; Matsumoto, *Shusenji no kaiso*, BKSS; Nishihara, *Shusen no keii*, vol. 1, pp. 215–218.

53. "Kido kokyosho," *Shusen shiroku*, vol. 5, pp. 19–20; *Kido nikki*, vol. 2, p. 1225.

54. *Daihonei rikugunbu* (10), pp. 492; Nishihara, *Shusen no keii*, vol. 1, pp. 203–205.

55. Toyoda Soemu, "Ayamarareta gozenkaigi," *Bungei shunju*, Jan. 1950, p. 58; Toyoda Soemu, *Saigo no teikoku kaigun* (Tokyo: Sekaino nihonsha, 1950), pp. 216–218; Nishihara, *Shusen no keii*, vol. 1, pp. 203–205.

56. Togo gaiso no kojutsu hikki, "Shusen ni saishite," *Shusen shiroku*, vol. 5, pp. 20–21; Nishihara, *Shusen no keii*, vol. 1, p. 205.

57. Shimomura, *Shusenki*, pp. 138–145; Abe Genki naiso dan, "Shusen naikaku," *Shusen shiroku*, vol. 5, pp. 38–39; Nishihara, *Shusen no keii*, vol. 1, pp. 206–207; *Ikeda shuki*, 13 Aug. 45.

58. Oya, *Nihon no ichiban nagai hi*, p. 36. For Sakomizu's fear of Soviet expansion, see Sakomizu Hisatsune, *Shusen no shinso* (n.p.: Dotoku kagaku kenkyujo, 1955), pp. 76–77.

59. "Inaba Masao chinjutsuroku," in Kurihara and Hatano, *Shusen kosaku*, vol. 2, p. 472; Nishihara, *Shusen no keii*, vol. 1, pp. 211–213; Takayama Nobutake, *Arao Okikatsu san o shinobu* (Takayama Nobutake, 1978), pp. 38–54. Hirohito believed that Arao was involved in the plot. See *Showa Tenno dokuhakuroku*, p. 134.

60. Sakomizu, *Kikanju ka no shusho kantei,* pp. 284–285; Sakomizu, *Shusen no shinso,* pp. 58–59; Nishihara, *Shusen no keii,* vol. 1, pp. 213–214.

61. Takeshita, "Kimitsu sakusen nikki," pp. 759–760; *Daihonei rikugunbu* (10), p. 498; "8-gatsu 13-nichi no Rikugunsho," Kurihara and Hatano, *Shusen kosaku,* vol. 2, pp. 475–476; Hayashi, "Shusen gorono Anami san," pp. 167–168; Oya, *Nihon no ichiban nagai hi,* pp. 37–38.

62. Forrestal Diary, 11 Aug. 45, Mudd Library, Princeton University, p. 432.

63. McCloy Diary, 13 Aug. 45. Takagi noted that an American broadcast threatened the use of an atomic bomb on Tokyo unless the United States received Japan's answer soon. Takagi, *Shusen oboegaki,* p. 56.

64. Odd Arne Westad, *Cold War and Revolution: Soviet-American Rivalry and the Origins of the Chinese Civil War, 1944–1946* (New York: Columbia University Press, 1993), pp. 52–53; Documents No. 708, 711, RKO, pp. 182–184, 189–192; Hoo Papers, pp. 70–74.

65. *Kido Koichi nikki: Tokyo saibanki* (Tokyo: Tokyo daigaku shuppankai, 1980), p. 422; *Kido nikki,* vol. 2, p. 1226.

66. Kase Toshikazu shuki, "Potsudamu sengen judaku made," *Sekai,* Aug. 1945, quoted in *Shusen shiroku,* vol. 5, p. 59; Sakomizu, *Kikanju ka no shusho kantei,* p. 289; Sakomizu Hisatsune, *Dainihon teikoku saigo no 4-kagetsu* (Tokyo: Oriento shobo, 1973), pp. 227–228; Shimomura, *Shusen hishi,* pp. 122–127.

67. Shimomura, *Shusenki,* pp. 148–152; Shimomura, *Shusen hishi,* pp. 122–127; Sakomizu, *Shusen no shinso,* p. 61; Nishihara, *Shusen no keii,* vol. 1, pp. 231–235; Ikeda shuki, 14 Aug. 45, "Gozenkaigi"; Toyoda, "Ayamarareta gozenkaigi," p. 60.

68. "Oi Atsushi shuki," *Shusen shiroku,* vol. 5, p. 123; Nishihara, *Shusen no keii,* vol. 1, pp. 211–213.

69. Takeshita, "Kimitsu Sakusen nikki," p. 760; Takashima Tatsuhiko, *Shusen chokuzen no togun* (typewritten manuscript, BKSS), p. 7; Fuwa Hiroshi, *Kyujo senkyo jiken* (typewritten manuscript, BKSS), pp. 54–55; Nishihara, *Shusen no keii,* vol. 1, pp. 228–229.

70. *Daihonei rikugunbu* (10), pp. 504–505; Nishihara, *Shusen no keii,* vol. 1, pp. 236–237.

71. Takeshita, "Kimiktsu sakusen nikkii," p. 762. For the ideological justification for the coup, see Ida Masataka, "Kyujo jiken ni kansuru shuki," in Nishihara, *Shusen no keii,* vol. 2, pp. 32–43; Oya, *Nihon no ichiban nagai hi,* pp. 50–51, 60–63; *Daihonei rikugunbu* (10), pp. 511–512.

72. *Daihonei rikugunbu* (10), pp. 510–512; Oya, *Nihon no ichiban nagai hi,* pp. 51–52, 77–79, 80–83; Nishihara, *Shusen no keii,* vol. 1, pp. 241/1–241/4, vol. 2, pp. 22–23; Huwa, *Kyujo senkyo jiken,* pp. 57–58; Ida Masataka, *Shuki* (typewritten manuscript, BKSS), p. 43.

73. Sakomizu Hisatsune, "Kofukuji no shinso," *Jiyu kokumin,* February Special Issue, 1946, quoted in *Shusen shiroku,* vol. 5, p. 62; Oya, *Nihon no ichiban nagai hi,* pp. 88–90, 98–100, 103–104, 109–110, 114–115. For details of the amendments, see *Shusen shiroku,* vol. 5, note 3, pp. 66–67.

74. Huwa, *Kyujo senkyo jiken,* pp. 58–59; Nishihara, *Shusen no keii,* vol. 2, pp. 23–24; "Ida Masataka shuki," *Shusen shiroku,* vol. 5, pp. 504–505; Oya, *Nihon no ichiban nagai hi,* pp. 144–149.

75. Togo to Kase, 14 Aug. 45, *Shusen shiroku,* vol. 5, pp. 73–74; Shimomura,

Shusen hishi, pp. 140–142; Oya, *Nihon no ichiban nagai hi,* pp. 155–159, 164–166.

76. Takeshita, "Kimitsu sakusen nisshi," p. 764; Oya, *Nihon no ichiban nagai hi,* pp. 169–172, 175–178, 180–181; Ida, *Shuki,* pp. 48–51; Ida, *Chinjutsusho,* (23 May 50); "Ida Masataka shuki," *Shusen shiroku,* vol. 5, pp. 507–508; Nishihara, *Shusen no keii,* vol. 2, pp. 21–22, 49–50; Huwa, *Kyujo senkyo jiken,* pp. 58–60, 66; "Shusen to hoso," pp. 644–645. For the details of the assassination of Mori, see the fascinating detective work of Iio Kenji, *Jiketsu: Mori konoe shidancho ansatsu jiken* (Tokyo: Shueisha, 1982).

77. Takeshita, "Kimitsu sakusen nikki," pp. 765–767; Oya, *Nihon no ichiban nagai hi,* pp. 190–194, 226–230; Huwa, *Kyujo senkyo jiken,* pp. 60, 64; Ida, *Shuki,* pp. 12–27, 52; Nishihara, *Shusen no keii,* vol. 2, pp. 23–24; Ida Chinjutsusho (23 May 50), BKSS.

78. Takeshita, "Kimitsu sakusen nikki," pp. 767–778. For various comments on Anami's suicide, see Takeshita chinjutsusho, pp. 7–8, BKSS; Takeshita's testimony in Nishihara, *Shusen no keii,* vol. 2, pp. 6–11; Ida, *Shuki,* pp. 18–19, also Takagi's unflattering appraisal, *Takagi nikki,* 15 Aug. 45, vol. 2, p. 928.

79. General Tanaka committed suicide on August 24 for assuming responsibility for the coup. Huwa, *Kyujo senkyo jiken,* p. 77.

80. This translation is from Robert J. C. Butow, *Japan's Decision to Surrender (Stanford: Stanford University Press, 1954),* Appendix 1, p. 248. For the Japanese text, see *Shusen shiroku,* vol. 5, pp. 70–71, and its translation into contemporary Japanese, pp. 86–88. Also see "Shusen to hoso," pp. 646–647; *20 seiki hososhi,* vol. 1, p. 194.

81. "Naikaku kokuyu," *Shusen shiroku,* vol. 5, pp. 145–146.

82. "Rikukaigunjin ni tamawaritaru chokugo," *Shusen shiroku,* vol. 5, p. 115.

83. Truman, *Memoirs,* vol. 1, pp. 435–436, 438; Walter Brown Diary, Potsdam Folder 602, Clemson Library; Leahy Diary, August 14, Library of Congress; Byrnes, *Speaking Frankly,* p. 210.

7. AUGUST STORM

1. Truman to Stalin, 15 Aug. 45, RGASPI, f. 558, op. 1, d. 372, l. 93 (Russian trans.), l. 94 (English original); Truman to Attlee, 14 Aug. 45, Papers of Harry S. Truman, SMOF, Naval Aide to the President, 1945–1953, Box 7, HSTL; *Pravda,* 16 Aug. 45, quoted in *Krasnoznamennyi dal'nevostochnyi: istoriia krasnoznamennogo Dal'nevostochnogo voennogo okruga* (Moscow: Voennoe izdatel'stvo, 1985), p. 221.

2. BKSS, *Senshi Sosho: Kantokuen, Shusenji no taiso sen* (Tokyo: Asagumo shinbunsha, 1974), pp. 453–455, 459–460 [hereafter Kantogun (2)]; Kawabe Torashiro, *Sanbo jicho nisshi,* 26 July–25 Sept. 45 (handwritten manuscript, BKSS), pp. 188, 198, 201; "Sanbo jicho no nikki," Kawabe Torashiro, *Kawabe Torashiro Kaisoroku* (Tokyo: Mainich shinbunsha, 1979), pp. 261, 263, 265; Hando Kazutoshi, *Soren ga Manshu ni shinko shita natsu* (Tokyo: Bungen shunju, 1999), pp. 235–237.

3. *Krasnoznamennyi dal'nevostochnyi*, pp. 222–225; Document 366, VO, 7 (1), pp. 377, 383–384; also see Hull's telegram to MacArthur, No. 1532, 17 Aug. 45, War Department Classified Message Service, Truman Papers, "Japan Surrender 2 of 4," Naval Aide Files, 1945–53, Box 13, HSTL.

4. Vasilevskii to Yamada, 6 A.M., 17 Aug. 45, in *Daiichi kyokuto homengun no sento nisshi*. This is a document obtained by *Sankei shinbun* from the Soviet archive, translated into Japanese. I am thankful to Professor Hatano for making this valuable document available to me. Hereafter it will be referred to as *Daiichi kyokuto homengun*. Pavlychev to Kuznetsov, 17 Aug. 45, *Daiichi kyokuto homengun*.

5. *Kantogun (2)*, pp. 466–467; 20 Aug. Report, *Daiichi kyokuto homengun*.

6. Viktor Karpov, *Plenniki Stalina: Sibirskoe internirovanie Iaponskoi armii, 1945–1956 gg.* (Kiev-Lvov, 1997), p. 23.

7. Ivanov's order, in *Daiichi kyokuto homengun*, p. 5; Report of Military Action, 18 Aug. 45, *Daiichi kyokuto homengun*, pp. 17–18; Vasilevskii to the commander of the Transbaikal Front and the commander of the First Far Eastern Front, coded telegram no. 9023, 18 Aug. 45, *Daiichi kyokuto homengun*, p. 13; Vasilevskii to Bulganin and Antonov, *Daiichi kyokuto homengun*, also Document 343, VO, vol. 7, pt. 1, pp. 355–356; Vasilevskii, Trotsenko's order, Document 353, VO, vol. 7, pt. 1, p. 365.

8. Nakayama Takashi, *1945nen natsu: saigono nissosen* (Tokyo: Kokusho kankokai, 1995), p. 79. For the Soviet operation in southern Sakhalin, see David. M. Glantz, *Soviet Operational and Tactical Combat in Manchuria, 1945, August Storm* (London: Frank Cass, 2003), pp. 242–277.

9. B. N. Slavinskii, *Sovetskaia okkupatsiia Kuril'skikh ostrov (avgust-sentiabr' 1945 goda): dokumental'noe issledovanie* (Moscow: TOO "Lotos," 1993), p. 57.

10. Glantz, *Soviet Operational and Tactical Combat in Manchuria*, pp. 250, 267–269; Nakayama, *1945nen natsu*, pp. 102, 104, 113, 143–149; *Krasnoznamennyi dal'nevostochnyi*, pp. 230–234.

11. Slavinskii, *Sovetskaia okkupatsiia*, pp. 61–61, Glantz, *Soviet Operational and Tactical Combat in Manchuria*, pp. 258–260.

12. Hattori Tokushiro, *Daitoasenso zenshi* (Tokyo: Hara shobo, 1965), p. 975; Nakayama, *1945nen natsu*, pp. 137–144. For the Soviet account of the battle in Maoka, see Slavinskii, *Sovetskaia okkupatsiia*, p. 62; Glantz, *Soviet Operational and Tactical Combat in Manchuria*, p. 273.

13. Slavinskii, *Sovetskaia okkupatsiia*, p. 62; Glantz, *Soviet Operational and Tactical Combat in Manchuria*, pp. 273–274.

14. "Meeting of the United States and Soviet Chiefs of Staff, Thursday, July 26, 3 P.M.," *FRUS: Potsdam*, vol. 2, pp. 410–411.

15. Slavinskii, *Sovetskaia okkupatsiia*, pp. 73, 81; No. 10542, 15 Aug. 45, MO TsVMA, f. 129, d. 26770, l. 119; Document No. 402, VO, vol 7, pt. 2, p. 24.

16. Marshall to Deane, 14 Aug. 45; "Exchange of Notes between Swiss Charge and Secretary of State," "Japanese Acceptance of Potsdam Declaration," Harriman Papers, Moscow Files, 13–16 Aug. 45, Library of Congress.

17. Sakhalinskii kraevedchekii arkhiv, f. Gnechko, *Zhurnal boevykh deistvii voisk Kamchatskogo oboronitel'nogo raiona po ovladeniiu ostrovami severnoi chasti Kuril'skoi griady v period 15–31.8.1945 g.* (hereafter

Gnechko, *Zhurnal*), pp. 1–3, 9–11. This is the report of the Kuril operation written by Gnechko. See also Iumashev's order, Boevaia direktiva MR/SP, 15.8.45, attached in Gnecko, *Zhurnal* (no page number).

18. Slavinskii, *Sovetskaia okkupatsiia*, pp. 83–84; Nakayama, *1945nen natsu*, p. 176; Gnechko, *Zhurnal*, pp. 5–6, 9–11. For the Soviet operation plan, see Glantz, *Soviet Operational and Tactical Combat in Manchuria*, pp. 286–293.

19. Slavinskii, *Sovetskaia okkupatsiia*, p. 87; Glantz, *Soviet Operational and Tactical Combat in Manchuria*, pp. 293–294.

20. For the battle of Shimushu, see Slavinskii, *Sovetskaia okkupatsiia*; Nakayama, *1945nen natsu*; John Stephan, *Kuril Islands: Russo-Japanese Frontier in the Pacific* (Oxford: Clarendon Press, 1974), pp. 158–164; V. N. Bagrov, *Iuzhno-Sakhalinskaia i Kuril'skaia operatsii (Avgust 1945 goda)*(Moscow: Voennoe izdatel'stvo, 1959), pp. 82–101; "Otchetnye dokumenty po zakhvatu Kuril'skoi griady," MO TsVMA, f. 129, d. 26770; Document 403, *VO*, vol. 7, pt. 2, pp. 23–32.

21. See Slavinskii, *Sovetskaia okkupatsiia*, pp. 91–103; Nakayama, *1945nen natsu*, pp. 180–200; Gnechko, *Zhurnal*, pp. 13–29; Tsutsumi Fusaki, *Kitachishima heidan no shusen* (typewritten manuscript, BKSS); Interview with Iwao Sugino, handwritten manuscript, *Chishima sakusen choshu shiryo*, vol. 8, BKSS; Interview with Risaburo Takuma, Kyushiro Kawada, *Hoppogun, Dai5homengun Kankei choshuroku*, BKSS.

22. Gnechko, *Zhurnal*, p. 6; Slavinskii, *Sovetskaia okkupatsiia*, p. 80; Nakayama, *1945nen natsu*, p. 170. Glantz, who uncritically uses earlier Soviet accounts but ignores Slavinskii, Soviet archival sources, and Japanese sources, provides a rosy picture of the battle that favors the Soviets. For instance, he writes: "By 0500 hours the detachment's main force had completed the landing without firing a single shot or losing a single soldier." Glantz, *Soviet Operational and Tactical Combat in Manchuria*, p. 294.

23. See Richard Frank, *Downfall: The End of the Imperial Japanese Empire* (New York: Random House, 1999), chaps. 8, 11, 13, and 20. The number of troops comes from p. 203, and the quote comes from p. 343.

24. MacArthur to Deane, 19 Aug. 45, "Japan Surrender 2 of 4," Truman Papers, Naval Aide Files, 1945–53, Box 13, HSTL; John R. Deane, *The Strange Alliance: The Story of Our Efforts at Wartime Co-operation with Russia* (New York: Viking Press, 1946), pp. 281–282. Deane confuses Shimushu for Shimushiri. This confusion indicates how little the Americans were concerned about the Kuril operation. See MacArthur to Deane, 23 Aug. 45, C35915, War Department Classified Message Center, Incoming Classified Message, "Japan Surrender 3 of 4," Papers of Harry S. Truman, Naval Aide Files, 1945–53, Box 13, HSTL.

25. Deane's Letter to Antonov, 15 Aug. 45, Harriman Papers, Moscow Files, 13–16 Aug. 45, Library of Congress; Memo for Record, OPD, 17 Aug. 45, OPD 336 TS, Case 132, Box 144, RG 165, NA; Antonov to Deane, 16 Aug. 45, Harriman Papers, Moscow Files, 13–16 Aug. 45, Library of Congress.

26. Telephone conversation between General Hull and Admiral Cooke, 1733, 16 Aug. 45, OPD, Executive File #17, item 35A, Folder #2, RG 165, NA; Marshall to Deane and MacArthur, 16 Aug. 45, OPD 336 TS, Case 132,

356 Notes to Page 265

Box 144, RG 165, NA; Memo for Record, OPD, 17 Aug. 45; Memo for Record, OPD, 18 Aug. 45, OPD 336 TS, Case 132, Box 144, RG 165, NA.

27. At 12:30 P.M. Washington time on August 9, which was after the Soviet tanks rolled into Manchuria, General Arnold of the army air force sent a top-secret telegram to the commanding general of the Alaskan Advance Command Post, repeating exactly the same demarcation line that had been agreed on at Potsdam. Arnold to Commanding General of the Alaskan Advance Command Post (Adak, Alaska), 9 Aug. 45, Records of the U.S. Joint Chiefs of Staff, Central Decimal File, 1942–45, CCS, 381 Japan (10-4-43), Sec. 4, USSR Collaboration against Japan, RG 218, NA; CCS, Japan (10-4-43), Sec. 9, USSR Collaboration against Japan, RG 218, NA. For the Joint Chiefs of Staff's order to Nimitz, see Joint Chiefs of Staff 1467/1, Instrument for the Surrender of Japan, Report by the Joint Staff Planners, 13 Aug. 45, Entry 421, Box 505, RG 165, NA; Memorandum for the SWNCC, "Instruments for the Surrender of Japan," SM-2866, Japan (2-7-45), Sec. 2, Unconditional Surrender of Japan, Box 137, RG 367, NA.

28. Joint Chiefs of Staff, Instruments for the Surrender of Japan, General Order No. 1, Joint Chiefs of Staff 1467/2, 17 Aug. 45, Top Secret ABC File, ABC, 387 Japan (15 Feb. 45), Box 504, RG 165, NA; "Unconditional Surrender of Japan," Enclosure, General Order No. 1, Military and Naval, ABC 387, Japan (2-7-45), Sec. 2–4, Box 137, NA, RG 218; General Order No. 1, Military and Naval, LM 54, SWNCC, Case File 19, 23 Sept. 44–Dec. 48, Reel 3, NA, RG 59; Appendix D, Corrigendum to Joint Chiefs of Staff 1275 (Washington), OPD, Entry 421, Box 505, RG 165, NA. Appendix E stipulates: "In accordance with the means, priorities and schedules, prescribed by the Supreme Allied (United States) Command, evacuate all Japanese armed forces personnel and their civilian auxiliaries from . . . (4) Kurile Islands (Chishima)." Appendix E, Corrigendum to Joint Chiefs of Staff 1275 (Washington), p. 13, OPD, Entry 421, Box 505, RG 165, NA. Incidentally, it also stipulates: "Prohibit and prevent in all territories listed in the Article: (1) the forced evacuation of any non-Japanese inhabitants; (2) the harming of the inhabitants or the damaging of their property; (3) the removal of animals, stores of food, forage, fuel or other provisions and commodities; and (4) pillaging, looting or unauthorized damage of any kind." Marc Gallichio asserts that it was Colonel Bonesteel who wrote the first draft of this order. Marc Gallichio, "The Kuriles Controversy: U.S. Diplomacy in the Soviet-Japan Border Dispute, 1941–1956," *Pacific Historical Review*, 60, no. 1 (1991): 83–84. According to Gallichio, although Bonesteel followed the demarcation line agreed upon at Potsdam, "his omission of the islands from the general order may be attributable more to design than [to] accident." Ibid., p. 84.

29. Lincoln's memorandum, 16 Aug. 45, OPD 336 TS, #126, Box 144, RG 165, NA; Stimson to Grew (undated), OPD, 336 TS (Section III), RG 165, NA; "U.S. Positions with Regard to General Soviet Intentions for Expansion," ABC, 092 USSR (15 Nov. 44), RG 165, NA; "Memorandum concerning U.S. Post-War Pacific Bases," Attachment in Hull's Message to Leahy, 3 July 45, and Lincoln, "Memorandum," 16 Aug. 45, OPD, 336 TS, #126, Box 144, RG 165, NA; Stimson to the President, 16 July 45,

FRUS: Potsdam, vol. 2, p. 1323; also see Gallichio, "The Kuriles Controversy," p. 80.

30. Gallichio, "The Kuriles Controversy," p. 84. Gallichio's assertion is based on Joint War Plans Committee, 264/8, 10 Aug. 45, CCS, 386.2, Japan (4-9-45), Sec. 4, RG 218, NA.

31. Gallichio, "The Kuriles Controversy," p. 84.

32. Minutes of Meetings of SWNCC, 1944–1947, SWNCC minutes, 21st meeting, 12 Aug. 45, T1194, NA; also Xerox 1597, Marshall Library; Draft: Report by Mr. Dunn, SWNCC Case File 19–23 Sept. 1944–Dec. 45, LM 54, Roll 3, RG 59, NA.

33. Bruce Cumings, *The Origins of the Korean War,* vol. 1: *Liberation and the Emergence of Separate Regimes, 1945–1947* (Princeton: Princeton University Press, 1981), pp. 120–121.

34. Hull and Cooke, Telephone Conversation, 12:00, 11 Aug. 45, OPD, Executive File #17, Item 35a, Folder #2, Entry 422, Box 101, RG 165, NA; McFarland's Memorandum for SWNCC, 14 Aug. 45, LM, SWNCC, Case File 19, 23 Sept. 45–Dec. 48, Reel 3, RG 59, NA; Hull and Cooke, Telephone Conversation, 13:40, 11 Aug. 45, OPD, Executive File #17, Item 35a, Folder #2, Entry 422, Box 101, RG 165, NA.

35. "Enclosure 'B'" Draft, LM54, SWNCC, Case File 19, 23 Sept. 44–Dec. 48, Reel 3, RG 59, NA. This policy followed George Lincoln's recommendation on August 12, which stated: "On Dairen, all we can say is 'The U.S. proposes to seize control immediately in the Japan Sea and the Yellow Sea, including the Gulf of Chihli, of U.S. naval forces and to secure key ports around the Yellow Sea," Lincoln's memorandum for McCloy, 12 Aug. 45, ABC, Japan 387 (15 Feb. 45), RG 165, NA.

36. Joint Chiefs of Staff to MacArthur, Nimitz, Wedemeyer, 15 Aug. 45, Plans and Operation Division, ABC Decimile File 1942–48, 387 Japan, RG 319, NA, Xerox 2380, Marshall Library. Interestingly, Appendix B for the memorandum, "Planning of Early Surrender of Japan," includes Otomari (Sakhalin) as one of the points that the United States was thinking of occupying. See Appendix B, Directives to Theater Commander concerning Operations upon Surrender of Japan Prior to Olympic, 17 Aug. 45, OPD, Entry 421, Box 505, RG 165, NA.

37. Document No. 363, Ministerstvo inostrannykh del SSSR, Perepiska predsedatelia soveta ministrov SSSR c prezidentami SShA i prem'erministrami Velikobritanii vo vremia Velikoi Otechestvennoi Voiny, 1941–1945 pp. [hereafter *Perepiska*] (Moscow: Gosudarstvennoe izd-vo politicheskoi literatury, 1957), vol. 2, pp. 263–264; RGASPI, f. 558, op. 1, d. 372, ll. 95–108; Stalin to Truman, trans., and the Russian original, Papers of Harry S. Truman, Files of the White House Naval Aide, HSTL; also ABC, Japan 387 (15 Feb. 45), Sec. 4, Box 506, RG 165, NA. For Stalin's telegram to Gromyko containing his answer to Truman, and the draft with the handwritten revision, see RGASPI, f. 558, op. 1, d. 372, ll. 109–110, 111 (emphasis added).

38. Document 633, *VO,* vol. 7, pt. 2, pp. 259–260.

39. Truman to Stalin, 17 Aug. 45, Truman Papers, Files of the White House Naval Aide, HSTL; also ABC, Japan 387 (15 Feb. 45), Box 506, RG 165,

NA; Document 364, *Perepiska,* vol. 2, p. 264. Actually, the first draft of Truman's reply included only his agreement to modify Order No. 1 to include the Kurils in the area where the Japanese forces were to surrender to the Soviet commander. Only in the second draft was the request for airbase rights added. ABC, 387, Japan (15 Feb. 45), Sec. 1-B, RG 165, NA.

40. Lincoln's memorandum, 16 Aug. 45, OPD 336 TS, #126, Box 144, RG 165, NA. Given the importance of Stalin's August 16 letter, which touched on such crucial issues as Dairen and Hokkaido, it is strange that no archival evidence has turned up about internal discussion of the letter.

41. "Occupation and Control of Japan in the Post-Defeat Period," ABC, 357 Japan (15 Feb. 45), Historical Documents Jap. Surrender 1945, RG 165, NA.

42. Lincoln and Gardner, Telephone Conversation, 18 Aug. 45, OPD, Executive File #17, item 35a, Folder #2, Entry 422, Box 101, RG 165, NA; McCarthy to Chief of Staff, 18 Aug. 45, Xerox 2380, Marshall Library.

43. Antonov to Vasilevskii, No. 145653, 20 Aug. 45, Volkogonov Papers, Reel 4, Library of Congress; Vasilevskii to Stalin (with a copy to Antonov), 20 Aug. 45, Volkogonov Papers, Reel 5, Library of Congress.

44. Draft Message, MacArthur and Nimitz, Info Wedemeyer, from Joint Chiefs of Staff, Microfilm 2350, Marshall Library; Cumings, *The Origins of the Korean War,* vol. 1, p. 121.

45. For instance, see Wada Haruki, "Nisso senso," in Hara Teruyuki and Togawa Tsuguo, eds., *Koza: Surabu no sekai,* vol. 8, *Surabu to Nihon* (Tokyo: Kobundo, 1995), p. 123; Wada Haruki, *Hopporyodo mondai; rekishi to mirai* (Tokyo: Asahi shinbunsha, 1999), p. 174.

46. Telegram 14/III from Vasilevskii and Trotsenko to Meretskov, 18 Aug. 45, Volkogonov Papers, Reel 4, Library of Congress; Document 405, *VO,* vol. 7, pt. 2, p. 36. "Shimushiru" referred to in this telegram must be the northern limit of the operation, since Shimushiri was in the central part of the Kurils. Slavinskii dates this telegram August 19 but does not cite his source. A photocopy in the Volkogonov papers clearly indicates the issuing date as August 18. Vasilevskii's report to the supreme commander (Stalin) on the conditions on August 17 also includes the exact same order. See Document 343, 18 Aug. 45, *VO,* vol. 7, pt. 1, pp. 355–356. Therefore, Stalin's order must have been issued on or before August 17, before he received Truman's answer. For operational plans see Document 343, *VO,* vol. 7, pt 1, p. 356; Documents, 406–409, *VO,* vol. 7, pt. 2, pp. 37–40.

47. Antonov to Vasilevskii, No. 14653, Volkogonov Papers, Reel 4, Library of Congress (italics added).

48. Vasilevskii's handwritten order, 21 Aug. 45, Volkogonov Papers, Reel 5, Library of Congress; Voroshilov to Commanders of the First and Second Far Eastern Fronts, Pacific Fleet, Air Force, 21 Aug. 45, Vasilevskii and Trotsenko's Order No. 20 (14726), 21 Aug. 45, "Zhurnal boevykh deistvii shtaba TOF. BFKP 5 'Skala,'" MO TsVMA, f. 129, d. 17752, ll. 149–150; Staff of the Pacific Fleet to Commander of the 16th Army, 21 Aug. 45, MO TsVMA, f. 79 (Sekretariat NKVMF), d. 38941.

49. Stalin to Truman, 22 Aug. 45, the English translation and the Russian original, Truman Papers, Files of the White House, Naval Aide, HSTL; Stalin to Truman, 22 Aug. 45, Harriman Papers, Moscow Files, 22–23 Aug. 45,

Library of Congress; also Molotov to Gromyko, RGASPI, f. 558, op. 1, d. 372, ll. 111–112; Document 365, *Perepiska,* vol. 2, p. 265.

50. Memorandum for General Hull, 21 Aug. 45, OPD, Executive File #17, Item #10, Navy Liaison (Folder #2), Col. McCarthy, Box 97, RG 165, NA.

51. Karpov, *Plenniki Stalina,* pp. 36–37.

52. Japanese Imperial General Headquarters to MacArthur, 24 Aug. 45, War Department Classified Message Center, Incoming Classified Message, "Japan Surrender 3 of 4," Papers of Harry S. Truman, Naval Aide Files 1945–53, Box 13, HSTL.

53. Ivanov to Iumashev, 27 Aug. 45, MO TsVMA, f. 129, d. 17752, l. 197; Dmitrii Volkogonov, *I. V. Stalin: Triomf i tragediia; politicheskii portret* (Moscow: Novosti), vol. 2, pp. 18–19; Document 635, *VO,* vol. 7, pt. 2, p. 263; Deane to War Department, 25 Aug. 45, War Department Classified Message Center, Incoming Classified Message, Xerox 2029, Marshall Library; Deane, *The Strange Alliance,* p. 281.

54. Telephone conversation, Hull and Cooke, 0823 (23 Aug. 45), Executive File #7, Item #35a, Folder #1, "Telephone Conversations (5 Aug. 45–25 Aug. 45)," RG 165, NA.

55. Harrison A. Gerhardt [Colonel, General Staff Corps, Executive to Assistant Secretary of War], Memorandum for the Assistant Chief of Staff, Operations, 23 Aug. 45, OPD 336TS, #126, Box 144, RG 165, NA.

56. Telephone Conversation, Hull and Cooke, 1710, 23 Aug. 45, OPD, Executive File #7, Item #35a, Folder #1, "Telephone Conversations (6 Aug. 45–25 Aug. 45)," RG 165, NA; also OPD 336TS, #126, Box 144, RG 165, NA. Etorofu and Kunashiri are the two adjacent islands, unless one counts Shikotan. But between Shikotan and Hokkaido was the Habomai group. What Cooke meant by two adjacent islands in addition to Etorofu is not clear, but his ignorance of geography indicates America's lack of interest in this issue.

57. Hull's memorandum for the Assistant Secretary of War, 24 Aug. 45, OPD 336TS, #126, Box 144, RG 165, NA; Telephone Conversation, Lincoln and Gerhard, 24 Aug. 45, in ibid.

58. Harriman's Draft Telegram to Byrnes (unsent), 19 Aug. 45, Harriman Papers, Moscow Files, 19–21 Aug. 45, Library of Congress; Byrnes to Harriman, 24 Aug. 45, Harriman Papers, Moscow Files, 22–23 Aug. 45, Library of Congress; Harriman's letter to Molotov, 24 Aug. 45, AVP RF, f. Referetura Iaponii, op. 29, d. 2, pap. 269, ll. 16–17; AVP RF, f. Molotova, op. 7, por. 743, pap. 47, delo Am-110-Iag, ll. 61–62.

59. Stalin and Antonov to Vasilevskii, Purkaev, Meretskov, and Iumashev, 18 Aug. 45, Volkogonov Papers, Reel 5, Library of Congress.

60. Vyshinskii to Harriman, 25 Aug. 45, AVP RF, f. Molotova, op. 7, por. 743, pap. 47, delo Am-110-Iag, Perepiska s Amerikanskim Pravitel'stvom po Iaponii, l. 63.

61. Harriman to Vyshinskii, 26 Aug. 45, AVP RF, f. Molotova, op. 7, por. 743, pap. 47, delo Am-110-Iag, Perepiska s Amerikanskim Pravitel'stvom po Iaponii, l. 68; also AVP RF. referatura po Iaponii, op. 29, d. 2, pap. 269, l. 19; Harriman to Byrnes, Paraphrase of Embassy Cable to Department #3073, 27 Aug. 45, Harriman Papers, Moscow Files, 24–27 Aug. 45, Library of Congress; Deane, *Strange Alliance,* p. 282.

62. Harriman to Molotov, 18 Aug. 45, RGASPI, f. 558, op. 1, d. 372, l. 112 (Russian trans.), l. 113 (English original).

63. William Craig, *Fall of Japan* (New York: Dial Press, 1967), pp. 204–217; Kawabe, "Sanbo jicho no nikki," pp. 265, 267–275.

64. William Manchester, *American Caesar: Douglas MacArthur, 1880–1964* (Boston: Little Brown and Co., 1978), pp. 441–442 (quote p. 441); Deane to Antonov, 21 Aug. 45, Harriman Papers, Moscow Files, Aug. 22–23, Library of Congress.

65. Deane to CINCPAC [commander in chief, Pacific Fleet], 26 Aug. 45, Harriman Papers, Moscow Files, 24–27 Aug. 45, Library of Congress; Deane to War Department, MX 5417, War Department Classified Message Center, Incoming Classified Message, "Japan Surrender 3 of 4," Papers of Harry S. Truman, Naval Aide File, 1945–53, HSTL.

66. Memorandum of Conversation, Kremlin, 27 Aug. 45, Harriman Papers, 24–27 Aug. 45, Library of Congress; also see Harriman to Byrnes, 29 Aug. 45, Department of State, Dean to War Department, MX 25430, 27 Aug. 45, Incoming Telegram, Papers of Harry S. Truman, Naval Aide File, "Japan Surrender 4 of 4, Box 13, HSTL; MacArthur to Deane, WARX 56898, 29 Aug. 45, War Department Classified Message Center, Outgoing Message, Papers of Harry S. Truman, "Japan Surrender 4 of 4," Naval Aide File, Box 13, HSTL; Hull to Deane, 29 Aug. 45, ABC 387, Japan (15 Feb. 45), Sec. 1-C, RG 165, NA (also in War Department Incoming Classified Messages, Xerox 2029, F. 52, Marshall Library).

67. White House Record, "Occupation of Kurile Islands by Russians," 22 Aug. 45, Papers of Harry S. Truman, Naval Aide File, "Stalin to Truman," Box 1, HSTL.

68. Personal message from the President to Generalissimo Stalin, Harriman Papers, Moscow Files, 24–27 Aug. 45, Library of Congress (italics added); Document 366, *Perepiska*, vol. 2, pp. 265–266.

69. Stalin to Truman, 30 Aug. 45 (English trans. and the Russian original), Papers of Harry S. Truman, Files of the White House Naval Aide, HSTL; Document 367, *Perepiska*, vol. 2, pp. 266–267. See David R. Jones, "The Rise and Fall of Aeroflot: Civil Aviation in the Soviet Union, 1920–1991," in Robin Highan, John T. Greenwood, and Von Hardesty, eds., *Russian Aviation and Air Power in the Twentieth Century* (London: Frank Cass Publishers, 1998), pp. 236–268, quoted in High S. Cunningham, http://www.cyberussr.com/rus/aeroflot.html.

70. Otchet po okkupatsii ostrovov Kuril'skoi griady, provedennoi v period 23 avgusta-5 sentiabria 1945 g., MO TsVMA, f. 129, d. 1777, ll. 3, 5; Slavinskii, *Sovetskaia okkupatsiia*, pp. 105, 106 (quoting from V. Akshinskii, *Kuril'skii desant* [Petropavlovsk-Kamchatkii, 1984], p. 25); Gnechko, *Zhurnal*, p. 29; Tsutsumi, *Kitachishima heidan no shusen*, pp. 38–39.

71. Gnechko, *Zhurnal*, pp. 29–30; Slavinskii, *Sovetskaia okkupatsiia*, pp. 106–108; Tsutsumi, *Kitachishima heidan no shusen*, pp. 41–42.

72. Vasilevskii to Iumashev, Document 415, VO, vol. 7, pt. 2, p. 43; Vice Admiral Andreev's report (handwritten draft copy), "Dopolneniia i zamechaniia shtaba STOF k otchetu komanduiushchego operatsiei po okkupatsii Kuril'skoi griady" [hereafter Otchet Andreeva], p. 1, Volkogonov Papers, Reel 5, Library of Congress; Slavinskii, *Sovetskaia okkupatsiia*, pp. 68, 69;

"Zhurnal boevykh deistvii shtaba TOF. BFKP 'Skala,'" MO TsVMA, f. 129, d. 17752, ll. 180–181.

73. "Otchet po okkupatsii ostrovov Kuril'skioi griady," MO TsVMA, f. 129, d. 17777, l. 4, quoted in Slavinskii, *Sovetskaia okkupatsiia*, pp. 69–71.

74. Gnechko, *Zhurnal*, p. 31; Slavinskii, *Sovetskaia okkupatsiia*, pp. 108–110.

75. Gnechko, *Zhurnal*, pp. 31–34; Slavinskii, *Sovetskaia okkupatsiia*, pp. 110–113.

76. Tsutsumi, *Kitachishima heidan no shusen*, pp. 42–43; Suizu Mitsuru, *Hoporyodo kaiketsu no kagi* (Tokyo: Kenkosha, 1987), pp. 22–24.

77. Otchet Andreeva, p. 2; Slavinskii, *Sovetskaia okkupatsiia*, p. 115.

78. Otchet Andreeva, pp. 2–3; "Dopolneniia i zamechaniia, Shtaba SVF po otchetu komanduiushchego operatsiei po okkupatsii Kuril'skoi griady" (hereafter "Dopolneniia i zamechaniia"), MO TsVMA, f. 129, d. 26770, l. 292; Slavinskii, *Sovetskaia okkupatsiia*, p. 115.

79. Otchet Andreeva, p. 4; "Dopolneniia i zamechaniia," l. 294; Slavinskii, *Sovetskaia okkupatsiia*, p. 115. Slavinskii's source, "Dopolneniia i zamezhaniia," which comes from MO TsVMA, f. 129, d. 26770, l. 292, is in all likelihood the same document as Otchet Andreeva in the Volkogonov Papers. The crucial question is the date of completion of the operation in this order. According to Slavinskii, it was September 3, but in my copy it was clearly September 2.

80. Otchet Andreeva, p. 3; "Dopolneniia i zamechaniia," l. 293; Slavinskii, *Sovetskaia okkupatsiia*, pp. 117–118; *Warerano Hopporyodo: soren senryo hen* (Sapporo: Chishima Habomai shoto kyojusha renmei, 1988), p. 153.

81. Otchet Andreeva, p. 3; "Dopolneniia i zamechaniia," l. 293; Slavinskii, *Sovetskaia okkupatsiia*, pp. 118, 119.

82. Slavinskii, *Sovetskaia okkupatsiia*, p. 120; Nakayama, *1945nen natsu*, p. 210; *Warerano Hopporyodo: Soren senryo hen*, p. 177.

83. Document 403, VO, vol. 7, pt. 2, p. 33; Slavinskii, *Sovetskaia okkupatsiia*, pp. 121–124.

84. Manchester, *American Caeser*, pp. 445, 448.

85. Truman, *Memoirs*, vol. 1, pp. 460–463.

86. "Obrashchenie tov. I. V. Stalina k narodu," 2 Sept. 45, Ministerstvo inostrannykh del SSSR, Vtoroi Dal'nevostochnyi otdel Istoriko-diploma-ticheskoe upravlenie, *Sbornik osnovnykh dokumentov po voprosam sovetsko-iaponskikh otnoshenii (1954–1972)* (Moscow: Ministerstvo inostrannykh del SSSR, 1973), p. 911; *Pravda*, 3 Sept. 45. For the original draft with revisions, see AVP RF, f. Molotova, op. 7, por. 901, pap. 55, l. 4.

87. *Sbornik osnovnykh dokumentov po voprosam sovetsko-iaponskikh otnoshenii*, p. 912. For a more detailed discussion, see Tsuyoshi Hasegawa, *The Northern Territories Dispute* (Berkeley: University of California, Berkeley, International and Area Studies Publication, 1998), vol. 2, chap. 14; Tsuyoshi Hasegawa, *Hopporyodo mondai to nichiro kankei* (Tokyo: Chikama shobo, 2000), chap. 1. "By force and greed" is the expression in the Cairo Declaration that referred to the territories Japan had acquired by war and aggression.

88. *Sbornik osnovnykh dokumentov po voprosam sovetsko-iaponskikh otnoshenii*, p. 912.

89. Otchet Andreeva, pp. 4–5, 6; Slavinskii, *Sovetskaia okkupatsiia*, pp. 121–122.
90. Slavinskii, *Sovetskaia okkupatsiia*, pp. 123–124.

CONCLUSION

1. Chairman's Office, *United States Strategic Bombing Survey, Summary Report (Pacific War)* (Washington, D.C.: U.S. Government Printing Office, 1946), p. 26. See Gar Alperovitz, *The Decision to Use the Atomic Bomb* (New York: Vintage Books, 1996), pp. 4, 321, 368–369, 464, 465.
2. Barton Bernstein, "Compelling Japan's Surrender without the A-Bomb, Soviet Entry, or Invasion: Reconsidering the U.S. Bombing Survey's Early-Surrender Conclusion," *Journal of Strategic Studies*, vol. 18, no. 2 (June 1995), pp. 101–148.
3. Ibid., p. 105.
4. Sadao Asada, "The Shocks of the Atomic Bomb and Japan's Decision to Surrender: A Reconsideration," *Pacific Historical Review*, 67, no. 4 (1998): 510–511.
5. Bernstein, "Compelling Japan's Surrender," p. 129.
6. Richard Frank, *Downfall: The End of the Imperial Japanese Empire* (New York: Random House, 1999), pp. 343–348.
7. The seven sources include Suzuki at the August 9 cabinet meeting, Shimomura on August 10, Togo at the August 10 imperial conference, Yonai on August 12, Sakurai at the August 13 cabinet meeting, Hirohito to three marshals on August 14, and the cabinet's statement on August 15.
8. *Asahi shinbun*, 11 Aug. 45, quoted in Kato Norihiro, *Amerika no kage: sengo saiken* (Tokyo: Kodansha, 1995), p. 291.
9. Ibid., pp. 290–292.
10. Gilbert Rozman, *Japan's Response to the Gorbachev Era, 1985–1991: A Rising Superpower Views a Declining One* (Princeton: Princeton University Press, 1992), pp. 12–13.
11. Asada, "The Shocks," p. 487.

Acknowledgments

This book was written in collaboration with two scholars: the late Boris Slavinsky, senior researcher at the Institute of World Economy and International Relations (IMEMO) in Moscow, and Sumio Hatano of Tsukuba University in Japan. My collaboration with Boris Slavinsky began during my four-month stay in Moscow in 2000. We had numerous discussions to outline our collaborative work, and he generously shared the massive archival materials that he had assiduously collected when the Soviet archives opened for a brief period after the collapse of the Soviet Union. Slavinsky was a courageous historian who challenged the orthodoxy that still prevails in the Russian historical profession even after the demise of the USSR. We were just about to begin writing our first draft of the book when he suddenly passed away in April 2002. His death was a great loss to this project.

Sumio Hatano made an invaluable contribution to this book. No one has better knowledge of historiography and sources related to Japan's surrender than Hatano. He tracked down numerous sources for me, some of which are used for the first time in this book, and answered my endless questions. He read the entire manuscript, provided me with useful comments, and corrected numerous mistakes that had slipped into the first draft.

My interest in the end of the Pacific War goes back to my graduate days, when I took Robert Butow's reading seminar at the University of Washington. Butow's classic work *Japan's Decision to Surrender,* published half a century ago, made an indelible impression on me. This book is in a way an overdue thank you to the mentor who inspired me many years ago.

I am indebted to my mentors at the University of Tokyo, Shinkichi Eto and Takashi Saito, who kindled my passion for international history when I was an undergraduate. My mentor in graduate school, the late Donald Treadgold, from whom I learned so much about the historical profession, would have been pleased to see this book. I also regret that my colleague and friend Seizaburo Sato did not live long enough to engage in discussion on various issues covered in this book.

Robert Scalapino, Gilbert Rozman, John Stephan, and David Holloway provided invaluable support at various stages of this project.

The colleagues and friends who helped me with this book are too numerous to be listed here individually. But a few deserve special mention. Richard Frank, with whom I disagree on a number of issues, has been a great supporter of this project. He shared information generously and read the manuscript with a critical eye, providing valuable comments. Barton Bernstein of Stanford University always welcomed my numerous telephone inquiries, some of which lasted for hours. I have also been fortunate to receive encouragement and comments from Gar Alperovits, who represents the opposite ideological wing from Frank. I am thankful for the warm support provided by these three scholars, all with different views on the highly contentious issue of the atomic bomb.

Dmitrii Slavinsky, Boris's son, graciously agreed to let me use his father's collection of sources, and he helped me locate many published materials and photographs in Russia. Kirill Cherevko, senior scholar at the Institute of Russian History of the Russian Academy of Sciences, also read the manuscript and made useful comments. I also thank Ernest May and Odd Arne Westad, who read the entire manuscript for Harvard University Press and provided valuable comments.

My colleagues and students at the Center for Cold War Studies and the Department of History at the University of California at Santa Barbara have been steady supporters of this project. Fred Logevall, now at Cornell University, was the very first person to suggest that I pursue this subject, and his encouragement and friendship greatly inspired me to complete this book. Jennifer See read the entire manuscript and provided useful comments on a number of topics. Chris Ziegler-MacPherson, Erik Esselstrom, Nobuko Kotani, Toshihiko Aono, and Yuriy Malikov worked as my research assistants. The staff at the Interdisciplinary Humanities Center and the Department of History at the University of California at Santa Barbara ably managed the grants and fellowships that supported this project.

My former colleagues at the Slavic Research Center of Hokkaido University in Japan, especially Shin'ichiro Tabata, provided me with valuable assistance in locating Japanese sources. My discussions with Japanese colleagues—especially Haruki Wada, Hiroshi Kimura, Teruyuki Hara, Takayuki Ito, Nobuo Shimotomai, Takashi Murakami, Nobuo Arai, Osamu Ieda, and Shinji Yokote—provided valuable information and inspiration for the book.

I am indebted to many librarians and archivists at the National Archives in College Park, the Harry S. Truman Library, the Franklin D. Roosevelt Library, the George Marshall Library, the Manuscript Division of the Library of Congress, the Hoover Institution Archives, the Houghton Library at Harvard University, the Sterling Library at Yale University, the Butler Library Oral History Collection at Columbia University, the Mudd Library at Princeton University, the Special Collections at the Clemson University Library, the Amherst College Library Archives and Special Collections, the Public Record Office (Kew Gardens, Britain), the Manuscript Collections of the Military History Division of the National Defense Institution (Boei Kenkyujo Senshishitsu) in Tokyo, the Foreign Ministry of the Russian Federation Archives (AVP RF), and the Russian State Archives of Social-Political History (RGASPI) in Moscow. I was extremely fortunate to receive invaluable help from John Taylor, whom I consider a national treasure, at the National Archives. I am also grateful to Dennis Bilger at the Truman Library, who went out of his way to assist me on this project.

This book was supported by generous grants and fellowships from the National Endowment for the Humanities, the United States Institute of Peace, the National Council for Eurasian and East European Research, the Japan Program of the Social Science Research Council, the International Research and Exchange Board (IREX), the Truman Library Fellowship Program, the University of California's Institute on Global Conflict and Cooperation (IGCC), the University of California's Pacific Rim Research Program, and the University of California at Santa Barbara Academic Senate Research Grant Program. I am also grateful to David Marshall, dean of Humanities and Fine Arts at UCSB's College of Letters and Sciences, for his support and encouragement.

Steve Brown, an artist at UCSB Artworks, produced the maps for this book. Kathleen McDermott of Harvard University Press has patiently shepherded the book from the time I submitted the manuscript to its publication. Christine Thorsteinsson of Harvard University Press, with her rigor and careful attention to detail, immensely improved the quality of the manuscript.

I am solely responsible for any errors of fact or shortcomings in this book.

My wife, Debbie, read the manuscript at various stages many times over. In fact, Debbie and my son, Kenneth, have lived with this project for many years. Without their constant encouragement, support, and love, this book would never have been written.

Index

ABCD (American, British, Chinese, Dutch) alliance, 15
Acheson, Dean, 81, 119, 291
Adrykhaev, N., 107
Air Force, U.S., 152
Alamogordo test site, 141, 160
Aleutian Islands, 280
Anami, Korechika, 48, 60; atomic bombs and, 184, 297; Big Six and, 72, 73, 74; Byrnes Note and, 231–233, 235–238; emperor's "sacred decision" and, 210, 214, 216; Kido's peace plan and, 102; last-ditch defense plans and, 211; military coup attempt and, 241–248; Moscow mediation plan and, 106, 127; Potsdam Proclamation and, 167, 203–204, 207, 209, 214; ritual suicide of, 247–248; Soviet declaration of war and, 200–201; war advocates and, 215, 230, 238, 240, 345n77
Ando, Yoshiro, 197, 228
Andreev, Vladimir A., 281, 283
Anglo-Japanese Alliance, 8
Anti-Comintern Pact, 13
Antonov, Aleksei I., 155, 177, 178, 270, 271, 332n6; General Order Number 1 and, 276–277; Hokkaido operation and, 274; Instrument of Surrender and, 278; plan to base U.S. bombers in Soviet Union and, 54–55; U.S. reaction to Soviet actions and, 264–265
Araki, Sadao, 13
Arao, Okikatsu, 237, 238, 241
Arisue, Seizo, 58
Army, U.S., 27–28, 78
Arnold, H. H. "Hap," 27, 67, 103, 356n27; atomic bombs and, 159; exclusion of Kyoto as atomic target, 150; ultimatum to Japan and, 148
Asada, Sadao, 295, 302
Asaeda, Shigeharu, 199, 201
Asai, Isamu, 58
Asaka, Prince, 350n42
Atlantic Charter, 17, 21, 22, 36; demand

for unconditional surrender and, 70–71, 145; Potsdam Proclamation and, 166; Soviet annexation of Kurils and, 301
Atomic bombs, 1, 3, 5, 211, 218, 239; as bargaining tool with Soviet Union, 139, 140; continuance of war in absence of, 294–295; demand for unconditional surrender and, 105, 135; determining targets of, 66–68; development of, 41–44; "Fat Man," 136, 140–141, 194, 201–203; final decision to use, 175–176; Hirohito's radio broadcast reference to, 249; Japanese surrender and, 296–298; justification for use of, 104, 135, 152, 158, 159, 169–170, 181–183, 202, 292, 299; Kyoto excluded as target of, 149–150; legacy in American memory, 298–300; "Little Boy," 179; myth concerning use of, 152, 170, 298–299; number of, 208, 297, 298; Operation Olympic and, 104, 335n44; reputation of United States and, 90; Soviet declaration of war and, 192, 194, 198–199, 200; Soviet intelligence about, 86, 128, 154, 192; Soviet project to develop, 44; testing of, 89, 140–141, 148–149, 179; ultimatum to Japan and, 119, 155–156; U.S.–Soviet relations and, 76–77. See also Hiroshima; Manhattan Project (S-1); Nagasaki
Attlee, Clement, 162, 267
August Storm, Operation, 260
Australia, 285
Axis powers, 13, 21
Ayers, Eben, 180, 181

Bagge, Widar, 53
Baldwin, Stanley, 12
Ballantine, Joseph, 22, 52, 81, 348n9; Japanese surrender acceptance and, 218, 221; Potsdam Proclamation and, 293–294; ultimatum to Japan and, 112, 118, 119

290; emperor system and, 82; General Order Number 1 and, 267, 269; Operation Olympic and, 103–104, 263; policy toward Soviet Union and, 64; proposed U.S. action in Asia and, 233–234; redefinition of unconditional surrender and, 97; Soviet entry into Pacific War and, 152–153; ultimatum to Japan and, 147, 148; U.S.–Soviet relations and, 55
Maruyama, Masao, 4
Marxism-Leninism, 1, 288
Mashbir, Sidney, 277–278
Matsudaira, Yasumasa, 28, 49, 324n13; Kido's peace plan and, 101; Moscow mediation plan and, 122; peace party and, 206, 239
Matsumoto, Shun'ichi, 165–166, 197, 207; Byrnes Note and, 227–228, 230, 232, 235; peace party and, 208; Potsdam Proclamation and, 217
Matsuoka, Yosuke, 7, 14, 16, 17, 191
Matsutani, Makoto, 28, 69; Big Six and, 74; Kido's peace plan and, 101; Moscow mediation plan and, 122; peace party and, 206, 239
McCarthy, Frank, 133
McCloy, John J., 50, 79; atomic bombs and, 76–77, 78, 149; General Order Number 1 and, 266–267; Japanese surrender acceptance and, 220, 222; Kuril Islands and, 275; Magic intercepts and, 134, 135; Operation Olympic and, 103, 105; Potsdam Proclamation and, 290, 294; redefinition of unconditional surrender and, 97–98; ultimatum to Japan and, 111, 112, 113–114, 148, 238–239
McCullough, David, 175
McDilda, Marcus, 208
Meiji Constitution, 3, 4, 211
Mellett, Lowell, 222
Meretskov, Kirill A., 116, 177, 195
Midway, Battle of, 20, 27
Mikasa, Prince, 80, 232–233
Mikoyan, Anastas, 178
Militarism, Japanese, 21, 22, 81, 87, 118; American goal to eliminate, 219, 291; emperor system and, 119, 211, 219, 220
Minobe, Tatsukichi, 4, 211, 212
Missouri, USS, 6, 284, 285
Miyakawa, Funao, 254
Miyazaki, Shuichi, 243
Molotov, Viacheslav M., 14, 19, 20, 50, 94, 144; Chinese Communists and, 51;

General Order Number 1 and, 276, 277; Hiroshima bombing and, 185, 186–187; Hirota-Malik talks and, 99, 107, 108, 109; Hokkaido operation and, 273; Japanese surrender and, 225, 226; Neutrality Pact and, 91–92; Potsdam Conference and, 120, 121, 124–125, 136; Potsdam Proclamation and, 160, 161–162, 163, 164, 171; preparation for war on Japan and, 23, 24, 25, 33, 178; renunciation of Neutrality Pact and, 45, 46–47, 48; Soviet declaration of war and, 189–191; Truman's meeting with, 63–66, 75; U.S.–Soviet relations and, 57; Yalta Agreement and, 34–35, 38–39, 63–66
Monarchy, constitutional: Allied occupation of Japan and, 81; Big Six and, 173, 291; Byrnes Note and, 294; emperor system and, 70, 105, 118, 127, 146–147, 212, 290–292; *kokutai* and, 60, 291; Meiji Constitution and, 4, 211; Potsdam Proclamation and, 169, 290–293; Stalin and, 293; ultimatum to Japan and, 89, 111, 117, 146–147, 148, 158
Mongolia, Inner, 29, 196, 224
Mongolia, Outer, 9, 32, 96; People's Republic, 275; Sino-Soviet negotiations and, 138, 188, 189, 224; Soviet sphere of interest in, 36, 73, 129; Yalta Agreement and, 34, 35, 36
Mori, Takeshi, 241, 245, 246, 249
Morishima, Goro, 61, 107
Moscow Declaration, 23, 163, 164, 193
Moscow Foreign Ministers' Conference, 21, 23, 24
Mukden, 8, 195, 238, 255
Müler-Grote, Gustav, 132
Munich Conference, 14, 15
Murase, Naoyoshi, 235
Mutanchiang, Battle of, 195, 196

Nagano, Osami, 242
Nagasaki, 1, 179, 180, 194, 201–203, 204; decision to destroy, 90; Japanese surrender and, 297, 298; selected as target, 152; standard American narrative about, 298–300
Naka, Akira, 168
Nambara, Shigeru, 99–100
Nanking Massacre, 13, 299
Nashi, Prince, 231
Nationalism, Japanese, 4, 301

Stimson, Henry L. *(continued)*
148–154; memorandum to Truman,
116–120; Potsdam Conference and, 131,
136, 265; Potsdam Proclamation and,
156–157, 290, 293–294; proposed suspension of bombing, 219; prospect of
additional atomic bombs and, 298;
redefinition of unconditional surrender
and, 97–98; Soviet entry into Pacific War
and, 152–153; U.S. policy toward Soviet
Union and, 64, 75–76
Sugiyama, Hajime, 16, 242
Suizu, Mitsuru, 281, 282–283
Sullivan, Mark, 222
Supreme Commander of Allied Powers, 52,
221, 222, 226
Supreme War Council, 95, 106, 121, 209,
345n78; Byrnes Note and, 229, 235–
236, 239; emperor and, 209, 210; Hiroshima bombing and, 185; Nagasaki
bombing and, 204; Potsdam Proclamation and, 203, 205, 213; Soviet declaration of war and, 198, 200. *See also* Big
Six
Supreme War Leadership Council, 28, 29,
38, 68, 72
Suzuki, Kantaro, 45, 215; Byrnes Note
and, 230–232, 235, 236–237, 294; cabinet of, 48–49, 88, 97, 249; German defeat and, 68; Hirohito's "sacred decision" and, 212–213, 240; Hiroshima
bombing and, 184, 185; Hirota-Malik
talks and, 102; on hypothetical absence
of atomic bombs, 295; Imperial Rescript
and, 245, 297; indecision of, 91; *kokutai*
and, 212, 250; "Mokusatsu" statement
of, 165–170; Moscow mediation plan
and, 106, 121; peace party and, 205,
239; Potsdam Proclamation and, 167,
170, 173, 183, 203, 204, 214; responsibility for war's delayed end, 301; Soviet
declaration of war and, 197, 198
Sweden, 53, 88, 135, 338; Japanese surrender acceptance and, 221; Potsdam Proclamation and, 169
Switzerland, 88, 135, 338; Japanese com-
plaint on use of atomic bombs and, 299;
Japan's surrender and, 250–251;
Potsdam Proclamation and, 169, 171

Taiwan, 8, 24, 59, 60, 71
Takagi, Sokichi, 28, 29–30, 53, 324n13;
Big Six and, 72, 106; Byrnes Note and,

232; Kido's peace plan and, 101; *kokutai*
defined by, 122; last-ditch defense of Ja-
pan and, 39–41; Moscow mediation
plan and, 106, 122; peace party and,
100, 239; Potsdam Proclamation and,
165, 203
Takagi, Yasaka, 100
Takamatsu, Prince, 38, 198, 205
Takashima, Tatsuhiko, 242
Takeshita, Masahiko, 230, 238, 242, 243,
247–248, 297
Tanaka, Shizuichi, 241, 242, 244, 247,
353n79
Tanakamaru, Yasuatsu, 322n99
Tanemura, Suketaka, 58, 59–60, 73, 107,
322n99
Target Committee, 67, 90
Teheran Conference, 21, 25, 31, 50
Tench, Charles, 278
Terauchi, Hisaichi, 233
Three Divine Objects, 102
Tibbets, Paul, 179
Tillitze, Lars, 87–88
Togo, Shigenori, 18, 49, 56; American in-
telligence intercepts of, 126, 127, 128,
134, 135; Big Six and, 72, 73–74; Byrnes
Note and, 227–228, 230–232, 236–237;
emperor's "sacred decision" and, 215;
German defeat and, 68; Hiroshima
bombing and, 184–185; Hirota-Malik
talks and, 107, 108–109, 110; Japanese
surrender and, 245; *kokutai* defined by,
212; Konoe mission and, 143–145; last-
ditch defense plans and, 96; Moscow
mediation plan and, 106, 121, 123, 124–
126, 322n99; peace party and, 100, 101;
policy toward Soviet Union, 61, 91–92,
94–95; Potsdam Conference and, 120;
Potsdam Proclamation and, 166–173,
203–205, 209, 211; responsibility for
war's delayed end, 301; Soviet declaration of war and, 197–198, 215–216; Soviet renunciation of Neutrality Pact and,
58; two-track policy to end war, 145
Tojo, Hideki, 18, 20, 28–30
Tokyo: incendiary bombings of, 80, 92,
119; as intended target of atomic bomb,
208, 352n63; Soviet proposal for occupation zone in, 268, 274
Toyoda, Soemu, 106, 127, 209; Byrnes
Note and, 229, 232, 236; emperor's "sacred decision" and, 210; Hiroshima
bombing and, 186; on hypothetical absence of atomic bombs, 295; Nagasaki

United States *(continued)*
  nese surrender, 277; press coverage of
  diplomatic maneuvers, 168; public opinion in, 23, 100, 113, 143, 220, 222–224,
  234, 291; Russo-Japanese relations and,
  7, 9; Sino-Soviet negotiations and, 234;
  "soft peace" advocates in, 40, 52, 100,
  223; Soviet alliance with, 16, 18, 23–25;
  Soviet operations against Japan and,
  256, 258, 264–267, 274–275; Stalin's
  bargaining with, 30–33; suspension of
  offensive operations, 252; ultimatum to
  Japan and, 111, 114, 115, 117
United States Strategic Bombing Survey,
  294–295
Unit 731, 299
Uruppu Island, 282, 287. *See also* Kuril Islands
Uspenskii, Captain, 285

Vasilevskii, Aleksandr M., 37, 85, 133,
  177–178, 187; cease-fire negotiations
  and, 254–255; Hokkaido operation and,
  271, 272; on Japanese surrender, 252;
  Kuril Operation and, 259, 281, 284; as
  proposed supreme commander, 226;
  Sakhalin operation and, 256, 257, 258;
  Soviet operations in Liaotung Peninsula
  and, 270
Vatican, 74
V-E Day, 70, 74, 80
Versailles Treaty, 9, 11
V-J Day, 286
Vladivostok, 7, 8, 32, 48, 273
Voronov, R. B., 283
Voroshilov, Kliment E., 187
Vostrikov, Lieutenant, 284
Voznesenskii, Nikolai A., 116
Vyshinskii, Andrei Ia., 178, 276–277

Wakamatsu, Tadakatsu, 243
Wakatsuki, Reijiro, 28
Wallace, Henry, 202
War criminals, 39, 68; Japanese appeal to
  Moscow and, 122–123; Potsdam Procla-
  mation and, 203–204; proposal to treat
  emperor as, 105; trials of, 127; U.S.–Jap-
  anese relations and, 112
War Department, U.S., 41, 66, 76, 111;
  American public opinion and, 223;
  atomic bombs and, 235; Civil Affairs Di-
  vision, 112; General Order Number 1

and, 269; Kuril Islands and, 274; na-
  tional objectives in Asia and, 98;
  Potsdam Proclamation and, 160; Soviet
  entry into Pacific War and, 79–80; ulti-
  matum to Japan and, 114, 161. *See also*
  Operations Division (OPD), War Dept.
Washburn, Stanley, 222
Washington Conference (1921–1922), 11
Washington Treaty system, 11
Weckerling, John, 112, 126–128, 134,
  330n92
Wedemeyer, Albert, 234
Wheeler, Burton K., 223
Wherry, Kenneth S., 223
White, Wallace H., 223
Wiley, Alexander, 194
Wilson, Woodrow, 223
World War I, 9, 11, 21
World War II, 14, 20, 37, 44, 45, 55. *See
  also* Pacific War

Yalta Agreement, 27, 41, 47, 83, 88; Big
  Three at conference, 34–37; China and,
  174; demand for Japanese surrender
  and, 53; General Order Number 1 and,
  266; Hirota-Malik talks and, 109; Japanese defense plans and, 38; renegotiation
  of, 75–80; Sino-Soviet negotiations and,
  192–193; Soviet dominance in Eastern
  Europe and, 43, 62; Soviet entry into
  Pacific War and, 115, 132–133, 137,
  161, 164, 189, 195, 253; Truman and,
  50, 63; U.S.–Soviet tension over, 2, 5,
  280
Yamada, Otozo, 253
Yamamoto, Isoroku, 17–18
Yokohama, 67
Yonai, Mitsumasa, 28, 49, 102, 207, 208;
  Big Six and, 72, 73, 74; Byrnes Note
  and, 230, 232, 236, 294; *kokutai* and,
  212; military coup plot and, 244; Moscow mediation plan and, 97, 106; peace
  party and, 53, 101, 215; Potsdam Procla-
  mation and, 167, 173, 203, 214; Soviet
  declaration of war and, 198
York, John, 75
Yoshizumi, Masao, 210, 214, 217
Yuhashi, Shigeto, 189, 191

Zacharias, Ellis, 53, 69–71, 145
Zakharov, S. E., 257, 258, 289
Zhukov, Georgii K., 116